COSMATESQUE ORNAMENT

FLAT
POLYCHROME
GEOMETRIC PATTERNS
IN ARCHITECTURE

COSMATESQUE ORNAMENT

FLAT POLYCHROME GEOMETRIC PATTERNS IN ARCHITECTURE

PALOMA PAJARES–AYUELA

Translation by
Maria Fleming Alvarez

W · W · NORTON & COMPANY · NEW YORK · LONDON

Printed in Singapore
First Edition

The text of this book is composed in Weiss with the display set in Trajan
Composition by Ken Gross
Manufacturing by CS Graphics Pte Ltd
Book design by Antonina Krass

Library of Congress Cataloging-in-Publication Data

Pajares Ayuela, Paloma
Cosmatesque ornament: flat polychrome geometric patterns in architecture/Paloma Pajares Ayuela; translation by Maria Fleming Alvarez.
p. cm.
Includes bibliographical references and index.
ISBN 0-393-73037-9
1. Decoration and ornament, Architectural—Europe. 2. Architecture, Medieval—Europe. 3. Architecture, Medieval—Italy—Rome. 4. Repetitive patterns (Decorative arts) in art. 5. Geometry in art. 6. Church decoration and ornament—Italy—Rome. I. Title.

NA3542.P35 2001
729—dc21 00-053696

W. W. Norton & Company, Inc., 500 Fifth Avenue, New York, N.Y. 10110
www.wwnorton.com

W. W. Norton & Company, Ltd., Castle House, 75/76 Wells St., London W1T 3QT

0 9 8 7 6 5 4 3 2 1

CONTENTS

INTRODUCTION

The Cosmati were a group of Roman artists who worked in Rome and the surrounding region of Latium during the second half of the Middle Ages. The essence of Cosmatesque art lies in its ornament, specifically in a particular type of flat polychrome geometric ornament. This book is a detailed study of this ornament.

The first challenge in studying the numerous examples of Cosmatesque art was to locate them. To find them all, I employed two complementary systems. The first, based on desk work in archives and libraries, consisted of consulting the scarce documentation with specific reference to the Cosmati. The second, based on field work, involved systematically visiting each of the medieval buildings in Rome and noting those that still contained Cosmatesque remains.

Once I had located all of the Cosmatesque monuments, I began to study in great detail those located in the city of Rome, which holds the majority and the most important of them. Through my field work, I acquired descriptive documentation (photographs and drawings), which complemented the historical information that I had obtained through my research in archives and libraries.

The introductory first chapter of this book discusses the general historical and geographic conditions of the period and places in which the Cosmati worked. It focuses as much on the sites with Cosmatesque ornament as on those sites in western medieval Europe with works of flat polychrome geometric ornament that, although similar to Cosmatesque works, are not in fact Cosmatesque, because the geometry that regulates their designs is not the same as that which regulates the Cosmatesque designs. Also included is a list of all the Cosmatesque monuments known to me, which are found grouped principally in Latium, the western region of central Italy. Rome, which is the Cosmatesque site par excellence, stands out among all of the Cosmatesque areas of concentration, as much for the number of monuments as for the quality of those monuments.

The second chapter is a comparative study of the morphological characteristics of the Cosmatesque monuments of that city. Because the Cosmati almost always worked in preexisting churches, I first address the fundamental steps in the development of these characteristics, which can be traced back to the early days of Christianity. I then study the characteristic forms that the churches of Rome displayed at the time of the Cosmati.

The third chapter compares Cosmatesque mosaics to earlier ones with similar formal characteristics. From this analysis it is inferred that the Cosmatesque artists integrated into their compositions elements inherited from the local classical tradition as well as others that were the product of Byzantine influence, the external tradition that had the greatest impact on the art of medieval Rome.

The fourth chapter analyzes in detail the underlying geometry of the Cosmatesque designs, identifying and defining the fundamental geometric motifs that are continually reiterated in all Cosmatesque work; in other words, the basic repertoire of constant geometric patterns. Also included is a list of terms and expressions that I consider indispensable in describing the Cosmatesque designs. Each of the integral components of a Cosmatesque tiling is defined, illustrated, and organized into different categories; and, when appropriate, the mathematical relationships that regulate the geometry of those components are noted. The chapter ends with a study of the process of fragmentation preferred by the Cosmati, which consists of inscribing within a figure its inverse. When the fragmented figure is a triangle, this process can be expressed in mathematical language by means of a classic fractal, Sierpinski's Triangle.

In the fifth chapter I attempt to shed some light on the meaning of the motif that dominates Cosmatesque composition: the quincunx. The underlying geometry of the quincunx is the double cross. This form is the foundation of a multitude of flat and spatial compositions, both medieval and Byzantine, to such a degree that one can speak of a true medieval "quincunx mania." To explain its meaning, I have compared the Cosmatesque quincunx with other medieval quincuncial compositions whose meaning we know, assuming that the signification of significants of similar formal characteristics ought to be the same, or at least similar. Thus, throughout the chapter, in addition to explaining the consecration ceremony of a medieval church, in which quincuncial sketches were drawn on the floor of the church, I link the Cosmatesque quincunx with the quincuncial composition that regulates the space of the centralized Byzantine church as well as the tessellation in *opus sectile* that is found under the dome of such a church. I further relate the Cosmatesque quincunx to other quincuncial forms derived from the medieval religious and cosmological world view (for example, the labarum, tetramorphs, Carolingian metalwork, imperial scepters, miniature manuscripts).

The sixth chapter examines in great detail the formal geometric characteristics of the floor paving of the schola cantorum of San Clemente in Rome, based on the survey that I carried out on a scale of 1:10 meters in 1993. The analysis of this tessellation employs the semantics and syntax explained in chapter 4. The detailed study of this mosaic explores the geometric and dimensional discrepancies that resulted from the use of spoliated materials in executing the pavement, as well as the manner in which the Cosmati addressed these nonconformities, ignoring or camouflaging them. Furthermore, the order in which the Cosmatesque artists must have executed the tessellation is made evident, attending to considerations of design and cost of execution, both in time and materials.

Chapter 1

PANORAMA

FLAT POLYCHROME GEOMETRIC ORNAMENT IN THE WESTERN EMPIRE DURING THE MIDDLE AGES

This book is dedicated to the study of a group of noteworthy works of art that exhibit a particular type of architectural ornament, namely, flat polychrome geometric ornament. This first chapter begins by outlining the most significant geographic and historical traits of the world in which these works were created. The artists who created them lived during the late Middle Ages (primarily from the beginning of the twelfth century until the first third of the thirteenth century), almost always in Rome and in the surrounding region of Latium. Among the authors who have written about these artists, the consensus has been to refer to them as "the Cosmati" or the "Cosmatesque artists," and to their work as "Cosmatesque architecture."[1]

Europe at the Time of the Cosmati

In the mid-twelfth century, Europe was a mosaic of geopolitical units. These units had been forming since the beginning of the Middle Ages. It is necessary, therefore, to go back to the time of the fall of the Roman Empire to understand the situation in Europe during the late Middle Ages.

Rome inherited and assimilated Greek culture in addition to incorporating within its boundaries the ancient cultures of Egypt, Syria, and Mesopotamia; to the west, it acquired European territories inhabited by primitive cultures. In each case, the empire introduced its political, social, economic, religious,

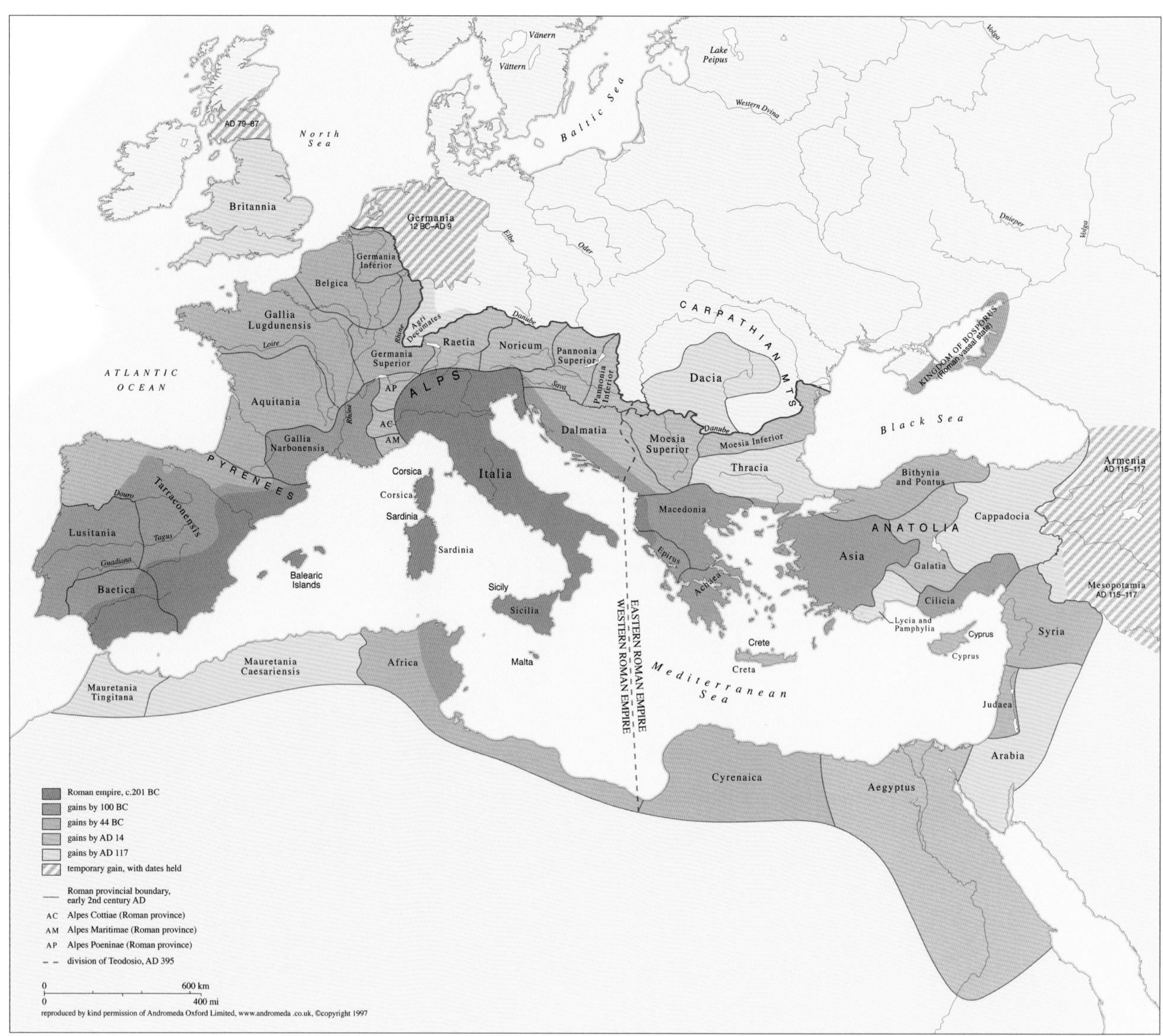

1-1. The Roman Empire.

administrative, and cultural structure, a unifying process known as Romanization.[2] The inequality of culture, agricultural wealth, and commercial development between the eastern and western regions of the Roman Empire became institutionalized in 395 when Theodosius divided the empire into two parts. From that time until the fifteenth century, the "pars Orientalis," with its capital in Constantinople, would be known as the Eastern Roman Empire, or Byzantine Empire,[3] while the "pars Occidentalis," of lesser cultural and organizational stature, would not resist barbarian attacks and would be invaded, ushering in the Middle Ages (fig. 1-1).

The western part of the empire, including Rome, came to occupy a position of secondary international importance in the medieval panorama, losing the influence it enjoyed during the time of the Roman Empire. The eastern part, however, did not lose the preeminence it had held while part of the empire and continued as a world power during the Middle Ages. Similarly, its principal rival, Islam, experienced a period of powerful expansion between the seventh and eighth centuries, occupying Byzantine territories in the east and in North Africa, as well as reaching southern Italy and the Pyrenees (fig. 1-2).[4]

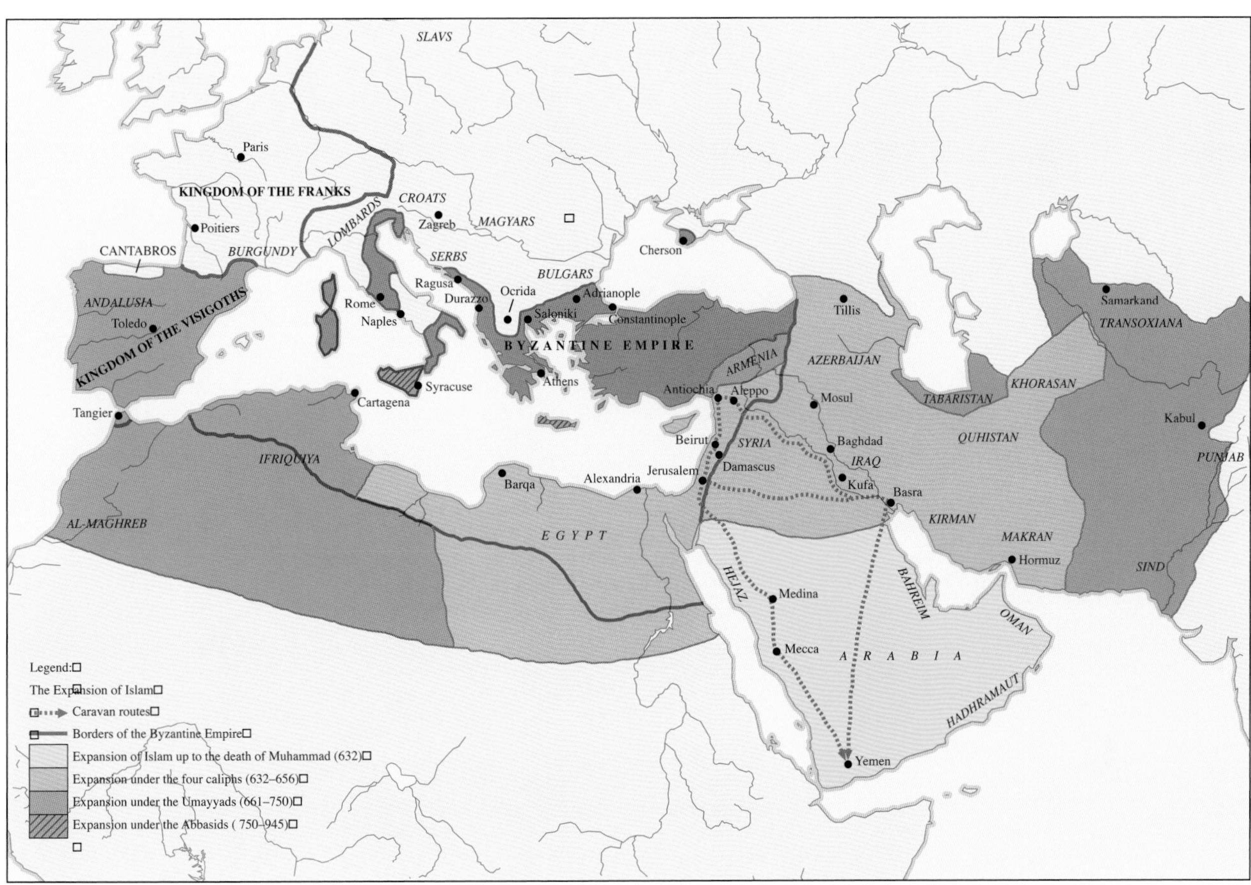

1-2. *The expansion of Islam.*

Europe, after an initial period of upheaval from the fifth century to the eighth century characterized by incessant changes of borders and population shifts, began a process of gradual stabilization. The territorial reorganization achieved by Charlemagne in the ninth century (labeled the second attempt at reconstruction of the Roman Empire, after Justinian's first attempt[5]) was a fundamental step in this process, which would continue into post-Carolingian times. By the eleventh century, Europe was enjoying a period of peace unknown since before the Germanic invasions of the fifth century, the immigration of Slavic and Steppe peoples, and the Norman displacement (ninth to eleventh century). This respite allowed for the political, economic, and cultural recuperation that Europe experienced during the late Middle Ages.

The territories now known as Italy were not indifferent to the general events just described. The Lombards invaded Italy in 568, occupying most of the region, except for some areas that remained under the protection of the Byzantine Empire: the band of central Italy that joins Rome with Ravenna (papal territories), the southernmost part of the peninsula (the "toe" and the "heel" of the Italian "boot"), Sicily, and a few cities, including Venice, Genoa, Florence, Pisa, Naples, and Gaeta (fig.1-3).

The Byzantine Empire had been responsible for defending the territorial interests of the Papacy since the time of the Lombard invasion of Italy. However, the popes had lost confidence in the Byzantine emperors, owing, in part, to the doctrinal disputes that had arisen over the Byzantine iconoclastic position (725–842).[6] Furthermore, in an age in which the Muslims posed a significant danger, threatening the territorial integrity of the empire, the

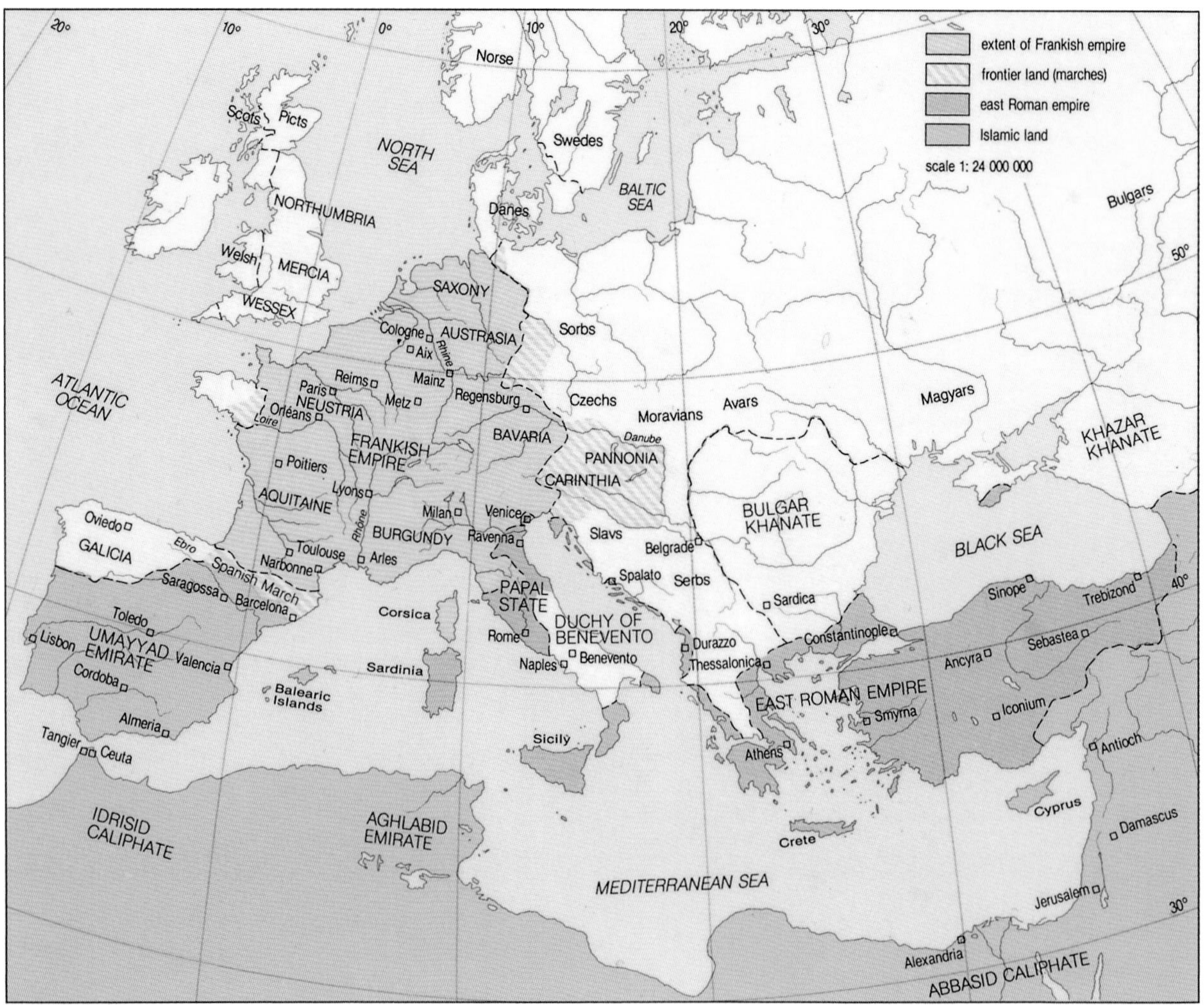

1-3. Europe in 800.

emperor lent only weak military support to his more distant territories at the center of the Italian peninsula. Instead, the emperor felt obliged to expend virtually all of his military energy in fighting against the powerful Islam, which lessened the urgency of attending to the petitions for help from Rome. Thus, by the eighth century, each time that the popes saw themselves in need of military support to protect their interests, they preferred to appeal to the western kings.

All this paved the way for Charlemagne, who left his native kingdom of Austrasia and led a territorial expansion that first made him the king of the Franks. Subsequently he came to personify the restitution of the imperial title of the West when, after conquering most of the Italian peninsula, he was crowned emperor by Pope Leo III in the year 800.[7] The papal territories were recognized as a state by Charlemagne and from that time on remained under the protection of the emperor of the West. The Byzantine domain in Italy was then limited to the extreme south of the peninsula (Calabria and the peninsula of Otranto), Sardinia, Sicily, and a few cities (Venice, Naples, Gaeta).[8] Sicily would fall into Muslim hands toward the middle of the ninth century, before being reclaimed for the west by the Normans in the late eleventh century.

The relative stability enjoyed by the Western Empire during the ninth century under Charlemagne enabled a cultural revival, the "Carolingian renaissance," which is considered the first attempt at the recovery of the culture of antiquity.[9] Charlemagne's empire would not withstand his death, owing to the successive partitioning of the territory among his descendants. The first division took place at the Treaty of Verdun (843), which divided the empire among Charlemagne's three surviving grandsons: Charles the Bald, king of France; Lothair, king of Lorraine; and Louis the German, king of the eastern portion, the future seat of the German kingdom. The eldest brother, Lothair, inherited the Middle Kingdom, which encompassed all of the key points of the empire—Rome, Pavia, Aachen—as well as a significant portion of the family holdings in Austrasia.

The period of peace that began in Europe at the start of the eleventh century paved the way for an economic and cultural revival in the Western Empire during the twelfth century. This recovery, accompanied by Church reform,[10] was very vigorous in Rome and its territory, the Papal State, where a renaissance of the culture of antiquity emerged, the second such movement, after the Carolingian renaissance. The terms *renaissance, renewal, renovatio,* and *new rebirth* have also been employed in referring to the twelfth-century resurgence of the antique in Rome.[11] The work of the Cosmati is an outstanding example of the artistic production of that renaissance, since they worked principally between the papacies of Gregory VII (1073–85) and Honorius III (1216–27), ornamenting buildings in the city of Rome and its environs.

The European map in the late Middle Ages, and in particular, during the time of the Cosmati, was dominated by three forces. The Byzantine Empire and Islam were the dominant geopolitical units of the European Mediterranean during the twelfth and thirteenth centuries, as well as throughout the remainder of the Middle Ages. Their preponderance was as much political and economic as cultural. They were the two world powers of the period, and they clashed incessantly in defending their respective territorial and religious interests. The geopolitical unit that followed these two world powers in importance, though at a certain distance, was the Western Empire. The Western Empire had always been politically, economically, and culturally inferior to either of the two heavyweights of the time. However, when it was banded together with them, a triumvirate of force was created that shaped the world during the second half of the Middle Ages.

The international panorama of which Italy was a part in the mid-twelfth century was a mosaic composed of a multitude of pieces (fig. 1-4). The most important pieces were the Eastern Empire to the east and the enormous territory of Islam to the south, which at that time still included most of the Iberian peninsula. Western continental Europe was occupied by the Plantagenet dynasty, which arose when the Normans, having settled in the northwest of France (dukedom of Normandy) upon their arrival from Denmark in 911, later extended their territories, taking over, in the middle of the eleventh century, the south of England and, in the middle of the twelfth century, the west of France (from Normandy to the Pyrenees). The Norman expansion also reached the Mediterranean: in 1030 the Normans established themselves in Aversa (near Naples), and in 1070 they conquered Palermo, which marked the end of Islamic rule in Sicily. In the middle of the twelfth century, under the government of the celebrated monarch Roger II, Sicily was one of the most significant cultural centers of the period.[12] The Norman kingdom in Sicily came to include not only the island itself but also the whole

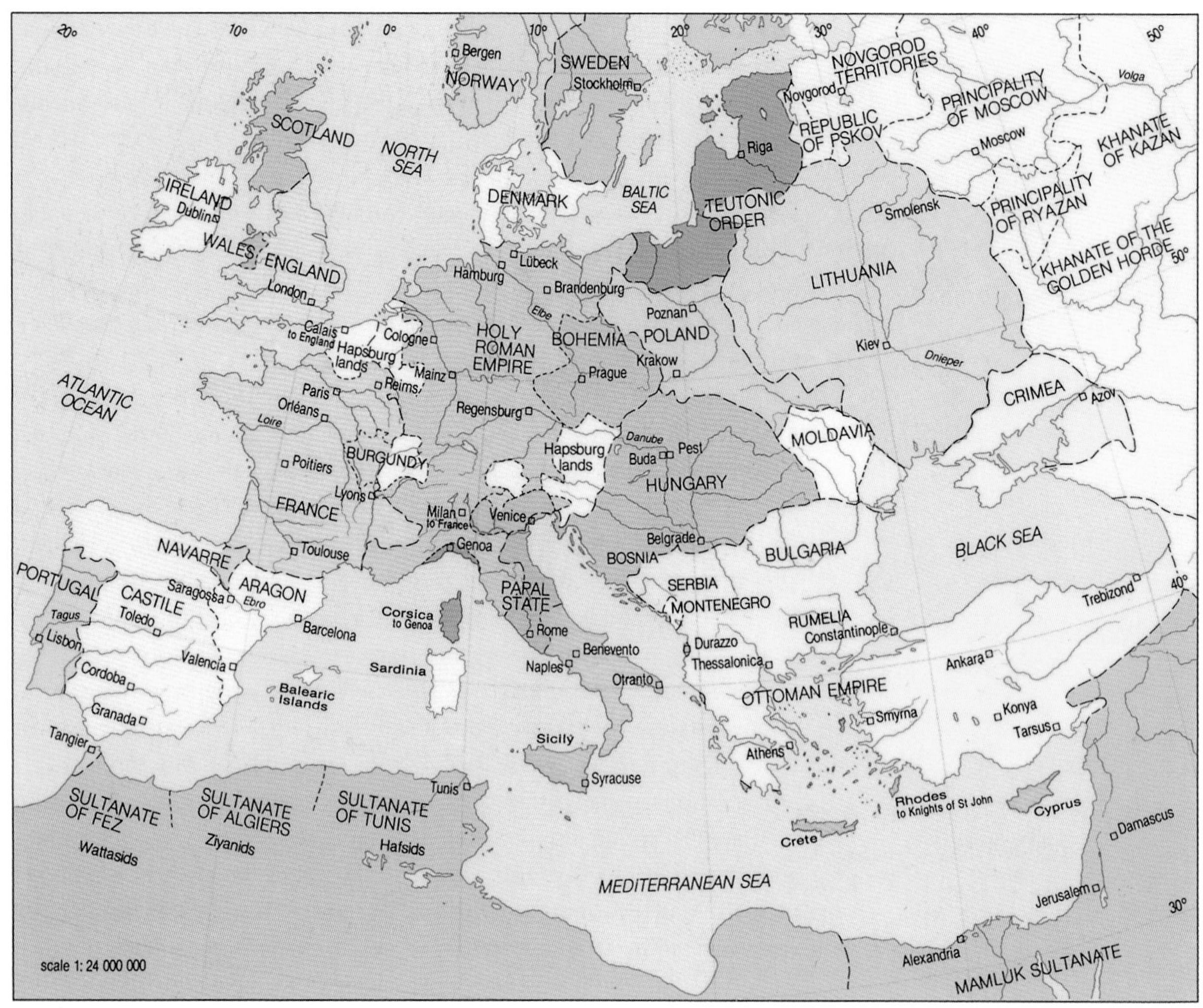

1-4. Europe circa 1150.

southern half of the Italian peninsula. The Normans snatched the northernmost portion (the dukedom of Benevento) from the Western Empire, and the extreme southern portion (the "toe" and "heel" of the Italian "boot"), as well as the semi-independent city-states of Gaeta, Naples, and Amalfi, from the Eastern emperor.[13]

During the eleventh and twelfth centuries, France of the Capetian dynasty, consisting of a multitude of feudal states, bordered the eastern side of the Plantagenet continental territories. Previously, during the tenth century, these French dominions formed, together with the westernmost territories of France, the westernmost of the three kingdoms which resulted from the division of Charlemagne's territories. In the twelfth century, the other two kingdoms of the immediate post-Carolingian period, the Middle Kingdom and the Eastern Kingdom, reunited to form the Holy Roman Empire. Thus, in the middle of the twelfth century, the Western Roman Empire included the kingdom of Germania, the kingdom of Italy (the northern half of the peninsula, which was Lombard territory until it passed into the hands of Charlemagne), and the Papal State (the western portion of the central band of the peninsula, with Rome as its center). Completing the map of Italy were the independent city-state of Venice and the Norman possessions, namely, the kingdom of Sicily (the southern half of the peninsula and Sicily).

The territories of Italy's central band, which unites Rome with Ravenna, had been liberated from Byzantine dominion in the ninth century, at

1-5. Departure for the Crusade; detail of 12th-century fresco from the Chapel of the Templars, Cressac, France.

which point they passed into the hands of Charlemagne, who recognized the western part of that region as the Papal State. From that time until the middle of the thirteenth century, the Papal State formed part of the Western Roman Empire. Thus, in the late Middle Ages, the king of Rome was also the German emperor. Friction between the pope and the emperor was frequent throughout this period because at that time the limits of their respective powers, regarding both temporal and spiritual matters, were still unclear. The principal issue in their struggle for power was the controversy over investitures, which created strife between the pope and the emperor for more than a century (1075–1177).[14] In the middle of the thirteenth century, relations between the emperor (Frederick II) and the pope reached a point of such tension that communication ceased, marking the beginning of the Papal State's independence.

A complete picture of the international geopolitical map at the time of the Cosmati must include mention of the Crusade states. These territories were won from the Muslims by the Christian world during the five military and religious expeditions which western Christianity, directed by the Papacy of Rome, sent to the Holy Land between the eleventh and the thirteenth centuries.[15] The preaching and the execution of the various Crusades were important events in the Middle Ages, and the fact that the conquests in the Middle East would become neither stable nor enduring did not diminish their importance (fig.1-5).

The territorial expansion carried out by the Crusaders was a sign of the recovery that Europe experienced in the late Middle Ages. Further indications included the rebirth of commerce and of cities and the resurgence of culture (the birth of universities) and of art (Romanesque, Gothic).[16] For the most part, the presence of the Far East was not felt in medieval Europe. However, there was contact with the Mongols, who were initially viewed as potential allies against the Muslims should missionaries successfully convert them to Christianity before Islam could claim them. Moreover, the Venetian inclination for adventure and commerce led to regular ventures to the easternmost regions of the Mediterranean as well as intrepid expeditions to the far-off Orient, as in the voyage carried out by Marco Polo to the court of Kublai Khan in 1275.

The physical appearance of Europe at the end of the Middle Ages is characterized by the stabilization of the western geopolitical units, namely the kingdoms of Portugal, Spain, England, and the Holy Roman Empire. The Holy Roman Empire, under the emperors of the house of Hohenstaufen (1125–1254), would come to dominate the entire Italian peninsula, including the islands of Corsica, Sardinia, and Sicily. At the end of the Middle Ages (fourteenth and fifteenth centuries), Italy remained divided in the north (Savoy, Milan, Genoa, Venice, Mantua, Modena, Ferrara, Lucca, Florence, and Siena), with its center occupied by the Papal State since its consolidation by Charlemagne, and its south under the crown of Aragon (which had conquered Sicily in 1282 and gained Naples in 1443).

In 1453 the Turks took the city of Constantinople, putting an end to the Byzantine Empire. This date also marks the end of the Middle Ages. The geographic discoveries of the fifteenth century would contribute to the fact that the Mediterranean ceased to be the "center of the universe" for the western world.[17]

The Principal Centers of Flat Polychrome Geometric Ornament in Western Medieval Europe

During the Middle Ages, especially from the ninth to the fourteenth centuries, the use of flat polychrome geometric ornament flourished in Italy (fig. 1-6).[18] The cities in which monuments with this type of ornament appear are grouped at various geographic focal points, the most important of which is found in the central region of the peninsula. With Rome as its heart, this area occupies all of the region of Latium and some of western Umbria and Abruzzi.[19] It is the Cosmatesque center par excellence, containing the vast majority of the cities in which the Cosmati worked.

1-6. Modern map of Italy; showing regions of the country today.

There are other notable centers of flat polychrome geometric ornament within Italy as well, as much in the northern half of the peninsula as in the southern half. In the northern half of the peninsula one can distinguish three focal points: one in the northeast (Upper Adriatic region), another in the north, and a third in the southeast. The focal point of the Upper Adriatic region includes some cities situated in Friuli-Venezia Giulia (Aquileia, Grado), Veneto (Venice, fig. 1-7), and Emilia-Romagna (Pomposa, Ravenna; fig. 1-8). The focal point in the north is in Lombardy (Como). The one in the southeast includes some cities in Tuscany (Florence, Pisa, Lucca).[20]

In the southern half of Italy are three other focal points, one to the southwest, another to the west, and the last to the southeast. The most important is the one in the southwest, which comprises cities in Sicily (Palermo, Monreale, Cefalù, and Messina; figs. 1-9 and 1-10). The center in the west follows in importance and is composed of cities in Campania (Naples, Benevento, and Cava de' Tirreni; fig. 1-11). The center in the southeast includes cities in Apulia (Otranto and Bari; fig. 1-12).[21]

1-7. *Marble floor, San Marco, Venice, 11th to 17th century. (Detail of a chromolithograph by* F. M. Hessemer, 1842)

1-8. *Marble pavements, San Vitale, Ravenna, mid-6th century. (Chromolithograph by* F. M. Hessemer, 1842)

1-9. Decorative mosaics, Cappella Palatina, Palazzo dei Normanni, Palermo, Sicily, 1132–40. The Islamic influence is evident in these two designs. (Chromolithograph by F. M. Hessemer, 1842)

1-10. Decorative mosaic, Duomo, Monreale, Sicily, 12th to 17th century. The Islamic influence is evident in this design. (Detail of a chromolithograph by F. M. Hessemer, 1842)

1-11. Decorative mosaics, top: Duomo, Naples, 13th century; center and bottom: Duomo, Benevento, 13th century. (Chromolithograph by F. M. Hessemer, 1842)

1-12. Fragment of the pavement from the choir, Basilica di San Nicola, Bari.

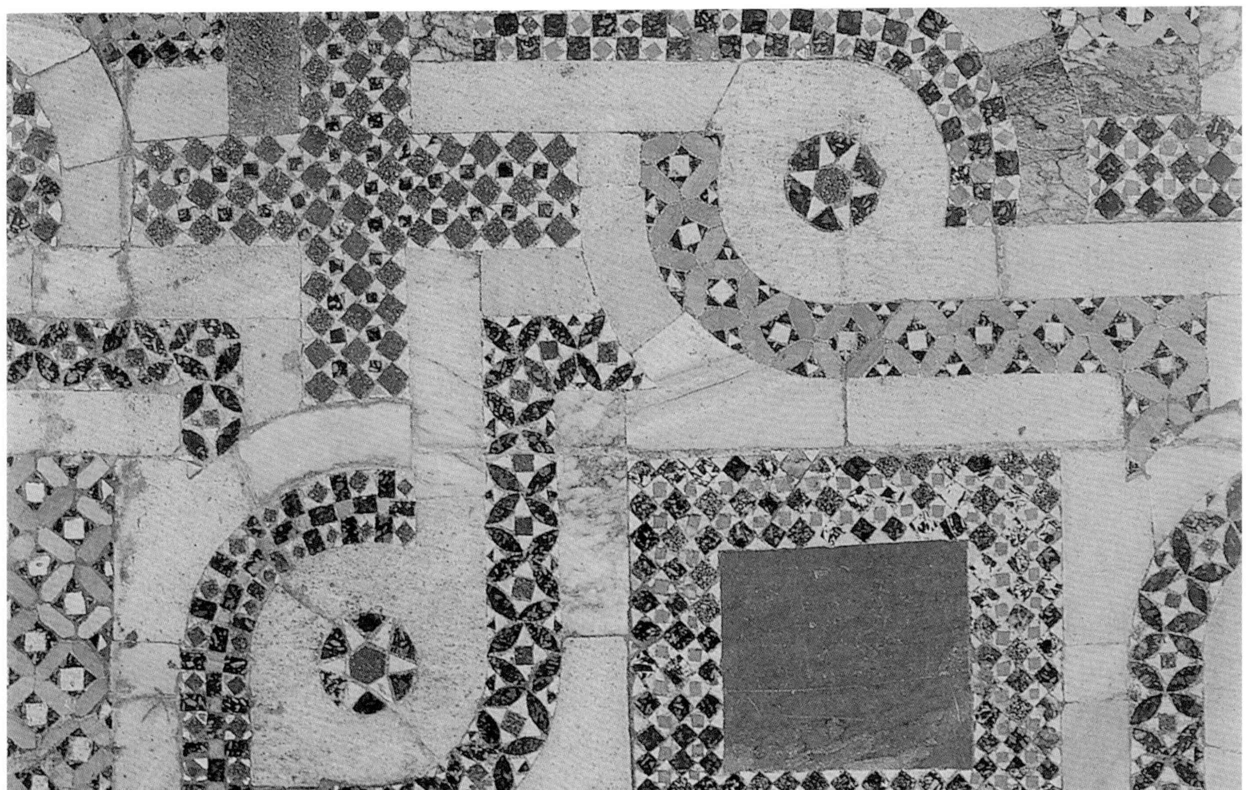

1-13. Detail of the pavement from Chapel of St. Thomas, Canterbury Cathedral.

Additional centers of flat polychrome geometric ornament can be found in transalpine Europe, as much in the continental region as in England. Two centers stand out in continental Europe, one to the southeast, in France (Saint-Benoît-sur-Loire), and another to the northeast, in Germany (Aachen, Metz). In England there is a focal point in the southeastern part of the island (London, Canterbury; fig. 1-13).[22]

The centers situated within Italian territory are the most significant.[23] They attest to the importance of flat polychrome geometric ornament in artistic production in Italy during the late Middle Ages, both in the multitude of architectural works which, more or less modified, have survived to the present, and works belonging to other artistic disciplines, such as painting. An example is the ingenious pictorial work of Giotto, full of beautiful images of architecture embellished with flat polychrome geometric ornament, copied from existing examples or invented by the artist (figs. 1-14, 1-15, 1-16, and 1-17).[24]

The geometric ornament of each center possesses particular characteristics that distinguish it from any other center. These characteristics are the result of a blending of local artistic tradition with external influences stemming from the cultural and commercial relations each center maintained, or had maintained, with neighboring and distant geographic areas.

The Byzantine Empire, Islam, and the Carolingian Empire were the most important external influences in Italy during the Middle Ages. These external influences mixed, to a greater or lesser degree, with the local classical tradition, inherited from the Roman Empire.[25] Islam, in its period of maximum expansion, succeeded in occupying the south of Italy, Sardinia, and Sicily; consequently, Arab influence is increasingly apparent southward along the peninsula.[26] Byzantine influence is present throughout the peninsula

1-14. Fresco of the life of Saint Francis: Saint Francis Honored by his Fellow Citizens, Giotto. Upper Church, San Francesco, Assisi.

1-15. Detail of Saint Francis Honored by his Fellow Citizens, Giotto.

1-16. Pentecost, Giotto. London, National Gallery (painting belonging to one of the panels from the church of Santa Croce, Florence).

1-17. Detail of Pentecost, Giotto. London, National Gallery.

and Sicily, but above all in the Upper Adriatic region, due as much to the close cultural, commercial, and military ties that Venice maintained with the eastern Mediterranean as to Ravenna's early role as the capital of the western Byzantine territories. The effects of the Carolingian Empire extend all through the territories conquered by Charlemagne, which is to say, the northern half of the peninsula, including Rome. The island of Sicily displays multiple influences, having been occupied successively by the Byzantines (sixth century), the Arabs (ninth century), and the Norman Danes (eleventh century). Sicily reached its greatest political and cultural splendor in the middle of the twelfth century, under the Norman king, Roger II, who was based in Palermo.

The classical, Byzantine, Carolingian, and Arabic traditions thus wielded the greatest weight in shaping medieval ornament. In designs of classical origin, regular partitions of the plane, which divide the surface in a homogeneous manner, abound. The Byzantine tradition exhibits a preference for sinusoidal intertwinings. In the Carolingian mosaics, chessboard patterns and designs with roundels in a quincuncial arrangement placed over a chessboard background appear frequently. The roundels do not appear connected by means of bands, as occurs in designs with a Byzantine component, but

1-18. General view of the pavement in its current state from the choir and transept, upper level, of Saint-Benoît-sur-Loire.

1-19. [Top] Detail of the pavement from the choir and transept; upper level, of Saint-Benoît-sur-Loire.

1-20. [Bottom] Detail of rectangular slab and porphyry roundels, pavement in the choir and transept, upper level, of Saint-Benoît-sur-Loire.

rather each floats in isolation over the chessboard background. Acute, sharp, and abrupt angles characterize the designs with Islamic influence; in them, the size of the tesserae is greatly reduced because the Muslims tended to "atomize" the patterns. Another sign of Arab influence is the occasional use of glazed ceramic pieces in pavements, rather than the more classic marble tesserae. The designs with Arab influence present greater complexity of geometry, mobility, and dynamism than the Byzantine and classical designs.

In the two centers of flat polychrome geometric ornament located in continental Europe, the dominant influence is Carolingian. It could not be otherwise in the palaces of Charlemagne, such as those in Aachen or Metz. In the pavement of the transept at Saint-Benoît-sur-Loire, the monolithic rounds of porphyry or circular slabs lie directly over a chessboard background; no curved white bands separate the roundels from the background (figs. 1-18, 1-19, and 1-20). This fact reveals a Carolingian influence, that also seems to blend with the classical.[27] The appearance of the pavement today is the result of successive work campaigns: new construction in the eleventh century, followed by reforms and additions from the medieval period (twelfth century) and the Renaissance (sixteenth and seventeenth centuries). It is known that in the sixteenth century, large porphyry roundels were ordered brought from Rome to improve the pavement, and it would not be surprising if some of the mosaicists also came from Rome, which would explain the classical traits present in the pavement.

Throughout the Italian peninsula as well as in Sicily, the influence of Byzantine art is evident in the local art. However, one can make various

1-21. [Left] Detail of part of the triumphal arch and portico, Santa Maria Maggiore (Duomo), Cività Castellana.
1-22. [Above] General view of the exterior, Santa Maria Maggiore (Duomo), Cività Castellana.

distinctions regarding the effect of eastern traditions as compared to the weight of the local and other imported influences.

In the focal point of flat polychrome geometric ornament situated in central Italy, the local tradition, which is to say, the classical tradition (including classical, late classical, and paleo-Christian), is dominant, although some mechanisms and elements of composition imported from the Byzantine tradition—the external tradition of greatest influence in medieval Rome—are also present. The designs in this region of central Italy combine the geometric compositions inherited from the ancient Roman mosaic with the gentle, sinusoidal curves probably learned from the interlacing designs of the Byzantine mosaics in *opus sectile* (marble intarsia, or mosaic, in which the design—usually a homogeneous geometric pattern—is entirely coincident with its constructive piecing). These Byzantine curves are, in turn, the product of the local tradition, for they revive the sinusoidal interlacings of the imperial Roman mosaics in *opus tessellatum* (mosaic built of small cubic tesserae; the design—figurative motifs or geometric patterns—is not entirely coincident with the constructive piecing). In chapter 3 there is a detailed study of the blending of local and Byzantine traditions in Cosmatesque mosaics. The magnitude and wealth of the sublime legacy from ancient Rome, therefore, did not go unnoticed by medieval Roman artists, who admired and studied its remnants, loading the artistic works of central Italy with flourishes of classicism. The reference to classical models is evident in a building like Santa Maria Maggiore in Cività Castellana (figs. 1-21 and 1-22), one of the few occasions in which the Cosmatesque artists had the opportunity to construct an entirely new building.[28] In Rome a few mosaics from the ninth century also remain as evidence of the Carolingian influence.[29] The most notable of these mosaics paves the Chapel of San Zenone in the

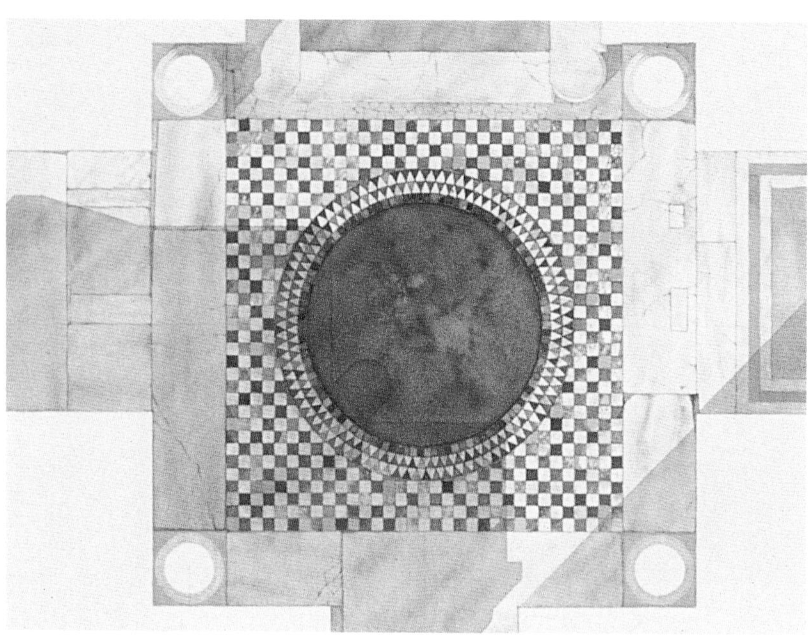

1-23. Pavement in the Chapel of San Zenone in the Church of Santa Prassede, Rome. (Detail of a watercolor on a scale of 1:10 meters, painted by P. Pajares, 1992–93)

Church of Santa Prassede, where an enormous porphyry roundel, 1.54 meters (5 feet) in diameter rests upon a background of tetrachrome chessboard pattern (fig. 1-23). (For further discussion of the chapel's pavement, see chapter 5.)

The northeastern focal point of flat polychrome ornament, located in the northern half of the Italian peninsula, that is, the High Adriatic region, is dominated by Byzantine tradition. This region was among those in which Byzantine rule lasted the longest and where, even when this dominion ended, intense commercial relations with the easternmost portion of the Mediterranean were maintained. Venice is the principal example of the weight of eastern influence, as evidenced by the very beautiful pavement of San Marco (figs. 1-24 and 1-25). In the art of the Comacini masters, who worked at the center in Como, the influence of Lombard art is apparent. Although Lombard influence predominates in the center in Tuscany, this source is blended with others. Thus, in Pisa the pavement of the baptistery owes some of its geometric characteristics to a slight Arab influence (fig. 1-26).[30] In Florence and Lucca are more tranquil examples, exhibiting the classical inheritance, making those works more similar to the Cosmatesque works in the center in Latium.

The characteristics of the flat polychrome geometric ornament of each of the three focal points situated in the southern half of the peninsula resulted from the blending of the different traditions of ornament of the peoples who successively occupied that territory during the Middle Ages: the Byzantines, the Arabs, and the Normans. The ornament of the center in Campania, because of the region's proximity to the center in Latium, presents classical-Byzantine characteristics, though mixed with those of Arab and Norman influence. In the center on the peninsula of Otranto, Byzantine influence dominates. In the southwestern center, the mix of influences reflects characteristics stemming from the triple tradition, Byzantine-Arab-Norman. This tradition led to medieval Sicily's singular artistic production, which is deserving of a specific name, although that name varies depending upon the art historian: "Sicilian-Norman," "Sicilian-Arab," or "Arab-Sicilian." The

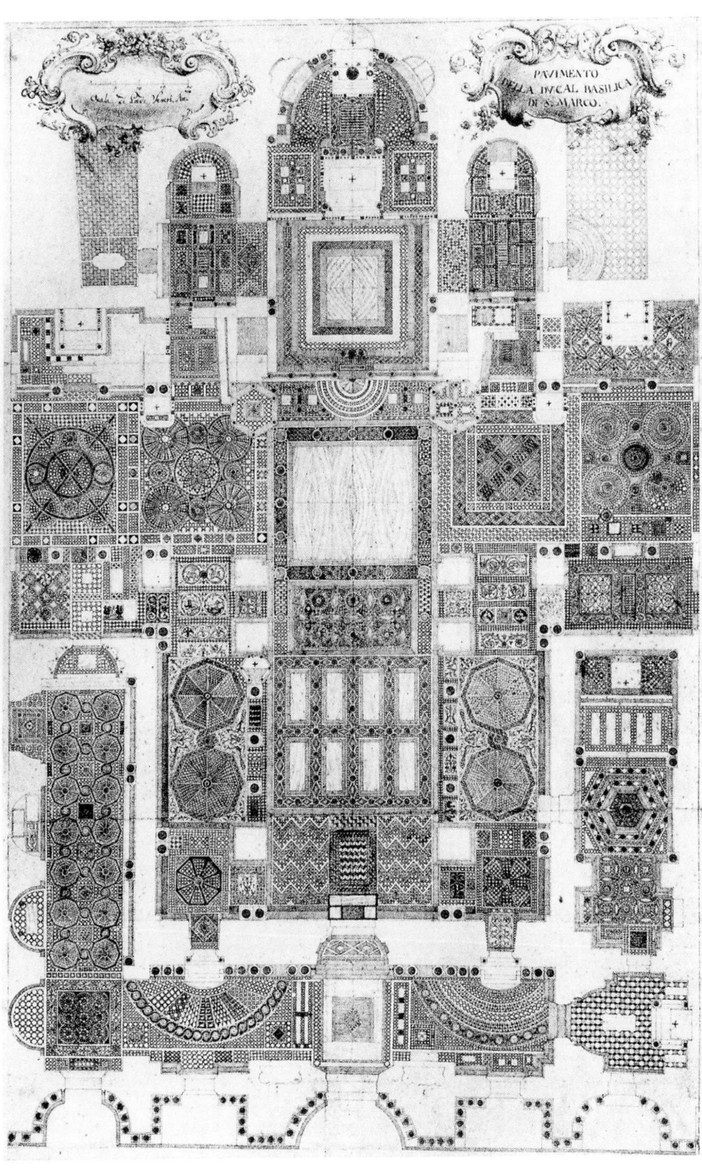

1-24. Pavement in the basilica of San Marco, Venice.

1-25. Detail of the pavement in the northwest corner of the basilica of San Marco (lower left corner of the previous figure).

1-26. Mosaic paving, Battisterio (baptistery), Pisa, 12th century. The Islamic influence is clear in this design. (Chromolithograph by F. M. Hessemer, 1842)

principal Sicilian monuments with flat polychrome geometric ornament are, in Palermo, the Palazzo dei Normanni (in the Cappella Palatina and Sala di Re Ruggero), La Martorana, the Cattedrale, the Chiesa de San Giovanni, and the Palazzo della Zisa; in Monreale, the Abadia (in the cathedral and cloister, figs. 1-27, 1-28, and 1-29); in Cefalù, the Cattedrale; and in Messina, the Chiesa dell' Annunziata dei Catalani.

It is noteworthy that in the areas of the Italian peninsula where Byzantine dominance was most enduring (the High Adriatic region, the central band that unites Rome and Ravenna, the "toe" and "heel" of the Italian "boot," Sicily), monuments with flat polychrome geometric ornament abound. In other words, the degree of "Byzantization" of a region is directly proportional to the number of monuments with flat polychrome geometric ornament that arise there. Similarly, the degree of "Islamization" of a region is directly proportional to the number of monuments produced in the region with that sort of ornament.

This section has thus far discussed the different centers of flat polychrome geometric ornament in medieval western Europe; the section that follows will provide additional information about some of the aforementioned centers, in particular, those in which the term *flat polychrome geometric* may be replaced by *Cosmatesque*. In an effort to link these two topics, I would first like to make some comments with respect to the appropriate use of the adjective *Cosmatesque*. Many authors, possibly owing to their general or limited knowledge of the topic about which they are writing, do not hesitate to employ

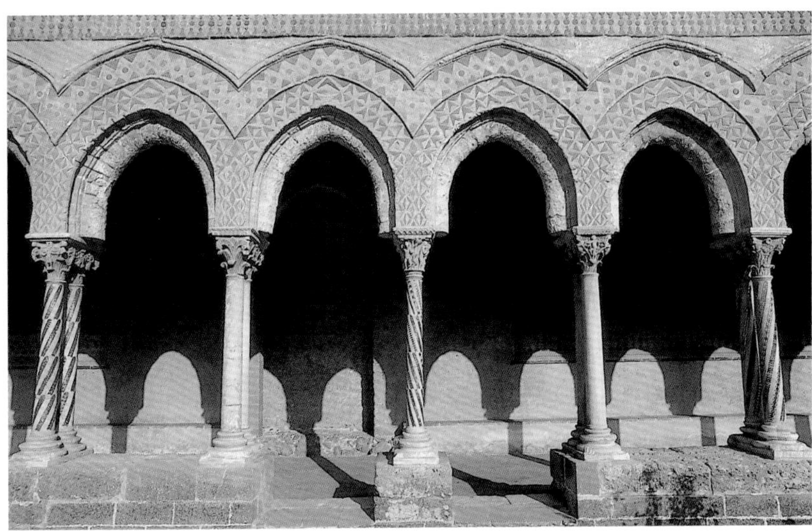

1-27. *Detail of one of the sides of the cloister of the abbey at Monreale.*

1-28. *Detail of the columns of the cloister of the abbey at Monreale.*

1-29. Decorative mosaic, cathedral, Monreale, 12th to 17th century. (Detail of a chromolithograph by F. M. Hessemer, 1842)

the qualifying adjective *Cosmatesque* to refer to any of the works contained in the numerous centers of flat polychrome geometric ornament cited up to this point. However, the marked differences among these works make it inappropriate to employ a single term in referring to all of them. Moreover, some experts, at the same time that they claim to employ the term *Cosmatesque* only because it is commonly accepted and used, recommend it be replaced by another, more suitable one. Thus, Goffredo Bendinelli, who studied the origin of the Cosmatesque mosaics, advocates the use of a new name to denote them, proposing *Byzantine-geometric* as the most fitting.[31] W. R. Lethaby, referring to the technique of these mosaics, prefers to employ the term *parcel mosaic* rather than the usual *Cosmati work*; on occasion, he also employs the term *opus alexandrinum* to refer to Cosmatesque pavements, possibly following the example of the postmedieval scholars who studied antiquity.[32] A. M. Bessone-Aurelj comments that these postmedieval scholars based their use of the term *opus alexandrinum* for the Cosmatesque pavements on the words of the historian Lampridio, who, when writing about an episode in the life of Alessandro Severo, recounted that the emperor ordered the creation of mosaic works made by assembling porphyry and serpentine.[33] Bessone-Aurelj uses the term *Cosmatesque* to describe the works of the centers in meridional Italy, although the author points out that these works are also laden with Sicilian-Arab influence.[34]

All of these labels appear to arise from the determination of each author to reveal the specific characteristics of the particular group of works that are the object of his or her study. My own use of the adjective *Cosmatesque* is explained in the section entitled "The Centers of Cosmatesque Ornament."

The Artists: Magistri Doctissimi Romani

Cosmatesque production flourished from late in the eleventh century, when Rome began to establish itself as the City of Popes, until 1305, at which time Clement V, a French pontiff, transferred the papal residence to Avignon. During the next 70 years the pontiffs remained in France as Rome fell into a state of abandonment and destitution which put an end to any commissions for work by the Roman marble workers. The most fruitful period for the Cosmatesque School coincided with the tenures of Paschal II (1099–1118), Honorius II (1124–1130), Innocent III (1198–1216), and Honorius III

(1216–1227), all of whom possessed a keen interest in rebuilding Rome and reviving the splendor which the city had held in pagan times. In order to achieve their goal, the pontiffs worked ceaselessly to promote the development of ecclesiastic construction, as much in the capital as in the rest of the papal territory.

The Cosmatesque artists were charged with the execution of those construction projects. They were Romans, proud of the glorious past of their city and committed to the local classical artistic tradition, which they eagerly studied for their own work. The buildings and ruins of Ancient Rome were their favorite subject. They worked as ornamenters, mosaicists, sculptors, and architects. They were excellent geometrists, capable of building their designs with rigor and exactness, by using precise technique. For their work, they used spoliated materials obtained from buildings in ruins. The headquarters of their guild seems to have been the church of SS. Quattro Coronati, specifically the chapel of S. Silvestro, which they probably used as a meeting hall. The majority of their workshops were located around the Via Lata and the neighborhood of Trevi. Sculptures and fragments of ancient buildings found in the ruins of many of these workshops were possibly collected and studied by the Cosmati as models for their own creations. Their pride in Roman citizenship and their fondness for study are evident in some of the inscriptions still visible in many of the Cosmatesque works whose authors signed their names followed by the title, "Magister Doctissimus Romanus," or simply, "Civis Romanus."

When these Roman masters were first studied, their work was commonly attributed to a single family, the descendants of Cosma. Hence the name, Cosmatesque. More recent research has clarified and completed the information regarding the *marmorari romani*. Today we know that several families were responsible for the creation of these works, each family with its own name and comprising numerous members who handed down their trade from father to son, generation after generation. Nonetheless, the term Cosmatesque is still used in referring to the artists collectively. We know the names, chronology, and genealogy of the Cosmatesque artists thanks to the study of the inscriptions which they themselves left on the majority of their works, as well as the study of written documents found in archives. The most outstanding of these families were: the Paolo family, who worked throughout the twelfth century; the Drudo da Trivio family, active in the first half of the thirteenth century; the Cosmati family (divided in two branches: the first being the Tebaldo family, active at the end of the twelfth century and beginning of the thirteenth century; and the second being the Mellini family, who worked in the second half of the thirteenth century); and finally, the Vassalletto family, contemporaries and emulators of the Cosmati. Other notable families of marmorari were: the Ranuccio family, who worked during the same period as the sons of Paolo; the Oderisio family, active in the second half of the thirteenth century. (Pietro Oderisio, or Petrus Odericius, who worked in England in Westminster Abbey and Canterbury Cathedral, was the most celebrated artist of this line); and the Salvati family, who worked from the twelfth century to the fourteenth century. Figure 1-30 lists the principal genealogical trees. Many other artists have been identified who seem to have worked independently: in the twelfth century, Pietro Amabili; in the thirteenth century, Pasquale, Pietro de Maria and his pupils

PAOLO
1108
GIOVANNI / PIETRO / ANGELO / SASSONE
1146 • 1148 • 1153
NICOLA D'ANGELO
1148 • 1153 • 1170 • 1180
JACOPO
1170

PIETRO MELLINI MARMORARO?
1200?
COSMA II
1246 • 1265 • 1279
JACOPO III / GIOVANNI / DEODATO / PIETRO / CARLO?
1293 • 1293 • 1299 • 1290 • 1332 • 1292 • 1297 • ?
LUCANTONIO (son of Giovanni)

DRUDO DA TRIVIO
1200 • 1240
ANGELO
1240

VASSALLETTO
1130 • 1154
PIETRO VASSALLETTO
1180 • 1225
VASSALLETTO (son of Pietro)
1215 • 1262

TEBALDO MARMORARO?
1100?
LORENZO
1162 • 1190
JACOPO
1205 • 1207 • 1210
COSMA
1210 • 1224 • 1231
LUCA / JACOPO
1234 • 1255 • 1231

RANUCCIO or RAINERIO DI GIOVANNI MARMORARO
PIETRO / NICOLA
1143 • 1143
GIOVANNI / GUITTONE
1166 • 1166
GIOVANNI
1209

1-30. Cosmatesque families. Dates refer to evidence from signed works.

(Nicola di Vassalletto, Alessio di Beraldo da Roma, Marco da Roma and Matteo), Andrea, Magister Cassetta, Giulano, Angelus filius Mailardi, Ognissanti de' Tederini, Rayno magister marmorarius, Alessio, Giacomello, Matteo da Narni; in the fourteenth century, Natio Stati, Marco Romano, Maestro Lorenzo Andreozzi, Magister Petrus, together with the group of artists who rebuilt the Abbey of Montecassino (e.g., Giovanni de Comes, Giovanni da Reims, Ugolino, Giovanni, Giovanni Moregia da Milano; Sisto da Alatri and his brother Antonio, Tizio and Cola di Tuzio da Piperno, Nicola di Alessandro, Colella di Giovanni di Sisto, Sisto di Giacomo da Alatri). Many other names should be added to this list since there is a multitude of works whose authors remain unidentified.[35]

The Centers of Cosmatesque Ornament

I regard any work of flat polychrome geometric ornament as a work of Cosmatesque ornament as long as its general composition is regulated by some specific geometric rules. These rules, described in chapter 3, regulate the flat polychrome geometric ornament of the group of works found in the focal point of central Italy. With this in mind, in addition to the center of central Italy, three other centers can be qualified as Cosmatesque: that in Tuscany, that in Campania, and that in the southeast of England. Figure 1-31 lists the centers of Cosmatesque ornament outside central Italy.

TUSCANY
Florence: Opera del Duomo
Lucca: S. Frediano
Pisa: Battisterio, Campo Santo, Duomo

CAMPANIA
Cava de Tirreni: Badia della Santissima Trinità
Naples: Santa Chiara

ENGLAND
London: Westminster Abbey

1-31. The centers of Cosmatesque ornament outside of central Italy.

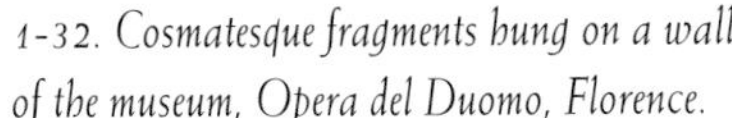
1-32. Cosmatesque fragments hung on a wall of the museum, Opera del Duomo, Florence.

1-33. Pavement behind the altar. Battisterio, Pisa.

Of the four principal centers of Cosmatesque ornament, the most important, by far, is the one of central Italy, that is, the center consisting of the collection of works of flat polychrome geometric ornament that are found in Rome and the surrounding region, Latium. I am inclined to qualify this focal point in central Italy as the "genuinely Cosmatesque" or "classic Cosmatesque," since the works that it comprises owe their traits to a mix of local classical tradition and Byzantine influence. Thus, it follows that the three remaining centers could be called centers of "hybrid Cosmatesque" ornament because their monuments, in addition to the Byzantine influence common to all Cosmatesque works, display characteristics derived from other external influences, such as the Arab and/or the Norman. The Tuscan center comprises Florence (Opera del Duomo, fig. 1-32), Lucca (San Frediano), and Pisa (Battisterio, fig. 1-33; Campo Santo, Duomo). The center in Campania includes Cava de Tirreni (Badia della Santissima Trinità) and Naples (Santa Chiara). The center in England lies in London (Westminster Abbey).

Cosmatesque Ornament in England

The Cosmatesque works in Westminster are the only ones by the Roman artists outside of Italy.[36] The abbey contains several such works, all commissioned by the Plantagenet king of England Henry III (1216–72), from a Roman artist, Petrus Oderisius. One of these works is in the sanctuary, and the rest are in the Chapel of Saint Edward the Confessor. In the sanctuary, in front of the main altar, is a pavement signed by Odericus in 1268 (fig. 1-34). The Chapel of Saint Edward contains the following Cosmatesque works: the base of the reliquary, signed by "Petrus . . . Romanus Civis" (fig. 1-35); the pavement surrounding that reliquary; the tomb of Henry III; the tombs of the princes, John and Alfonso, and the princess, Katherine (all moved to the ambulatory); and the tombstones of John and Margaret of Valence.[37]

The pavement in the sanctuary of Westminster Abbey possesses a general geometric composition that, by virtue of its similarity to some of the motifs

1-34. Pavement in the sanctuary, Westminster Abbey, London.

1-35. Reliquary from the Shrine of Saint Edward the Confessor, Westminster Abbey, London. (Engraving by George Vertue, as reconstructed by Abbot Feckenham in the 1550s)

present in medieval pavements in Rome (such as San Crisogono), allows for its classification as Cosmatesque. However, the pavement shows other characteristics, such as the extreme subdivision of the pattern, proper to the works of Sicilian-Norman art; not surprising if one considers that England and Sicily maintained close political and cultural ties during the late Middle Ages when both territories found themselves under Norman rule.[38]

The pavement in the sanctuary at Westminster Abbey is an imported Cosmatesque pavement, given that both the master who executed it and the materials that compose it were brought from Rome.[39] The journey that Petrus made from Rome to London possibly put him in contact with some of the Romanesque works and artists of continental Europe, which might partially explain the stylistic peculiarities of the Cosmatesque mosaics that Petrus created on English soil.[40] Many authors, particularly English ones, have published studies about the Cosmatesque works in Westminster Abbey.[41] Among these studies Richard Foster's extensive monograph about the pavement in the sanctuary stands out; he analyzes in detail all aspects of the pavement, including its meaning. Foster discusses at length the cosmic symbolism of the pavement, which he perceives as a means of contemplating the higher order of the universe in its continuous expansion-contraction.

Cosmatesque Ornament in Central Italy

Each of the cities that form part of the classic Cosmatesque focal point, that is, the Cosmatesque center of central Italy, possesses one or more monuments worked on by Cosmatesque artists (fig. 1-36 lists these monuments) and each monument contains one or more works created by the Roman *marmorari*. In central Italy I know of sixty-two cities in which it is currently possible to see Cosmatesque ornament: fifty of them are found in the region of Latium (figs. 1-37 to 1-49), eight in Umbria (figs. 1-50 and 1-51), and four in Abruzzi.

The Cosmatesque center of central Italy is without doubt the most important of all the centers of flat polychrome geometric ornament cited thus far,

LATIUM

Acquapendente: San Francesco
Albano: Frattocchie, San Pietro
Amaseno: San Lorenzo
Anagni: Sant'Andrea, San Giacomo, Santa Maria (duomo; San Magnus crypt; museum), San Pietro in Vineis
Anticoli Corrado: San Pietro
Ardea: San Pietro
Arsoli: Castello Massimo
Bolsena: Santa Cristina
Castel Sant'Elia (near Nepi): Sant'Anastasio
Cave: San Carlo
Cività Castellana: Santa Maria Maggiore (duomo)
Cività Lavinia: Santa Maria Maggiore
Cori: Santa Maria della Pietà
Falleri (in Faleri Novi): Santa Maria di Falleri
Farfa in Sabina: Badia, Santa Maria di Farfa
Ferentino: Duomo, Sant'Ambrogio, Palazzo Episcopale
Fondi: Duomo
Foronovo: Santa Maria in Vescovio
Fossanova (near Sonnino): Badia
Frascati: San Rocco
Gaeta: Duomo
Genazzano: San Nicola, San Paolo
Grottaferrata: Badia, Santa Maria
Mentorella in Sabina (Vulturella, near Guadagnolo): Santa Maria in Mentorella
Montebuono: San Pietro
Monte SantAngelo in Arcese (near Maránola): San Michele Arcangelo
Nazzano: Badia di Sant'Antimo
Nepi: Duomo
Ninfa (near Norma): church outside walls
Orte: San Silvestro
Palestrina: Duomo, Sant'Agapito
Palombara Sabina: San Giovanni in Argentella
Ponzano Romano: Sant'Andrea in Flumine
Rieti: Cattedrale
Rignano Flaminio: Santi Abbondio ed Abbondanzio
Rome: See chapter 2
San Oreste: San Lorenzo
Segni: Duomo, San Pietro
Sermoneta: Santa Maria Della Pieve
Subiaco: San Benedetto, Santa Scholastica, Sacro Speco
Sutri: Assunta, Duomo, San Francesco, San Giacomo
Tarquinia: Santa Maria di Castello
Terracina: Duomo
Tivoli: Duomo, Sant'Andrea, San Lorenzo, Santa Maria Maggiore, San Michele, San Pietro (Chiesa della Carità), San Silvestro
Toffia: San Lorenzo
Tuscania: Santa Maria Maggiore, San Pietro
Velletri: Duomo, Santa Maria in Trivio
Veroli: Sant'Erasmo
Vetralla: San Francesco
Viterbo: Duomo, Museo Civico, San Francesco, San Lorenzo

UMBRIA

Assisi: San Francesco (Upper Church, Lower Church)
Bevagna: San Michele
Foligno: Duomo
Lugnano in Teverina: Santa Maria Assunta
Narni: Duomo, San Domenico, San Giovenale, Santa Maria in Penzola
Orvieto: Badia di Santi Severo e Martirio, Santa Maria del Piano, Santi Andrea e Bartolommeo, Duomo
Sassovivo (near Foligno): Badia
Spoleto: Assunta, Duomo, San Gregorio Maggiore

ABRUZZI

Alba Fucense: San Pietro
Basanello: San Salvatore
Rocca di Botte: Badia
Teramo: Duomo, San Francesco (Sant'Antonio)

1-36. The places and monuments with Cosmatesque ornament in central Italy (Latium, Umbria, and Abruzzi).

1-37. Detail of one of the motifs in the pavement covering the longitudinal axis of Santa Maria Maggiore, Tivoli.

1-38. View of the interior, Santa Maria Maggiore, Tivoli.

1-39. Detail of the central eyelet of the quincunx located on the longitudinal axis of the church, pavement, San Pietro (Chiesa della Carità), Tivoli.

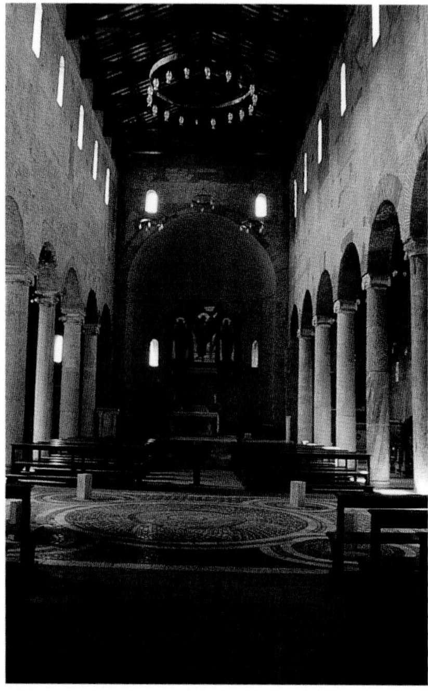

1-40. View of the interior, San Pietro (Chiesa della Carità), Tivoli.

1-41. Details of the pavement,
San Pietro (Chiesa della Carità), Tivoli.

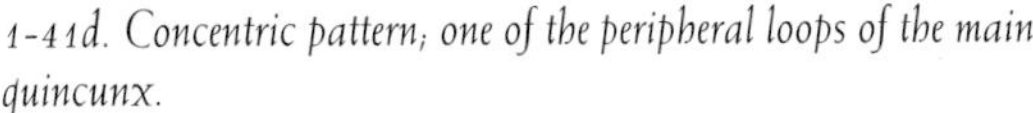

1-41d. Concentric pattern; one of the peripheral loops of the main quincunx.

1-41a. Chessboard pattern; every other square bearing an hourglass of two semicircles.

1-41e. Detail of the center of a concentric pattern; one of the loops of the main quincunx.

1-41b. Triaxial pattern of six-pointed stars forming lozenges.

1-41f. Row of tangent circles; each circle formed by four tangent spindles.

1-41c. Chessboard pattern; every other square bearing its inverse.

1-41g. Series of adjoined broken lines.

1-42. Detail of the rose window of the façade, Santa Maria Maggiore, Tuscania.

1-43. Façade, Santa Maria Maggiore, Tuscania.

1-44. Rose window of the façade. San Pietro, Tuscania.

1-45. Central portion of the façade, San Pietro, Tuscania.

1-46. Detail of the Cosmatesque mosaics that ornament the base of the door's arch, San Pietro, Tuscania.

1-47. Door. San Pietro, Tuscania.

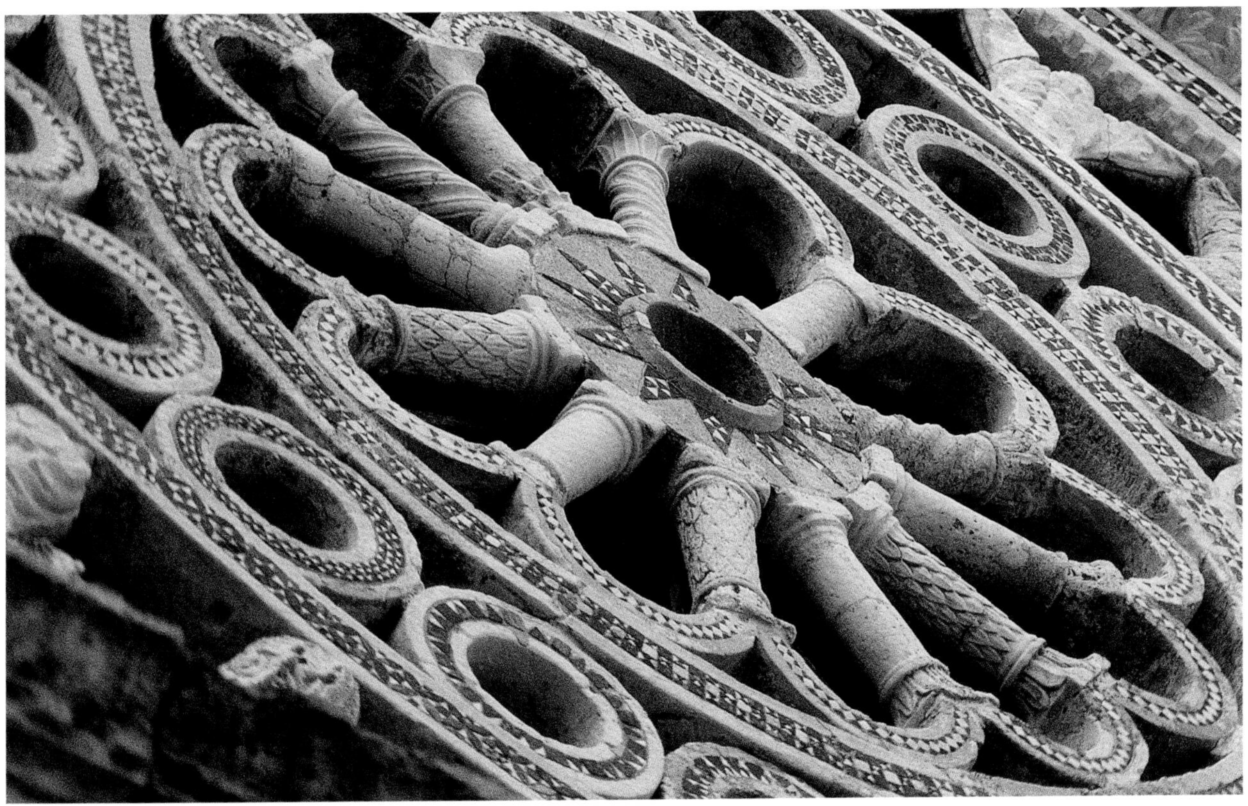

1-48. Detail of the central portion of the rose window of the façade. San Pietro, Tuscania.

1-49. Details of the mosaics that ornament the door frame, San Pietro, Tuscania.

1-49a. Linear pattern that ornaments the sides of the door jambs. Row of stars of six lozenges and equilateral hourglasses.

1-49b. Linear pattern that ornaments the front of the jambs. Row of tangent circles composed of four spindles.

1-50. Mosaic decorations in the basilica of San Francesco, Assisi, 13th century. (Detail of a chromolithograph by F. M. Hessemer, 1842)

1-51. Detail of the façade, Duomo, Orvieto.

not only because it has the greatest number of works, but also because it covers uniformly a region of considerable extent, while the remaining centers consist of either isolated works or of clusters comprising a very small number of works.

If one marks on a contemporary map of Italy all of the cities containing buildings with remains of works created by the medieval Roman marble artists, the small centers or groups in Tuscany and Campania appear, as well as the large group comprising numerous cities in central Italy (fig. 1-52). This central group or cluster presents a dense nucleus with faint branches; the nucleus covers practically all of the region known today as Latium, while the branches are shaped by some of the western cities of Umbria and Abruzzi. The heart of the nucleus is Rome, which is, furthermore, the densest site, commanding a very large number of monuments with Cosmatesque ornament.

By studying a map of the geopolitical units that shaped Italy around 1150, which is to say, the map of Italy from the time of the Cosmati (see fig. 1-4), one can see that the region of central Italy was occupied at that time by the

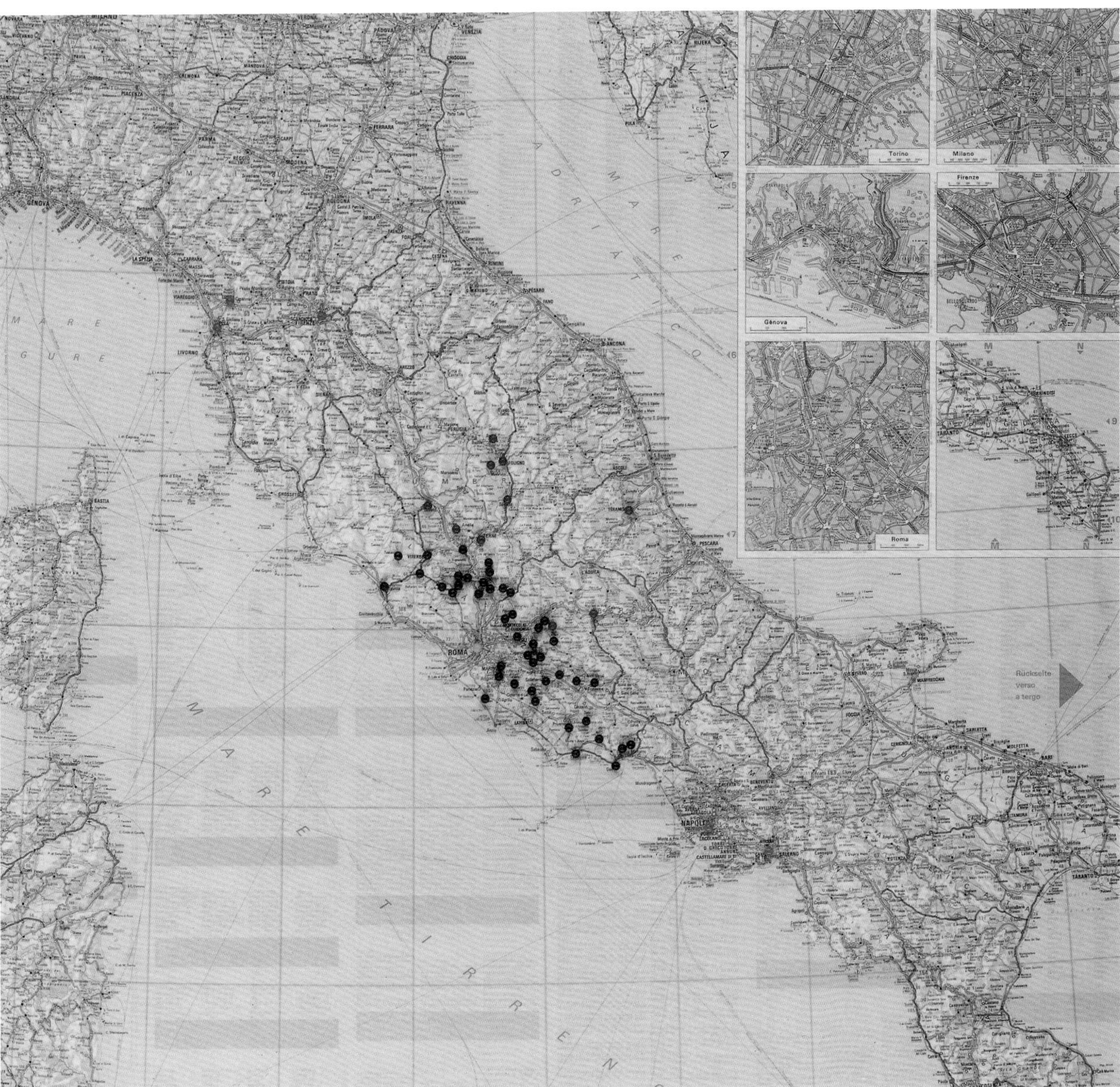

1-52. Sites with Cosmatesque ornament in Italy, marked with colored points: yellow, Rome; black, Latium; blue, Umbria; green, Abruzzi; red, Tuscany; orange, Campania. (Map, 1:1,000,000, 90 by 131 cm, Kümmerly+Frey, Bern, Switzerland. © Kümmerly+Frey AG, CH-3052 Zollikofen-Bern.)

Papal State. The Papal State, like all the medieval states, had unstable borders, occupying, at times of maximum expansion, the territories in the strip of central Italy that unites Rome with Ravenna (which had been property of the Byzantine emperor until Charlemagne conquered these territories in the ninth century) and in its moments of least expansion, the western zone of the central strip, that is, the region surrounding Rome, known today as Latium (fig. 1-53).

In comparing the two previous maps of Italy, the territory occupied by the cluster of cities in central Italy, where we can still contemplate Cosmatesque works today, clearly coincides with the territory of the Papal State in the Middle Ages. The portion of Italian geography in which we currently find the classical or principal Cosmatesque center, with its nucleus in Latium and its branches to the northeast, coincides therefore with the area occupied by the pontifical territories at the time of the Cosmati (fig. 1-54).[42]

The existence of such a large number of monuments with shared stylistic characteristics, geographically concentrated almost exclusively in the Papal

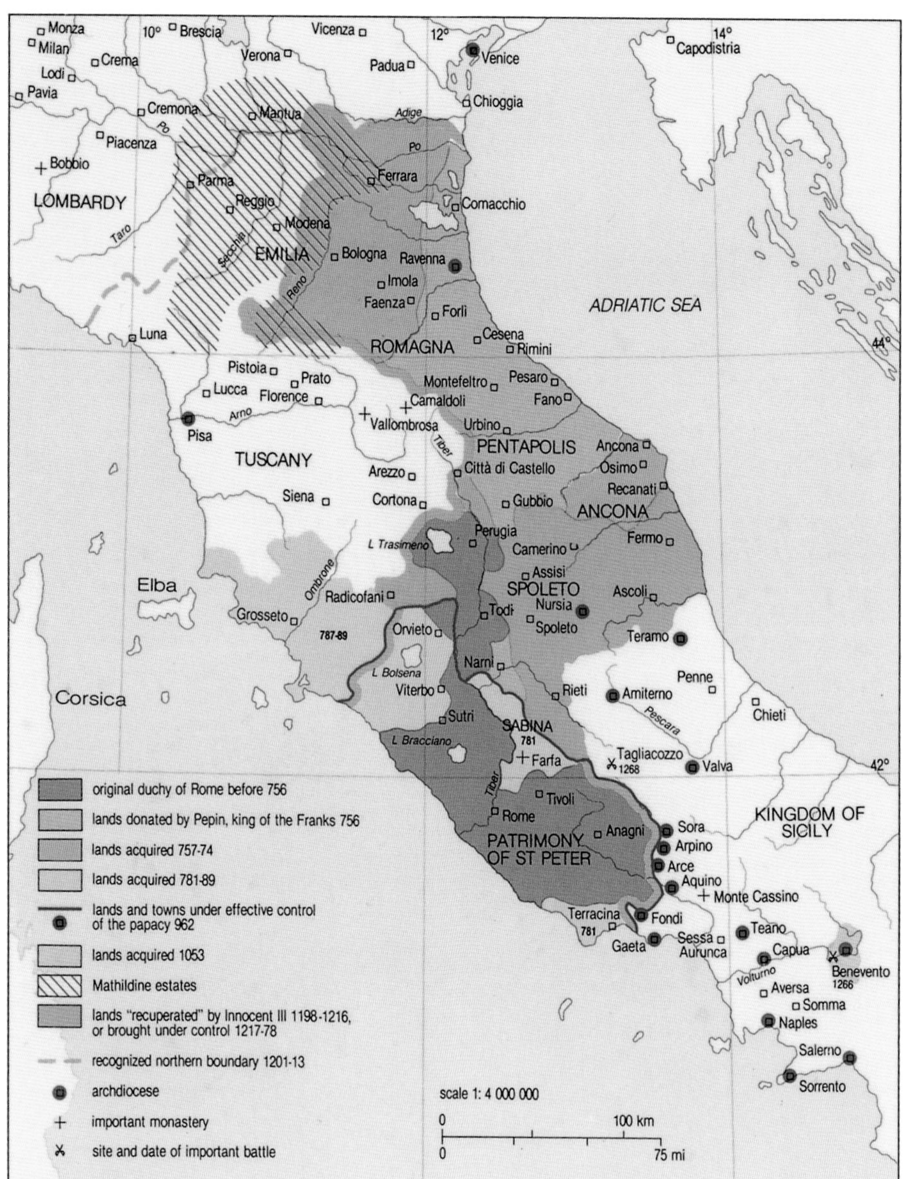

1-53. The development of the Papal State. The territories of present-day Latium were, in the Middle Ages, the nucleus of the Papal State; the territories of the band that joins Rome and Ravenna were the preferred area of expansion of the Papal State.

State and covering that area in its entirety, leads one to think that the Cosmatesque works were undertaken through an active building program promoted and/or financed by the Papacy and embracing its entire territory; in other words, a state-funded nationwide building program.

This program launched the construction of new churches, principally in rural population centers, in addition to the improvement and embellishment—today we would say "rehabilitation"—of existing churches, in monasteries and towns as well as in the great city of Rome, where innumerable churches had been popping up since the early times of Christianity and which now required renovation and improvement. The reform of these buildings arose in conjunction with the spiritual "antiabuse" and "anticorruption" reforms that the church was undergoing at the time.[43] There is no doubt that the hierarchy within the church, by promoting, throughout its territory, the construction of new places of worship and the rehabilitation and embellishment of those already in existence, sought to contribute to the material and spiritual development of the whole Papal State. However, one should not dismiss additional motives, of a propagandist nature, in the

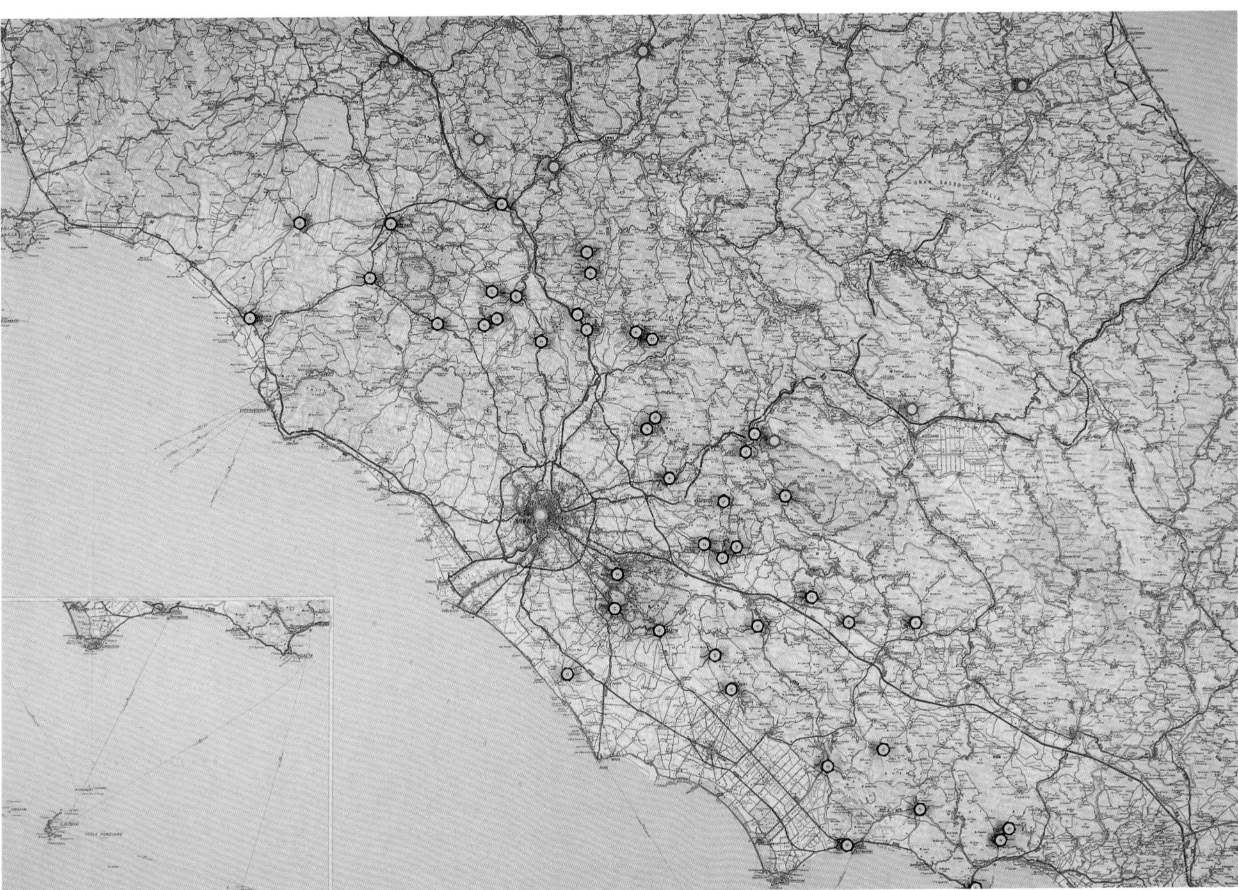

1-54. Sites with Cosmatesque ornament in and near Latium, marked with colored points: yellow, Rome; black, Latium; blue, Umbria; green, Abruzzi.(Map, 1:200,000, 135 by 93 cm, Touring Club Italiano, Milan)

building activity promoted by the Papacy since Cosmatesque work possibly represented for the church authorities one, perhaps the best, means within their reach to affirm before the faithful the preeminence of the pope's power—spiritual and temporal—in the face of other rival powers within the local panorama (Roman aristocracy), the national panorama (the emperor of the West), or the international panorama (the Byzantine Empire, Islam).

The papal building program (whose prolific results have survived to the present, presumably quite reduced with the passage of time and in part altered by the restorations of the sixteenth to seventeenth and the nineteenth to twentieth centuries[44]) flourished thanks to the relative economic and political stability that the Papal State enjoyed as of the eleventh century. Such stability permitted the revival of culture and art. The work of the Cosmati belongs to this period of recuperation, the Roman renaissance or *renovatio* of the twelfth century; in it one can observe a resurgence of classical models, relearned through the study of those ruins and buildings of the Roman Empire that survived in medieval Rome. The recovery of a classical language, associated and associable with the times in which Rome was the "queen of the world," must have seemed supremely appropriate at that time in the eyes of the Papacy, with its determination to affirm its primacy and that of its city. The pride of being Roman, mixed with nostalgia for the better times of the past and the will to revive them, seemed to be present as much in the spirit of those who promoted the Cosmatesque works as in the spirit of the artists themselves. It was not unfounded that the Cosmati, upon signing their works, frequently added to their name the postscript "Roman Citizen."

Chapter 2

ROME

COSMATESQUE SITE PAR EXCELLENCE

Of the sixty-eight cities that have Cosmatesque ornament, sixty-two form a cluster in central Italy. Three of the six remaining cities are in Tuscany, two in Campania, and one in England. The principal focal point of Cosmatesque ornament, central Italy, thus is home to 91 percent of the Cosmatesque cities. The sixty-two cities of central Italy contain 183 Cosmatesque monuments (see chapter 1 for a list of these cities and monuments); 85 of these lie within the capital city of Rome (fig. 2-1).[1] Hence, Rome contains 46 percent of the monuments of the principal Cosmatesque focal point (fig. 2-2). Moreover,

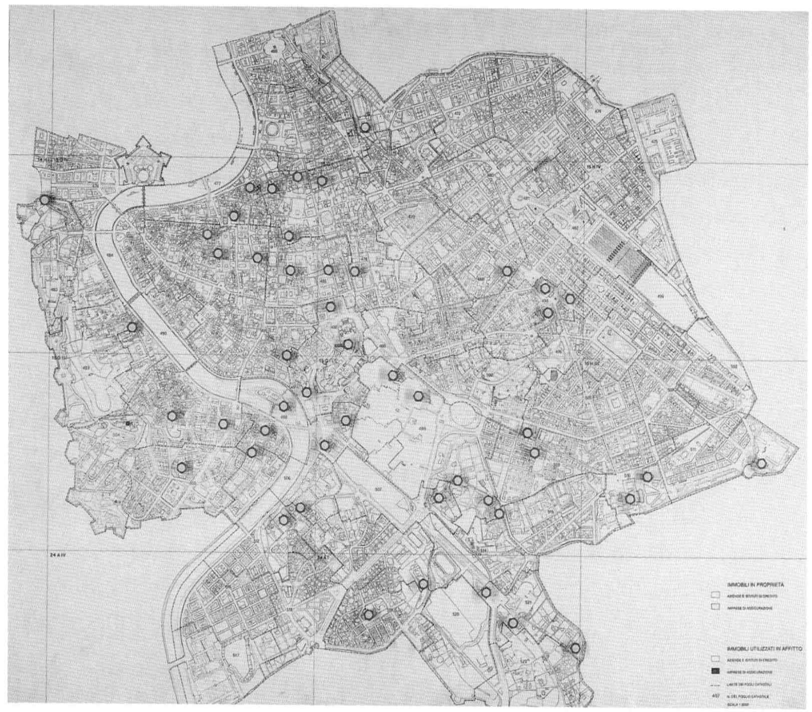

2-1. The locations of the principal monuments with Cosmatesque ornament in Rome, marked with blue push pins. (Map of Rome, historic center, 1:5,000, 106 by 90 cm, Carta delle Propietà nel Centro Storico di Roma. SPQR—Comune de Roma—Ufficio Speciale per gli Interventi sul Centro Storico [S.A.R.A. NISTRI], Árgos, Roma, 1992)

Chiesa dell'Addolorata
Sant'Adriano
Sant'Agnese in Agone (Piazza Navona)
Sant'Alessio (Santi Bonifacio e Allessio in Aventino)
Sant'Ambrogio in Pescheria
Sant'Anselmo
Sant'Antonio Abate
Annunziatella (fuori porta San Sebastiano)
Sant'Apollinare (Piazza Navona)
Santi Apostoli
Appartamento Borgia
Santa Balbina
San Bartolommeo all'Isola Tiberina
San Benedetto in Piscinula
Cappella Sistina (Vatican City)
Casina di Pio IV (Vatican City)
Santa Cecilia in Trastevere
San Cesareo
San Clemente
San Cosimato in Trastevere
Santi Cosma e Damiano
San Crisogono
Santa Croce
Santa Croce in Gerusalemme
Sant'Eusebio
Sant'Eustachio
Santa Francesca Romana al Foro Romano
San Giacomo all Lungara (San Giacomo in Settignano)
San Giorgio in Velabro
San Giovanni in Laterano
Santi Giovanni e Paolo
San Giovanni a Porta Latina
San Giuseppe
San Gregorio Magno (San Gregorio al Celio)
Sant'Ivo dei Brettoni
San Lorenzo in Lucina
San Lorenzo fuori le Mura
Madonna del Rosario
San Marco
Santa Maria in Aquiro
Santa Maria in Aracoeli
Santa Maria in Cosmedin
Santa Maria in Domnica (Santa Maria della Navicella)
Santa Maria Egiziaca a Bocca della Veritá
Santa Maria della Luce in Trastevere
Santa Maria Maggiore
Santa Maria sopra Minerva
Santa Maria in Monticelli
Santa Maria della Pace
Santa Maria del Priorato
Santa Maria Scala Coeli (Abbazia delle Tre Fontane)
Santa Maria in Trastevere
Santa Maria in Via Lata
Santi Michele e Magno
Santi Nereo ed Achilleo
San Nicola in Carcere
San Nicola dei Prefetti
San Pancrazio
San Paolo fuori le Mura
San Pietro Vaticano and Grotte Vaticane
San Pietro in Vincoli
Santa Prassede
Santa Prisca
Santa Pudenziana
Santi Quattro Coronati
Santi Quirico e Giulitta
Santi Rufina e Seconda (Via della Lungaretta)
San Saba sul Celio
Santa Sabina
Sacro Cuore del Sufragio
San Salvatore alle Cappella
Scala Santa (Sancta Sanctorum Cappella)
San Sebastiano
San Silvestro in Capite
San Sisto Vecchio
Santo Spirito
Stanza della Segnatura (Stanze di Raffaello, Vatican City)
Santo Stefano del Cacco
Santo Stefano Rotondo sul Celio
Tempietto di Bramante
San Tommaso in Formis
Trinità dei Monti
Sant'Urbano
Palazzo Venezia
Santi Vincenzo ed Anastasio (Abbazia delle Tre Fontane)

2-2. *The Cosmatesque monuments in Rome.*

the Cosmatesque monuments in Rome are the most important, as much for their dimensions as for their quality of design and execution. Rome is, without doubt, the Cosmatesque site par excellence, and for that reason warrants special attention in any research on the work of the Cosmati. The irrefutable importance of Rome as a Cosmatesque site has led me to dedicate a substantial part of this book to the detailed study of the Cosmatesque monuments in that city and to leave a comparable study of the other Cosmatesque monuments for another occasion.

Included among the Cosmatesque monuments of Rome are those that constitute genuine Cosmatesque production—that is, the collection of works produced by Roman artists during the period from the Papacy of Gregory VII (1073–85) to the Papacy of Honorius III (1216–27).[2] Also included are those monuments that display works with undeniably Cosmatesque traits, although they were executed after the thirteenth century. Some of these "late-Cosmatesque" works were built in the fifteenth and sixteenth centuries (for example, the pavements of the Cappella Sistina (Sistine Chapel), Tempietto di Bramante, Appartamento Borgia, Stanze di Raffaello, the room of Cardinal Giuliano della Rovere in Santi Apostoli). Others, which I call "neo-Cosmatesque," appeared in the nineteenth century and early twentieth centuries (for example, Chiesa dell'Addolorata, San Giuseppe, Santa Croce, Sacro Cuore del Suffragio, Madonna del Rosario). The latter, referred to by A. M. Bessone-Aurelj as "modern imitations," are the products of the eclectic art of the nineteenth century.[3] The Cosmatesque revival that occurred in Rome during that period was one of the many "revivals," including the Greek Revival and Gothic Revival, that took place in Europe at that time.

Rome in the Late Middle Ages

A constant struggle for power among the pope, the emperor, and the local aristocracy dominated life in medieval Rome.[4] At the end of the eleventh century and throughout the twelfth century, during the time of the Cosmati, the conflict between the emperor and the pope reached a climax, as evidenced by the Controversy of the Investitures (1075–1177), which was partially resolved by the Concordat of Worms (1122), the agreement that laid the foundation for recognition of the pope as the supreme spiritual as well as temporal authority. In about the year 1130, the Papacy saw the emperor subordinated to the pope, when it was accepted that the pope conceded temporal power to the emperor through the act of coronation.

It was during the time of the Cosmati, therefore, that the popes won the battle against the Hohenstaufen emperors in their struggle for temporal power. This period also marked the beginning of the struggle of the Roman citizens—with the support and representation of their nobles—against the temporal authority of the pope. By the twelfth century, the citizens of Rome had grown wealthy and naturally claimed political power. In 1143 a city revolt produced the proclamation of a republic and the establishment of a senate. Thereafter, the pope and the emperor together would contrive to prevent the citizens of Rome from attaining their goal of full self-government. Conflict continued, with short-lived periods of reconciliation, until the reign of Pope Clement III, a Roman citizen himself, who came to a final agreement with the city of Rome in the Concordat of 1188. This compromise succeeded because it made concessions to both sides: it restored all temporal rights to the pope while at the same time recognizing the city as a commune. The base for the new revival that Rome experienced from the end of the twelfth until the middle of the thirteenth century was thus established.

Under Innocence III (1198–1216) and Honorius III (1216–27), efficient and powerful rulers, the medieval Papacy reached its peak. The politics of Innocence III centered on the maintenance, restructuring, and expansion of the papal territories in central Italy, with Rome as the locus of power. These ambitions were possible because of an effective, reorganized administration and wise fiscal policy, which convinced the citizens to support the Papacy. The economically strong citizenry of Rome consisted of a variety of social groups: artisans and small merchants, the great landowners of Latium, the urban aristocracy of managers and financiers, as well as the landowners who had become merchants and overseas shippers. In addition, tourists and pilgrims continued to visit the monuments and churches of Rome, above all the seven principal churches: San Giovanni in Laterano, San Pietro, San Paolo fuori le Mura, San Lorenzo fuori le Mura, Santa Maria Maggiore, Santa Croce in Gerusalemme, and San Sebastiano. During the twelfth century, Rome also consolidated its position as the leading European center of finance. In the first decades of the thirteenth century, Rome was the "head of the world," *caput mundi*; through the Papacy, the city had become a force in politics, law, and finance. The popes and cardinals accumulated enormous fortunes, and the Church stored the collected goods in the houses of the Templars or the Tuscan bankers. This economic zenith was reflected in the size and splendor of the churches, which would be rehabilitated and redecorated or reornamented to achieve a sumptuousness not previously displayed. The nobles, the magnates of the church, and their relatives would invest their fortunes in urban development as well as in the lands of the Roman countryside, where monasteries and churches would flourish, emulating those of Rome.

At about this time, the popes adopted the outward signs of maximum temporal power, which previously had been at the exclusive disposition of the emperors, in addition to the signs of maximum spiritual power, which the popes had already been employing. The change was evident in their liturgical ceremonies, vestments, insignia, and furnishings, and, of course, in the architecture they promoted and financed. These imperial symbols included, for example, the use of the color purple, resulting in the employment of porphyry as a building material. Another example was gemmed anagrams of an underlying geometry analogous to the arrangement of five points on a die, which in architecture appear in the quincunx of Cosmatesque interlacings.

The ornament of the Cosmatesque churches symbolized the power, both temporal and spiritual, that the Papacy achieved during the twelfth century. In fact, for the medieval pontiffs, Cosmatesque art was the principal means of promoting their power, as evidenced by the proliferation of Cosmatesque churches throughout the Papal State and the great importance of those medieval churches, especially in Rome.

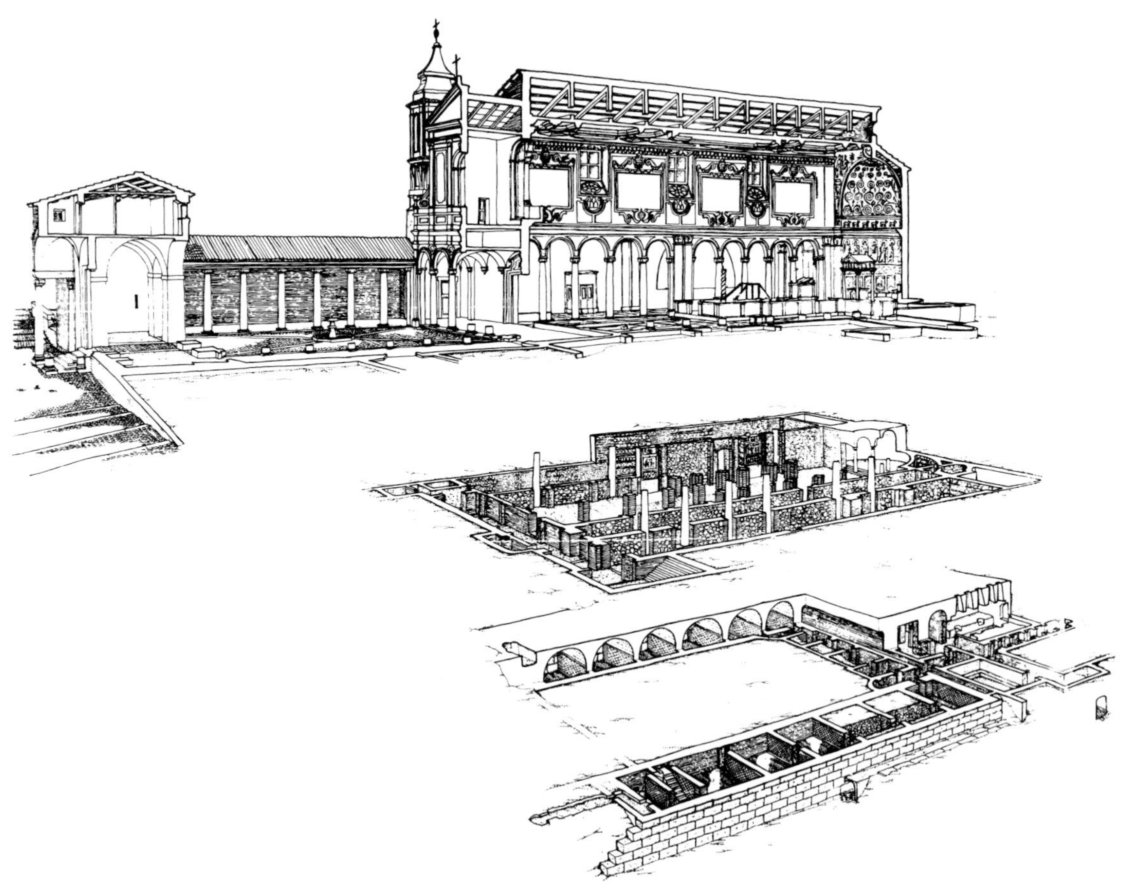

2-3. *San Clemente, Rome—sectional perspective of three levels: lower level, first to third or fourth century; intermediate level, third or fourth century to twelfth century; upper level, twelfth to twentieth century.*

The Genesis of the Churches of Rome

In the second half of the Middle Ages, the vast majority of Christian churches in Rome were not built from the ground up. They were, rather, the cumulative result of successive work campaigns—the original construction plus enlargements, reforms, and repairs—that had been carried out over the course of centuries (fig. 2-3).

To understand the origin of many of the medieval Christian buildings, it is necessary to refer back to the late Roman Empire. In Rome the first Christians gathered in modest settings of a completely domestic and private nature: apartments, blocks of multiple homes (*insulae*), mansions (*domi*), simple naves of recent construction, prayer rooms in private homes. These were rented, bought, or donated by their owners for use as communal centers dedicated to religious endeavors and social welfare. Thus arose the many *tituli* of Rome, identified by the name of the original owner of the title of the building (such as *titulus Clementis, Anastasiae, Caeciliae, Chrysogoni*). As a result, many of the oldest parishes of Rome began as former Roman homes that were subsequently enlarged and reformed, adapting to the growing needs of the Christian communities that gathered in them.

Emperor Constantine (306–37) was the first to give a public dimension to the Christian meeting centers. At his command, construction of the first and largest basilicas in Rome began: San Pietro (figs. 2-4 and 2-5), San Giovanni in Laterano (fig. 2-6), the chapel on the site of San Paolo fuori le Mura, the covered cemetery on the site of San Lorenzo fuori le Mura, and other smaller Christian buildings (such as Santa Croce in Gerusalemme, San Sebastiano,

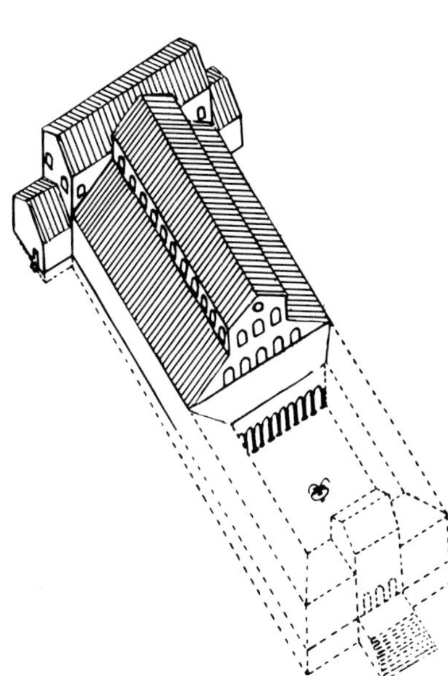

2-4. *Basilica of San Pietro. Reconstruction, as it was circa 330.*

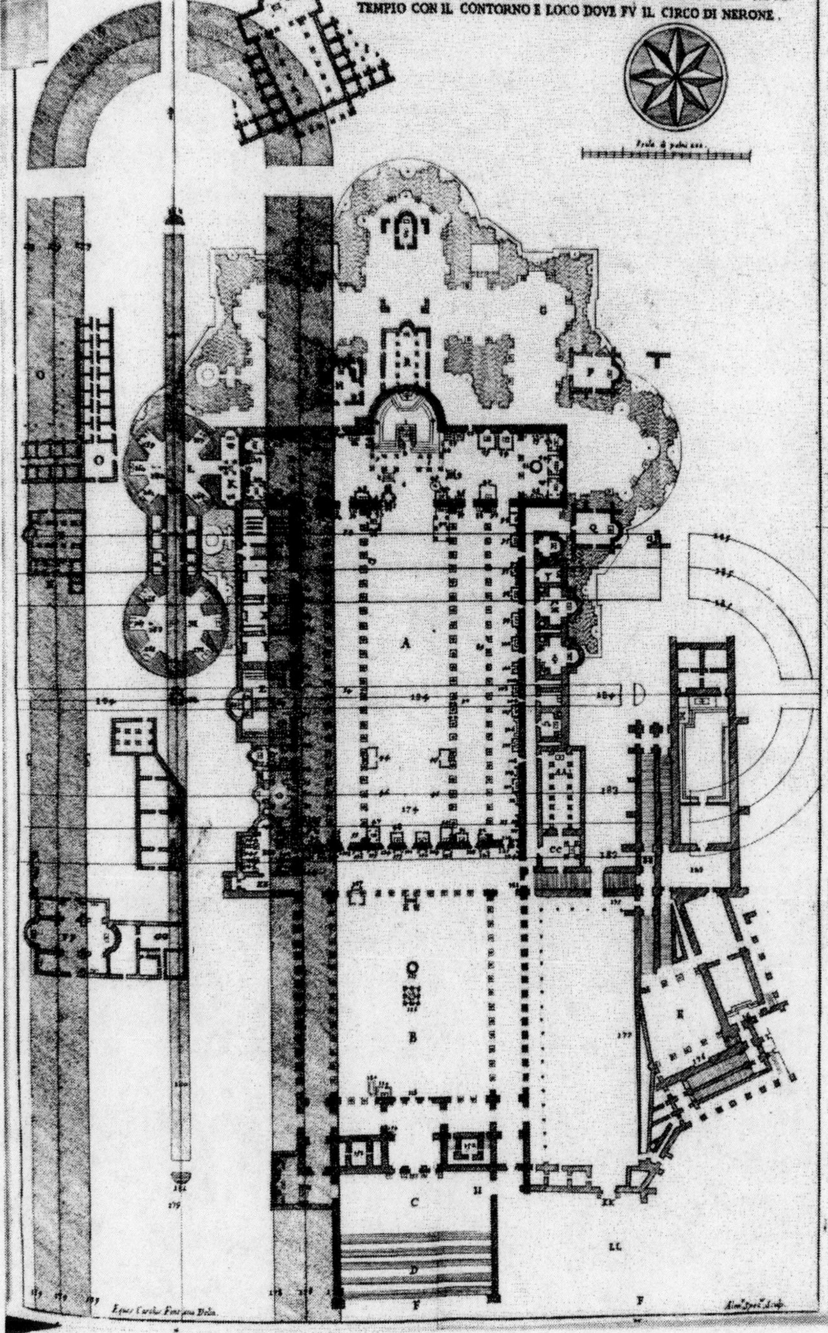

2-5. *Floor plan of the basilica of San Pietro, highlighting the Circo di Nerone, the Constantinian basilica, and the present basilica.*

Santa Constanza). The great Constantinian basilicas were public buildings that competed in size, decoration, and content with the most magnificent constructions of Rome. Constantine intended that they serve as propaganda for the power of the "new God" and therefore to propagate the new faith, promoted by the emperor. However, of these great buildings, only two, San Giovanni in Laterano and Santa Croce in Gerusalemme, were located *entro le mura* (within the city walls), and only at the edge of the city, in the green belt; the rest lay *fuori le mura* (outside the walls). Constantine was obliged to use private imperial lands, outside the walls, for their construction because the Senate and the citizens of Rome were still primarily pagan and totally opposed to the imposition of Christian buildings within the heart of their city. In the context of a still-pagan Rome, the emperor gave a public dimension to his Christian buildings, but without any ostentation. Hence the

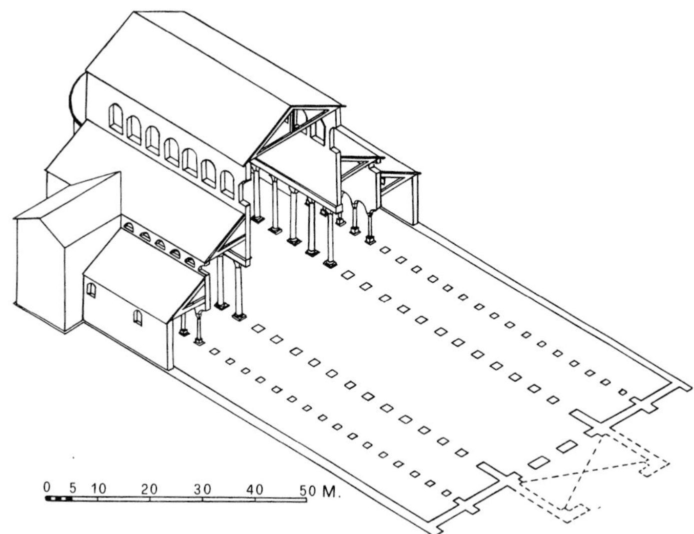

2-6. *Basilica of San Giovanni in Laterano. (Reconstruction by Waddy, revised by Lloyd)*

tremendous simplicity of the exteriors of the Constantinian constructions, which contrasts with the sumptuousness of their interiors. This hidden luxury, which gave a new image to Christianity, remained concealed from the general public and reserved only for the faithful who gathered in these new buildings.

Constantine abandoned Rome in 330, establishing himself in Byzantium, renamed Constantinople, which would become the Christian capital of his Christian empire. In Rome paganism would survive until the beginning of the fifth century, when the pagan aristocracy lost its battle with the Church, which had garnered the support of the emperor and the masses.

Throughout the fourth century, Rome experienced a process of Christianization, marked by a succession of imperial decrees that supported and promoted the consolidation of the Christian cult in the city. The first of the series of imperial provisions arose in 313, when the Edict of Milan initiated tolerance for the Christian cult in the empire. In 346 public pagan worship in Rome was prohibited. In 356 the temples were closed. In 364 the temples' revenues were confiscated. In 408 it was mandated that all the temples be dedicated to new secular uses. A key link in the chain of decrees appeared in the year 395, when an official order suppressed paganism in Rome, obliging the remaining members of the pagan resistance, primarily aristocrats, to convert.

This series of events allowed Christian churches to flourish during the fourth and fifth centuries, not only in the center of the city, but in places of importance. They were given the status of significant public architecture and neighbored the most exceptional ancient monuments. Churches arose in those places where Christian communal centers of worship had previously existed, replacing or incorporating the preexisting structure (for example, Santi Giovanni e Paolo, Sant'Anastasia, San Lorenzo in Lucina). Many others were established on new sites, such as the churches that were sponsored by the bishop of Rome (the pope), or by powerful donors and clergy, built in the urban mansions of interested families on privileged locations throughout the city (including San Vitale, San Marco, the ancient church now beneath Santa Maria in Trastevere, Santa Sabina, San Pietro in Vincoli). In general, these churches represented the characteristic Roman type: basilica with three naves, with a semicircular apse, an enclosure for the clergy, *solea* (a long, narrow enclosure, situated at the longitudinal axis of the

2-7. *San Paolo fuori le Mura, interior after the fire of 1823. (Engraving by L. Rossini)*

2-8. *San Paolo fuori le Mura, view of the interior. (P. M. Letarouilly)*

church, which served as a path to the presbytery), narthex, atrium, and protiro (a more detailed analysis of Roman churches can be found later in this chapter). The Christians created these buildings with materials and architectural elements taken from the ruins and debris of the pagan structures. The frenzy of building at the end of the fourth century continued into the beginning of the fifth. During this period two of the most significant Christian buildings were constructed in Rome: San Paolo fuori le Mura, begun in 384 (figs. 2-7 and 2-8), and Santa Maria Maggiore, begun circa 420.

The construction of new Christian buildings did not result in the cessation of repairs, reconstruction, redecoration, and remodeling of older religious buildings, civic buildings, and infrastructure. The pagan temples and buildings were respected and protected as monuments and as fiscal property. Rome jealously guarded these architectural treasures, which gave evidence of its glorious past as the capital of an empire. Associating the Church with the resplendent classical past of Rome would permit the revitalization of the city, now in competition with Constantinople, offering the new Rome as the Christian and classical capital, leader of the civilized world, city of God, capital to the successor of Saint Peter.

While Rome Christianized itself, the Church simultaneously Romanized itself, becoming the heir and protector of the local classical tradition. The artistic tastes of the magnates of the Church, now cultured, rich, and members of the great families of Rome, strayed little from those of their predecessors, the pagan Roman nobles, in whose eyes Christian art was merely plebeian, lacking in rigor and limited to conglomerations of heterogeneous elements. Although Christian art was not initially classical—and could be considered anticlassical—as the artists' patrons and promoters, the popes, began to Romanize themselves, more refined works that integrated the classical Roman tradition began to appear throughout the fifth century, such as Santa Maria Maggiore, the reform of the Battisterio of San Giovanni in Laterano, San Paolo fuori le Mura, Santa Pudenziana, Santa Sabina, and Santo Stefano Rotondo. At the beginning of the fifth century, the popes took charge of all ecclesiastical construction in Rome and continued to oversee it thereafter.

The fifth-century Papacy concentrated its building activity primarily on the papal headquarters at San Giovanni in Laterano, the official center of Christian Rome. The additions, reforms, and improvements of the Laterano were a response to the growing competition from another religious center of enormous weight, San Pietro (Saint Peter's), which although not the official center of Christianity, was becoming more popular than the Laterano.

The image Rome had presented in the fifth century, both Christian and Roman, still carried some grandeur, but warfare and natural catastrophes in the last two-thirds of the sixth century accelerated the physical deterioration of the city, and the city arrived at the end of the sixth century in a state of dramatic physical decline, a reflection of its many economic and social calamities. Rome—which had become but one more city in the Byzantine Empire, governed from Ravenna—suffered Lombard invasions, floods, epidemics, hunger, poverty, and unemployment. The population diminished (the plebeians were decimated by poverty; the aristocrats left for Ravenna or Constantinople), and the physical urban fabric (infrastructure, services, civic buildings, and housing) reached a state of near collapse.

Ancient Rome, upon "falling to pieces," became the victim of despoilment. Despite repeated imperial vetoes, temples and other public buildings were dismembered and demolished; bronze statues, melted; marble, lead, and brass, snatched. The same occurred with many of the abandoned great mansions. Ancient Rome became a huge quarry.[5] In the year 459, the pillaging of buildings in a state of irreversible deterioration was legalized. The Church would benefit greatly from the plunder of materials.

The majority of Rome's inhabitants were forced to live on the lower floors of their residential buildings because the advanced deterioration of these structures made the upper floors uninhabitable. Nonetheless, the skeleton of the city survived; the walls, the streets, and many of the aqueducts and public baths continued in use. The construction activity of the Church continued uninterrupted, and during the last two-thirds of the sixth century, numerous new churches were built, including Santi Quirico e Giulitta, Santi Apostoli, San Giovanni a Porta Latina, Santi Nereo ed Achilleo, and a church over the tomb of San Lorenzo, the presbytery of the current basilica.

From the fifth century forward the decimated Roman population was concentrated in a small area, covering Trastevere and the region east of the

Tiber, between the Teatro di Marcello, the base of the Capitolio, and the line of what is today the via Arenula. This compact populated space, the *abitato,* contrasted with the rest of the city, the *disabitato,* which had become a large, open, and indistinct unpopulated area, consisting of a jumble of fields, ruins, vineyards, and small farms. Such disparate land usage would characterize the image of Rome far beyond the Middle Ages.

The severe deterioration of Rome's physical fabric was compounded by the severe deterioration of its public system of social welfare. Neither the Byzantine emperor nor the local government responded to this issue, leaving the Church to assume responsibility and take on the role of a temporal authority to resolve the problems of the Romans. The Church, which had been acquiring land since its creation, was the principal landowner in Italy during the sixth century. The Church was also the only power with the economic and human resources to ensure, on the one hand, the creation and function of centers of charity or welfare, and, on the other hand, the maintenance of the public monuments of the city.

The majority of the churches founded in the sixth century and the early seventh century were located around the Forum, the Sacra Via, and the Palatino (including Santi Quirico e Giulitta, Santi Apostoli, Santa Maria Antiqua, and Santi Luca e Martina—located within the Senate building). For the first time, new Christian buildings were being built in the very heart of imperial Rome, contributing to the revitalization of the dead monument zone. Moreover, the Church was now taking over and occupying public Roman buildings, converting them and financing their maintenance. Santi Cosma e Damiano (526–30), for example, was converted from an audience hall of a city prefect; Santa Maria Antiqua (635–42), from a ceremonial hall. Closed since 356, the pagan temples were reopened and Christianized, as in the case of the Pantheon, consecrated as the church of Santa Maria Rotonda (609), and the Tempio della Fortuna Virile a Bocca della Verità, consecrated as Santa Maria Egiziaca (872–82). The Church also claimed and gave new use to private properties that were costly to maintain, such as the great mansions, which became monasteries, and their reception halls, which became churches (for example, San Gregorio Magno, located in the familial home of its donor, the pontiff Gregory I, and Santi Quattro Coronati, whose foundation includes the walls of a mansion).

2-9. *Santa Maria in Cosmedin, view of the interior, looking toward the entrance.*

During his pontificate (590–604), Gregory I would undertake a series of practical measures designed to satisfy the basic needs of the inhabitants of Rome (residents, pilgrims, visitors, refugees). He developed an efficient administrative organization and created a network of centers for public assistance, the *diaconia*, which, although equipped with chapels, had as their principal function the provision and distribution of food. These charity centers were served by monastic communities and were located in Roman buildings that had provided similar administrative services, namely the distribution and storage of provisions. The diaconates also offered baths and operated as inns for pilgrims, the poor, and the sick. The remains of these centers survive in such churches as Santa Maria in Cosmedin (fig. 2-9), San Giorgio in Velabro, and Santa Maria in Via Lata.

New diaconates, or centers of charitable assistance for the poor, were created in the seventh and eighth centuries in an effort to meet the needs of the multitude of pilgrims who visited Rome, by then the spiritual center of

Christian western Europe. The pilgrims and tourists arrived from around the world, though primarily from other parts of Europe (where Gregory had sent missionaries), with the intention of visiting the tombs and relics of the martyrs, and in particular the tomb of Saint Peter. Many diaconates were located close to the principal pilgrimage destinations (San Pietro, San Paolo fuori le Mura, San Lorenzo fuori le Mura, San Pancrazio), in response to the demand for accommodations, provision and distribution of food, care and lodging for the poor and the elderly, medical attention, and baths. Other centers were located in or at the edge of the *abitato* with the customary mission of distributing food (for example, Sant'Angelo in Pescheria, and those annexed to the churches of Santa Maria Antiqua, Santi Cosma e Damiano, and Sant'Adriano). Some of the churches were designed to serve the colonies of foreigners—Saxons, Lombards, Franks—who visited Rome (such as San Michele in Borgo, which served the Frankish colony), while other buildings, such as basilicas with galleries (the Basilica Pelagiana of San Lorenzo fuori le Mura, Sant'Agnese fuori le Mura) and semiannular crypts (San Pietro, San Pancrazio, San Crisogono), were built to improve conditions for the pilgrims who visited the tombs of the saints.

In the second half of the seventh century and in the eighth century, numerous "Greek" refugees arrived in Rome, coming from the southern and eastern regions of the empire. Many of them were monks or hermits who had fled Middle Eastern and North African territories conquered by the Muslims in the middle of the seventh century or who had abandoned the Byzantine Empire because of iconoclastic persecution. Eastern monastic congregations settled in a few of the monasteries in Rome, such as San Gregorio, Abbazia delle Tre Fontane, and San Silvestro in Capite. The Byzantines brought with them their artistic and liturgical traditions, which fused with local traditions and became Romanized. The Byzantine or Hellenistic influence is most clearly evident in the mosaics and painted murals, which acquired a rigid, flat, lineal appearance. Other signs of Byzantine influence included the pulpit, the schola cantorum (a shorter, wider enclosure for the choir than the solea, which it replaced), the architraved colonnade, or iconostasis, in the enclosure of the presbytery, and icons (panels with images that, if painted, were positioned over the trabeated colonnade; if engraved in silver, were tied to the architrave). Also imported from the east were floor plans for churches, including the basilica with galleries, the church with a three-sided exterior apse (such as San Giovanni a Porta Latina), the church with three apses at the eastern end (including Sant'Angelo in Pescheria, Santa Maria in Cosmedin, and Santa Maria in Domnica), and the church with towers flanking the apse (such as Santi Nereo ed Achilleo).

In the middle of the eighth century, the pope, with the support of his militias, the great families of Rome, the masses, and the clergy, achieved a degree of temporal power that allowed him to turn his back on the Byzantine emperor. With the strength of the Franks behind him—the only plausible defense against the military threat of the Lombards—the pope became the maximum spiritual authority in Europe and the governing sovereign of the patrimony of Saint Peter. Thus, Rome was transformed into the spiritual capital of western Europe as well as the temporal capital of central Italy. The East had been excluded from the new image that Rome presented to the world.

Thanks to the protection of the Franks, Rome felt safe at the end of the eighth century, defeating the Lombards and eliminating the Byzantine presence in central Italy. Then began a period of revitalization, the Carolingian period, which would last from the end of the eighth century through the middle of the ninth century, its start coinciding with the pontificate of Adrian I (772–95). The passage of time, the final Lombard attacks, and floods had left Rome in a state of tremendous physical deterioration. Adrian I, much like Gregory the Great two centuries earlier, found himself forced to undertake the renovation of his city, seeking the repair of ecclesiastic buildings (churches, diaconates, monasteries, chapels) and of infrastructure (walls, aqueducts, baths). In an effort to ensure the supply of food for the city, he established rural units of agrarian production, *domus cultae,* within Latium, easily accessible to Rome; many of these "church farms" were located at ancient Roman villas. He put into action an ambitious plan for the overall restoration of the churches in Rome, improving and repairing (especially the roofs) those within as well as those beyond the city walls. Following the example of Constantine, he took care to embellish them luxuriously, providing valuable fabrics (curtains for the intercolumniations of the naves, the triumphal arch, the enclosure of the presbytery, and the main entrance door; runners for the altar), icons, lamps, paschal candelabra, silver furnishings, and other elements of the ecclesiastic trousseau. By the end of the eighth century, the churches of Rome had attained an interior luxury not seen since the time of Constantine. Adrian I also had the remains of the martyrs from the devastated cemeteries and catacombs transferred to the security of churches situated within the Roman walls (such as San Silvestro in Capite and Santa Maria in Cosmedin). Rome was beginning to muster the will to revive the most glorious times of its Christian past, the time of the empire of Constantine.

An attack by the Saracens in 846, which reached San Pietro and San Paolo, alerted the Papacy to the need for self defense and independence. From 847 to 853, under the pontiff Leo IV, the Leonine walls were constructed, enclosing the basilica of San Pietro and the surrounding buildings. In about 880 a fortification was built around San Paolo as well.

The first half of the ninth century marked the high point of the Carolingian renaissance in Rome. The principal goal of the Papacy was to restore Rome to its former Christian splendor, to which end Adrian's successors repaired and constructed innumerable churches while continuing to enrich the churches and papal palaces with valuable gifts. During this era, luxurious improvements embellished the halls and oratories of the Lateran Palace, instigated by the enduring competition with the Great Imperial Palace of Constantinople. The pope, Paschal I (817–24), initiated a new program of renovation for the city and its monuments, following the Constantinian models. He constructed Santa Prassede (fig. 2-10), Santa Maria in Domnica, Santa Cecilia in Trastevere, and Santi Quattro Coronati, referring to the basilicas of San Pietro and San Paolo as prototypes. The paleo-Christian renaissance inspired the revitalization of Byzantine influence in the mosaics on walls and vaults (for example, the Chapel of San Zenone in Santa Prassede). Churches were built to replace the old communal centers and diaconates, as well as oratories in bad condition, and to provide protection for the remains of the bodies of the saints, which were then transported,

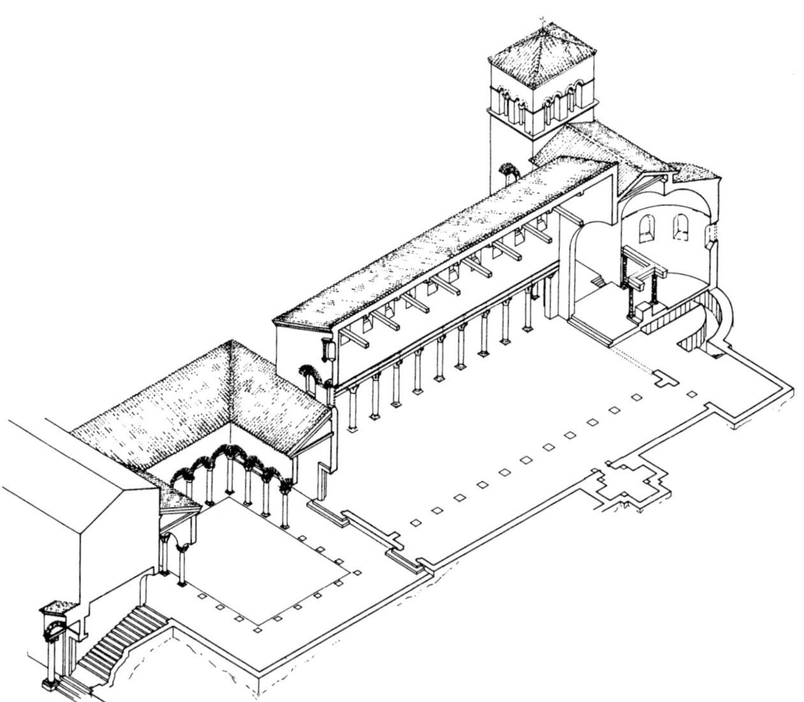

2-10. *Santa Prassede, isometric reconstruction.* (*Spencer Corbett*)

individually or in cart loads, from the outlying catacombs to churches within the walls. All these reforms arose in response to Rome's aspiration to present a brilliant image, worthy of the capital of an empire. Among the churches of this era are San Martino ai Monti, Santa Maria Nova (constructed to replace Santa Maria Antiqua, which was buried in a landslide in 847), Santa Cecilia in Trastevere, Santa Maria Domnica, San Giorgio in Velabro, and San Marco. All possessed a semiannular crypt and confessio in which were housed the relics and remains of the saints. The majority of the churches built in the ninth century lie at the edge of the *abitato* or in the *disabitato,* which is to say, on the outskirts of the city. Therefore, although they had decisive economic and political influence in their time, these churches did not have a significant impact on the core of the urban fabric of Rome. The Carolingian ecclesiastic constructions arose with the objective of reviving the best of the Roman Christian tradition, just as that legacy had initially formed from the fifth to the eighth century. The more recent Byzantine influence of the seventh and eighth centuries was not considered incongruous to that effort.

From the end of the ninth century to the beginning of the twelfth century, Rome was the center of a tense and prolonged struggle between the pope and the emperor for temporal power. During this period, marked by the Reform of the Church and the Controversy of the Investitures, the physical deterioration of Rome accelerated. The inhabitants of Rome, sufficiently preoccupied by the frequent and turbulent confrontations between the papal and imperial clans, left great architectural endeavors for another age. After the wave of Carolingian building, which ended in about 860, the construction of churches in Rome stopped almost completely. Only a few minor projects were undertaken: establishing chapels in the ancient ruins (for example, Sant'Agnese in Piazza Navona, Santa Barbara dei Librai), decorating Christianized temples with murals (such as Santa Maria Egiziaca), or constructing new diminutive chapels in an apsed nave (such as Santa Maria in Pallara and Santa Maria in Capella). Finally, in the last third of the eleventh century, new churches began to appear (including San Stefano del Cacco and San Giovanni a Porta Latina), the majority of them situated in the *abitato*, between the Corso and the bend in the Tiber. The prevailing type, which was common for over a century, was a small basilica containing three naves and an apse.

In conclusion, Christian churches opened steadily throughout the Middle Ages, integrating themselves into the fabric of the city, gradually but without pause. The initial Christian gathering places were centers of a domestic nature, unpretentious, inconspicuous, and unremarkable in the context of the surrounding urban architecture. Later, in the Constantine era, the churches acquired the status of public architecture, although located on the outskirts of the city, either in the suburbs or at the edge of the walls. The churches progressively made their way into the heart of the city, settling in private buildings within the walls. Having penetrated the inner city, they continued advancing, progressively conquering more central locations, approaching the important public pagan buildings. Ultimately they invaded the Forum and its surroundings, the true heart of imperial Rome. Once all the geography of the city was conquered, the occupation of ancient monuments followed; Christian churches began to establish themselves in significant public pagan buildings, and eventually they even assimilated the pagan temples. Having colonized the public monuments of the city, Christian structures began to appear everywhere, designed to satisfy every sort of need: the urban distribution of social welfare, the administration and management of rural units of agrarian production, the transfer of the remains of martyrs. Then, as the network of churches in Rome solidified, the projects of improvement and repair became paramount. Ancient Rome had fallen at the feet of a new Christian Rome, constructed in the ruins, and with the ruins, of pagan Rome.[6]

Morphological Characteristics of the Churches of Medieval Rome

Given the process of gestation that gave rise to the Roman churches of the twelfth century, the Cosmatesque artists who worked in the city rarely did so in completely new structures, but rather in existing buildings in varying states of disrepair: whole or semiruined, complete exterior and incomplete interior, or an interior and exterior in need of improvements and additions. The assignments that the Cosmati undertook varied, depending primarily upon the condition of the preexisting structure. Some churches needed specific additions, such as a portico, a campanile, a cloister, an atrium, or a protiro. More frequently, however, interior redecoration or improvements were required; then the Cosmati constructed all the elements necessary for the complete ornamental program of a church: the paving, all the fixed liturgical furnishings (the altar, the ciborium, the ambos, and the episcopal throne), the partitions of the different liturgical enclosures (schola cantorum; enclosure of the presbytery, with architraved colonnade), the tombs, the monuments, and the tombstones. Some churches needed reconstruction throughout, such as those that were practically in ruins after fires or floods (for example, San Clemente, Santa Maria in Trastevere, Santi Quattro Coronati); in these cases the Cosmati acted as genuine architects, adapting the design of the new structures to the demands of contemporary liturgical uses. The Cosmatesque artists addressed both the construction of the buildings and the procurement of the necessary architectural pieces, which required despoiling the ancient buildings and subsequently reusing the materials. They carefully selected architectural elements in the ruins and remains of pagan buildings for later use, either directly or, if necessary, by carving imitations. Thus, the Cosmati constructed arcades and architraved colonnades; they reformed structures, adding a crypt or a confessio; and they restructured existing buildings, inserting or raising the transept of paleo-Christian basilicas (for example, San Pietro, Santa Croce in Gerusalemme, Santa Maria Maggiore, San Giovanni in Laterano) or adding piers to support transverse diaphragm arches. The Cosmati also created sculptures, when they decorated—with figures of lions, eagles, and other creatures—entablatures for cloisters, screens, and portals. To produce their ample and varied work, they fulfilled a multitude of roles: architect, interior decorator, builder, curator, restorer, sculptor, engraver, lime and marble worker, mosaicist, warehouseman, and exporter of materials.

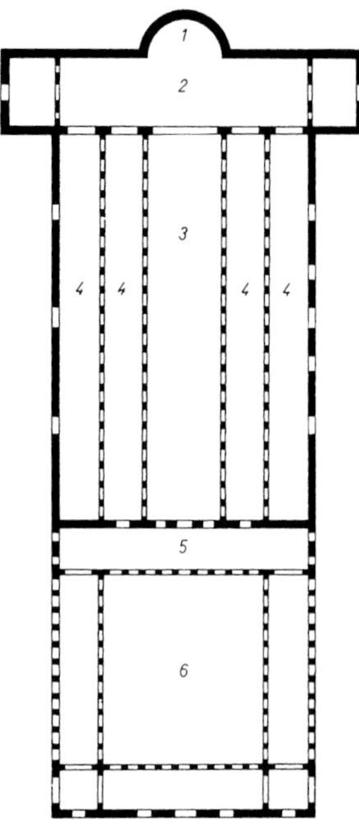

2-11. *Floor plan of the Western paleo-Christian basilica: (1) apse; (2) transept; (3) nave; (4) lateral and co-lateral aisles; (5) narthex; (6) atrium.*

The morphological characteristics of the Cosmatesque churches were a composite of structures before the Cosmati and those that they themselves carried out. The exteriors of these churches had a simple, austere, almost monochrome appearance, far from ostentatious. Their interiors, however, were rich, polychrome settings, typically Roman, which resulted from the melding of the simplest architecture and the most luxurious ornamentation.[7]

The majority of the Cosmatesque churches were basilicas with three naves, with a semicircular apse at the east end and, at the west end, a narthex, atrium, protiro, and campanile (figs. 2-11 and 2-12). The walls were of exposed brick with a concrete core, constructed with despoiled red bricks (fig. 2-13). Windows with latticework opened onto the façade of the church (fig. 2-14); the stretches between them frequently were decorated with mosaic murals on the outside and fresco paintings on the inside. The door to the church, closed with hanging curtains, opened in the lower portion of the façade, preceded by a portico or narthex, whose walls were sometimes decorated with mural paintings. The portico opened onto a four-sided atrium with trabeated colonnades; the access door to this quadriportico was usually protected by a protiro, or gabled porch.

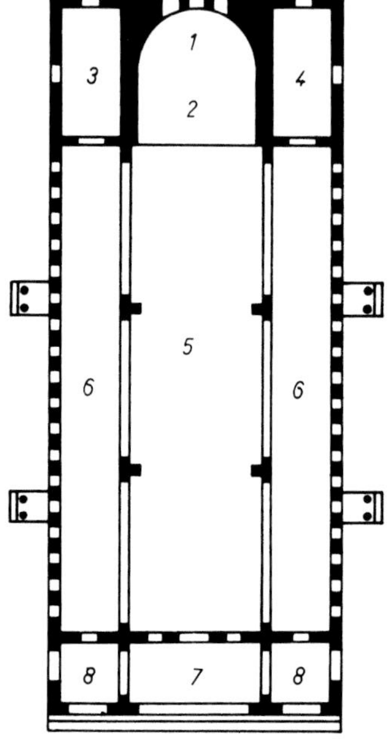

2-12. *Floor plan of the Eastern paleo-Christian basilica: (1) apse; (2) bema; (3) diaconicon; (4) prothesis; (5) nave; (6) lateral aisles; (7) narthex; (8) towers.*

The interior space presented a tripartite division, with a central nave and two lateral aisles, joined occasionally by two additional co-lateral aisles (figs. 2-15 and 2-16). The aisles were separated by architraved colonnades, or by arcaded colonnades, and in the intercolumniation hung curtains made from exquisite cloth (woven with strands of purple silk, or wool; embroidered with gold and silver; with lively designs of birds and other figurative or geometric designs of Byzantine inspiration). Thus, the interior was arranged in three parallel but separate chambers. They used despoiled columns, many having fluted shafts (with flutes and fillets in the lower third). The capitals were frequently Ionic, some from ruins, others carved in the twelfth century, imitating the ancient ones (fig. 2-17). Sometimes there were lateral chapels decorated with rich floors in *opus sectile*, painted murals, and mosaics in the vaulted roof (figs. 2-18 and 2-19). The two-sided roof of

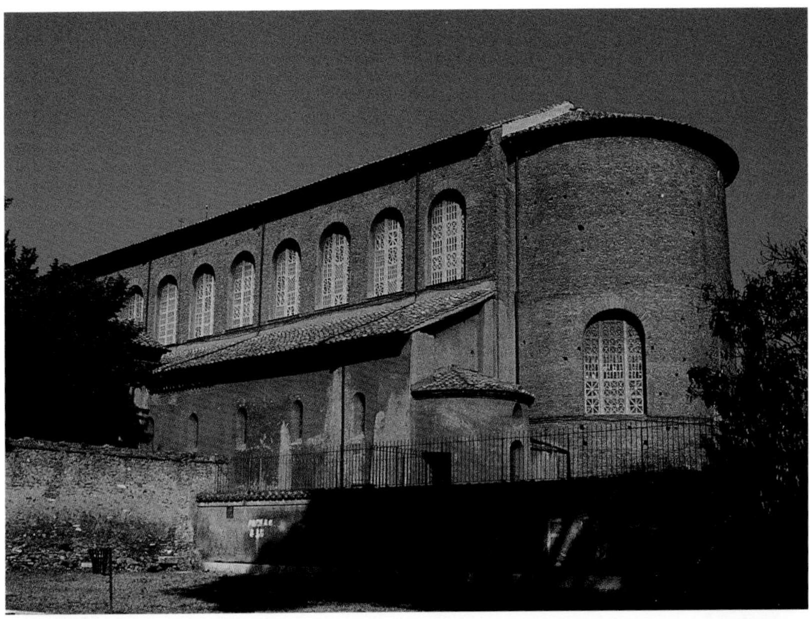

2-13. *Exterior of Santa Sabina.*

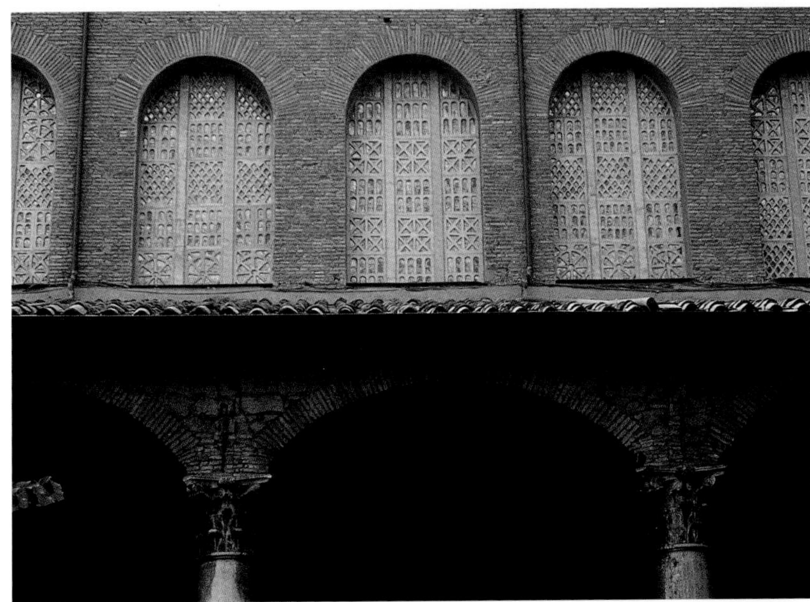

2-14. *[Right] Lattice windows of Santa Sabina.*

2-15. *[Below] Co-lateral aisle of San Paolo fuori le Mura.*

2-16. *[Below, right] Lateral aisle of Santa Maria in Cosmedin.*

2-17. [Far left] Ionic capital on a fluted column at San Giovanni a Porta Latina.

2-18. [Left] Interior of the Chapel of San Zenone in Santa Prassede.

2-19. Design of the mosaics of the vault in the Chapel of San Zenone in Santa Prassede.

2-20. [Far left] Interior of San Saba, with ceiling of exposed trusses.

2-21. [Left] Corinthian capitals in Santa Sabina; in the background, coffered ceiling decorated with stars.

2-22. *[Top, left] The head of the nave of Santa Maria in Trastevere.*

2-23. *[Top, right] Vault of the apse of San Paolo fuori le Mura.*

2-24. *[Above, left] Apse of Santa Sabina.*

2-25. *[Above, right] Triumphal arch of Santa Prassede.*

the central nave rested on wooden trusses (fig. 2-20). The beams, if they were left exposed, were gilded; otherwise, they remained hidden behind a flat or coffered wooden ceiling, which was gilded or adorned with golden stars (fig. 2-21). The furnishings of the church included valuable pieces of metalwork (such as lamps, candelabra, reliquaries, furniture, dishes, and utensils of gold and silver) whose designs were inspired by Byzantine models. The vertical panels of the pieces of fixed furniture and of the funeral monuments were encrusted with mosaics of red, blue, and gold glass tesserae, displaying minute designs. At the head of the nave lay a semicircular apse and a vault with a quarter-sphere shape, also decorated with glass mosaics (figs. 2-22 and 2-23). The walls of the apse contained lattice windows and were lined with marble or painted with frescoes (fig. 2-24). The transept was deep, continuous, as tall as the nave. At its center rose the triumphal arch, the archivolt and intrados decorated with mosaics and supported by porphyry columns, also hung with luxurious curtains (fig. 2-25). The central nave presented

2-26. *[Far left] Nave of Santa Prassede, with diaphragm arches.*

2-27. *[Left] San Pietro Vaticano, reconstruction of the presbytery.*

three liturgical sections, which sometimes were emphasized by interruptions in the colonnades, indicated by changes in the type of capitals (as in Santa Maria in Trastevere), by massive rectangular piers (Santa Maria in Cosmedin), or by diaphragm arches (Santi Giovanni e Paolo, Santa Prassede, fig. 2-26). The first section, the area reserved for the officiating clergy, was the enclosure of the presbytery, raised and separated from the rest of the nave by screens, above which was sometimes an architraved colonnade also hung with curtains (fig. 2-27). The following section, reserved for the choir, was the schola cantorum, enclosed by screens and flanked by ambos. The remaining section, situated at the entrance to the nave, was an open space reserved for the people attending the mass. The floor of the church was covered with tetrachrome marble mosaics, in *opus sectile*; the design of the pavement followed and emphasized the three liturgical divisions of the nave. In the enclosure of the presbytery lay the altar, under a ciborium or tabernacle, and behind it at the back of the apse sat the bishop's chair. Beneath the altar, visible through the transenna, or screen, of the confessio, was hidden the crypt, which held the remains and relics of saints. Over the colonnades of the nave rested the walls of the clerestory, onto which opened windows. The stretches between the openings were decorated with painted murals, just like the walls of the aisles. The windows of the clerestory were arched and elongated, endowed with latticework made either of stone plates with numerous perforations (fig. 2-28) or of wood and grayish white stucco gratings (fig. 2-29), with translucent panels of selenite, mica, alabaster, or colored glass (figs. 2-30 and 2-31). The windows allowed only a tenuous and diffuse light to reach the interior, nonetheless creating a vibrant and impressionistic atmosphere as the light reflected off the gilded and polychrome surfaces of the ceiling, mosaics, frescoes, cloths, furniture, and pavement (figs. 2-32 and 2-33). At night, the interior of the building shimmered with the tremulous light of candles and oil lamps.

Many of the churches of Rome have retained the majority of the characteristics from the time of the Cosmati, augmented by others acquired later through works of postmedieval redecoration, preservation, maintenance, or restoration, such as those of the seventeenth century (a new roof added to Santa Maria in Trastevere), eighteenth century (Santa Croce in Gerusalemme

2-28. *Lattice windows in the openings of the façade of San Giovanni a Porta Latina, seen from the interior.*

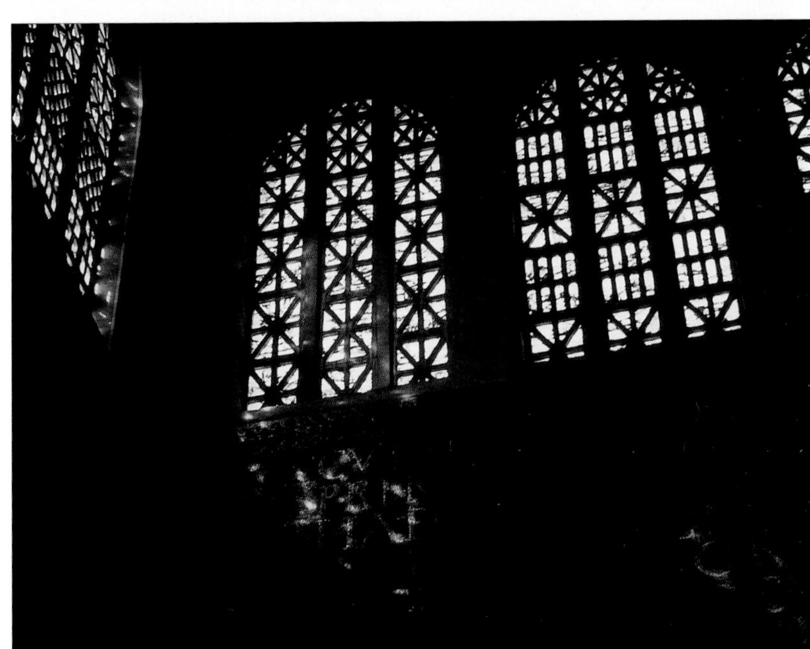

2-29. *Lattice windows in the openings of the façade of Santa Sabina, seen from the interior.*

2-30. *[Below] Window in San Paolo fuori le Mura.*

2-31. *[Below, right] Windows in the clerestory of San Paolo fuori le Mura, seen from a side aisle.*

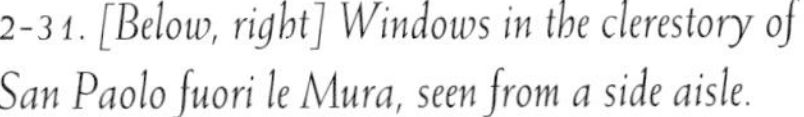

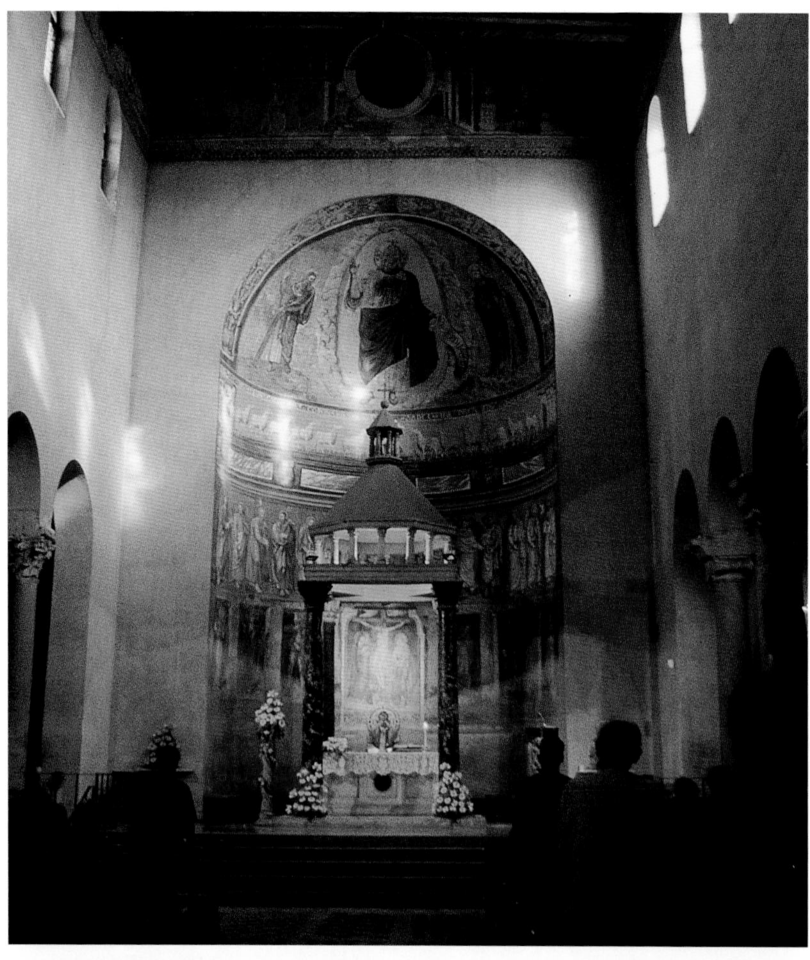

2-32. *Interior of San Saba.*

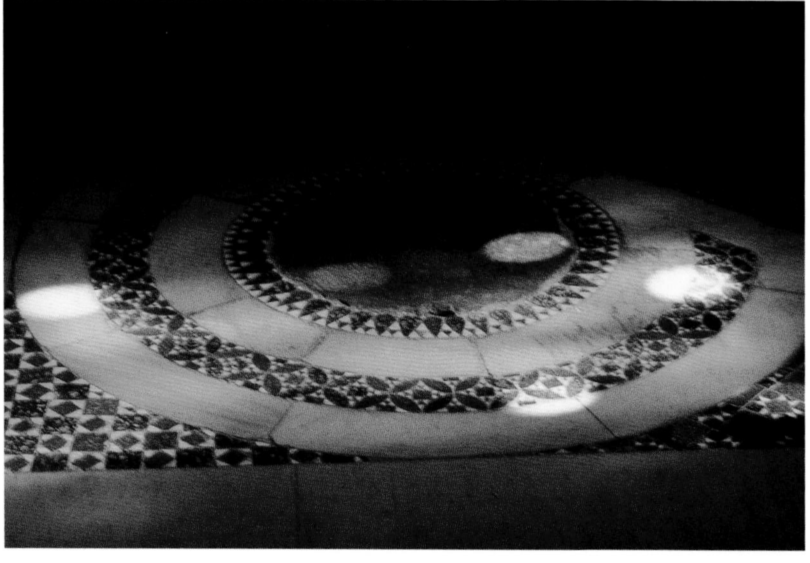

2-33. *Detail from the pavement in the presbytery of Santa Maria in Trastevere.*

remodeled), nineteenth century (resetting of the pavement in Santa Maria in Trastevere), and twentieth century (Santa Maria in Cosmedin restored).

The principal Cosmatesque components of a twelfth-century Roman church follow. This step-by-step tour begins at the exterior of the church and advances through the main door to the interior, continuing to travel along the longitudinal axis from the start of the nave to the back of the sanctuary. The general morphological characteristics of the Christian churches of medieval Rome result from assembling the following components.

CAMPANILES

The campanile is a bell tower, generally at the west end of the church, to one side of the façade. Some are situated in front of the church, atop one end of the transept or inserted in an aisle. Originally campaniles were all of exposed brick, although some are now stuccoed over. Some are very slender, others are not. Campaniles are divided into several floors—generally five—separated by small cornices. Each cornice or small eave is formed by three bands: those at the edges consist of alternating rows of brick sleepers and sawtooth patterns; the central band is a string of dentils of white stone. Each floor is perforated with arches—some supported by brick pillars and others by small columns of white stone—grouped to form double and triple windows. The arches of the lower floors are usually blind. Some campaniles are decorated with small roundels and crosses made from marble, porphyry, serpentine, and majolica of different colors. Occasionally campaniles contain a small aedicule intended to house an image, painted or sculpted, of the Virgin Mary or a saint. At the crest of the four-sided roof, a bronze rooster crowns the bell tower. Many campaniles were constructed in the time of the Cosmati; most remarkable are those of Sant'Alessio, Santa Balbina, San Bartolomeo, Santa Cecilia in Trastevere, San Crisogono, Santa Croce in Gerusalemme, Santa Francesca Romana, San Giorgio in Velabro, San Giovanni in Laterano, Santi Giovanni e Paolo (figs. 2-34 and 2-35), San Giovanni a Porta Latina (figs. 2-36 and 2-37), San Lorenzo in Lucina, San Lorenzo fuori le Mura, Santa Maria in Cosmedin, Santa Maria Maggiore, Santa Maria in Trastevere, Santi Michele e Magno, Santa Pudenziana, and San Silvestro in Capite (fig. 2-38). The proliferation of campaniles profoundly changed the profile of medieval Rome, producing the fierce appearance of the city characteristic of the Romanesque period.

2-34. *[Top] Campanile of Santi Giovanni e Paolo.*

2-35. *[Above] Detail of the lower portion of the campanile of Santi Giovanni e Paolo.*

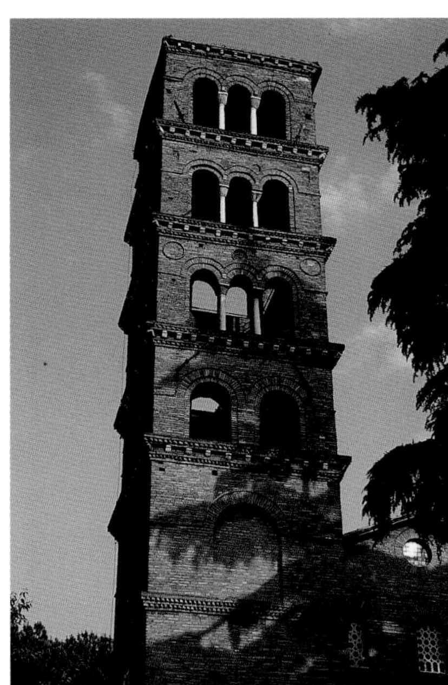

2-36. *Campanile of San Giovanni a Porta Latina.*

2-37. *Detail of the campanile of San Giovanni a Porta Latina, seen from its base.*

2-38. *Campanile of San Silvestro in Capite.*

2-39. *[Above] Protiro of San Clemente.*

2-40. *[Left] Protiro of San Clemente. (P. M. Letarouilly)*

Protiros or Porches

The protiro is a porch with a two-sided cover, consisting of a small structure made of brick that rests on a semicircular arch supported by two marble columns. Not many protiros have survived to the present day. The few that remain shelter the door that gives access to the portico, the atrium, or the entrance patio, as in San Clemente (figs. 2-39 and 2-40), Santa Prassede (fig. 2-41), Santa Maria in Cosmedin (fig. 2-42), and San Cosimato.

2-41. *[Below, left] Protiro of Santa Prassede.*

2-42. *[Below] Protiro of Santa Maria in Cosmedin.*

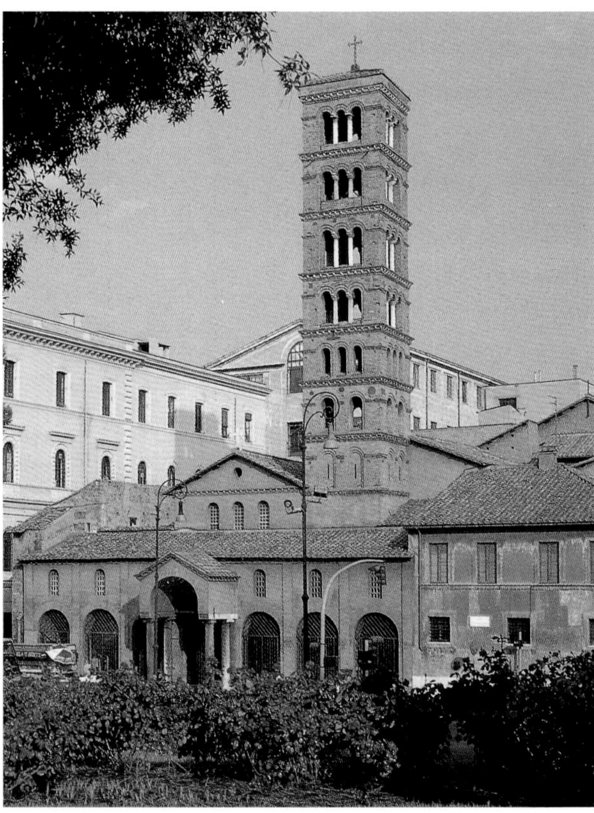

Atriums or Entrance Patios

The atrium is an enclosure surrounded by porticoes in front of the church. At the center of the atrium lies a fountain, used for purifying ablutions before entering the church. When the four sides of the atrium are porticoes, the atrium is called a quadriportico. The atria of San Paolo fuori le Mura and San Clemente are examples of quadriporticoes (figs. 2-43 and 2-44). Atria are rare in Rome, given the limited space available in the densely constructed urban fabric. The few that remain are very remodeled and usually possess only one portico, the narthex, which precedes the façade of the church, while the other sides are simply blank walls, as in the case of the atrium of San Silvestro in Capite and of Santa Cecilia in Trastevere (fig. 2-45). Some atria, such as that in Santa Prassede, have been reduced to patios, as they only preserve the central space without the porticoes on the sides. Some churches include an enclosed area at the entrance that serves as a courtyard or garden, as at San Cosimato, San Tomaso in Formis, San Saba, and San Giovanni a Porta Latina. In all of these churches, the edge of the courtyard is a solid brick wall, except San Giovanni a Porta Latina, whose entrance enclosure (which has a well rather than a fountain) is surrounded by a metal fence.

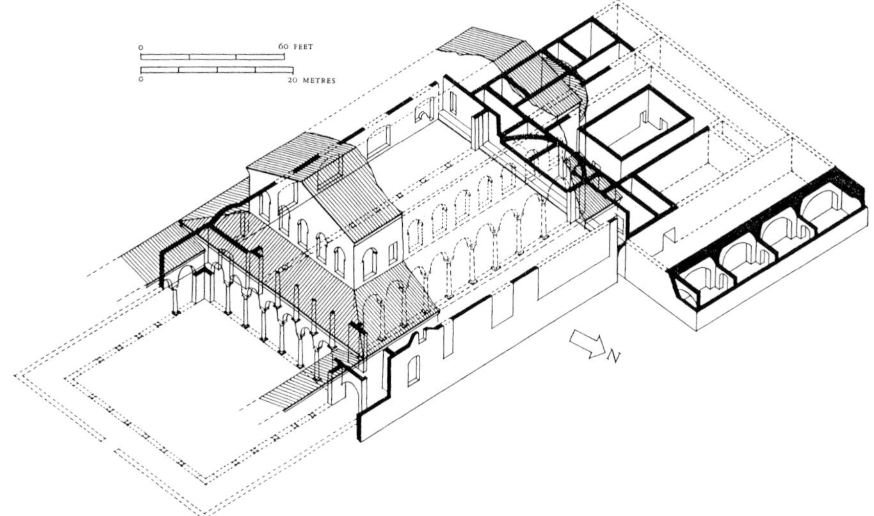

2-43. *[Right] Isometric view of San Clemente.*

2-44. *[Below, right] Atrium of San Clemente.*

2-45. *[Below] Atrium of Santa Cecilia in Trastevere.*

EXONARTHEXES

The exonarthex is the name given to the portico that precedes the façade of the church when the portico forms one of the sides of a porticated atrium. In Rome these are as scarce as atriums. In some instances, a colonnade sustains an architrave, as at San Clemente, Santa Cecilia in Trastevere, and San Paolo; while others have an arcade, as at San Silvestro in Capite and Santi Quattro Coronati (fig. 2-46). The exonarthex of the Cosmatesque churches derives from the paleo-Christian narthex. In the fourth and fifth centuries, the narthex or exonarthex opened onto an architraved colonnade leading toward the atrium, while the façade opened onto the narthex with arcades. Thus, the narthex acted as exo- and esonarthex, endowed with two parallel rows of columns, the interior hung with curtains (fig. 2-47). After 430 this type of narthex disappeared in Rome, replaced by one that led to the nave only by means of doors.[8]

2-46. *Exonarthex of Santi Quattro Coronati.*

2-47. *Reconstruction of the narthex and interior of San Vitale. (Drawing by Leporini)*

PORTICOES

The portico is a very common element in the medieval churches of Rome. It is a gallery set in the lower part of the façade of the church, protecting the access door or doors to the interior. The gallery is sustained by a row of columns made from despoiled materials (shafts of white marble, Ionic capitals), above which rests the entablature, comprising an architrave, frieze, and cornice. The architrave is straight, made of marble. In the oldest porticoes, the frieze consists of load-bearing segmental arches, executed in brick, while the more recent ones are decorated with lineal, geometric, or figurative designs laid in mosaic. In the early porticoes, the cymatium of the cornice is composed of alternating rows of brick sleepers and saw-toothed bricks. The corona is denticulated, containing a series of white stone corbels. Later porticoes have a cornice consisting of a band of sculpted stone with bas-relief (for example, geometricized plant motifs, lion heads). The angular supports of the portico are great rectangular brick piles, unless the sides of the portico are walls, in which case the extreme supports are embedded within. The porticoes that best preserve these characteristics are those of Santa Cecilia in Trastevere, San Giorgio in Velabro (figs. 2-48 and 2-49),

2-48. *[Far left] Exterior and portico of San Giorgio in Velabro.*

2-49. *[Left] Detail of the portico of San Giorgio in Velabro.*

2-50. [Right] Detail of the portico of Santa Maria Scala Coeli.

2-51. [Below, left] Detail of the portico of San Lorenzo fuori le Mura.

2-52. [Below, right] Exterior and portico of San Lorenzo fuori le Mura.

2-53. [Bottom, left] Interior of the portico of San Lorenzo fuori le Mura, decorated with wall paintings.

2-54. [Bottom, right] Portico of San Giovanni a Porta Latina.

Santi Giovanni e Paolo, San Lorenzo in Lucina, Santa Maria Scala Coeli (fig. 2-50), and San Lorenzo fuori le Mura (figs. 2-51, 2-52, and 2-53). Though unusual, there are also porticoes consisting of a series of arches supported by columns, such as those of Santa Maria in Cosmedin, Santa Sabina, and San Giovanni a Porta Latina (fig. 2-54). More rare still are the porticoes that, instead of having columns for support, have prismatic pillars of brick, such as that at Santa Balbina, which has an arcade, and that at San Saba, which is architraved. Frescoes decorate the walls of the portico.

Doors or Portals

The door, generally protected by a portico, is the main entrance to the interior of the church, opening at the center of the lower part of the façade. The Cosmatesque artists frequently embellished the marble frame of the door with bands of polychrome small-piece mosaic, containing an abundance of golden tesserae, as seen in Sant'Alessio, San Saba, and San Giovanni a Porta Latina (fig. 2-55). Some doors, in addition to having a frame decorated in mosaic, are flanked by sculptures of lions, for example, those of San Lorenzo in Lucina and Santi Giovanni e Paolo (figs. 2-56 and 2-57).

The portal, or grand entrance door, generally a semicircular arch, gives access to the forecourt that precedes the church. The portal appears in various forms. The one in the Abbazia delle Tre Fontane is a heavy arch of brick upon which rests a short tower (fig. 2-58). The one in San Saba is a porch or protiro that shelters a lunette decorated with a figurative mosaic. That in San Tomaso in Formis is a marble arch upon which rests a tabernacle covering a figurative mosaic (figs. 2-59 and 2-60). The portal of San Pancrazio is similar to the one in San Tomaso, but the tabernacle covers a fresco instead of a mosaic.

2-55. *Door of San Giovanni a Porta Latina.*

2-56. *[Above] Door of Santi Giovanni e Paolo.*

2-57. *[Left] Detail of the mosaic band that ornaments the door frame of Santi Giovanni e Paolo.*

2-58. [Right] Portal to the Abazzia delle Tre Fontane.

2-59. Portal to San Tomaso in Formis.

2-60. [Right] Detail of the tabernacle over the portal to San Tomaso in Formis.

Façades

The façade of a Cosmatesque church is a wall crowned with the symmetrical slopes of the gabled roof. This wall is made of brick and usually has a circular window at its center. Under the round opening, and above the portico or the narthex, are three arched windows, closed with latticework. The churches that best preserve all or some of these characteristics are San Lorenzo fuori le Mura, Santa Maria Scala Coeli, Sant'Anselmo, Santa Prassede (fig. 2-61), and San Giovanni a Porta Latina (fig. 2-62). On occasion, bright mosaics with figures of saints on a golden background shine from the upper part of the façade, as in Santa Maria Maggiore, San Paolo fuori le Mura (fig. 2-63), and Santa Maria in Trastevere (figs. 2-64 and 2-65).

2-61. [Above] Detail of the façade of Santa Prassede.

2-62. [Below, right] San Giovanni a Porta Latina.

2-63. [Below, left] Façade of San Paolo fuori le Mura.

2-64. [Bottom, right] Façade of Santa Maria in Trastevere.

2-65. [Bottom, left] Detail of the façade of Santa Maria in Trastevere.

2-66. *[Right] Exterior of San Saba.*

2-67. *[Below] Detail of architectural fragments on the floor of the portico of San Saba.*

2-68. *[Right] Interior of the portico of San Saba.*

2-69. *[Bottom] Detail of the interior of the portico of San Lorenzo fuori le Mura.*

Other Exterior Elements

In studying the exterior of a particular church, other elements may be observed, such as the structure with windows and a crowning arcade that rests on the portico of San Saba (fig. 2-66), or the protuberances caused by small side chapels, such as the Chapel of San Zenone in Santa Prassede. Architectural fragments from prior eras may also be detected (such as pieces of cornices, capitals, sarcophagi, tombstones, plaques with inscriptions); these are usually found resting on the ground or embedded in the walls of the portico, as at San Saba (figs. 2-67 and 2-68) and in San Lorenzo fuori le Mura (fig. 2-69), or embedded in the walls of the atrium, as at San Silvestro in Capite.

Esonarthexes

The esonarthex, endonarthex, or inner narthex is a gallery at the base of the nave, which serves as a vestibule. In the bays between the columns or pillars of the inner narthex were hung curtains that, together with the doors or curtains in the openings of the façade, served to limit or close access to the nave of the church. Although very remodeled, the inner narthex of San Silvestro in Capite (fig. 2-70) and that of Santa Cecilia in Trastevere (fig. 2-71) have survived to the present.

2-70. *Interior of San Silvestro in Capite, seen from the esonarthex.*

2-71. *Interior of Santa Cecilia in Trastevere, seen from the esonarthex.*

Pavements

The tetrachrome marble pavings in *opus sectile* laid by the Cosmati appear in the majority of the medieval churches of Rome. The design of these pavements responded to the functional and symbolic needs of the staging of medieval Christian ceremonies. The pavement covered the entire floor of the church, as much in the central nave as in each of the aisles, with the paving of the central nave being richer and more sophisticated, especially along the longitudinal axis of the church (figs. 2-72 through 2-76). In general, just as the church exhibited three distinct zones, so did the pavement of the central nave: the zone closest to the entrance, reserved for the use of the faithful or seculars, called the *sancta*; the zone at the east end of the church, for the exclusive use of the clergy or officiants, called the *sancta sanctorum*; and the intermediate zone where the choir was located, called the *schola cantorum*. The Cosmatesque pavements of the twelfth century displayed a great ornamental motif at the center of the space reserved for the faithful, in the middle of the sancta (figs. 2-77 and 2-78). This motif, which

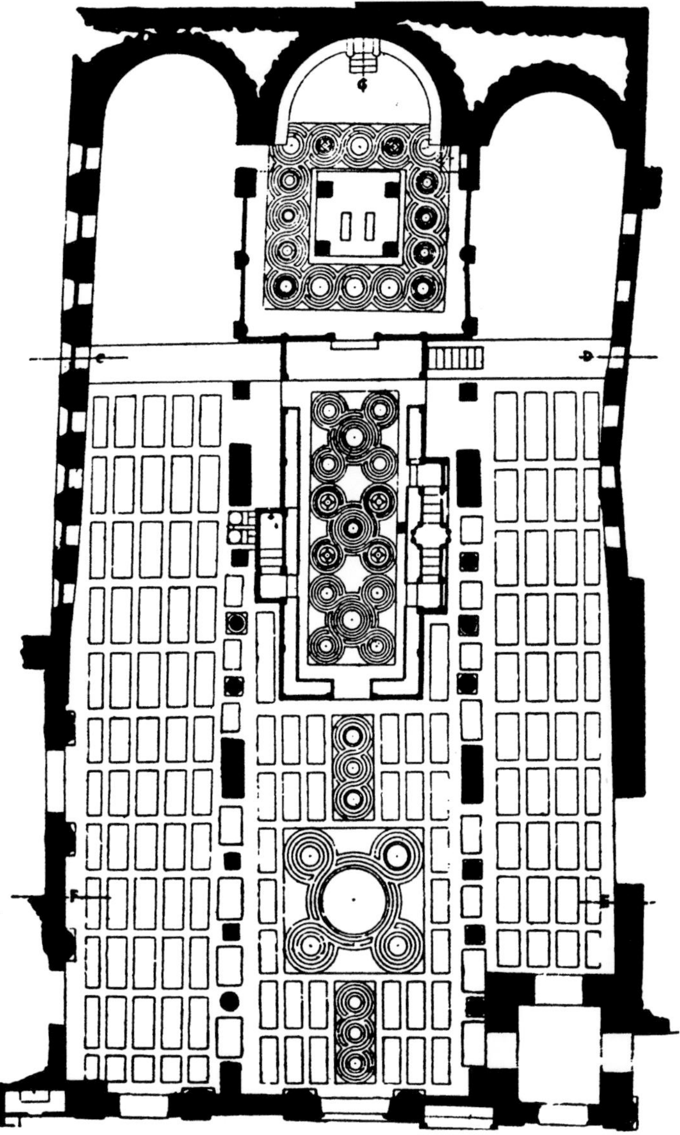

2-72. *Floor plan of Santa Maria in Cosmedin.*

2-73. *[Above] Pavement in the nave of San Lorenzo fuori le Mura.*

2-74. *[Left] Pavement in the nave of Santa Maria in Cosmedin.*

2-75. *[Below, left] Pavement in the right aisle of San Clemente.*

2-76. *[Below, right] Pavement in the right aisle of Santa Sabina.*

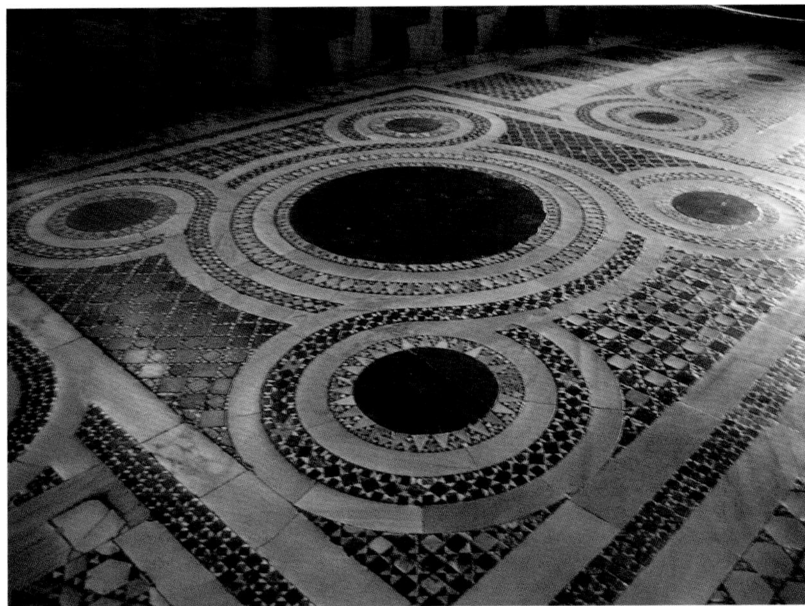

2-77. *Pavement at the center of the sancta of Santa Croce in Gerusalemme.*

2-78. *[Right] Pavement at the center of the sancta of Santa Maria in Cosmedin.*

2-79. *[Below] Pavement from the schola cantorum of San Clemente.*

2-80. *[Below, right] Pavement from the schola cantorum of Santi Quattro Coronati.*

was almost always a quincunx, was connected to the other zones of the church by means of lineal ornamental designs, usually sinusoidal braids. The paving of the schola cantorum was generally a rich design of quincuncial or braided arrangements (figs. 2-79 and 2-80). Although rare, in some churches the pavement of the transept looks different from that of the rest of the nave. Sometimes the design of the pavement itself indicates the presence of an illustrious tomb, frequently situated along the longitudinal axis of the church, before and at the foot of the altar (figs. 2-81 and 2-82). The presbytery, or the space reserved for the officiants, often is enriched with Cosmatesque mosaics that sometimes surround the altar (fig. 2-83) or appear behind it, over the longitudinal axis of the church at the foot of the bishop's throne (figs. 2-84 and 2-85). The Cosmatesque artists also paved the crypts of many medieval churches (fig. 2-86).

The buildings of Rome that preserve their original Cosmatesque pavement almost entirely, that is, covering the entire floor, are San Clemente,

2-81. *[Above, left] Tomb at the foot of the altar of San Clemente.*

2-82. *[Above, right] Detail of the tomb at the foot of the altar of San Clemente.*

2-83. *[Left] Pavement surrounding the altar of San Lorenzo fuori le Mura.*

San Crisogono (fig. 2-87), San Gregorio Magno, San Lorenzo fuori le Mura, Santa Maria in Cosmedin, Santi Quattro Coronati, the Chapel of San Silvestro in Santi Quattro Coronati, San Saba (fig. 2-88), and the Sancta Sanctorum Cappella. In some churches, such as Santa Maria Maggiore (fig. 2-89), San Giovanni in Laterano (fig. 2-90), Santa Maria in Trastevere (fig. 2-91), and Santa Prassede (fig. 2-92), the Cosmatesque pavement has been restored, reset, or redone; however, the original Cosmatesque design remains intact. The pavement designs of Santa Maria in Aracoeli and Santa Sabina are intact but anomalous, displaying an orthogonal reticular partition formed by great slabs of marble bordered by bands of mosaic, rather than the design mentioned previously (fig. 2-93). Other structures retain only part of their original Cosmatesque design. This occurs in churches whose present pavement, made from tiles or bricks, has some bands and panels of Cosmatesque mosaic, such as Sant'Alessio, Santa Balbina (mixed with ancient Roman mosaics), Santi Giovanni e Paolo, and Santi Michele e

2-84. *[Right] Pavement behind the altar of Santa Maria in Trastevere, as seen from the episcopal throne.*

2-85. *[Far right] Pavement behind the altar of San Lorenzo fuori le Mura, as seen from the episcopal throne.*

2-86. *[Below, left] Pavement in the crypt of Sant'Agnese in Agone.*

2-87. *[Below, right] Interior of San Crisogono.*

2-88. *Interior of San Saba.*

2-89. *Pavement at Santa Maria Maggiore.*

2-90. *Pavement at San Giovanni in Laterano.*

2-91. *Interior of Santa Maria in Trastevere.*

2-92. *Interior of Santa Prassede.*

2-93. *[Left] Pavement of Santa Maria in Aracoeli.*

2-94. *[Below, left] Detail of the pavement in the vestibule of the Casina di Pio IV.*

2-95. *[Below, right] Interior of the vestibule of the Casina di Pio IV, Vatican City.*

2-96. *[Bottom] Pavement in front of the tomb of San Pietro (Saint Peter), in the semiannular crypt of San Pietro Vaticano.*

Magno. Other buildings only contain fragments or remnants of Cosmatesque paving, such as San Benedetto in Piscinula, San Bartolomeo all'Isola, the Casina di Pio IV (medieval Cosmatesque panels inserted into the posterior floor, figs. 2-94 and 2-95), San Giovanni a Porta Latina, San Marco, Sant'Ivo dei Bretonni, Santa Maria sopra Minerva (side chapel), Santa Maria della Pace (side chapel), the Grotte Vaticane (chapels in the semiannular crypt, fig. 2-96), and San Silvestro in Capite (side chapels). Fragments of Cosmatesque pavements also appear set into or hanging on walls, as in Santa Croce in Gerusalemme.[9] In addition to the pavements just cited, one can see other earlier and later examples of Cosmatesque pavements in Rome. A pre-Cosmatesque pavement from Carolingian times covers the floor of the Chapel of San Zenone in Santa Prassede. Late Cosmatesque pavements—designed and laid during the Renaissance by the same methods and with the same technique as the medieval Cosmatesque

2-97. *Pavement from the Cappella Sistina (Sistine Chapel), seen from the entrance.*

2-98. *Pavement from the Cappella Sistina, seen from the altar.*

2-99. *Interior of the Stanza della Segnatura, Vatican City.*

pavements—can be found in the Cappella Sistina (figs. 2-97 and 2-98), the Stanza della Segnatura (fig. 2-99), and the Tempietto di Bramante (figs. 2-100, 2-101, and 2-102). Such pavements are the only form of Cosmatesque art that continued to be produced after the disappearance of the medieval Cosmatesque school, which expired with the transfer of the Papacy to Avignon.

2-100. *View of the exterior of the Tempietto di Bramante. (P. M. Letarouilly)*

2-101. *Detail of the pavement of the Tempietto di Bramante, seen from the entrance.*

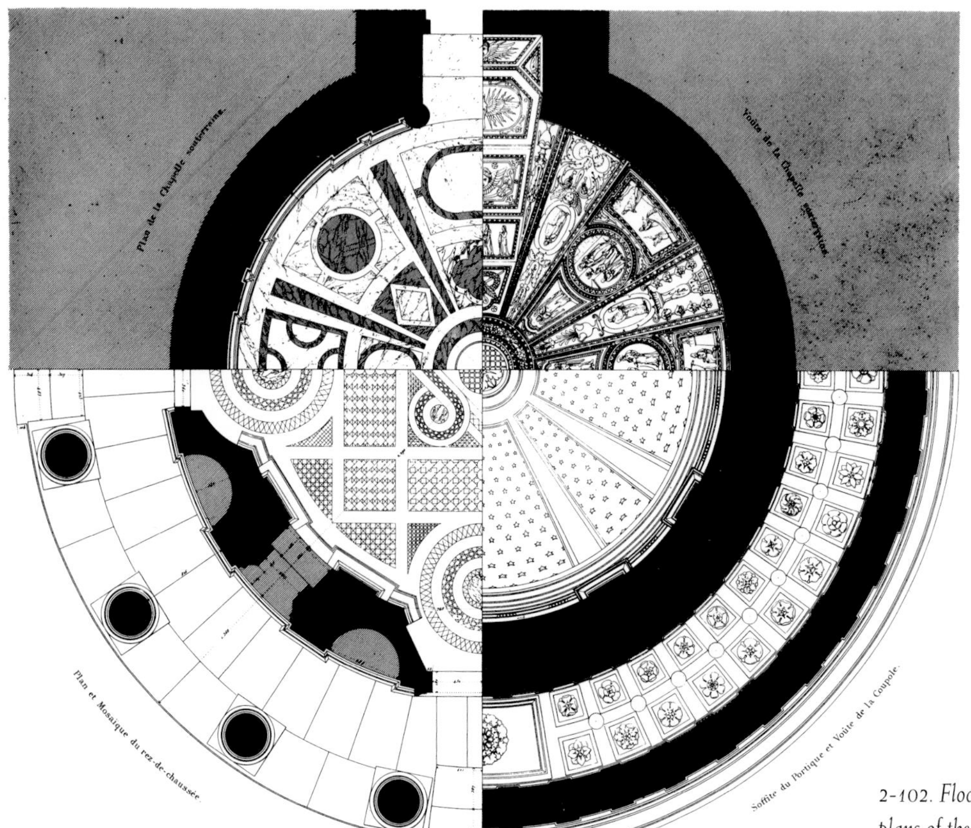

2-102. *Floor plans and reflected ceiling plans of the church and crypt of Tempietto di Bramante. (P. M. Letarouilly)*

Screens, Plutei, and Iconostases

The areas closed to the secular public, such as the schola cantorum and the presbytery, are separated from the rest of the church by means of dividing walls called *screens*. The Cosmatesque artists sometimes used spoliated materials to construct these partitions; for this reason, the screens occasionally contain a combination of marble panels decorated with bas-relief from the paleo-Christian or late ancient era, to which the Cosmati then added multicolored mosaic insertions, as can be seen in the schola cantorum of San Clemente (figs. 2-103 and 2-104). Some screens have no mosaic decoration, for example, those of the schola cantorum in Santa Maria in Cosmedin. When a screen is perforated (lacework), it is called a *transenna*; there are transennae in the presbytery of Santa Maria in Trastevere and remains of transennae in the chancel of Sant'Anselmo.

The term *plutei* refers to enclosure panels that are very rich in materials and design. Whereas the knee walls called screens mark the limits of the schola cantorum, plutei generally separate the presbytery from the rest of the church. The plutei typically are decorated with a grid of newel posts that form rectangular compartments filled with slabs of porphyry and serpentine, and are flanked by twisted columns adorned with polychrome mosaics. Whole plutei or their remnants can be found in the churches of San Cesareo,

2-103. *[Above] Screen at the lower right of the schola cantorum of San Clemente.*

2-104. *[Right] Detail of the lower right screen of the schola cantorum of San Clemente.*

2-105. *[Far left] Detail of the right half of the pluteus, Santi Nereo ed Achilleo.*

2-106. *[Left] Presbytery of Santi Nereo ed Achilleo, seen from the right aisle.*

2-107. *[Above] Pluteus of San Saba.*

2-108. *[Above] Detail of pluteus of San Saba.*

San Lorenzo fuori le Mura (at the back of the presbytery, with the episcopal throne centered in the pluteus), Santi Nereo ed Achilleo (figs. 2-105 and 2-106), San Pietro Vaticano (the altar of one of the chapels of the semiannular crypt is built with the remains of a pluteus), and San Saba (the remains of a pluteus are embedded in the wall of the right aisle, figs. 2-107 and 2-108).

Some of the churches have retained an architraved structure sustained by a row of columns or pillars that, in the manner of a screen, separate the presbytery from the nave. Such a structure is called an *iconostasis.* In Rome the iconostasis of Santa Maria in Cosmedin, made of ancient fragments, has survived to the present and extends along the aisles, separating them from the presbytery (figs. 2-109, 2-110, and 2-111). Remnants of disassembled iconostases can also be found—for example, the two columns decorated with mosaics that today stand behind the high altar of Sant'Alessio, which originally belonged to the iconostasis of San Bartolomeo all'Isola (figs. 2-112 and 2-113).

2-109. *[Above, left] Nave of Santa Maria in Cosmedin, with iconostasis at the end.*

2-110. *[Above, right] Side aisle of Santa Maria in Cosmedin, with iconostasis at the end.*

2-111. *[Right] Reconstruction of the presbyterial division of Santa Maria in Cosmedin. (F. Mazzanti)*

2-112. *[Below, left] Bishop's throne at Sant'Alessio.*

2-113. *[Below, right] Detail of one of the columns from the bishop's throne at Sant'Alessio.*

Ambos

The ambo is a pulpit or gallery, generally located on either side of the choir and used for the chant or the readings from the Gospels and the Epistles, respectively. The decoration of the ambos grew richer over time. The most luxurious ambos have parapets or guardrails decorated with great slabs or rounds of porphyry and serpentine, framed by moldings of white marble inlaid with polychrome mosaic. There are two types of ambo: asymmetric and symmetric. The asymmetric ambo has one set of stairs; the symmetric ambo has two, facing each other. In both cases, the stairs lead to a central landing on which the officiant stands when reading, resting the sacred books on a stone book rest that sits on the parapet, which often boasts a sculpted eagle in high relief. The Cosmatesque churches generally have two ambos, one symmetric and the other asymmetric, one on either side of the schola cantorum; examples include Santa Maria in Cosmedin, San Lorenzo fuori le Mura (figs. 2-114 through 2-119), and San Clemente (figs. 2-120 and 2-121). Santa Maria in Aracoeli (figs. 2-122 and 2-123) and San Cesareo are examples of churches with a pair of asymmetric ambos. These ambos are not the originals, but rather the result of reforms or restorations in which the original symmetric ambo was taken apart, creating two.

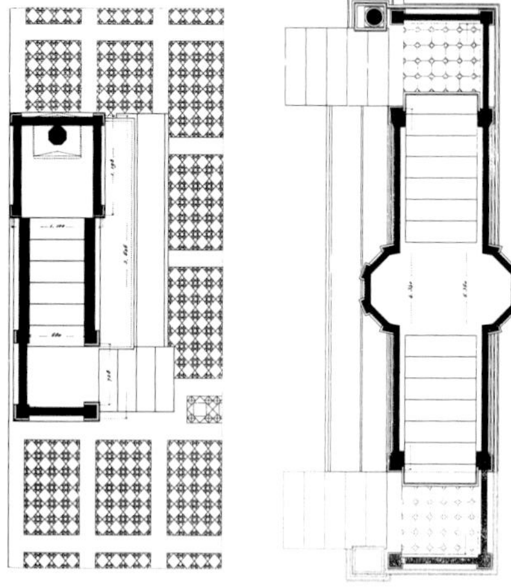

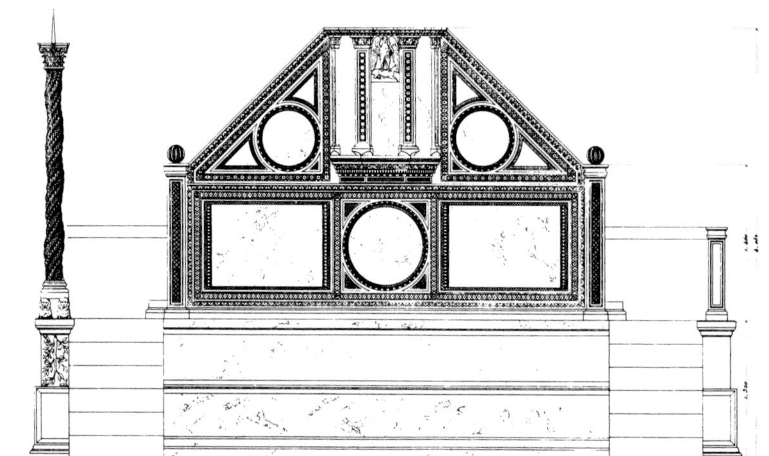

2-114. [Above, left] Plan of the left ambo of San Lorenzo fuori le Mura. (P. M. Letarouilly)

2-115. [Above, right] Plan of the right ambo of San Lorenzo fuori le Mura. (P. M. Letarouilly)

2-116. [Left] Elevation of the right ambo of San Lorenzo fuori le Mura. (P. M. Letarouilly)

2-117. [Below, left] Right ambo of San Lorenzo fuori le Mura.

2-118. [Below, right] Detail of the right ambo, San Lorenzo fuori le Mura.

2-119. *Interior of San Lorenzo fuori le Mura. (P. M. Letarouilly)*

2-120. *(Right) Left ambo of San Clemente.*

2-121. *[Far right] Right ambo of San Clemente.*

2-122. *[Right] Left ambo of Santa Maria in Aracoeli, seen from the altar.*

2-123. *[Far right] Right ambo of Santa Maria in Aracoeli, seen from the altar.*

Paschal Candelabra

The paschal candelabrum holds the Easter candle. The Cosmati candelabra display a free column, with a Corinthian capital and a twisted shaft encrusted with bands of polychrome mosaic; sometimes a sculpted lion appears at the base. Originally the candelabrum was placed on the guardrail of one of the landings of the symmetrical ambo, as can still be seen in San Clemente (fig. 2-124), San Lorenzo fuori le Mura, and Santa Maria in Cosmedin (fig. 2-125). Some candelabra have been moved and today are found to one side of the altar, resting on the screen that separates the presbytery from the rest of the church or on the floor of the presbytery, as in Sant'Anselmo (figs. 2-126 and 2-127), Santa Cecilia in Trastevere (fig. 2-128), Santa Maria in Trastevere, and San Saba.

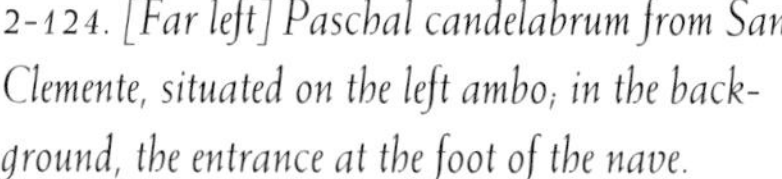

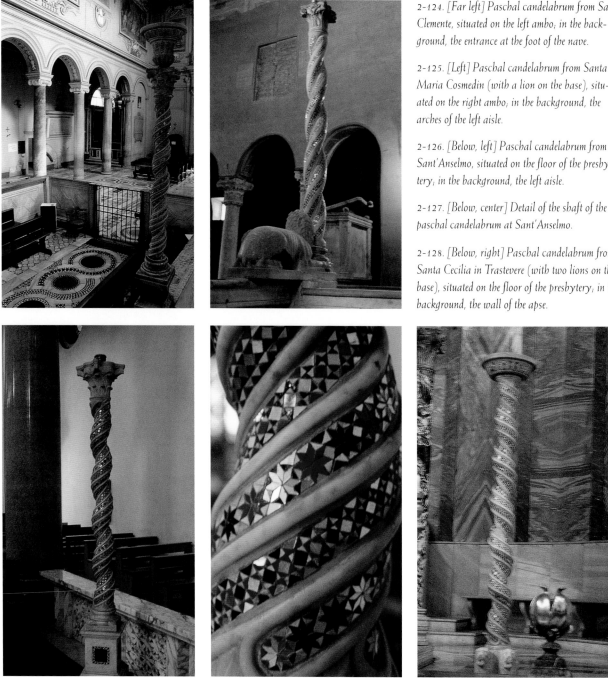

2-124. *[Far left] Paschal candelabrum from San Clemente, situated on the left ambo; in the background, the entrance at the foot of the nave.*

2-125. *[Left] Paschal candelabrum from Santa Maria Cosmedin (with a lion on the base), situated on the right ambo; in the background, the arches of the left aisle.*

2-126. *[Below, left] Paschal candelabrum from Sant'Anselmo, situated on the floor of the presbytery; in the background, the left aisle.*

2-127. *[Below, center] Detail of the shaft of the paschal candelabrum at Sant'Anselmo.*

2-128. *[Below, right] Paschal candelabrum from Santa Cecilia in Trastevere (with two lions on the base), situated on the floor of the presbytery; in the background, the wall of the apse.*

2-129. Marble column from San Paolo fuori le Mura.

Marble Column

The great free-standing marble column with sculpted bas-relief covering its shaft serves both as candelabrum and as a commemorative pillar for relevant historic-religious events. In Rome there is only one such column, in the basilica of San Paolo fuori le Mura (fig. 2-129).[10]

Altar Tables, Tombs, and Paliottos

The altars of the Cosmatesque churches take various forms. The simplest consist of a solid stone prism that supports a stone panel, or tabletop. On the front of the support is a cross made with encrusted mosaic. This sort of altar appears in some of the side chapels of Santa Balbina and San Giovanni a Porta Latina. Somewhat more sophisticated altars, such as those found in a few of the side chapels of San Silvestro in Capite, have two supporting pilasters decorated with bands of mosaic (fig. 2-130). The majority of the Cosmatesque high altars, in addition to serving as a Eucharistic table, contain the relics and mortal remains of saints in their interiors. These altars, which serve as table, reliquary, and sarcophagus, have the form of a bulky, straight, and hollow prism, in proportions similar to a cube. Some of them are simply decorated, such as the one in San Lorenzo fuori le Mura, which consists of a prism with sides of porphyry slabs, or that in San Giorgio in Velabro, decorated only with bands of mosaic on the corner pilasters (fig. 2-131). Others,

2-130. [Right] Detail of the altar in one of the side chapels of San Silvestro in Capite.

2-131. [Far right] Altar and confessio of San Giorgio in Velabro.

2-132. *Paliotto of the altar of Santi Nereo ed Achilleo.*

the most luxurious, have a front or anterior face, or *paliotto*, that is profusely decorated with panels (square, rectangular, triangular, and circular) of porphyry and serpentine, bordered with bands of white marble that are in turn encrusted with mosaics; the most notable Cosmatesque paliottos are those of San Cesareo, Santa Prassede, and Santi Nereo ed Achilleo (fig. 2-132).

2-133. *Tabernacoletto of San Crisogono.*

Tabernacoletti

The small Cosmatesque tabernacle, or *tabernacoletto*, consists of a miniature temple structure formed by two twisted columns that support a small pediment. Both the shafts of the small columns and the tympanum and edges of the pediment are decorated with mosaics of colored glazes and gold. The purpose of the tabernacoletto is to hold the relics and protect sacred images. This small temple sits in the area closest to the presbytery in the wall of one of the aisles, as in San Crisogono (fig. 2-133), or in the wall of the presbytery, to one side of the apse, as in Santa Maria in Domnica and San Clemente (figs. 2-134 and 2-135). There are also remains of tabernacoletti in Santa Cecilia in Trastevere, San Nicola in Carcere, Santa Sabina, and San Pietro Vaticano (moved to the foot of the altar of one of the chapels of the semiannular crypt).

2-134. *[Below, left] Apse of San Clemente, with tabernacoletto at the front of the right side.*

2-135. *[Below] Detail of the lunette of the tabernacoletto of San Clemente. Boniface VIII and his nephew (1299).*

Confessios

The confessio is a cell in the semibasement, situated under the altar, in which the remains of one or several martyrs are interred. Their origin stems from the need to hide the holy tombs for fear of desecration. Thus, their only access is a small window, the *fenestella confessionis*, which is sealed with a transenna (stone screen decorated with lacework) and found under the frontal of the altar. The medieval pilgrims would push pieces of cloth through the holes of the confessio until the cloth touched the floor of the tomb of the martyr, thus converting the rags into holy relics. The Cosmatesque artists remodeled numerous confessios in Rome; the most notable are found in San Lorenzo fuori le Mura, San Clemente (fig. 2-137), San Cesareo, San Giorgio in Velabro (see fig. 2-131), and Santi Nereo ed Achilleo (fig. 2-136); the latter three still have the bands of polychrome mosaic with which the Cosmati decorated the frame and the mullions of the transenna.

2-136. *Ciborium, altar, and confessio of Santi Nereo ed Achilleo.*

2-137. *Ciborium, altar, and confessio of San Clemente.*

Ciboria

The ciborium, or baldachin, is a structure in the form of a canopy over the altar, which rests on four columns. One can distinguish two varieties of Cosmatesque ciboria: the classic ciborium and the Gothic ciborium. The former were constructed in the twelfth century; the latter, in the second half of the thirteenth century. In general, the classic Cosmatesque ciborium consists of four columns with shafts of red porphyry (occasionally of red granite, black-white marble, white marble, or green antico) and gilded Corinthian capitals (occasionally of serpentine or white marble) that support a straight architrave of white marble decorated with lineal designs of polychrome mosaic. Resting on the architrave are one or two galleries of alternately square and octagonal floor plan, shaped by small white columns. The finishing touch of the ciborium is a small lantern with an octagonal floor plan and a pyramidal cover crowned by a ball on which rests a Latin cross. The ceiling of the cibo-

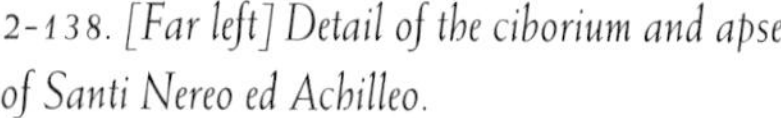

2-138. [Far left] Detail of the ciborium and apse of Santi Nereo ed Achilleo.

2-139. [Left] Ciborium and pluteus of San Cesareo.

2-140. [Below, left] Ciborium and part of the schola cantorum of San Clemente.

2-141. [Below, center] Ciborium and apse of Santa Maria in Trastevere.

2-142. [Below, right] Ciborium of San Saba.

rium is painted with golden stars on a blue background. The most notable classic ciboria that remain in Rome are those of Santi Nereo ed Achilleo (fig. 2-138), San Cesareo (fig. 2-139), San Clemente (fig. 2-140), Santa Maria in Trastevere, very remodeled (fig. 2-141), San Saba (fig. 2-142), San Pancrazio, although excessively restored (figs. 2-143 and 2-144), San Giorgio in Velabro (figs. 2-145 and 2-146), and San Lorenzo fuori le Mura, which is the prototype of the classic ciborium in Rome (fig. 2-147). There were also ciboria in the churches of San Bartolomeo all'Isola, Santa Croce in Gerusalemme, Santi Giovanni e Paolo, and San Marco, although nothing remains of them.

In the Gothic Cosmatesque ciborium, the pointed arch appears, accompanied by pinnacles and lobed arches. The churches with Gothic ciboria are Santa Maria in Cosmedin (fig. 2-148), Santa Cecilia in Trastevere (fig. 2-149), San Paolo fuori le Mura (fig. 2-150), and San Giovanni in Laterano (figs. 2-151 and 2-152).

2-143. [Below, left] Ciborium of San Pancrazio.

2-144. [Below, right] Detail of the ciborium of San Pancrazio.

2-145. [Bottom, left] Ciborium of San Giorgio in Velabro.

2-146. [Bottom, right] Detail of the ciborium of San Giorgio in Velabro.

2-147. *[Above, left] Ciborium of San Lorenzo fuori le Mura.*

2-148. *[Above, middle] Ciborium of Santa Maria in Cosmedin.*

2-149. *[Above, right] Ciborium of Santa Cecilia in Trastevere.*

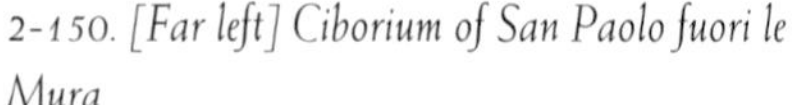

2-150. *[Far left] Ciborium of San Paolo fuori le Mura*

2-151. *[Left] Ciborium of San Giovanni in Laterano.*

2-152. *Detail of the ciborium of San Giovanni in Laterano.*

Episcopal Thrones

The cathedra or bishop's throne is the seat in the presbytery designated for the bishop or the officiant during the liturgical ceremony. The Cosmati situated the chair at the back of the apse of the central nave, elevated above three to five steps. Occasionally the throne is found inserted into plutei, which decorate the chancel of the church, although generally the chair is freestanding. The bishop's chair usually has a head piece with a great circular motif, a frontal embellished with a porphyry plaque, and armrests sculpted with standing lions that bear the seat on their backs. The decoration of the episcopal throne is sumptuous, with backgrounds and bands of polychrome mosaic, twisted columns with mosaic insertions, small twin pilasters, carved cornices, and slabs (circular, rectangular, and square) of such precious materials as porphyry, serpentine, black porphyry, and green

2-153. *[Below, left] Bishop's throne of Santa Balbina.*

2-154. *[Below, right] Detail of the bishop's throne of Santa Balbina.*

2-155. *[Bottom, left] Bishop's throne inserted into plutei at San Lorenzo fuori le Mura.*

2-156. *[Bottom, right] Bishop's throne at San Lorenzo fuori le Mura.*

granite. It is not unusual to find cathedrae with inscriptions that recall the name of the occupant-donor of the chair or the name of the artist who made it or both. The Cosmatesque episcopal thrones that survive in Rome were created in the medieval era or later. One can see early medieval cathedrae, that is, those executed before or during the twelfth century, in Santa Balbina (figs. 2-153 and 2-154), San Lorenzo fuori le Mura (inserted or embedded in plutei, figs. 2-155 and 2-156), and Santa Maria in Cosmedin. The chairs of San Clemente and San Silvestro in Capite (today in the cloister of the Laterano, fig. 2-157), that are also from the same early era, are made of ancient fragments. The late-medieval thrones, those constructed in the thirteenth century, have a dais or Gothic gable, as can still be seen in San Cesareo (remade with ancient pieces), the Grotte Vaticane, and Santi Nereo ed Achilleo (restored in the sixteenth century, fig. 2-158). The following survive from the postmedieval era: the throne of San Saba (figs. 2-159 and 2-160), which is a reconstruction from medieval pieces, and a few thrones that have been redone or overrestored in recent centuries, including those of Sant'Anselmo (fig. 2-161), San Giovanni in Laterano (fig. 2-162), Santa Maria in Trastevere, and Santa Sabina.

2-157. *[Top] Remains of the bishop's throne of San Silvestro in Capite, now in one of the galleries of the cloister of San Giovanni in Laterano.*

2-158. *[Above, left] Back of the bishop's throne of Santi Nereo ed Achilleo.*

2-159. *[Above, center] Bishop's throne of San Saba.*

2-160. *[Above, right] Detail of the bishop's throne of San Saba.*

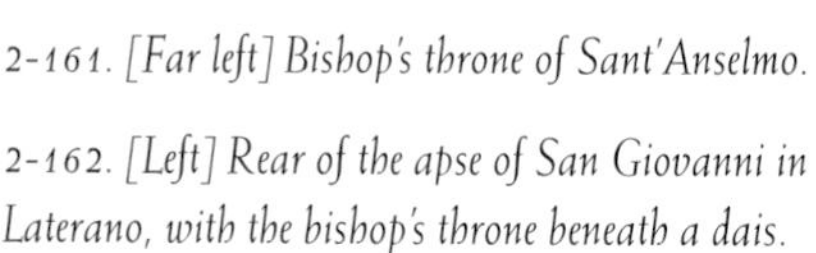

2-161. *[Far left] Bishop's throne of Sant'Anselmo.*

2-162. *[Left] Rear of the apse of San Giovanni in Laterano, with the bishop's throne beneath a dais.*

Tombs and Monuments

In the second half of the thirteenth century and the first decades of the fourteenth century, the Cosmati created tombs and sepulchral monuments for illustrious personages, generally bishops, cardinals, and popes. All of these works present, to greater or lesser degree, Gothic traits, except the tomb of the Cardinal Fieschi in San Lorenzo fuori le Mura, which is also the earliest (mid-thirteenth century) and displays classical forms instead. This particular tomb consists of a platform beneath two Ionic columns, which serve as support for a straight architrave which in turn supports a gallery of small columns, over which rests a dais in the manner of a pediment. On top of the platform lies an ancient pagan sarcophagus sculpted with a nuptial scene in high relief. Murals decorate the wall between the sarcophagus and the dais (fig. 2-163).

There are two types of Gothic Cosmatesque tombs: those without and those with a dais. The first consist of a platform decorated with mosaics,

2-163. *Tomb of Cardinal Fieschi at San Lorenzo fuori le Mura.*

2-164. *[Above, left] Tomb of Cardinal Anchero de Troyes at Santa Prassede.*

2-165. *[Above, right] Detail of the tomb of Cardinal Anchero de Troyes at Santa Prassede.*

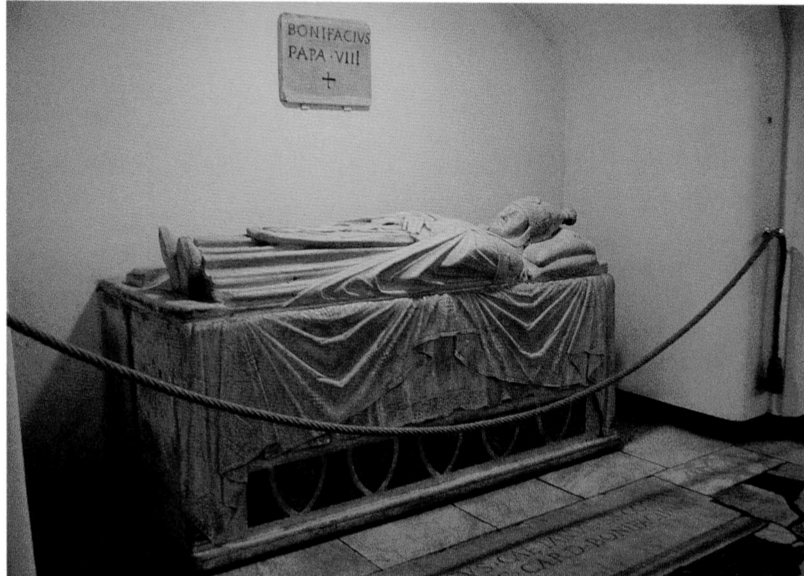

2-166. *[Left] Tomb of Boniface VIII at the Grotte Vaticane.*

2-167. *[Below, left] Tomb of Cardinal Stefano de Surdi at Santa Balbina.*

2-168. *[Below, right] Detail of the tomb of Cardinal Stefano de Surdi at Santa Balbina.*

which serves as the base of a sarcophagus, decorated with coats of arms and mosaics, above which rests the effigy of the deceased. The latter have, in addition to the above elements, two small pilasters decorated with mosaics that rest on the platform and sustain a trefoil arch with a gable and pinnacles over a mosaic or a figurative fresco in the wall. In Rome one can still see Gothic Cosmatesque tombs in Santa Prassede (figs. 2-164 and 2-165), the Grotte Vaticane (fig. 2-166), Santa Balbina (figs. 2-167 and 2-168), Santa Maria in Aracoeli (fig. 2-169), Santa Maria sopra Minerva (fig. 2-170), Santa Maria Maggiore (fig. 2-170), San Giovanni in Laterano, Santa Maria del Priorato, and Santa Maria in Trastevere.

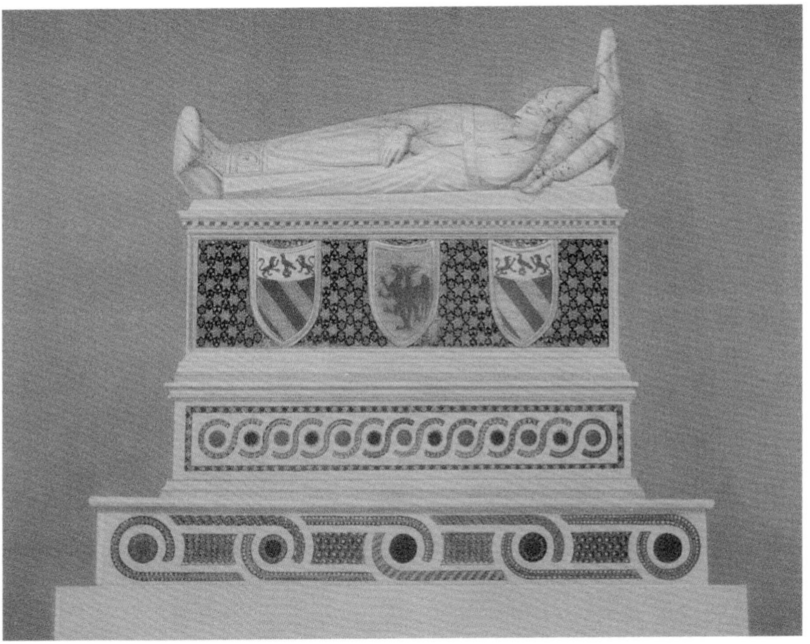

2-169. *Tomb of Pope Honorius IV at Santa Maria in Aracoeli. (G. B. De Rossi)*

2-170. *Tomb of Cardinal Gugliemo Durante at Santa Maria sopra Minerva (left); and tomb of Cardinal Consalvo Rodríguez at Santa Maria Maggiore (right). (G. B. De Rossi)*

TOMBSTONES

The tombstone is a rectangular stone slab, generally of marble, which serves as the cover to a grave. Tombstones can have bas-relief, inscriptions, and emblems in intarsia of colored marbles. Many Cosmatesque pavements are interrupted by tombstones: in San Clemente, where there are several tombstones, one replacing a quincunx in the center of the space reserved for the faithful (fig. 2-171) and others in the lateral naves (fig. 2-172); in Sant' Alessio, where the presbytery holds a tombstone with a bas-relief image of a recumbent human figure (fig. 2-173); in Santa Sabina, where many of the great white marble slabs of the reticular pavement are in fact gravestones (fig. 2-174); and in Santa Maria Maggiore, where several tombstones with inscriptions rest over the longitudinal axis of the church (fig. 2-175). Santa Prassede also contains the remains of tombstones, now relocated on the walls of one of the side chapels.

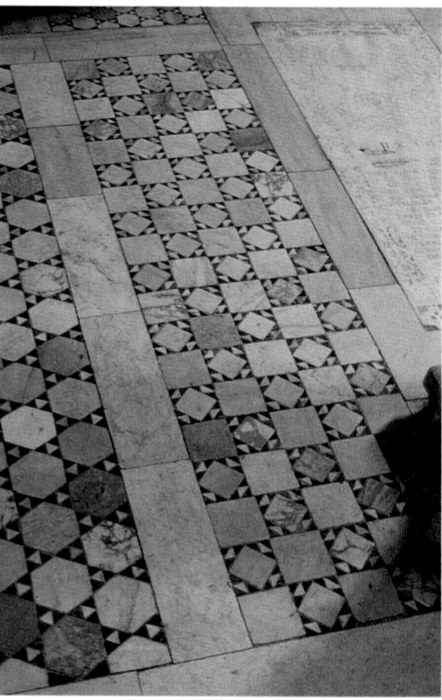

2-171. *[Left] Interior of San Clemente; there is a tombstone in the middle of the pavement of the sancta.*

2-172. *[Above] Pavement in the left aisle of San Clemente, with tombstone.*

2-173. *Pavement from the presbytery of Sant'Alessio, with tombstone.*

2-174. *Pavement in Santa Sabina, with tombstones.*

2-175. *Pavement on the longitudinal axis of Santa Maria Maggiore, with tombstones.*

Sculpture

The Cosmatesque artists used figurative sculptures to ornament the many elements of their architectural works, not only on the exteriors but in the interiors as well. They employed a variety of motifs, although the most characteristic are the lion, the sphinx, and the eagle. They created sculptures of medium to large size, such as the angels that today stand in the Grotte Vaticane (figs. 2-176, 2-177, and 2-178), the sculptural collection of saints whose remains are preserved in the cloister of the Laterano, and numerous sculptures of lions that can still be seen on doors, cloisters, thrones, and paschal candelabra. Figures of half lions, lying down, seated, or standing, rest attached to the foot of the flanks of the doors of Santi Giovanni e Paolo (figs. 2-179, 2-180, and 2-181), San Lorenzo in Lucina, and San Lorenzo fuori le Mura (figs. 2-182, 2-183, and 2-184). At San Bartolomeo all'Isola and Santi Apostoli, the lions that originally sat at the entrance door of the church have been relocated in other parts of the building (fig. 2-185). On the sides of the thrones of Santi Nereo ed Achilleo and San Saba reside sculpted lions, as do lions on the ends of the continuous side bench of the presbytery of San Lorenzo fuori le Mura (fig. 2-186). Two seated lions flank the arch that gives access to the center of the cloister of San Giovanni in Laterano (fig. 2-187). There are also lions on the feet of the paschal candelabra of San Lorenzo fuori le Mura and Santa Maria in Cosmedin. Large sphinxes remain in one of the arches that give access to the center of the cloister of San Giovanni in Laterano, while others of smaller dimensions decorate the door of Sant'Antonio Abate and the ambo of San Cesareo (fig. 2-188). Small figures of eagles extend their wings under the book stand of the ambos of

2-176. Tomb of San Pietro (Saint Peter) in the crypt of San Pietro Vaticano. Angels in high relief flank the arch, and lions lie at the feet of the arch (the lions originally formed part of the throne of San Pietro).

2-178. Eastern end of one of the chapels of the crypt at San Pietro Vaticano. Angels in high relief flank the altar.

2-177. Tomb of San Pietro in the crypt of San Pietro Vaticano; detail of the angel and lion to the right of the arch.

2-179. *Detail of the bottom of the door of Santi Giovanni e Paolo, with lions resting against the frame.*

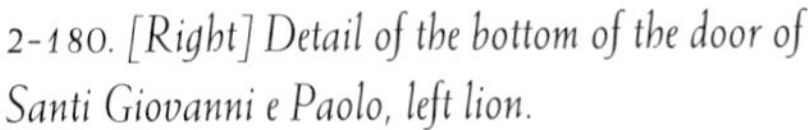

2-180. *[Right] Detail of the bottom of the door of Santi Giovanni e Paolo, left lion.*

2-181. *[Far right] Detail of the bottom of the door of Santi Giovanni e Paolo, right lion.*

2-182. *[Below, left] Door of San Lorenzo fuori le Mura.*

2-183. *[Below, middle] Detail of the bottom of the door of San Lorenzo fuori le Mura, left lion.*

2-184. *[Below, right] Detail of the bottom of the door of San Lorenzo fuori le Mura, right lion.*

San Lorenzo fuori le Mura (fig. 2-189) and Santa Maria in Aracoeli (fig. 2-190), as well as on the lintel of the door of Santi Giovanni e Paolo. In addition to lions, sphinxes, and eagles, the Cosmati sculpted, in high relief and in bas-relief, many other small figures, including small leonine heads, human heads, dog or wolf heads, repetitive geometricized plant motifs, and other small representations of animals, people, and plants (lambs, small eagles, birds, leaves, the Virgin, the Christ child and saints, Adam and Eve next to the Tree of Knowledge, and so on). These various decorations appear on the cornices of the porticoes, as in San Giorgio in Velabro (see fig. 2-49) and San Lorenzo fuori le Mura; on plutei, as in San Lorenzo fuori le Mura and San Saba; on ambos, as in San Cesareo and San Lorenzo fuori le Mura; on tabernacoletti, as in San Clemente; on Gothic ciboria, as in Santa Maria in Cosmedin; on the cornices of cloisters, as in San Giovanni in Laterano (fig. 2-191) and San Paolo fuori le Mura (figs. 2-192, 2-193, and 2-194); and at the bases of columns in cloisters, as in San Paolo fuori le Mura (fig. 2-195).

2-185. *[Above, left] Detail of reclining lion embedded in the left side of the steps of the right apse of San Bartolomeo all'Isola.*

2-186. *[Above, middle] Detail of a reclining lion that serves as the right arm of the bench that extends along the right side of the presbytery of San Lorenzo fuori le Mura.*

2-187. *[Above, right] Entrance arch to the center of the cloister of San Giovanni in Laterano, flanked by lions.*

2-188. *Detail of the ambo in San Cesareo, with figures of sphinxes.*

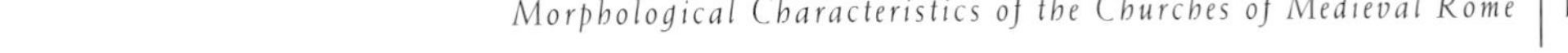

2-190. *Detail of the left ambo in Santa Maria in Aracoeli, with figure of an eagle.*

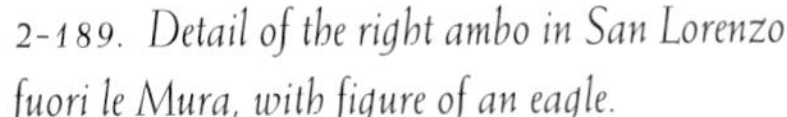

2-189. *Detail of the right ambo in San Lorenzo fuori le Mura, with figure of an eagle.*

2-192. *Detail of the entablature of a pilaster from the cloister of San Paolo fuori le Mura. Small leonine heads are on the cornice.*

2-191. *Detail of the arcade and entablature from the cloister of San Giovanni in Laterano. Small leonine and human heads are on the cornice.*

2-193. Detail of the entablature in the cloister of San Paolo fuori le Mura. Small human and leonine heads are on the cornice.

2-194. Detail of the entablature of a pilaster from the cloister of San Paolo fuori le Mura. Small leonine heads, which act as gargoyles, are in the corners of the cornice.

2-195. Detail of a twin column from the cloister of San Paolo fuori le Mura. A small figure of a recumbent lion is at its base.

Crypts

The crypt is the underground space, situated beneath the presbytery, that serves as the burial ground for one or several martyrs. Crypts responded to the need to build tombs that ensured the security of their contents while facilitating comfortable and orderly visits for pilgrims. Many of the crypts that survive in Rome still have remnants of Cosmatesque mosaic in the floor, on the altar, or both. In Rome the crypt is typically semiannular. A staircase descends to a curved hallway that follows the arch of the apse and connects with a straight corridor. This passage continues to a wall, behind which lies the tomb of the martyr. At the other extreme of the curved corridor is the ascending staircase. The first crypts of this design were those of San Pietro Vaticano and San Paolo, by order of Gregory the Great (590–604). Semiannular crypts or their remains survive in San Pietro Vaticano, with many examples of remains of Cosmatesque mosaics on the floors and altars of the surrounding chapels (figs. 2-196 through 2-199); Santi Quattro Coronati (fig. 2-200); Santa Prassede, with a Cosmatesque paliotto (fig. 2-201); San

2-196. [Below, left] Curved corridor from the semiannular crypt of San Pietro Vaticano.

2-197. [Below, right] Semiannular crypt of San Pietro Vaticano (isometric reconstruction).

2-198. [Bottom, left] Interior radiating chapel in the semiannular crypt of San Pietro Vaticano; Cosmatesque panels were inserted in the pavement.

2-199. [Bottom, right] Exterior radiating chapel in the semiannular crypt of San Pietro Vaticano; the altar contains Cosmatesque fragments.

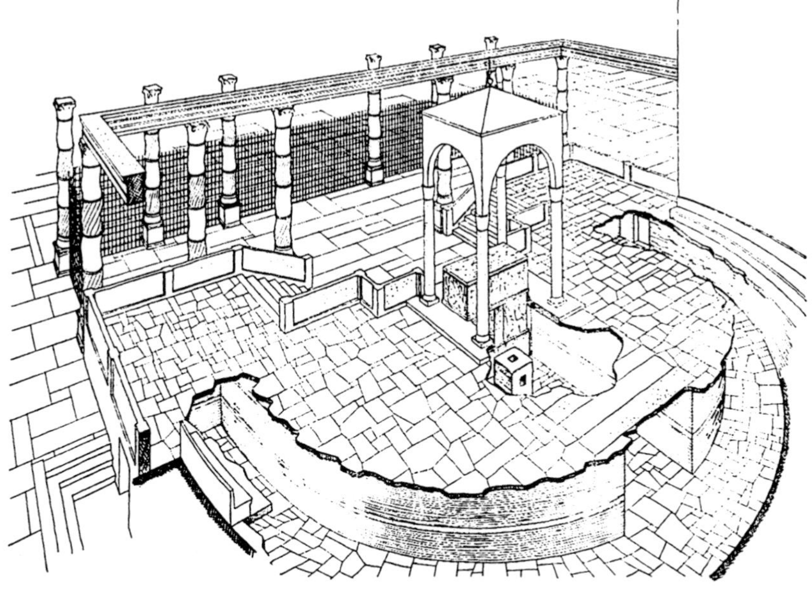

Crisogono, with wall frescoes containing quincuncial designs; San Pancrazio; Santa Cecilia in Trastevere, with the remains of a Cosmatesque floor in the vestibule of the neo-Cosmatesque crypt constructed in 1900 by Giovanni Battista Giovenale (fig. 2-202); San Marco; and San Saba. Some crypts take the shape of a small underground basilica, such as those of San Lorenzo fuori le Mura (very remodeled at the end of the nineteenth century, when the architect Raffaele Cattaneo built the funerary chapel of Pius IX, with mosaics by Lodovico Seitz) and Santa Maria in Cosmedin. Other crypts contain small oratories, including those in Sant'Agnese in Agone, with Cosmatesque pavement (fig. 2-203); Sant'Apollinare, with Cosmatesque pavement at the foot of the altar (figs. 2-204 and 2-205); Santi Giovanni e Paolo; and Santa Maria Scala Coeli, with remnants of Cosmatesque mosaics on the altar. Finally, some crypts consist of an opening in front of the altar accessible by means of lateral stairs, as in San Silvestro in Capite, with remains of Cosmatesque mosaics on the altar (fig. 2-206), and Santa Maria Maggiore.

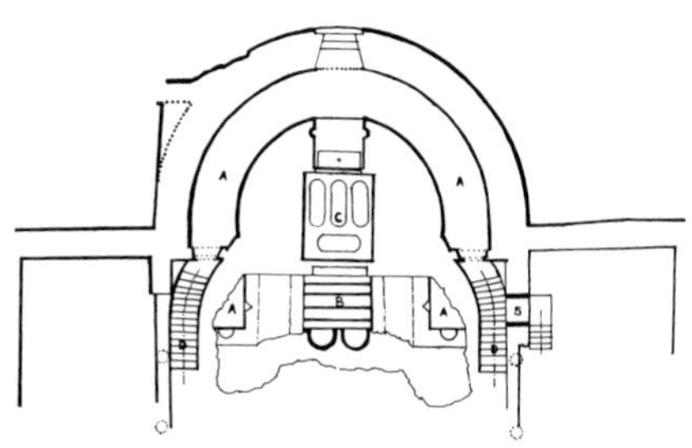

2-200. *Floor plan of the semiannular crypt of Santi Quattro Coronati.*

2-201. *Crypt of Santa Prassede; at the rear, a thirteenth-century Cosmatesque paliotto.*

2-202. *[Far left] Neo-Cosmatesque crypt in Santa Cecilia in Trastevere.*

2-203. *[Left] Crypt from Sant'Agnese in Agone with Cosmatesque pavement; altar in the background.*

2-204. *Crypt of Sant'Apollinare.*

2-205. *Crypt of Sant'Apollinare; detail of the paved platform at the foot of the altar.*

2-206. *Crypt of San Silvestro in Capite.*

Cloisters

The cloister is a gallery of arches around a rectangular or square patio, joined to the church. Each arm or side of the cloister is composed of a group of arcades divided by rectangular piles. Each arcade is, in turn, composed of several arches. The arches rest on paired columns and support the entablature. Two groups of Cosmatesque cloisters are distinguishable—early, executed in the twelfth century, and late, executed in the first third of the thirteenth century. To the first group belong the cloisters of Santi Quattro Coronati (figs. 2-207 through 2-211), Santa Cecilia in Trastevere, San Cosimato (figs. 2-212 and 2-213), San Lorenzo fuori le Mura (figs. 2-214 through 2-217), and Santa Sabina. To the second belong those of San Paolo fuori le Mura (figs. 2-218 to 2-235) and San Giovanni in Laterano (figs. 2-236 through 2-246). The early cloisters are cruder and of poorer quality than the later examples. In the cloisters of the twelfth century, the entablature consists of a band of marble dentils arranged in a series, flanked by rows of brick sleepers that alternate with rows of saw-toothed bricks. In the cloister of Santi Quattro Coronati, the open spaces between the stone corbels of the

2-207. *Galleries in the cloister of Santi Quattro Coronati.*

2-208. *Detail of the paired columns in the cloister of Santi Quattro Coronati.*

cornice are decorated with lively geometric designs in mosaic. The cloister of San Lorenzo fuori le Mura is the only one in Rome that has an upper level with elegant multiple windows supported by individual and paired columns. In the later cloisters, the cornice or entablature displays a rich frieze decorated with linear geometric compositions (for example, mixed braid, series of connected figures) made in marble and vitreous mosaic. In the spandrels between arches sit small sculptures, frequently grotesque (warriors, small birds, dogs, hunters, Adam and Eve near the Tree of Knowledge, masks of various shapes). The top of the cornice is a band of marble carved with a variety of figures in bas-relief (such as palmettes and other geometricized plant motifs, human heads, leonine heads). The columns differ widely: fluted, geminated, ophidian, wreathed, and turned.[11] Frequently their shafts are embellished with mosaics of marble tesserae (white, yellow, red, and green) and glazed tesserae (white, red, blue, black, and gold), and their capitals imitate foliage. On the bases of the colonettes were sometimes carved small reclining animals. The largest sculptures are the lions that flank the central arches at each side of the cloister, which grant access to the center of the cloister.

2-209. *[Below] Center of the cloister of Santi Quattro Coronati.*

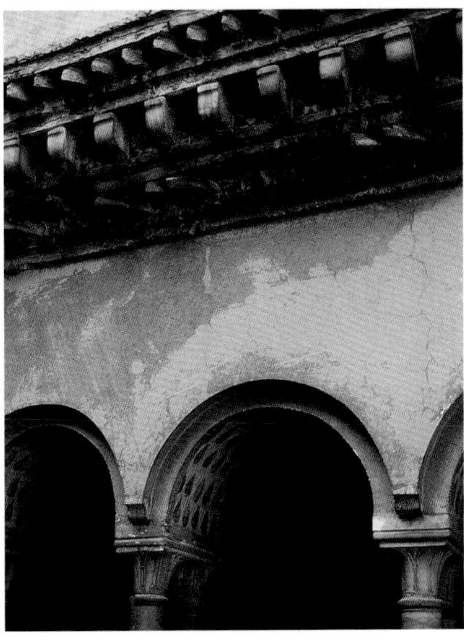

2-210. *[Above, left] Detail of arches and cornice in the cloister of Santi Quattro Coronati.*

2-211. *[Above, right] Detail of the cornice in the cloister of Santi Quattro Coronati.*

2-212. *[Right] Patio of the cloister of San Cosimato.*

2-213. *[Below] Galleries of the cloister of San Cosimato.*

2-214. *Galleries of the cloister of San Lorenzo fuori le Mura.*

2-215. *[Left] Patio, with second floor, in the cloister of San Lorenzo fuori le Mura.*

2-216. *[Below, left] Detail of a multiple window on the upper level of the cloister of San Lorenzo fuori le Mura*

2-217. *[Below, right] Detail of one side of the patio in the cloister of San Lorenzo fuori le Mura.*

2-218. *Galleries in the cloister of San Paolo fuori le Mura.*

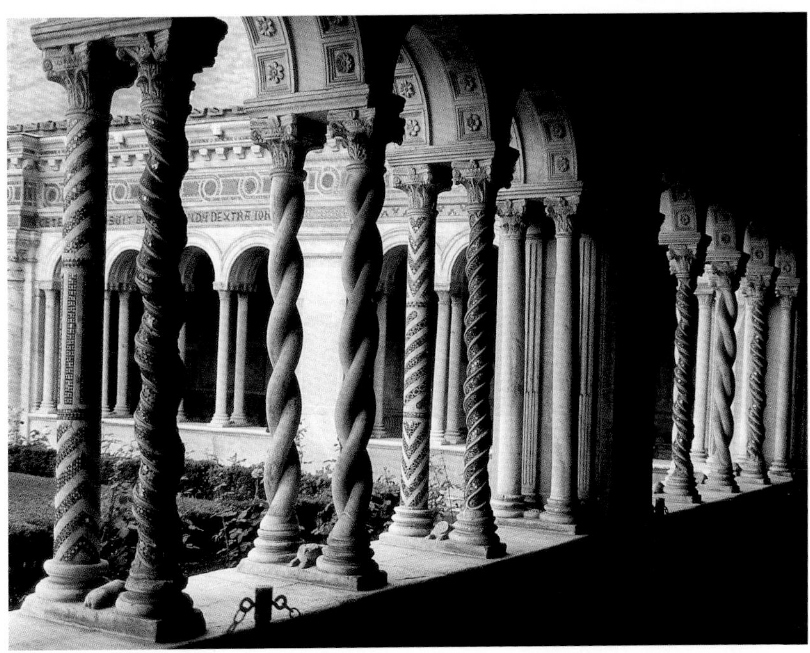

2-219. *Galleries, with paired columns, in the cloister of San Paolo fuori le Mura.*

2-220. *Patio in the cloister of San Paolo fuori le Mura.*

2-221. *[Far left] Detail of Cosmatesque fragments found in one of the galleries in the cloister of San Paolo fuori le Mura.*

2-222. *[Left] Detail of the central arch of one side in the cloister of San Paolo fuori le Mura.*

2-223. *[Above] Elevation of one side of the patio in the cloister of San Paolo fuori le Mura.*

2-224. *Detail of an archivolt in the cloister of San Paolo fuori le Mura.*

2-225. *[Far left] Detail of the entablature over an embedded column in the cloister of San Paolo fuori le Mura.*

2-226. *[Left] Detail of the entablature above a pilaster in the cloister of San Paolo fuori le Mura.*

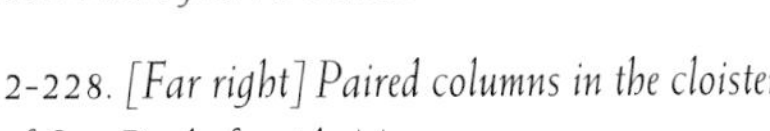

2-227. *[Right] Paired columns in the cloister of San Paolo fuori le Mura.*

2-228. *[Far right] Paired columns in the cloister of San Paolo fuori le Mura.*

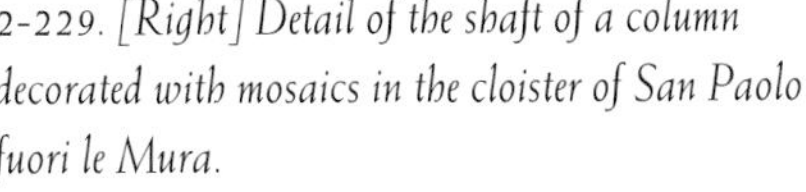

2-229. *[Right] Detail of the shaft of a column decorated with mosaics in the cloister of San Paolo fuori le Mura.*

2-230. *[Far right] Detail of the shaft of a column decorated with mosaics in the cloister of San Paolo fuori le Mura.*

2-231. *[Below, left] Arcade in the cloister of San Paolo fuori le Mura.*

2-232. *[Below, center] Capitals in the cloister of San Paolo fuori le Mura.*

2-233. *[Below, right] Shafts of columns in the cloister of San Paolo fuori le Mura.*

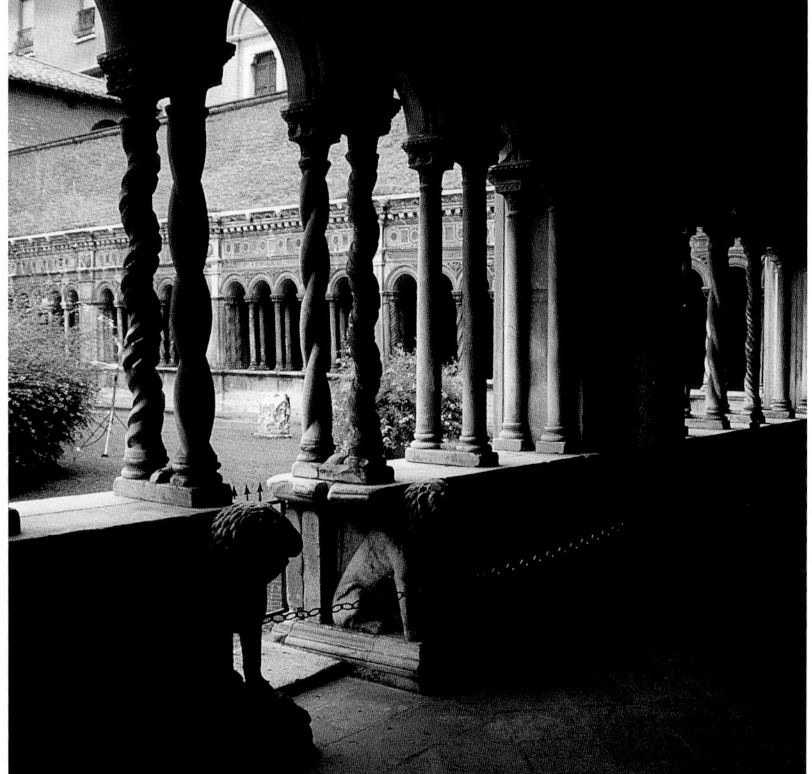

2-234. *[Above, left] Detail of the shaft of a column decorated with mosaics in the cloister of San Paolo fuori le Mura.*

2-235. *[Above, right] Detail of the shaft of a column decorated with mosaics in the cloister of San Paolo fuori le Mura.*

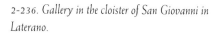

2-236. *Gallery in the cloister of San Giovanni in Laterano.*

2-237. *[Above] Patio in the cloister of San Giovanni in Laterano.*

2-238. *[Right] Arcade of five arches in the cloister of San Giovanni in Laterano.*

2-239. *Shafts of paired columns decorated with mosaics in the cloister of San Giovanni in Laterano.*

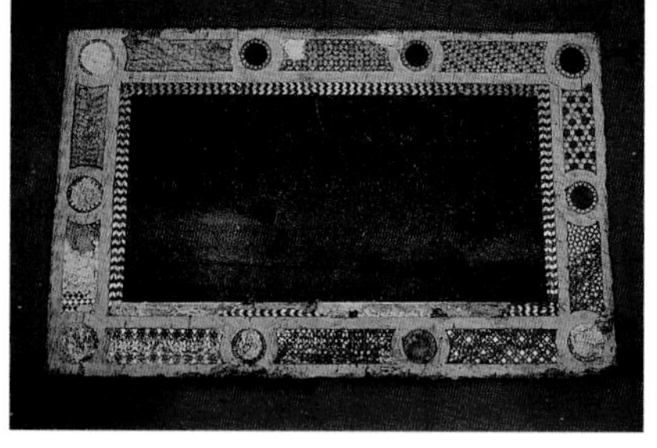

2-240. *[Left] Detail of Cosmatesque fragment (front of tomb) in the cloister of San Giovanni in Laterano.*

2-241. *[Top] Cosmatesque fragment (front of tomb), today hung on the wall, in the cloister of San Giovanni in Laterano.*

2-242. *[Above] Cosmatesque fragment (panel), today hung on the wall, in the cloister of San Giovanni in Laterano.*

2-243. *[Far left] Corner of the patio in the cloister of San Giovanni in Laterano.*

2-244. *[Left] Arches, frieze (decorated with mixed braid), and cornice in the cloister of San Giovanni in Laterano.*

2-245. *[Right] Detail of the shaft of a column decorated with mosaics in the cloister of San Giovanni in Laterano.*

2-246. *[Far right] Detail of the shaft of a column decorated with mosaics in the cloister of San Giovanni in Laterano.*

Other Interior Elements

In addition to the elements just cited, the interiors of Cosmatesque churches include other components. These, already discussed earlier in the initial description of these churches, include glass mosaics in the apse, starred wooden ceilings, latticework in the arched windows, wall paintings, curtains, lamps, relics, and pavements in the side chapels.

The Cosmati, by joining all of the aforementioned components, created opulent places of worship, reflecting the spirit of a new era. The Cosmatesque artists took paleo-Christian and late antique prototypes as models, both for their building plans and their ornamental programs. They revived above all the paleo-Christian models of the Constantinian era, in particular the basilica of San Pietro, which they considered the ideal archetype. The Cosmati played a leading role in the medieval renaissance of antiquity, which was nourished in part by the contact that the artists had with works of classical tradition, through the study of the innumerable and sublime remains from that period still extant in Rome, and through the relationship of the Roman artists with the masters of the school of Montecassino and of southern Italy, who familiarized them with the elements, techniques, and designs of Byzantine ornamental art.

The insistence with which the Roman artists of the late Middle Ages looked to the past, always at the same ancient models, produced two results. On the one hand, it left Rome outside the predominant trends of transalpine art of the period (Romanesque, Gothic). On the other hand, despite the common criticism of Cosmatesque art as conservative, insular, unimaginative, retrograde, and monotonous, it anticipated the rediscovery of, and the consequent cult of, classical antiquity that would soon take place, in the artistic period that has come to be known as the Renaissance.

Chapter 3

ANTECEDENTS

LOCAL TRADITION AND BYZANTINE INFLUENCE

The expansion of the Roman Empire gave rise to the Romanization of the Mediterranean region. One aspect of Roman cultural influence was the generalization of an ornamental practice, originally Greek, that might well be considered the true Roman national art: the geometric mosaic in marble (fig. 3-1).

The customary use of marble mosaic was disseminated from Rome to all points of the empire, either through the export of works and models created in the city or by the dispatch of artists and marble cutters who executed mosaics, of the typical Roman geometric repertoire, in other parts of the empire. Upon reaching the different destinations, the traditional Roman geometric pavement would gradually incorporate local traditions, both cultural and technical. The new works resulted from the meshing of the classic Roman mosaic tradition with preexisting construction techniques, local ornamental motifs, and indigenous materials.

In later eras the process reversed. The Rome that in antiquity had exported construction techniques and repertoires of ornamental designs for marble revetments became the importer of ornamental motifs developed in other parts of its former empire. Just as the different regions conquered by Rome did in their day, Rome assimilated the external influences while retaining local traditions; the local traditions have always carried enormous weight in the art of the city of Rome, which was always consciously determined to preserve its "Romanness" and was a jealous protector of the continuity of its ancient tradition.

By the Middle Ages, Rome had lost most of its power. Political, economic, and cultural preponderance in the Mediterranean emanated from the *pars Orientalis* of the ancient empire. The eyes of Rome were fixed on the center of its rival power, Byzantium—the Greek name for Constantinople. The forms of Byzantine art, in whose development Roman art had participated, became the source of inspiration for the artistic creations of medieval Rome (figs. 3-2 and 3-3).

3-1. Pompeiian ornament. (Chromolithograph by Owen Jones, 1856)

This cycle of ebb and flow or export and import of ornamental motifs repeated incessantly for centuries in the Mediterranean region, a natural consequence of the permanent relationship between the different cultural-artistic traditions of the peoples who lived there. This phenomenon complicates the identification of the place of origin of many of the ornamental motifs typical of this geographic area, since the process that led to the gestation of those motifs is characterized by the accumulation of influences whose sources indicate contrary directions.

Identifying the origin of the ornamental motifs found in the geometric mosaics of the city of Rome is further complicated by Rome's position as a powerful radiating center during antiquity, exporting to the world its geometric repertoire. Therefore, when Rome subsequently imported ornamental motifs elaborated upon in any of the lands previously under its protection or influence, the material inevitably reflected both the latest trends of the autonomous tradition that had developed and refined them as well as features

3-2. *[Above, left] Byzantine ornament. (Chromolithograph by Owen Jones, 1856)*

3-3. *[Above, right] Byzantine ornament. (Chromolithograph by Heinrich Dolmetsch, 1883)*

of Rome's own ornamental tradition. The search for the antecedents of Cosmatesque ornamentation must fit within this framework.

At the beginning of the twelfth century, the Cosmatesque mosaics were born and quickly consolidated in the city of Rome. It is necessary to look back to the ninth century to find, in the right aisle of Santi Quattro Coronati, an example that seems to be the successor of a discrete series of geometric *opus sectile* that flourished in Rome in the Carolingian age.[1]

In the city of Rome examples of *sectilia* that might be considered immediate precedents to the Cosmatesque mosaics of the twelfth century no longer exist. Such examples would be of great help in providing a thorough explanation of the development of each of the elements that characterize the geometric forms of Cosmatesque ornament. Therefore, one must consider, at least in part, the influence of ornamental production outside Rome, while proceeding with an attentive examination of examples produced by the ancient local tradition.

Of great interest are the results of the research conducted by Alessandra Guiglia Guidobaldi in which she summarizes, amplifies, and on occasion, rectifies the conclusions reached by other authors who had addressed the topic previously, although with less depth and detail. Guiglia Guidobaldi divides her 1984 text, *Tradizione locale e influenze bizantine nei pavimenti Cosmateschi* (Local traditions and Byzantine influence in the Cosmatesque pavements), into four sections: (1) motifs with roundels and interlacings; (2) reticular partition by means of marble bands; (3) geometric motifs used to fill the intervals; and (4) chromatic taste.[2] In each section she examines in particular those features that she perceives to be the principal stylistic and iconographic components of the Cosmatesque works.

The content of this chapter is divided in the same way. Each section addresses the considerations that seem most pertinent, including and complementing those already examined by Guiglia Guidobaldi.

The Motifs with Roundels and Interlacings

These motifs can be divided into two fundamental types. One is a simple row of roundels occupying the eyelets of a sinusoidal two-strand guilloche. The other is a quincunx composed of five roundels joined by means of interlacing bands; the largest roundel is located within an imaginary square, occupying the exact center, and each of the four remaining roundels is tangential to two sides of the square, with one roundel at each of the angles of the residual space left free by the central roundel.

Guiglia Guidobaldi reviews the diverse hypotheses maintained by various authors about the sources of these motifs. Primitive antecedents of these designs may be found in the mosaics of imperial Rome.[3] They may have arisen from Byzantine models.[4] The mosaics of the late imperial Rome may have influenced these motifs, as may paleo-Christian and early medieval pavements from the Venetian area, considered direct inheritors of the decorative tradition of Rome, with some Byzantine influence.[5] Or antecedents of the Cosmatesque guilloche and quincunx may be identified in some examples of local painting and sculpture (the eighth-century frescoes on the walls of the crypt of San Crisogono contain interlacing designs, also apparent in early medieval Roman sculpture). With no example identical to the Cosmatesque quincunx in the mid-Byzantine artistic production, perhaps a pavement, no longer in existence, served as the inspiration for the masters of the Capella Palatina in Sicily, as well as for the Cosmati in Rome.[6]

Despite these various hypotheses, when the time comes to identify the most immediate antecedent of the Cosmatesque pavements, no one hesitates to point to the pavement in the Church of the Abbey of Montecassino (Latium), consecrated in the year 1071. The sources expressly cite the fact that Desiderio, the abbot of Montecassino in the eleventh century, ordered that masters be brought from Constantinople and Alexandria to execute the pavement, which supports the thesis of total or partial reliance of the Cosmatesque style on Byzantine cultural matrices.[7]

A fundamental image among those compiled as antecedents of the Cosmatesque pavements is the drawing by E. Gattola from 1773, the only evidence available until a few decades ago of the existence of the Montecassino pavement from the eleventh century, hidden beneath another pavement from the eighteenth century (fig. 3-4). A. Pantoni verified the veracity of Gattola's drawing in conscientious studies of the ample remains of the original pavement, revealed during the restoration of the abbey after its destruction during the Second World War.[8] In the museum of the abbey one can see, recomposed in panels of cement, numerous fragments from the ancient *sectile*. Some are also found in other areas of the Benedictine complex.

3-4. *Drawing of the pavement in the Church of the Abbey of Montecassino.* (E. Gattola, 1733)

The pavement of Montecassino shows, over the longitudinal axis of the church, two examples of a motif that is basically a square circumscribing a wheel of eight circlets ensconced in the angles between four roundels. This motif, if in fact it might be considered a relative of the Cosmatesque quincunx, is at best a distant one, given that both the relative proportions of the roundels and the detail of the pattern of the bands that tie the roundels together are very different from those of the Cosmati. The same can be said of the two motifs inscribed in a poised square that appear in the left aisle, near the west end of the church. This position, in the aisle, is totally contrary to the practice of the Cosmati, and the motifs that might be considered analogous are found in few Cosmatesque works (such as San Crisogono). Furthermore, the artists of Montecassino refrained from using guilloches laden with aligned roundels. Thus, it is necessary to continue to

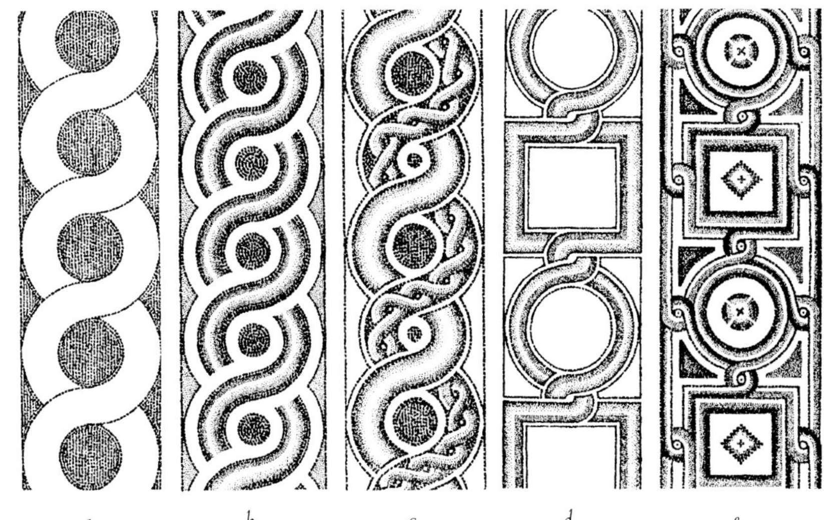

3-5. Interlacings in opus tessellatum from antiquity. (Drawings by Richard Prudhomme)

3-5a. Rome: Baths of Diocletian, in situ, gardens, Museo Nazionale Romano.

3-5b. Apamea, Syria. (V. Verhoogen, 1965, plate 12)

3-5c. Sardes, Turkey. (Turk Arkeoloji Dergisi, 1962, fig. 8, plate XXXV)

3-5d. Jerusalem, Israel. (L. Budde., 1972, 212, fig. 259)

3-5e. Khaldé, Lebanon. (M. H. Chebab, 1959, plate LXV, I)

search elsewhere for examples that contain interlacing designs similar to those commonly found in Cosmatesque works.

The imperial age, especially the late-ancient period, and the paleo-Christian age produced a rich repertoire of interlacing ornament in numerous examples dispersed throughout the Mediterranean region. Examples appear as much in mosaic pavements as in other artistic manifestations, including painting, sculpture, miniatures, and weavings.[9] It is important to keep in mind that during antiquity the various interlacing motifs appeared only in mosaic pavements of *opus tessellatum*; pavements executed in *opus sectile* never contained interlacing designs.

Finding mosaics in *opus tessellatum* from the imperial and paleo-Christian age with interlacing motifs comparable to those of the Cosmati is an easy task.[10] However, that identity exists only in the basic geometric design, not in the decorative effect: the *three dimensionality* that is often emphasized, through the use of shade and shadow, in a design built in *opus tessellatum* is flattened when the same design is built in *opus sectile* (fig. 3-5). Rendered in *opus sectile*, according to different canons of taste, the mosaic is redirected almost exclusively toward *two dimensionality*. The Cosmatesque interlacings exhibit the two dimensionality inherent to *opus sectile*, which does not occur in the interlacing motifs of the mosaics in *opus tessellatum* of the ancient age.

In the shift from the paleo-Christian age to the Middle Ages, the repertoire of interlacing motifs experienced varying fortunes in different cultural regions. Although these motifs survive in various artistic manifestations in Rome,[11] they do not fall within the ornamental repertoire used in the pavements, given that from the fourth century on, those pavements were executed preferably in *opus sectile*, a technique that, as previously noted, had not produced interlacing motifs and continued not to do so around Rome.[12]

In the Byzantine region, the situation differed. The ancient repertoire of interlacings continued to be used and enriched with multiple variations, appearing not only in the mosaics but in other ornamental works as well (fig. 3-6).[13] For the first time, in the sixth century, pavements appear in *opus sectile* with simplified motifs of interlacing. Guiglia Guidobaldi considers them a true Byzantine "invention." Examples throughout the middle-Byzantine age—Saint John of Ephesus, sixth century; the Basilica of the Mount of

3-6. Saint Michael Archangel: eleventh-century silver icon gilded with enamel and precious stones, originally from Constantinople.

Olives in Jerusalem, sixth century; the mausoleum attached to Saint Eufemia in Constantinople, sixth and seventh centuries; the Kalenderhane Camii in Constantinople, seventh century; the Church of Yacacik in Bithynia,[14] eighth to tenth centuries—testify to the continuity of this type of mosaic, which grew in strength until almost entirely replacing the ancient traditional art of mosaic in *opus tessellatum*.

According to Goffredo Bendinelli, the interlacings in *sectile* stem from the ability of the Byzantine artists to make schematic the mosaic designs from imperial Rome (mosaics that he considers the last source of the Cosmatesque motifs in interlacing), reducing them to their geometric skeleton through a process of simplification and abstraction characteristic of the evolution of design forms in general as they passed from the classical age to the medieval age.[15] In studying the process of geometrization which the interlacing motif underwent, the aspects of design described above must be considered jointly with the following constructive aspects. In the imperial age the eyelets in the guilloches were filled with figurative motifs (animal and plant) or geometric motifs executed in *opus tessellatum*. During the sixth

3-7. *Eleventh-century pavement in the Church of the Nea Moni on the Greek island of Chios.*

century in the Byzantine regions, the marble cutter began to replace the mosaicist in the execution of pavements so as to economize time and labor. As a result, the round interspaces soon came to be occupied by large monolithic porphyry roundels and the classic guilloche was gradually reduced to rigid geometric designs set in *opus sectile*.[16]

By the tenth century, the marble cutter had completely replaced the mosaicist. During this time the glorious Macedonian dynasty flourished in Constantinople (865–1025), under which Byzantine art and culture became highly developed. The new decorative style spread farther and farther, both west (Thessalonica, Macedonia, Greece, Upper Adriatic region, Rome) and east (Asia Minor and Syria, to Palestine). This diffusion led to the nearly simultaneous appearance of artistic manifestations of the same genre or style in the east and in the west. The examples of pavements with interlacing became frequent throughout Byzantium: the Monastery of Iviron on Mount Athos, tenth century; the Church of the Koimesis at Nicaea, eleventh century; the Church of the Nea Moni on the island of Chios, eleventh century (fig. 3-7); the Church of Saint Nicholas at Olynthus, eleventh century (fig. 3-8); the mausoleum of Orhan Gazi at Bursa, eleventh century; the Church of Saint Nicholas at Myra, eleventh century (see chapter 5 for additional discussion and illustration of the Church of Saint Nicholas at Olynthus and the mausoleum of Orhan Gazi at Bursa). Such widespread adoption demonstrates the definitive assimilation of a genre of paving that would continue in use until the end of the Byzantine age, which contained motifs similar to those of the Cosmatesque pavements.[17]

G. Bendinelli suggests that, rather than the name *Cosmatesque* for mosaics of this type that developed in the area of Rome, one should say *Byzantine geometric,* given the developed geometric component of the articulated repertoire of interlacing during the Macedonian age and the extension of that type of decoration throughout the Mediterranean.[18]

It is reasonable to assume that the masters from Constantinople who traveled to Montecassino collaborated in the transfer of the interlacing motifs in *sectile* from the Byzantine world to the Roman world. One could hypothesize that their contact with the local masters (from Campania[19] and from Rome), through the exchange of ideas, designs, or sketches, and through work on

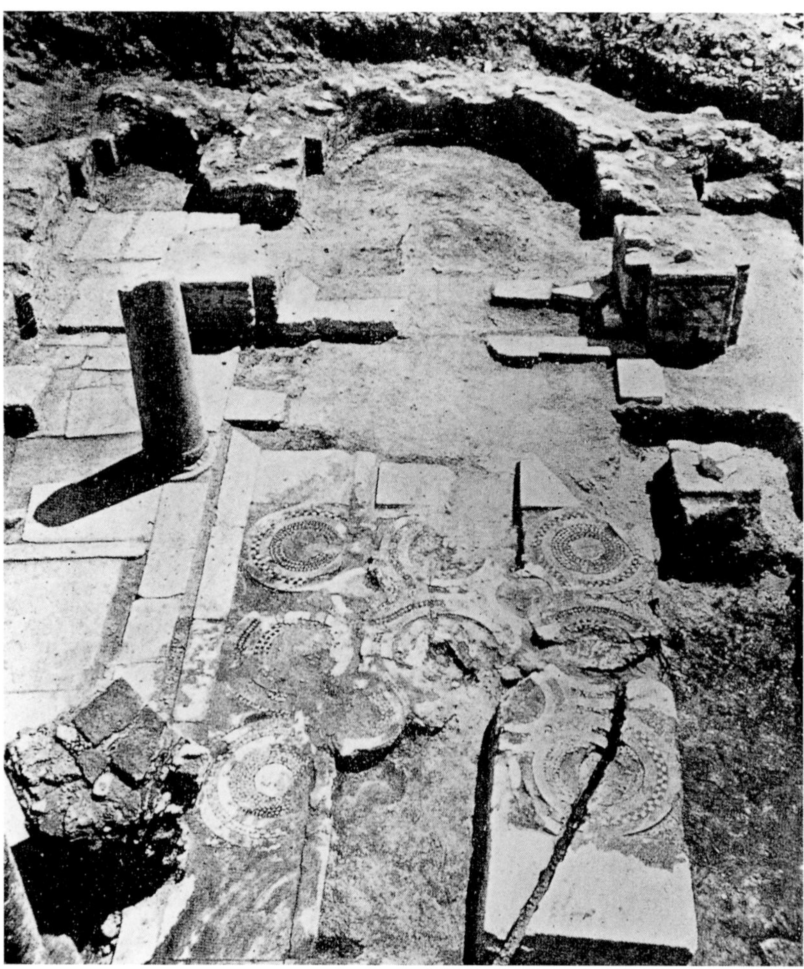

3-8. *The Byzantine church of Saint Nicholas at Olynthus, seen from the west. (David M. Robison, 1946, plate 263)*

the pavement in the Church of the Abbey, could have contributed to the assimilation by local masters of the technique and guiding principles of the regulating geometry of these ornamental designs, more than the study of a model or concrete example could have done. This knowledge would in turn enable them to design or select an appropriate repertoire of motifs, a repertoire that would be limited, decidedly self-contained, because it would be realized on the bases of two fundamental conditions: first, the significance or symbolism of the ornamentation and its relation to the program of liturgical use of the church, and, second, the availability of techniques and materials, given the need to reuse ancient marbles, especially the large monolithic rounds of porphyry.[20]

Reticular Partition Using Bands of Marble

A characteristic feature of the Cosmatesque pavements is compartmentalization of the surface with marble bands. Numerous examples testify to the continuity of this practice in the area of Rome from the sixth to the twelfth century. Remains from sixth-century pavements have survived in the area of the presbytery in Santa Maria Antiqua (fig. 3-9); in two spaces on the south side of the Basilica Emilia in the Roman Forum: the entry vestibule and Taberna VIII (fig. 3-10); in the apse of the primitive oratory of San Saba; in the apse of San Lorenzo fuori le Mura; and in the second basilical phase of

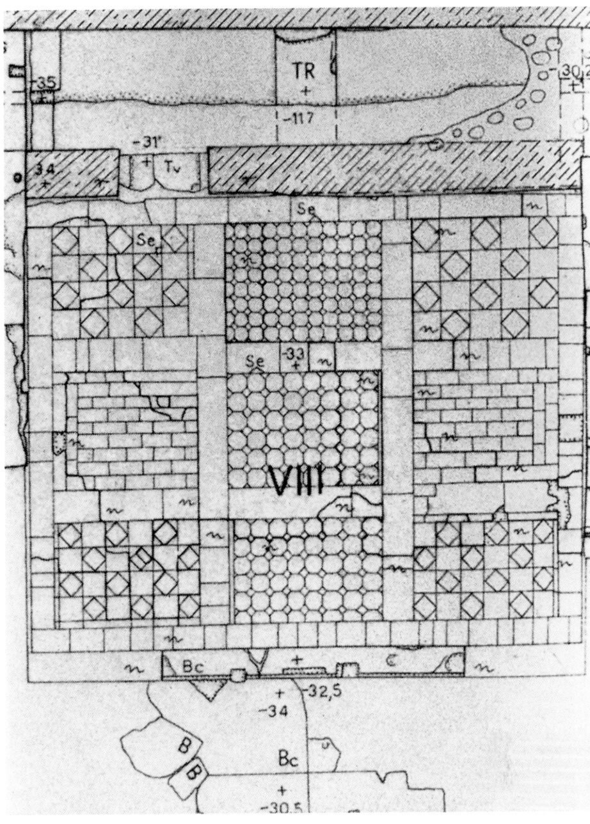

3-9. [Above, left] Sixth-century pavement from the presbyteral area of the Church of Santa Maria Antiqua in Rome. (Detail of the floor plan by A. Petrignani at the time of excavation, 1901)

3-10. [Above, right] Sixth-century pavement in the Taberna VIII of the Basilica Emilia at the Roman Forum. (Detail from the floor plan by H. Bauer).

San Marco.[21] From the ninth century come examples in the Abbey of Farfa, San Giorgio in Velabro, and Santi Quattro Coronati.[22]

Surviving examples of *sectile* from the sixth century are very scarce in Rome, whereas the selection of pavements in *sectile* from the twelfth century is abundant and can still be seen in churches embellished by the Cosmati. It is important to realize that the pavements from the sixth century that have survived to the present were hidden during the twelfth century (by the ruin or burial of the building or because they lay beneath other constructions or pavements). Therefore, Guiglia Guidobaldi hypothesizes that the materials from whole sets of pavements from the sixth century were reused by the marble cutters of the twelfth century, who transferred them to pavements of the churches that they were decorating.[23] Only those few mosaics that were hidden remained at their original location, which explains the current scarcity of pavements from the sixth century. This would imply that the pavements of the Cosmati were a "cut-and-paste" affair. They created them from scraps, using previous pavements or parts of them to fill some of the compartments of the reticular partitions of the new "patchwork" composition.

It seems very likely that the practice, common in Rome as of the sixth century, of compartmentalizing the surface to be ornamented with marble bands was imported from the Byzantine region prior to the sixth century. During the fifth century and especially during the Justinian period, this type of geometric *sectile* had been disseminated throughout the eastern Mediterranean region (for example, in Cyprus, in the sixth-century pavement of the northern aisle of the episcopal basilica of Kourion).

Among the examples in the Byzantine regions prior to the sixth century, the small basilica of Heraclea Lynkestis in Pelagonia (Upper Macedonia) is of particular interest. Peco Srbinovski is inclined to date this building, which

3-11. *Pavement from the small basilica of Heraclea Lynkestis in Pelagonia.*

is the transformation of a Roman monument, to late antiquity, the fourth century.[24] Its pavement exhibits a reticular partition with marble bands (fig. 3-11). Here again one could wonder if the origin of that type of partition stems from the local Hellenistic tradition or from the influence of Roman tradition, since by that time Roman colonists had settled in Macedonia. The geometric patterns observable in the aforementioned pavement from the fourth century are identical to those found in pavements in the aisles from the twelfth century executed by the Cosmati. The overall layout, by suggesting a directional space superposed on the longitudinal axis of the building, could be considered a prelude to the clear differentiation of directional spaces and static spaces found in the Cosmatesque designs.[25]

This differentiation can also be observed at an emerging stage in the directional designs that emphasize the longitudinal axis in the decoration of the High Adriatic compositions, which D. F. Glass selects as probable antecedents to the Cosmatesque works: the pavements of the Theodoran

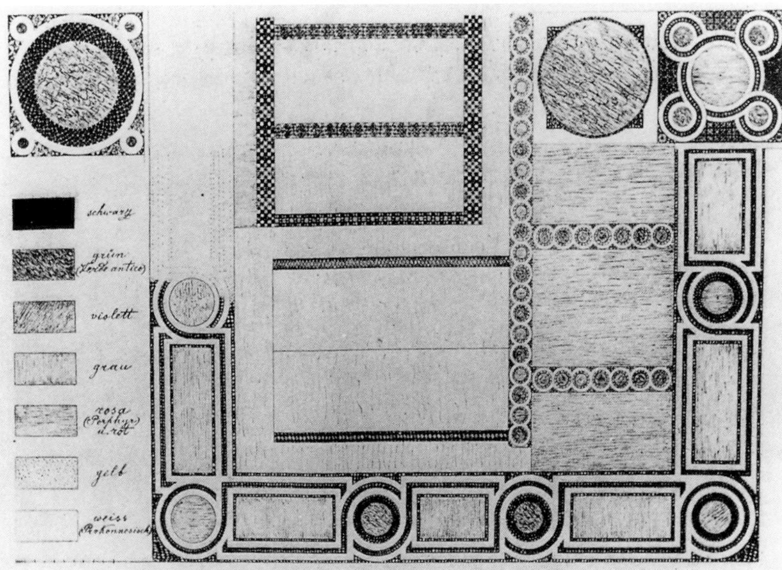

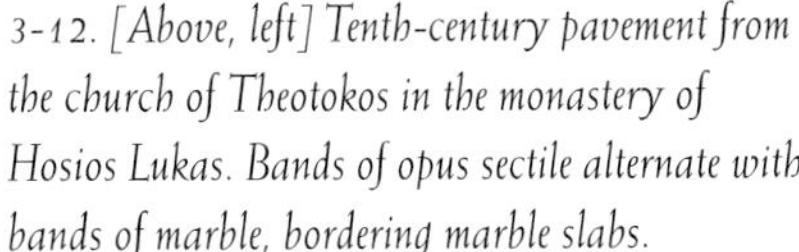

3-12. [Above, left] Tenth-century pavement from the church of Theotokos in the monastery of Hosios Lukas. Bands of opus sectile alternate with bands of marble, bordering marble slabs.

3-13. [Above, right] Eleventh-century pavement from the church of Koimesis in Nicaea. Bands of opus sectile alternate with bands of marble, bordering marble slabs.

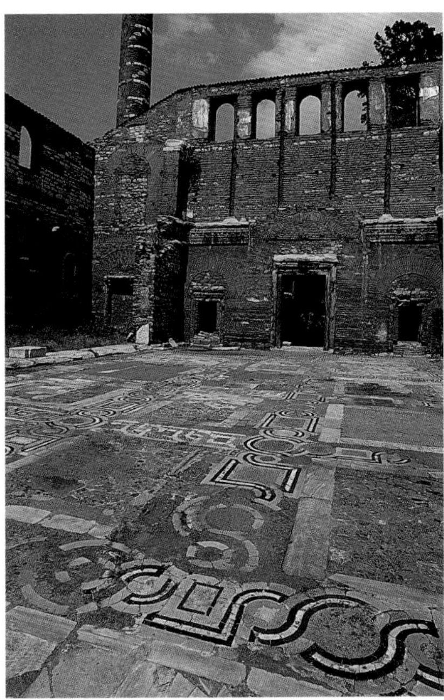

3-14. Eleventh-century pavement from the church of Saint John of Stoudios in Istanbul. Interlacing bands border large marble slabs.

basilica of Aquileia, and the sixth-century pavement in Sant'Eufemia of Grado.[26]

Until the seventh century, marble bands were commonly used in Byzantine ornament to create the reticular partition of the pavements, accompanied by the filling of the resulting intervals with geometric patterns in *opus sectile*. This practice was abandoned in the Macedonian age, in the seventh century, replaced by one that could be described as the "negative" of its predecessor: bands in *opus sectile* or interlacing were used to draw the grid of the pavement, with large marble slabs covering the rectangular interspaces, as in the monastery of Hosios Lukas, in the tenth-century pavement of the church of the Theotokos (fig. 3-12) and in the eleventh-century pavement of the church of the Katholikon; in Nicaea, in the eleventh-century pavement of the church of the Koimesis (fig. 3-13); and in Istanbul, in the eleventh-century pavement of the church of Saint John of Stoudios (fig. 3-14).[27]

Alessandra Guiglia Guidobaldi asserts that, in this particular aspect of their designs, the Cosmatesque artists referred to their most immediate predecessors, as much in time (the eleventh century) as in space (Latium), tying their work to the local tradition and not to the far more distant Byzantine creations previous to the seventh century. Guiglia Guidobaldi bases this assertion on the one hand upon the uninterrupted presence in the area of Rome, from the sixth to the twelfth century, of the practice of compartmentalizing the pavement with a grid drawn by means of bands of marble, and on the other hand upon the discontinuation of this practice by Byzantine artists beginning in the seventh century.

Keeping in mind the diverse character of the group of masters who worked on the eleventh-century pavement in the Church of the Abbey of Montecassino (traveling from Rome, Campania, Constantinople, and Alexandria), it follows that the reticular partition by means of marble bands that organizes the pavement stems from the local masters (from Rome and Campania), not from the Byzantine masters who, according to Guiglia Guidobaldi, would not have been likely to recover a model that had been in disuse in their ornament for more than four centuries.

The Geometric Motifs within the Intervals

Now that we have examined the origin of the marble bands that divide the surface to be ornamented, let us consider the antecedents of the geometric mosaics in *opus sectile* that cover the spaces created by those bands.

The intervals fall into two groups, determined by their shape and size. In the first group are the rectangular compartments created by the grid of orthogonal bands. In the second group are, on the one hand, the interstitial spaces between the marble bands of the orthogonal reticle and the bands of marble that constitute the edges of the strands of the interlacing motifs; on the other hand, the interstitial spaces between the parallel bands of marble that border and subdivide the strands of the motifs in interlacing. The intervals of the second group are much smaller than those of the first group and usually have one or more curved sides.

To begin with a study of the antecedents of the mosaics that fill the intervals of the first group, it is necessary to refer back to the sixth century to find geometric *sectile* in Rome that are essentially identical to those employed by the Cosmati in the rectangular intervals.[28] These pavements from the sixth century inherited the repertoire of geometric *sectile* from the imperial age, which in turn exhibit regulating patterns whose geometry is designed just like those of the mosaics in *opus tessellatum* from the ancient age.[29]

As noted previously, the transition from *opus tessellatum* to *opus sectile* in the interlacing motifs occurred in the sixth century in the Byzantine regions. The shift from *opus tessellatum* to *opus sectile* in the isotropic geometric patterns took place earlier, in late antiquity. As of the fourth century in Rome, pavements were preferentially executed in *opus sectile*.

Keeping in mind the evolution of the porphyry/marble mosaic pavements of Rome and its environs,[30] as well as the repertoire of isotropic surface patterns in *opus tessellatum* of the ancient Roman mosaic,[31] I contend that the "black-white mosaic" (*opus tessellatum* in two counterchanged colors, namely black and white) is the bridge that connects the *opus tessellatum* with the *opus sectile*. The black-white mosaic was the direct progenitor of the "bichrome mosaic" (*opus tessellatum* in two counterchanged colors) and, in the case of chromatic splitting, of the *opus tessellatum* in four counterchanged colors.[32] Each of these represents different moments in a transition that has two distinct fundamental phases. First came the step from one dimension to another, while maintaining the same building technique, in other words, the step from *three-dimensional opus tessellatum—opus tessellatum* in multiple colors, playing with visual effects of perspective and volume through changes of color and tonal gradations—to *two-dimensional opus tessellatum*, a black-white, bichrome, or tetrachrome mosaic of flat visual effect. Second came the step from one building technique to another, but within the same dimension, that is, the step from *two-dimensional opus tessellatum* to *two-dimensional opus sectile* (*opus sectile* of flat visual effect)[33] (figs. 3-15 through 3-33).

From the ancient era to the sixth century, the geometric mosaics in *opus sectile* in Rome display decorative continuity. Beginning in the seventh century, this technique for building mosaics fell into disuse, making it impossible to find examples of geometric *sectile* in Rome that immediately precede those of the Cosmati. Such was not the case in Byzantine mosaics, where the distant classical matrix common to the decorative repertoires of the East and

3-15. *Isotropic pattern of spindles: the steps from opus tessellatum (of three-dimensional effect) to opus sectile (of two-dimensional effect).*

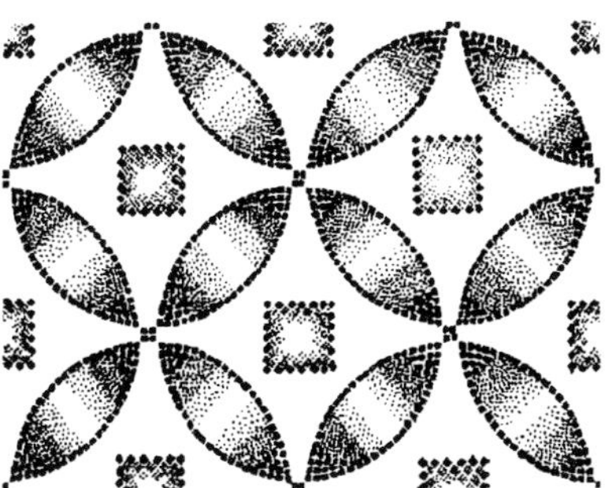

3-15a. *Roman mosaic, Khaldé, Lebanon: polychrome opus tessellatum with tonal gradations.*

3-15b. *Roman mosaic, Beirut, Lebanon: trichrome opus tessellatum with the effect of depth.*

3-15c. *Roman mosaic, Mandeure, France: bichrome opus tessellatum (black-white mosaic) with a flat visual effect.*

3-15d. *Cosmatesque mosaic, Rome: tetrachrome opus sectile (bichrome with chromatic splitting) with a flat visual effect.*

West persevered in the geometric *sectile* in a continuous and uninterrupted manner from the classical age through the late ancient and Byzantine periods, until the Macedonian age.

While the geometric *sectilia* which cover the rectangular interspaces of the Cosmatesque mosaics present a dimensional design and modules that are comparable to those of the Roman *sectile* of the sixth century, they show a more varied compositional repertoire and a tendency toward the fractionation of the basic unit of design. These last two characteristics are attributable to the influence of the Byzantine tradition and in particular to the influence of the eleventh-century pavement in the Abbey of Montecassino where the taste for minute design and division of motifs is evident, not only in the panels but also, and more markedly, in the curved or interlacing motifs.[34] This does not mean that the Cosmatesque repertoire is derived only from the Eastern tradition, since motifs that are analogous to those of Rome in the ancient age appear in the works of the Cosmati but do not appear in the Byzantine pavements.

Thus, the intervals from the first group owe the geometric patterns that cover them to the joint influence of the local tradition and the Byzantine tradition.

To determine the relative contributions of each tradition, it would be necessary first to have an inventory of the geometric motifs used by the Cosmati. With such an inventory in hand, one would then have to determine if and how often Cosmatesque motifs appear in each of those traditions. However, a complete and systematic inventory of Cosmatesque motifs has yet to be undertaken. Moreover, the few studies of Cosmatesque motifs in each

3-16. [Left] Isotropic pattern of lozenges: the steps from opus tessellatum (of three-dimensional effect) to opus sectile (of two-dimensional effect).

3-17. [Right] Isotropic pattern of poised squares: the steps from opus tessellatum (of three-dimensional effect) to opus sectile (of two-dimensional effect).

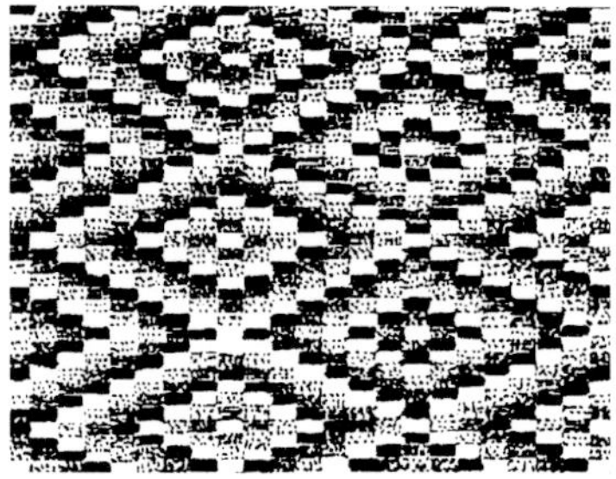

3-16a. Roman mosaic, Acholla, Tunisia: polychrome opus tessellatum with tonal gradations.

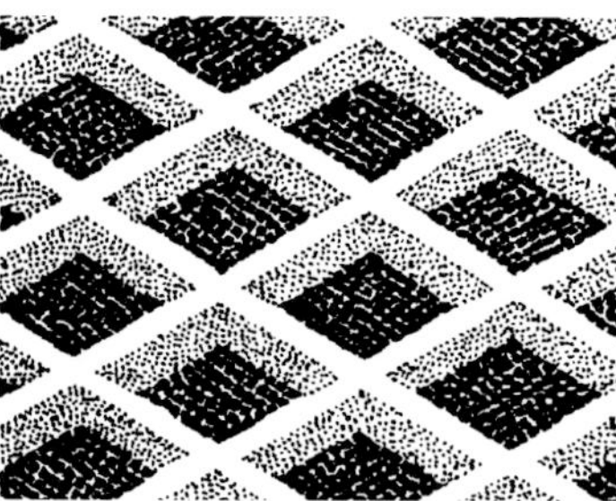

3-16b. Roman mosaic, Lucus Feroniae, Italy: trichrome opus tessellatum with the effect of perspective.

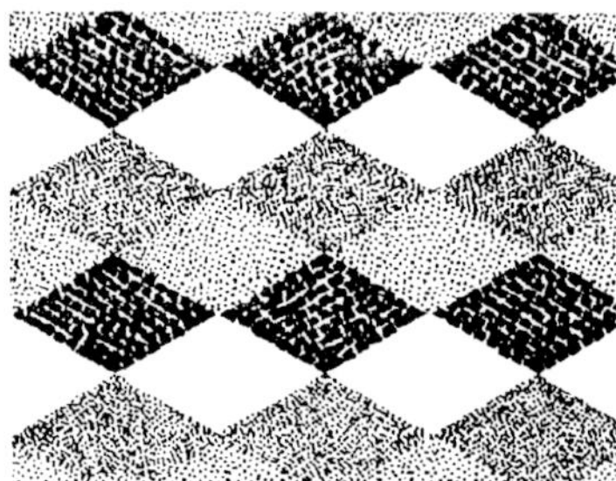

3-16c. Roman mosaic, Lyon, France: tetrachrome opus tessellatum with a flat visual effect.

3-16d. Roman mosaic, Biches, France: bichrome opus tessellatum with a flat visual effect.

3-16e. Cosmatesque mosaic, Rome: tetrachrome opus sectile (bichrome with chromatic splitting) with a flat visual effect.

3-17a. Roman mosaic, Canosa, Italy: polychrome opus tessellatum with tonal gradations.

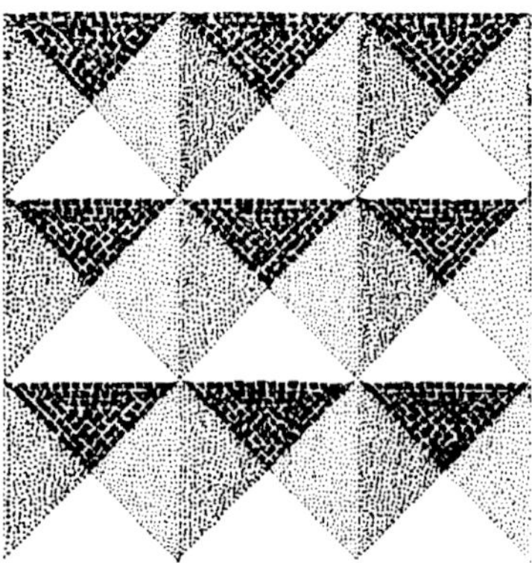

3-17b. Roman mosaic, Pergamum, Turkey: tetrachrome opus tessellatum with the effect of volume.

3-17c. Roman mosaic, Autun, France: bichrome opus tessellatum (black-white mosaic) with a flat visual effect.

3-17d. Cosmatesque mosaic, Rome: tetrachrome opus sectile (bichrome with chromatic splitting) with a flat visual effect.

3-18 [Right] and 3-19 [far right]. Isotropic patterns: the steps from opus tessellatum to opus sectile can be seen by comparing figures 3-18 (opus tessellatum) and 3-19 (opus sectile). Each lettered piece of 3-18 corresponds to the same-lettered piece in 3-19. (Drawings in 3-18 in black-and-white by R. Prudhomme)

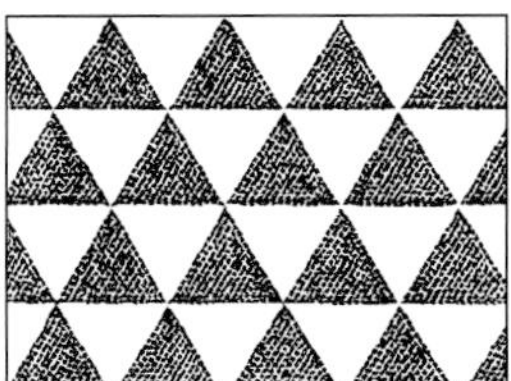

3-18a. Roman mosaic, Utique, Tunisia

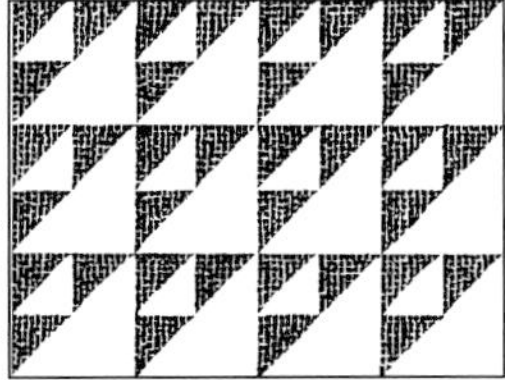

3-18b. Roman mosaic, Ouzouër-sur-Trézée, France

3-18c. Roman mosaic, Trieste, Italy

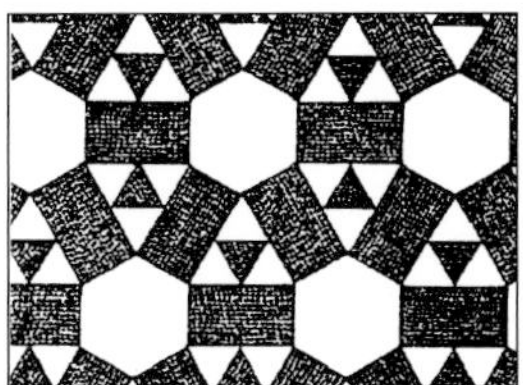

3-18d. Roman mosaic, Trieste, Italy

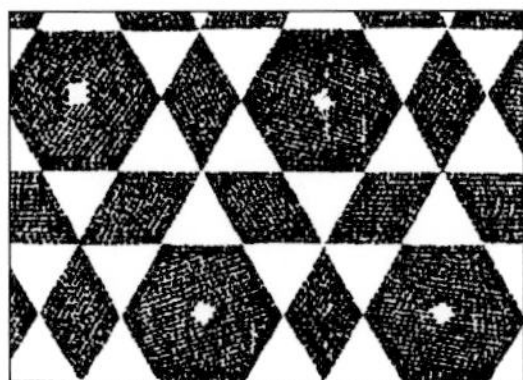

3-18e. Roman mosaic, Italica, Spain

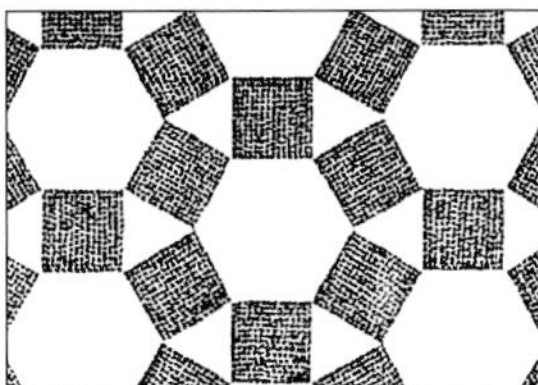

3-18f. Roman mosaic, Ostia, Italy

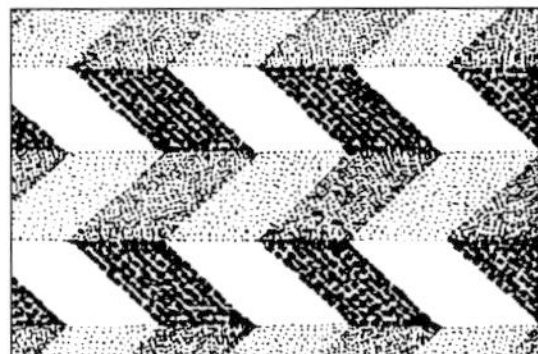

3-18g. Roman mosaic, Hammam Guergour, Algeria

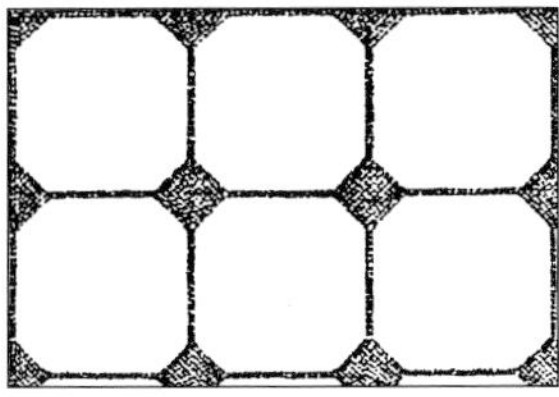

3-18h. Roman mosaic, Fréjus, France

3-19a. Cosmatesque mosaic, Rome

3-19b. Cosmatesque mosaic, Rome

3-19c. Cosmatesque mosaic, Rome

3-19d. Cosmatesque mosaic, Rome

3-19e. Cosmatesque mosaic, Rome

3-19f. Cosmatesque mosaic, Rome

3-19g. Cosmatesque mosaic, Rome

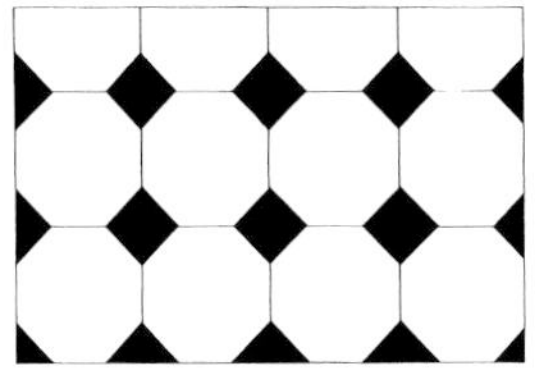

3-19h. Cosmatesque mosaic, Rome

3-20a. Roman mosaic, Besançon, France

3-20b. Roman mosaic, Zliten, Libya

3-20c. Roman mosaic, Rome

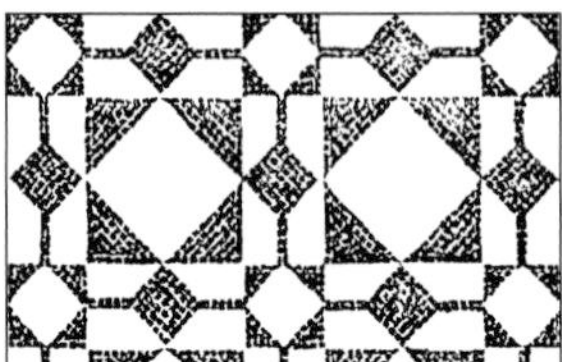
3-20d. Roman mosaic, Serravalle Scrivia, Italy

3-20e. Roman mosaic, Aix-en-Provence, France

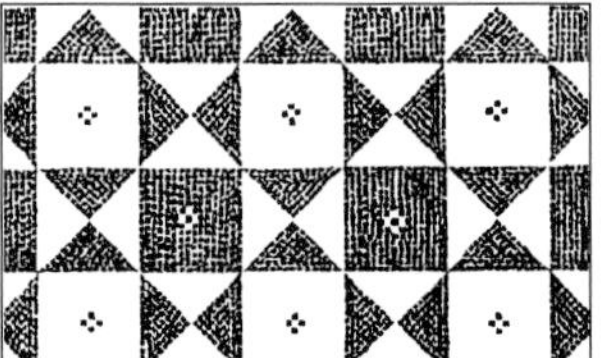
3-20f. Roman mosaic, Este, Italy

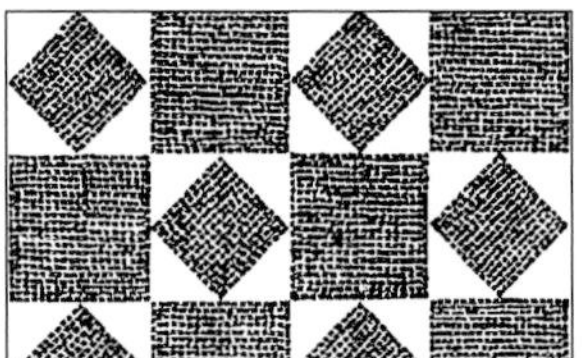
3-20g. Roman mosaic, Ampurias, Spain

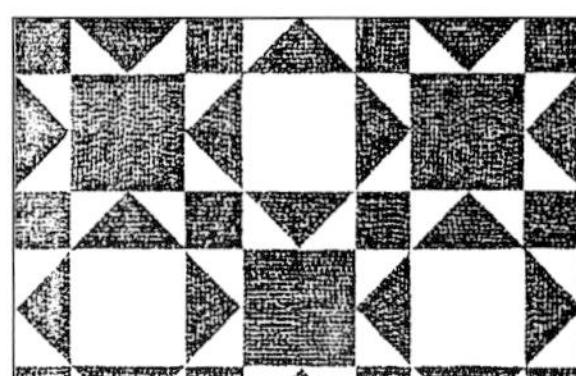
3-20h. Roman mosaic, Trieste, Italy

3-21a. Cosmatesque mosaic, Rome

3-21b. Cosmatesque mosaic, Rome

3-21c. Cosmatesque mosaic, Rome

3-21d. Cosmatesque mosaic, Rome

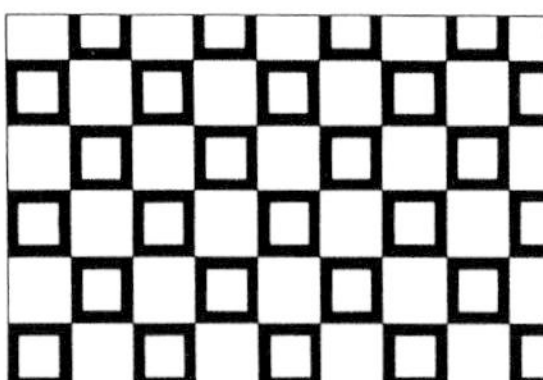
3-21e. Cosmatesque mosaic, Rome

3-21f. Cosmatesque mosaic, Rome

3-21g. Cosmatesque mosaic, Rome

3-21h. Cosmatesque mosaic, Rome

3-20 [Far left] and 3-21 [Left]. Isotropic patterns: the steps from opus tessellatum to opus sectile can be seen by comparing figures 3-20 (opus tessellatum) and 3-21 (opus sectile). Each lettered piece of 3-20 corresponds to the same-lettered piece in 3-21. (Drawings in 3-20 in black-and-white by R. Prudhomme)

3-22 [Right] and 3-23 [far right]. The steps from opus tessellatum to opus sectile. Each lettered piece of 3-22 (opus tessellatum) corresponds to the same-lettered piece in 3-23 (opus sectile).

3-22a. Roman mosaic, Pompeii, Italy

3-23a. Cosmatesque mosaic, Rome

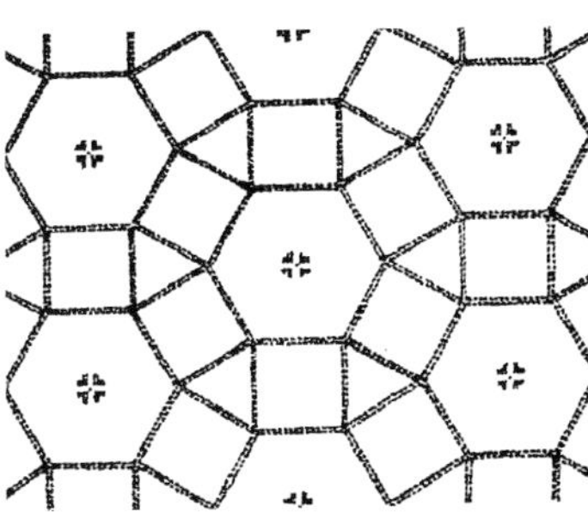

3-22b. Roman mosaic, Pompeii, Italy

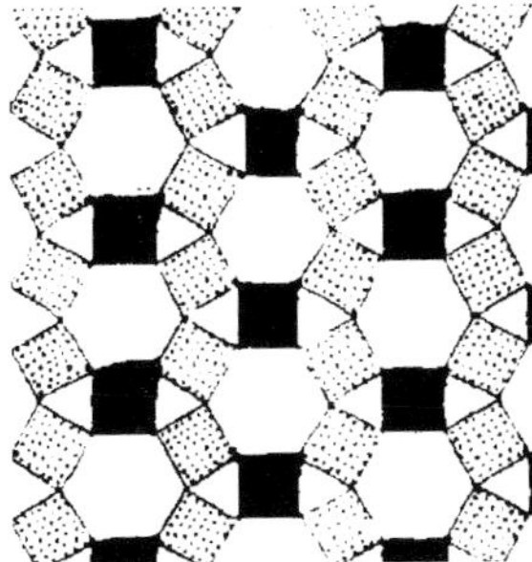

3-23b. Cosmatesque mosaic, Rome

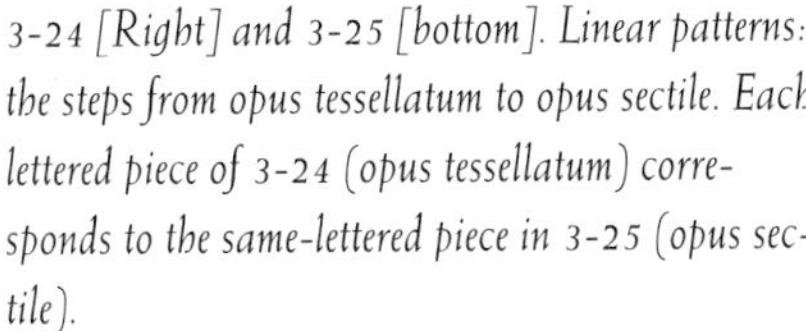

3-24 [Right] and 3-25 [bottom]. Linear patterns: the steps from opus tessellatum to opus sectile. Each lettered piece of 3-24 (opus tessellatum) corresponds to the same-lettered piece in 3-25 (opus sectile).

3-24a. Roman mosaic, Licenza, Italy

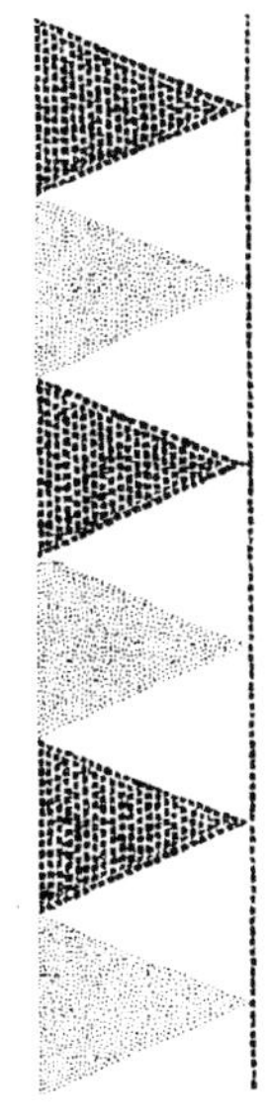

3-24b. Roman mosaic, Tittmoning, Germany

3-24c. Roman mosaic, Sainte-Colombe, France

3-24d. Roman mosaic, Lyon, France

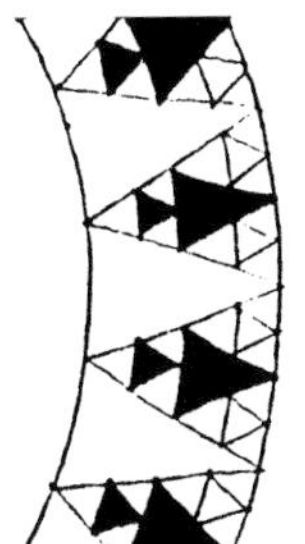

3-25a. Cosmatesque mosaic, Rome

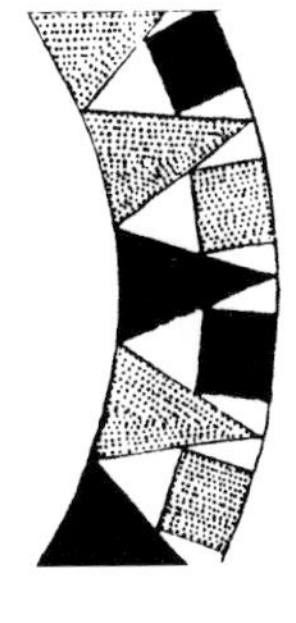

3-25b. Cosmatesque mosaic, Rome

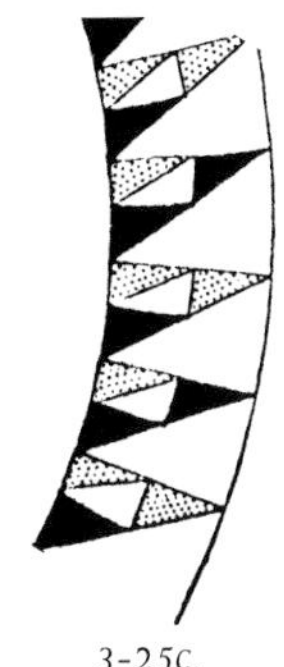

3-25c. Cosmatesque mosaic, Rome

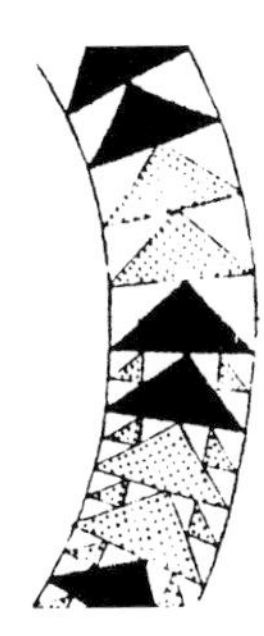

3-25d. Cosmatesque mosaic, Rome

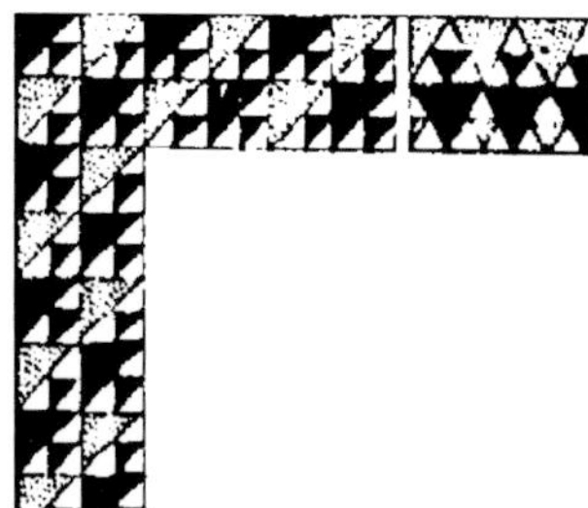

3-26*a*. *Cosmatesque mosaic, Rome*

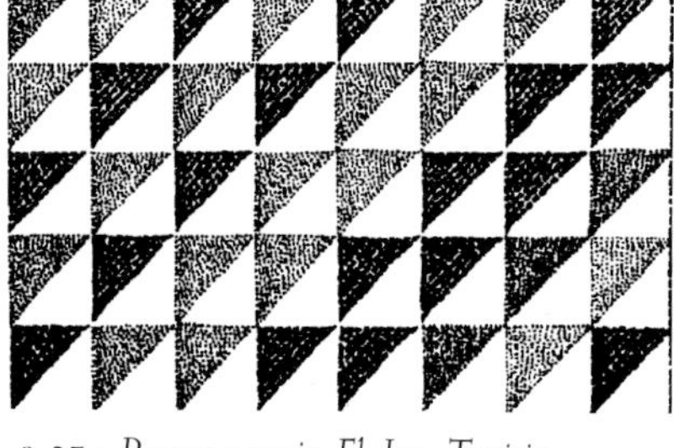

3-27*a*. *Roman mosaic, El-Jem, Tunisia*

3-26 and 3-27. The steps from opus tessellatum to opus sectile. Each lettered piece of 3-26 (opus sectile) corresponds to the same-lettered piece in 3-27 (opus tessellatum).

3-26*b*. *Cosmatesque mosaic, Rome*

3-27*b*. *Roman mosaic, Aquileia, Italy*

3-28 and 3-29. Linear patterns: the steps from opus tessellatum to opus sectile. Each lettered piece of 3-28 (opus tessellatum) corresponds to the same-lettered piece in 3-29 (opus sectile).

3-28*a*. *Roman mosaic, Salzburg, Austria*

3-28*b*. *Roman mosaic, Parma, Italy*

3-28c. *Roman mosaic, Anse, France*

3-28*d*. *Roman mosaic, Antioquia, Turkey*

3-29*a*. *Cosmatesque mosaic, Rome*

3-29*b*. *Cosmatesque mosaic, Rome*

3-29c. *Cosmatesque mosaic, Rome*

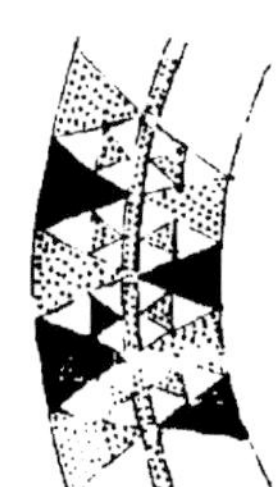

3-29*d*. *Cosmatesque mosaic, Rome*

3-30 and 3-31. Linear patterns: the steps from opus tessellatum to opus sectile. Each lettered piece of 3-30 (opus tessellatum) corresponds to the same-lettered piece in 3-31 (opus sectile).

3-30*a*. *Roman mosaic, Apamea, Syria*

3-30*b*. *Roman mosaic, Pompeii, Italy*

3-30*c*. *Roman mosaic, Acholla, Tunisia*

3-30*d*. *Roman mosaic, Montmorot, France*

3-31*a*. *Cosmatesque mosaic, Rome*

3-31*b*. *Cosmatesque mosaic, Rome*

3-31*c*. *Cosmatesque mosaic, Rome*

3-31*d*. *Cosmatesque mosaic, Rome*

tradition are not conclusive, because some study only partial aspects, while others are based upon assumptions that are too general.[35]

To consider the antecedents of the mosaics that fill the intervals of the second group, one must recall that these intervals—the interspaces adjacent to and contained within the interlacing motifs—are of much smaller extent than the intervals of the first group, and they usually have one or more curved sides. Consequently, the tesserae that cover them are of much smaller dimensions than the tesserae that fill the rectangular intervals of the first group. The smaller size of the tesserae is due not only to style considerations but to construction restraints as well.[36]

The *sectile* of the intervals of the second group contain motifs similar to the larger ones in the intervals of the first group and are characterized by division and subdivision of the basic motifs, on a scale notably inferior to that of the mosaics of the ancient age. In the geometric *sectile* associated with the interlacings in the pavement of the Abbey of Montecassino, these characteristics are very marked, implying that, in this respect, the Desiderian pavement is the direct antecedent of the Cosmatesque mosaics.

3-32*a*. *Roman mosaic, Reims, France*

3-32*b*. *Roman mosaic, Langres, France*

3-32*c*. *Roman mosaic, Tivoli, Italy*

3-32*d*. *Roman mosaic, Cologne, Germany*

3-33*a*. *Cosmatesque mosaic, Rome*

3-33*b*. *Cosmatesque mosaic, Rome*

3-33*c*. *Cosmatesque mosaic, Rome*

3-33*d*. *Cosmatesque mosaic, Rome*

3-32 *and* 3-33. *Linear patterns: the steps from opus tessellatum to opus sectile. Each lettered piece of* 3-32 *(opus tessellatum) corresponds to the same-lettered piece in* 3-33 *(opus sectile).*

Because the polychrome geometric patterns in *sectile* flanking the white bands of the interlacings (both the surface patterns adjacent to the outer bands and the linear patterns contained within the concentric bands) form a whole with those interlacings, they can be attributed to the same cultural antecedents as those interlacings. Therefore, they share the characteristics and origins of the interlacings in *sectile* that, from the sixth to the eleventh centuries, are continually present in the Byzantine ornamental repertoire, as discussed earlier in this chapter.

The smaller size of the tesserae and the division of the basic motifs in the Cosmatesque geometric *sectile*—as much in the rectangular panels as in the interlacing designs, although more markedly in the latter—when compared with the *sectile* of the ancient mosaic, can be explained not only in terms of the cultural conditioning factors described above, but also, and I should say primarily, in terms of the material limitations facing the artists. Quarried marble was scarce when the Cosmatesque artists worked, and the great majority of the spoliated pieces available were small in size.

Given the lack of materials and the difficulty in obtaining them, efficient use of the available materials was a principal objective for the Roman marble workers. The fragmentary nature of the marbles available to the Cosmati required the subdivision of the patterns to achieve optimal efficiency.

In the general regulating schemata of their geometric *sectile*, the Cosmatesque artists used large dimensional modules, a legacy from the mosaics of the ancient age. This compositional tradition clashed with the reality of the available materials. The Cosmati resolved this conflict by using techniques of fragmentation (regulated by fractal laws; see chapter 4), which dictate that a figure is subdivided by inscribing in it its inverse. These techniques allowed the Cosmati to carry the subdivision of a geometric pattern to infinity without distorting the original regulating geometry. This system enabled the Roman marble cutters to make the most of the material available without abandoning the dimensional modules that formed part of their ornamental tradition. Thanks to the extreme fractionating of the pattern, they were able to use not only the marble spolia that they collected from the ruins of Rome but also the marble remnants that they themselves generated during the elaboration of a pavement, recycling *all* the material at hand and taking advantage of even the smallest leftovers.

Chromatic Taste

The use of color is one of the most obvious characteristics of the Cosmatesque pavements. The balanced distribution of red and green porphyries next to ancient yellow and other light-colored marbles allowed the Cosmati to integrate the iconographic components of diverse origins that establish the basic design, achieving a homogeneous and unmistakable result.

There is no doubt about the local roots of the chromatic taste associated with the four dominant colors in the works of the Cosmati: red, green, yellow, and white. In Rome this tetrachrome tendency had dominated the decoration in *sectile* since ancient times. The continuity of this chromatic choice is evident in numerous examples: the Neronian *sectile* in the Palatino,[37] the parietal *sectile* in the building at the exterior of the Porta Marina in Ostia (fig. 3-34),[38] the examples of *sectile* of square module with complex motifs from late antiquity (for example, that of the cemetery of Santi Pietro e Marcellino), the pavements in panels from the sixth and seventh centuries (as much in *opus sectile* as in *sectile tessellatum*), the pavements from the eighth and ninth centuries with motifs in chessboard pattern,[39] particularly the pavement of the Chapel of San Zenone in Santa Prassede.[40]

The preference for the frequent, regular use of porphyries was shared by the Byzantine artists, but their compositions show a more muted chromatic tone with less incisive contrasts than those of the Roman masters. The choice of marbles in the mid-Byzantine pavements is less rigid than in Rome, where the traditional chromatic coupling is inviolable, respected to the point of becoming one of the most fundamental components of the Cosmatesque pavements.

3-34. Wall mosaics in opus sectile from the late fourth-century villa at Ostia fuori Porta Marina.

3-34a. [Left] Opus mixtum from the left wall of the exedra.

3-34b. [Above, left] Detail of the chessboard pattern of the exedra.

3-34c. [Above, right] Detail of a false window in the left wall of the exedra.

3-34d. [Left] Detail of the opus mixtum of the exedra.

In summary, the Cosmatesque stylistic matrix stems from both Byzantine experience and local tradition. From the Byzantine tradition came the interlacing designs and the fractionalized geometry of the regulating schemata. The latter characteristic is present in both the large rectangular intervals and in the small intervals (those intervals adjoining and contained within the interlacings), although more markedly in the small intervals. The local tradition contributed the organization of large surfaces in panels, defined by a reticle drawn with bands of marble. Also of local origin is the chromatic choice, which successfully integrates the diverse elements of the composition. The joint Byzantine and Roman influence becomes evident in the varied repertoire of basic geometric motifs and in the technique of execution.

The pavement of the Church of the Abbey of Montecassino attests to the convergence of the two traditions. It should not be considered an isolated case of such a convergence, but rather an early example of what would become a more common merging of the two traditions during the final decades of the eleventh century in the area between Latium and Campania.

Chapter 4

THE REGULATING GEOMETRY

THE BASIC REPERTOIRE OF CONSTANT GEOMETRIC MOTIFS

A series of continually reiterated fundamental geometric motifs appears throughout the works of the Cosmatesque artists. This chapter identifies and defines these fixed motifs, elaborating on the basic repertoire of geometric designs that characterizes the most classic work of the Cosmati, that is, the work executed from early in the twelfth century to the first third of the thirteenth century.

Glossary

A systematized language allows for mutual understanding, a basic requirement when embarking upon any descriptive effort. Tackling the description of the geometry that regulates the Cosmatesque pavements requires vocabulary appropriate for the task. I have adopted as a model the semantics and syntax employed in a widely accepted, exhaustive description of ancient Roman mosaic compositions, *Le décor géométrique de la mosaïque romaine: Répertoire graphique et descriptif des compositions linéaires et isotropes* (The geometric decoration of Roman mosaic: Graphic and descriptive repertoire of linear and isotropic patterns).[1]

What follows is a selection of definitions of the most useful terms and expressions for describing the geometric forms employed by the Cosmatesque artists.

adjacent: Two figures exterior to one another, contiguous on one side (≠ spaced, staggered, tangent).

adjoined: Two opposed linear figures or patterns, normally not discordant, which present to one another the part accepted as the "back" (= opposed back to back; ≠ confronted). *See also* opposed.

angle (in): A figure located within another figure, at one of the enclosing figure's angles (= in recessed corner, in reentrant angle; ≠ in corner, in projecting corner, in salient angle).

bearing: A figure that contains another or others (= containing, laden with).

betraying: This term is used to link two expressions that describe the same pattern in two different ways; the second expression provides specifics about or complements the first.

biaxial geometric pattern: *See* orthogonal pattern.

bounded by: *See* linked by.

chessboard pattern: A pattern of adjacent squares in counterchanged colors.

chessboard pattern of X: A surface pattern composed of identical elements that are adjacent, oriented in one or two directions only, and arranged in counterchanged colors.

chevron: A motif consisting of two equal segments of fillets or bands forming a right angle or an acute angle.

compartment: (1) In a chessboard pattern, one of the component squares. (2) The square interspaces created by the lineal structures that constitute a grid. *See also* chessboard pattern, grid.

concordant: Lines of the same nature whose rhythms are the same (≠ discordant).

confronted: Two opposed linear figures or patterns, normally not discordant, which present to one another the part accepted as the "front" (≠ adjoined, opposed back to back). *See also* opposed.

connected by: *See* linked by.

containing: *See* bearing.

contiguous: Two figures that have at least one point of contact and do not cut each other.

corner (in): A figure located at one of the angles of another figure, on the exterior (= in projecting corner, in salient angle; ≠ in angle).

counterchanged colors (in): Patterns in which the outline of the figures is made evident by the meeting of surfaces of two different colors. *See also* three counterchanged colors (in).

dart: An oriented figure with a tip formed by two straight segments in an acute angle and a base that is a semicircle or semihexagon, the latter with a side perpendicular to the longitudinal axis of the figure (fig. 4-1).

decussate: *See* saltire (in).

discordant: Rows of the same nature whose rhythms are out of phase.

dog's-tooth pattern: A row of isosceles triangles that are juxtaposed, tangent, and that rest on their bases, with the two equal sides of each triangle greater than the base and shorter than three times the base (fig. 4-1). This pattern is usually reversible (≠ points, sawtooth pattern).

écoincon (in): Position of a figure situated in a triangular residual interspace of one or two concave sides (= in spandrel).

effect of: The expression "creating an effect of" is used when a particular design suggests to the eye a particular figure without actually forming the figure in question.

enclosed: A figure contained in another without touching it or touching only at one point or along one side.

4-1. Curvilinear band of a row of darts (interior) and a dog's-tooth pattern (exterior). The row of darts forms equilateral triangles, creating a saw-tooth patten. Detail of the paving, San Crisogono, Rome.

ensconced in the angles between: Indicates that other figures are located at the angles of the figure under discussion, on its exterior (≠ on angle, in *écoincon,* flanked by).

eyelet: *See* eyelet hole.

eyelet hole: The residual opening between the strands of a guilloche (= eyelet).

flanked by: Indicates that other figures are located to the sides of the figure in question, on the exterior.

forming: A geometric design is frequently described as a foreground pattern set against residual background figures. In this sense, the foreground pattern is defining or *forming* the background figures (for example, a grid pattern of tangent circles forming poised squares with concave sides).

four-pointed star: A star of eight sides and four reentrant angles. When it is bearing an inscribed square, the square usually is inscribed by the vertices; otherwise *inscribed by the sides* is specified. *See also* star.

grid: A surface pattern, usually orthogonal, composed of fillets, bands, or linear patterns; in the last case, more than one element should occur between two consecutive intersections of the grid. A grid normally

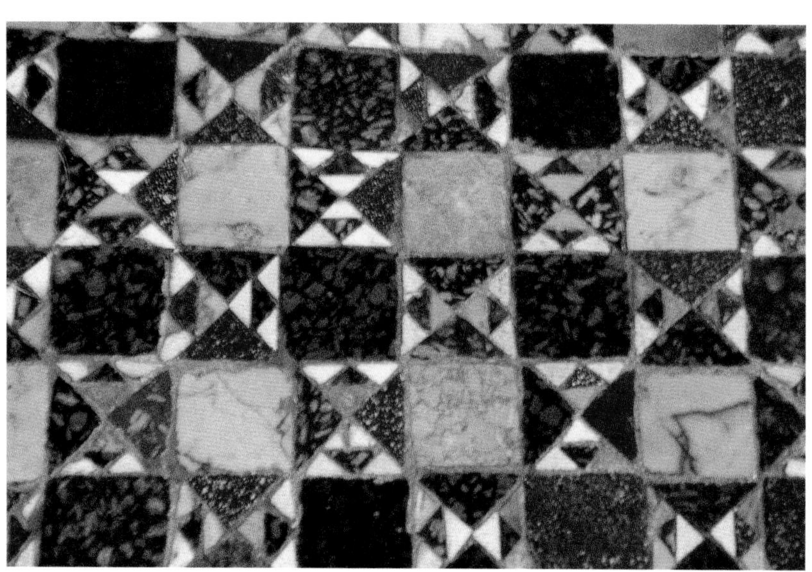

4-2. Oblique grid pattern. Detail of the paving, San Crisogono, Rome.

forms square compartments; when this is not the case, the shape of the compartments/intervals is specified: rectangles, lozenges, parallelograms. The term *oblique grid* indicates that, in a single pattern composed of two grids, one grid has its axes turned 45 degrees in relation to the axes of the other grid (fig. 4-2). *See also* grid pattern.

grid of bands: A grid of square-shaped intersections that are visible because of outline or counterchanged colors; the width of the bands should be inferior or equal to the side of the interval. The grid of bands, usually simple, can be called *grid of bands with a square at the intersections* when the square appears formed by the crossing of bands, and *grid of bands with an exceeding square or motif at the intersections* when the motif extends beyond the crossing.

grid pattern: A surface pattern composed of elements arranged along the axes of an orthogonal grid, such that there is only one element between two consecutive intersections of the grid. *See also* grid.

guilloche (two-strand, three-strand, multistrand): A linear pattern formed by two, three, or more sinusoidal threads, normally arranged in interlacing. When the strands interloop, creating circular interspaces, the figure is a *guilloche of eyelets*.

herringbone: A linear pattern of superposed, adjacent chevrons in which the arms of a single chevron are of different colors and the arms of the next chevron are of those colors in reverse. *See also* chevron.

hexagon: Normally regular, a six-sided parallelogram in which all the sides and angles are equal. For irregular hexagons, *see* oblong hexagon, scutum, short hexagon.

honeycomb: A triaxial pattern of adjacent regular hexagons. By extension, the expression *oblong honeycomb* is used for a pattern of two nonperpendicular axes of adjacent oblong hexagons. *See also* honeycomb pattern.

honeycomb pattern: A surface triaxial pattern of elements, organized in groups of six or multiples of six, according to the design of a honeycomb, forming at its center a regular hexagon. *See also* triaxial pattern.

horizontal: In a linear pattern, an oblong element whose longest axis is parallel to the axis of the pattern (= recumbent; ≠ standing, vertical).

hourglass: A motif formed by two equal isosceles triangles (of coaxial heights) opposed at their apexes (fig. 4-3).

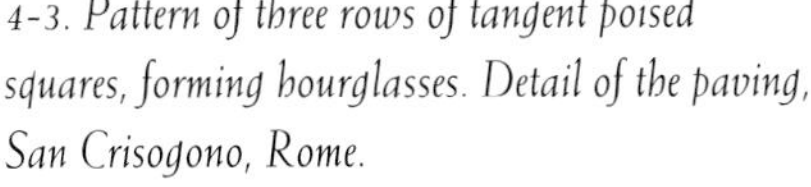

4-3. Pattern of three rows of tangent poised squares, forming hourglasses. Detail of the paving, San Crisogono, Rome.

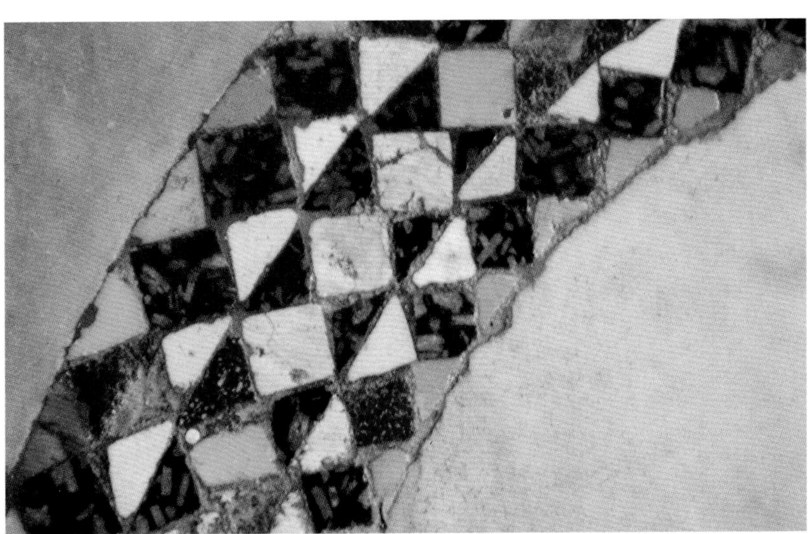

imbricated: Two figures in which the salient parts of one are fit into the reentrant parts of the other.

inscribed: A figure contained within another, touching it at two or more isolated points.

interlacing (in): Two figures or two linear structures formed by bands or fillets that alternately cross over and under, forming a hole or interval (= interlooped). *See also* eyelet hole.

interlooped: *See* interlacing (in).

intersecting: Two figures whose outlines cut each other (= secant).

intersections (at the): In a grid of bands, an element situated at the crossing of the bands.

interspace (in): The position of a figure situated in a residual space (= in interval).

interval (in): *See* interspace (in).

inverted: A figure inscribed or enclosed in a figure of the same nature, such that the vertices of one correspond to the midpoints of the sides of the other.

irregular octagon: An octagon, inscribable in a square, with sides of two different lengths. *See also* octagon.

isotropic, isotropous: A pattern that covers a plane or space in a homogeneous or uniform way without discontinuities.

juxtaposed: Elements arranged in a row and oriented such that the main axis of each of the elements is perpendicular or oblique to the axis of the row.

laden with: *See* bearing, containing.

lattice pattern: An isotropic surface pattern of elements whose arrangement is repeated according to two nonorthogonal intersecting axes (= oblique biaxial geometric pattern).

linked by: Two figures united by another joining element, such as a fillet, ring, or arc (= bounded by, connected by, tied by).

loop: In an interlacing figure, a coil comprising an eyelet hole together with the band or strands that border it. *See also* eyelet hole, interlacing (in).

oblique: In a linear pattern, an oblong element whose longest axis is neither parallel nor perpendicular to the axis of the pattern. In a surface pattern based on a grid, a second grid whose axes form an angle of 45 degrees with the axes of the first grid.

oblique biaxial geometric pattern: *See* lattice pattern.

oblong: A figure that is longer than it is wide.

oblong hexagon: An irregular hexagon in which the two sides that are parallel to the longitudinal axis are greater than or equal to the four remaining sides (≠ scutum, short hexagon). *See also* hexagon.

oblong octagon: An octagon, inscribable in a rectangle, with sides and/or angles of two different dimensions. *See also* octagon.

octagon: An eight-sided parallelogram that is usually regular (all its sides and angles are equal). *See also* irregular octagon, oblong octagon, stellate octagon.

opposed: Two oriented figures of the same nature, arranged symmetrically in relation to each other; also, two linear structures of the same nature, dissymmetric in relation to their longitudinal axis but symmetrically arranged in relation to one another. *See also* adjoined, confronted, opposed back to back.

opposed back to back: *See* adjoined.

orthogonal: *See* orthogonal pattern.

orthogonal biaxial geometric pattern: *See* orthogonal pattern.

orthogonal pattern: An isotropic surface pattern of elements whose arrangement is repeated according to orthogonal intersecting axes (= biaxial geometric pattern, orthogonal biaxial geometric pattern).

overlapping: Two figures in which a portion of one hides a portion of the other (= superimposing).

pattern of rows of X: An isotropic surface pattern that can be interpreted only as the repetition along parallel axes of linear patterns that are contiguous and superposed. If not contiguous and superposed, the pattern is specified as *spaced* or *discordant* (for example, a pattern of spaced rows of *X*). When the linear pattern has a name (such as waves or sinusoids), the pattern of rows is also specified as such (for example, a pattern of waves, a pattern of sinusoids).

pattern of X and Y: A surface pattern in which two elements alternate.

perspective (in): A system of representation that gives the illusion that the figures are seen in space.

points: A row of triangles, usually isosceles, that are juxtaposed, tangent, and that rest on their bases, with the two equal sides of each triangle equal to or greater than three times the base. When the triangles are right triangles, the vertical side of each triangle must be equal to or greater than three times the short side that serves as the base (≠ dog's-tooth pattern, sawtooth pattern).

poised: In a linear structure, a polygon of more than three sides in which one of the diagonals is perpendicular to the axis of the composition (≠ straight).

projecting corner (in): *See* corner (in).

rack: A row of tangent right triangles each resting on one side of the right angle, when the vertical side is less than three times the length of the short side that serves as the base.

recessed corner (in): *See* angle (in).

recumbent: *See* horizontal.

recumbent and standing: In a surface pattern, oblong elements whose primary axis alternates in two perpendicular directions.

reentrant angle (in): *See* angle (in), recessed corner (in) (≠ in projecting corner, in salient corner).

relief (effect of): Treatment of a figure, intended to suggest its volume by means of a gradation of colors or tones (≠ in perspective). *See also* shaded.

reversible: A pattern that creates a residual pattern identical to itself.

rhomboidal, rhomboidal pattern: *See* lattice pattern.

row of X: A linear pattern formed by elements arranged along a single axis (see fig. 4-3). *See also* pattern of rows of *X*.

row of X and Y: A linear pattern in which two elements alternate (fig. 4-4).

rows (of 2, 3, 4, n): The number of adjacent rows in which a chessboard band is organized (fig. 4-5).

salient angle (in): *See* corner (in).

saltire (in): A cruciform figure whose axes are oblique to those of the figure or pattern in which it is integrated (= decussate, in X-shaped cross; ≠ straight).

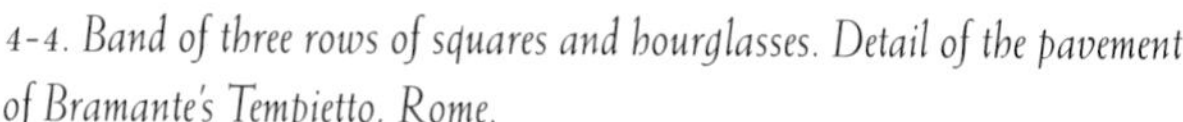

4-4. Band of three rows of squares and hourglasses. Detail of the pavement of Bramante's Tempietto, Rome.

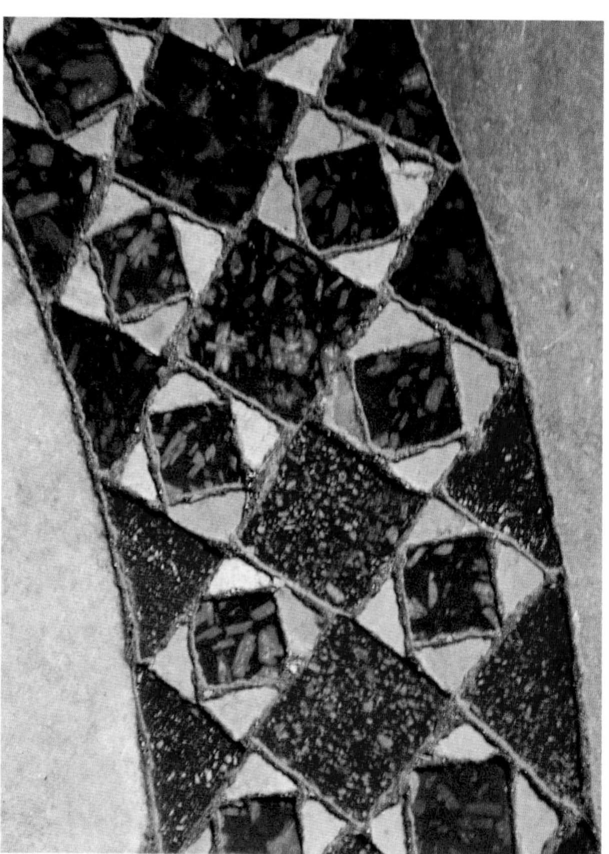

4-5. Chessboard band of two rows of poised squares. Detail of the pavement of Bramante's Tempietto, Rome.

sawtooth pattern: A row of equilateral triangles or of isosceles triangles that are juxtaposed, tangent, and rest on their bases, with the equal sides of each triangle shorter than the base (see fig. 4-1). This pattern is usually reversible (≠ dog's-tooth pattern, points).

scutum: An irregular hexagon in which the two sides that are perpendicular to the longitudinal axis are shorter than the four remaining sides (≠ oblong hexagon, short hexagon). *See also* hexagon.

secant: *See* intersecting.

shaded: A figure with a gradation of tones that creates an effect of relief. *See also* relief.

short hexagon: An irregular hexagon in which the two sides that run parallel to the longitudinal axis are shorter than the remaining four (≠ oblong hexagon, scutum). *See also* hexagon.

short isosceles triangle: An isosceles triangle in which the median that passes through the apex containing the two equal sides of the triangle is shorter than the side perpendicular to that median.

spaced: Figures that have no point of contact.

spandrel (in): *See* écoincon (in).

spindle: A closed figure composed of two symmetrical arcs of circle, each less than a semicircle.

standing: *See* vertical.

star: A polygon with a radiating arrangement that includes at least three reentrant angles (fig. 4-6). *See also* four-pointed star, star of two squares, star of two triangles.

4-6. Triaxial linear pattern with stars of six lozenges. Detail of the pavment, San Crisogono, Rome.

star of two squares: A star of eight points, obtained by the superposition of two equal squares, such that the axis of one is turned 45 degrees in relation to the axis of the other; otherwise it is called *irregular.*

star of two triangles: A star of six points, obtained by the superposition of two equal triangles, such that the axis of one is turned 180 degrees in relation to the axis of the other.

stellate octagon: A figure consisting of a central octagon flanked by eight adjacent squares or rectangles, each with a side equal to the side of the octagon, and ensconced in the angles between eight lozenges, each tangent to the octagon and adjacent to the said squares or rectangles. *See also* octagon.

straight: A polygon of more than three sides in which one median is perpendicular to the axis of the composition (≠ poised). Also, a cruciform element whose axes are parallel and perpendicular to those of the figure or pattern in which it is contained (≠ in saltire).

stuffed: A figure enclosed by another of the same nature, when said figures are concentric and when their outlines are parallel; in other words, a form contained in another that is homothetic and of the same orientation.

superimposing: *See* overlapping.

superposed: Elements arranged in a row and oriented such that the main axis of each of the elements coincides with the axis of the row.

tangent: Two figures exterior to one another that touch at one or more isolated points (≠ adjacent).

thorns: A row of tangent superposed triangular shapes each having two equal concave sides. When the triangular shapes are isosceles triangles the thorns are called *rectilinear thorns.* Without further specification, the thorns are long (with the equal sides of each triangular shape equal to or greater than the base); otherwise the thorns are called short.

three counterchanged colors (in): Patterns in which the outline of the figures is made evident by the meeting of surfaces of three different colors.

tied by: *See* linked by.

triaxial geometric pattern: *See* triaxial pattern (fig. 4-7).

triaxial pattern: An isotropic surface pattern of elements whose arrangement is repeated according to three axes intersecting at 120 degrees (= triaxial geometric pattern).

4-7. Triaxial linear pattern from the door frame of San Saba, Rome.

upright: *See* straight.
vertical: In a linear pattern, an oblong element whose longest axis is perpendicular to the axis of the pattern (= standing, upright; ≠ horizontal).
X-shaped cross (in): *See* saltire (in).

The Fundamental Components of a Cosmatesque Pavement

The fundamental components of a typical Cosmatesque pavement are the *framework* and the *interstitial fabric*. A detailed analysis of these components has led me to establish the categories noted in figure 4-8.

The Framework
- **The Gross Framework**
- **The Light Framework**
  - Pointed Interlacing Designs
    - *The Quincunx and the Quincunx-in-square*
    - *The Decussate Quincunx and Its Derivatives*
  - Linear Interlacing Designs
    - *The Guilloche and the Guilloche-in-rectangle*
    - *The Mixed Guilloche*
    - *The Series of Tangent Quincunxes*
    - *The Series of Linked Quincunxes*
    - *The Series of Linked Figures*
  - Surface Interlacing Designs
    - *The Pattern of Linked Roundels*
    - *The Grid of Guilloches*

The Interstitial Fabric
- **The Elements of Composition and the Regulating Design**
- **The Geometric Patterns**
  - The Roundels
  - The Centered Geometric Patterns
  - The Linear Geometric Patterns
  - The Surface Geometric Patterns
  - The Cosmatesque Process of Fragmentation Expressed in the Language of Fractals: The Case of the Sierpinski Triangle

4-8. *The fundamental components of a Cosmatesque pavement.*

The Framework

The framework is a skeleton, comprising bands of white marble, which supports the ornamental fabric that covers the floor of the church. This skeleton consists of a *gross framework* of straight geometry, which houses a thinner framework of curved and mixed geometry, the *light framework*. The gross framework is an *orthogonal reticle*, while the light framework consists of interlacing designs (such as the quincunx, the guilloche, and variations and combinations thereof).

The Gross Framework

This structure of straight geometry is an orthogonal grid forming square and rectangular intervals, drawn with bands of white marble in lines

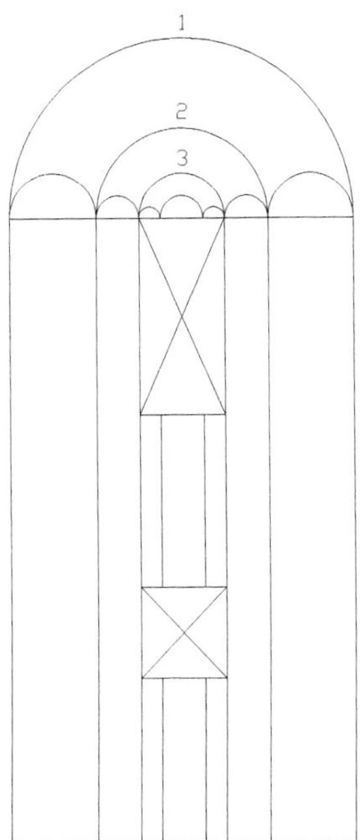

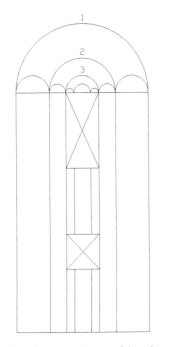

4-9. The triple tripartite division of the orthogonal grid. The first division into three rectangles is indicated by the number 1 above; the second division, of the resulting middle rectangle, is indicated by the number 2; the third division, by the number 3.

parallel and perpendicular to the longitudinal axis of the church (the principal axis).

The orthogonal grid results from a centripetal compartmentalization parallel to the principal axis and is created by means of three successive operations of tripartite division such that each tripartite division divides the central area resulting from the previous tripartite division. The remaining intervals, those that are not central, are divided into a whole number of rectangles through two successive operations of division, perpendicular among themselves, the first parallel to the principal axis and the second perpendicular to that axis (fig. 4-9).

The first of the three operations of tripartite division concurs with the architectural partitioning of the Christian basilica, in the placement of three rectangles in the floor plan of the building, the central rectangle (the nave) being wider than the other two (the aisles).

The second operation of division splits the central rectangle resulting from the previous division (the nave) into three rectangles parallel to the longitudinal axis of the church. The central rectangle resulting from this second operation of division is divided by lines perpendicular to the principal axis, thus creating, in its center, a square and, in its eastern extreme, a rectangle. In both are inscribed designs of curved geometry, that is, interlacings. The square, which occupies the center of the nave, bears a quincunx; the rectangle, upon which rests the schola cantorum, generally is ornamented with guilloches or a series of quincunxes.

The third operation of division separates the remainder of the central rectangle resulting from the preceding division into three rectangles parallel to the principal axis. In the central interval resulting from this third and final tripartite division are inscribed interlacing designs, generally guilloches, which contribute to the "carpet" that, superposed on the principal axis, connects the entrance of the church with the altar.

All of the residual lateral rectangles created by the successive tripartite divisions are compartmentalized, by means of bands parallel to the longitudinal axis of the church, into very long rectangles which, in turn, are divided, by means of bands perpendicular to the same axis, into a whole number of rectangles of nearly equal size. These final rectangles are filled with ornamental geometric patterns.

The Light Framework

The light framework is a substructure consisting of interlacing designs of curved and mixed (curved and straight) geometry, which, drawn with bands of white marble narrower than the bands that mark the orthogonal grid, are inscribed in the central intervals; that is, those superimposed on the principal axis and created by the gross framework. The light framework takes the form of *pointed, linear,* and *surface* interlacing designs.

POINTED INTERLACING DESIGNS

There are various types of pointed interlacing designs. The most notable are the *quincunx* and the *quincunx-in-square* and the *decussate quincunx* and its derivatives.

The Quincunx and the Quincunx-in-square The quincunx, shown in figure 4-10, is the king of ornaments in Cosmatesque designs; in fact, all of chapter 5 is dedicated to a detailed description of it, as well its underlying geometry, origins, and signification.

The quincunx-in-square is a square bearing an inscribed quincunx. Among the forms that the quincunx can take, the quincunx-in-square best characterizes Cosmatesque pavements. Chapter 5 also examines the quincunx-in-square. Examples of it in Rome include Santa Maria Maggiore (fig. 4-11), Santi Quattro Coronati (fig. 4-12), Santa Maria in Cosmedin (fig. 4-13), San Saba (fig. 4-14), and Santa Croce in Gerusalemme (fig. 4-15); and in Ferentino, Sant'Ambrogio (fig. 4-16).

4-10. *[Far left] Diagram of a quincunx.*

4-11. *[Left] Detail of the pavement from the Basilica Liberiana, Santa Maria Maggiore, Rome. (G. B. De Rossi)*

4-12. *Quincunx-in-square. Detail of the pavement, Santi Quattro Coronati, Rome.*

4-13. Quincunx-in-square. Detail of the pavement, Santa Maria in Cosmedin, Rome.

4-14. Quincunx-in-square. Detail of the pavement, San Saba, Rome.

4-15. Quincunx-in-square. Detail of the pavement, Santa Croce in Gerusalemme, Rome.

4-16. Quincunx-in-square. Detail of the pavement, Sant'Ambrogio, Ferentino.

4-17. [Far left] Example of a "Dumbo" quincunx, San Saba, Rome.

4-18. [Left] Example of a quincunx "of large center," Santa Maria in Cosmedin, Rome.

In taking the measurements of different pavements and comparing them, it is evident that the relationship between the diameter of the central roundel and the diameters of the roundels in angle of the same quincunx differs depending on the pavement. Thus, there are "Dumbo" or "big-eared" quincunxes, in which the size of the peripheral roundels is close to the size of the central roundel, as in the pavement in San Saba (fig. 4-17), and there are quincunxes "of large center" in which the central roundel is much larger than those in the corners, as in the pavement at Santa Maria in Cosmedin (fig. 4-18).

Since *C* is the diameter of the central roundel (eyelet) of the quincunx, and *A* is the width of the imaginary square circumscribed around the quincunx,

4-19. *[Above] Diagram of a quincunx of poised-square center.*

4-20. *[Above, right] Row of three quincunxes-in-square. The central quincunx, of circular center, is flanked by two quincunxes of poised-square center. Detail of the mosaics from the sanctuary of Westminster Abbey, London.*

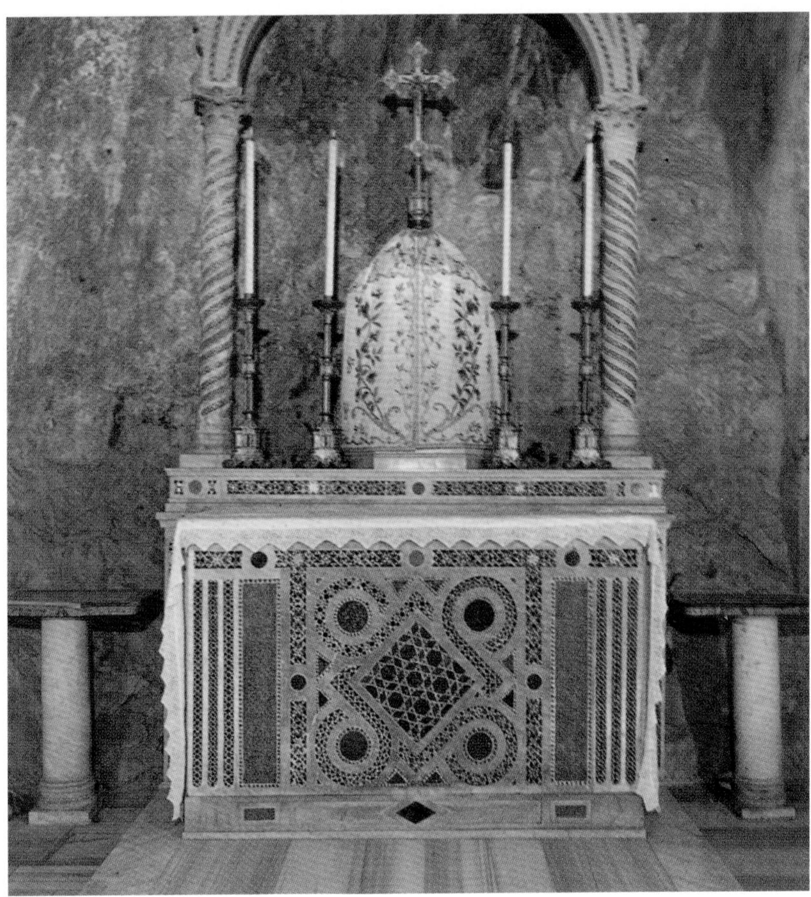

4-21. *Quincunx of poised-square center. Altar, Sacro Speco, Subiaco.*

in any Cosmatesque pavement the ratio of *C* to *A* always falls within the following limits:

$$1/3 \leq C/A \leq 1/2$$

In the Dumbo quincunx in San Saba, $C/A \approx 1/3$; in the one of large center at Santa Maria in Cosmedin, $C/A \approx 1/2$.

Thus far, only the quincunx consisting of a roundel ensconced in the angles between four roundels (quincunx or *quincunx of circular center*) has been discussed. However, the Cosmati also made use of quincunxes with centers that were not circular, but rather were a square (*quincunx of square center*), a poised square (*quincunx of poised-square center*; figs. 4-19, 4-20, and 4-21), or a rectangle (*quincunx of rectangular center*).

The Decussate Quincunx and Its Derivatives The decussate quincunx (from the Latin *quincunx* and *decŭssis*, the number ten, which in Roman numerals was X) is a poised quincunx, that is, a quincunx in which one of the diagonals is perpendicular to the principal axis of the ornamental composition (fig. 4-22). That axis, in the case of the Cosmatesque pavements, coincides with the longitudinal axis of the church. The center of the decussate quincunx is usually a circle (decussate quincunx or *decussate quincunx of circular center*), although there are examples in which a square appears at the center (*decussate quincunx of square center*).

A frequent motif consists of a square containing an inscribed quincunx whose center is an inscribed inverted square that, in turn, bears an inscribed decussate quincunx. This motif can simply be called a *decussate-quincunx-in-quincunx* (fig. 4-23). Among the churches with pavements that exhibit notable examples of this motif are: in Cività Castellana, Santa Maria Maggiore;[2] in Vetralla, San Francesco (fig. 4-24); in Rome, San Crisogono, Santa Francesca Romana (fig. 4-25), and the Cappella Sistina (Sistine Chapel); and in London, Westminster Abbey (fig. 4-26; see chapter 5 for a discussion of this type of quincunx at Westminster).

4-22. *Diagram of a decussate quincunx.*

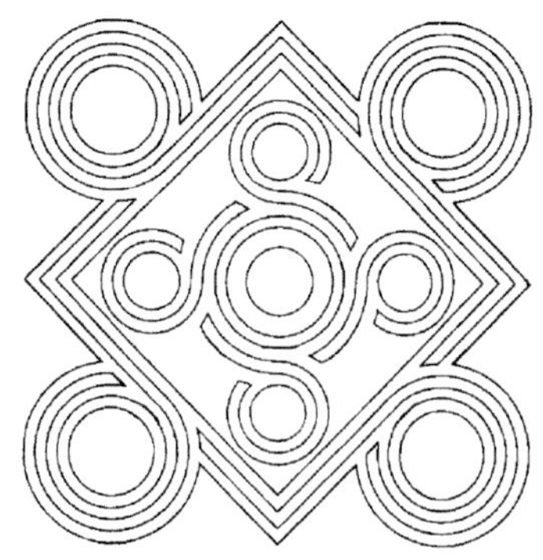

4-23. *[Above] Diagram of a decussate-quincunx-in-quincunx.*

4-24. *[Left] Decussate-quincunx-in-quincunx. Detail of the pavement, San Francesco, Vetralla.*

4-25. *[Left, below]Decussate-quincunx-in-quincunx. Detail of the pavement of the nave, Santa Francesca Romana, Rome.*

4-26. *[Above] Decussate-quincunx-in-quincunx. Pavement of the sanctuary, Westminster Abbey, London.*

4-27. *[Above] Row of three adjacent squares. Pavement of the nave, San Crisogono, Rome.*

4-28. *[Above, right] Square bearing an inscribed quincunx of poised-square center that in turn bears an inscribed decussate quincunx (decussate-quincunx-in-quincunx). Detail of the pavement, San Crisogono, Rome.*

4-29. *Square bearing an inscribed decussate quincunx of circular center that in turn bears an inscribed quincunx. Detail of the pavement, San Crisogono, Rome.*

4-30. *Square bearing a circular loop in each angle and, at the center, an inscribed decussate quincunx of square center that in turn bears an inscribed quincunx. Detail of the pavement, San Crisogono, Rome.*

The pavement in San Crisogono in Rome displays a full range of designs derived from the decussate quincunx in its many forms. The dominant design in the pavement of the nave is a row of three adjacent squares (fig. 4-27): the square closest to the entrance is a decussate-quincunx-in-quincunx (fig. 4-28); the central square bears an inscribed decussate quincunx of circular center, which in turn contains an inscribed quincunx (fig. 4-29); the square closest to the altar bears a circular loop in each angle and, at the center, an inscribed decussate quincunx of square center which in turn contains an inscribed quincunx (fig. 4-30).

LINEAR INTERLACING DESIGNS

There are various types of linear interlacing designs. The most notable ones are the guilloche, the guilloche-in-rectangle; the mixed guilloche; the series of tangent quincunxes; the series of linked quincunxes; and the series of linked figures.

The Guilloche and the Guilloche-in-rectangle The Cosmatesque guilloche is an interlacing of two strands, made from a pair of crossed, opposed sinusoids forming circular eyelets. Each strand consists of three parallel bands: the central band, in a linear geometric pattern in four counterchanged colors; and the plain white outer bands. The eyelets bear round tesserae, alternately in red and green.

A rectangle, drawn with white bands, circumscribes the guilloche. In *éco-incon* are surface geometric patterns in four counterchanged colors. This common form of the guilloche is the *guilloche-in-rectangle* (figs. 4-31 and 4-32).

The guilloche can be briefly described as a series of linked roundels, joined by interlacings.

As its principal trait, the Cosmatesque guilloche displays two interlaced sinusoidal threads (fig. 4-33). This type of braid is a very ancient motif whose origins, as can be deduced from archeological findings in Mesopotamia, Syria, and Greece, seem not to be found outside architecture. The oldest known remains are found in the Assyrian capital of Nimrud, in walls of polychrome glazed bricks that date from the ninth century B.C.[3]

D. F. Glass has demonstrated that the Cosmati of the twelfth century used a system of proportional measurement in which one of the most significant factors was the arrangement of the roundels (or *rotae*) contained in the principal motifs.[4] Glass measured the width of the rectangle circumscribing the guilloche (*a*) and the distance between the centers of two successive roundels in the guilloche (*d*) in several Cosmatesque pavements. The results,

4-31. [Above] Guilloche-in-rectangle. Detail of the Cosmatesque pavement from the schola cantorum, San Clemente, Rome.

4-32. Guilloche-in-rectangle. Detail of the Cosmatesque pavement from the nave, Santi Quattro Coronati, Rome.

4-33. Guilloche of two interlaced sinusoidal strands.

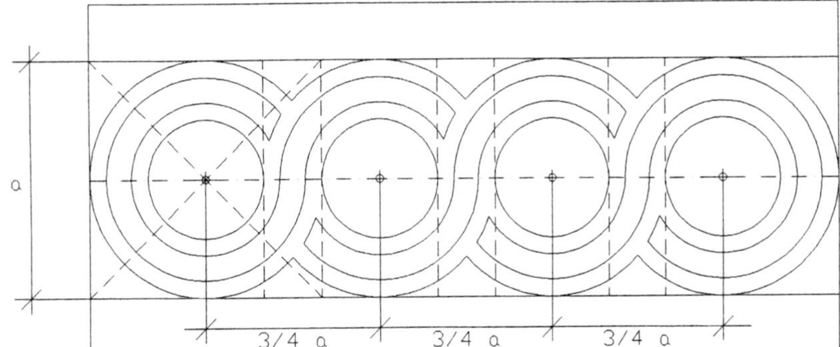

4-34. Measurements for the construction of a Cosmatesque guilloche.

in centimeters, are as follows: San Benedetto in Piscinula, Rome, a = 113, d = 88; San Clemente, Rome, a = 133, d = 99; Santi Quattro Coronati, Rome, a = 141, d = 107; Santa Croce in Gerusalemme, Rome, a = 137, d = 105; Sant' Anastasio, Castel Sant'Elia, a = 144, d = 110; Sant'Ambrogio, Ferentino, a = 129, d = 98; Santa Maria Maggiore, Cività Castellana, a = 163, d = 130. She then observed that $d/a \approx 0.75$ in all of them, which is equivalent to saying that

$$d \approx {}^{3}/_{4}\, a,$$

or the distance between the centers of two consecutive roundels of a guilloche is equal to three-quarters of the width of the rectangle circumscribing the guilloche.

The proportional ratio between the width of the circumscribing rectangle and the distance between the centers of two successive *rotae* is completely unrelated to the total number of roundels in the row, which implies that the total length of the circumscribed rectangle is not a significant factor in the overall measurements. This fact is apparent in the numerous Cosmatesque pavements with guilloches in which the final loop is incomplete.

Based on these findings, Glass explained the process the Cosmati used to construct a guilloche. Once the longitudinal axis of the nave was determined and the width of the rectangle intended to enclose the series of *rotae* had been decided, the width of the rectangle was set and its two diagonals were drawn. The intersection of the two diagonals marked the position of the center of the first roundel of porphyry. Next, the centers of the successive roundels were arranged at three-quarters of the width of the rectangle, until all the available space was filled (fig. 4-34). Then the *rotae* were joined by means of two strands, each of them composed of a central band in tetrachrome mosaic flanked by two bands in white marble.

Chapter 6 of this book, "Analysis of a Mosaic," offers an additional hypothesis about how the basic geometric design that regulates a Cosmatesque guilloche was executed, based on my own detailed measurements and analysis of a specific pavement. Although the essence of my interpretation coincides with Glass's hypothesis, it differs when put into practice. I believe that the Cosmati must have arranged the roundels of the guilloche by measuring the *distances edge to edge between the eyelets bearing roundels of the same color* (that is, every other roundel), rather than the distances between the centers of the *rotae*, without forgetting that the distances are a function of the diameter of the eyelet and the width of the rectangle that circumscribes the guilloche.

The dimensional ratios derived from the material studied in chapter 6, in conjunction with the proportions observed by Glass that relate the width of the circumscribed rectangle to the distance between the centers of two consecutive roundels, led me to discover this fundamental relationship:

a = width of the rectangle circumscribed around the guilloche
b = diameter of the eyelet (the "hole")
d = distance between the centers of two successive roundels

$$d = \tfrac{1}{2}(a + b)$$

$$d \approx \tfrac{3}{4} a$$

$$\tfrac{1}{2}(a + b) \approx \tfrac{3}{4} a$$

$$b \approx \tfrac{1}{2} a$$

$$a \approx 2b$$

Thus, the width of the rectangle circumscribed around the guilloche is approximately equal to double the diameter of the eyelet.

Knowledge of this basic ratio allowed me to develop two of the relations postulated in my study of the guilloche in the pavement in the schola cantorum of San Clemente (see chapter 6):

c = width of a strand
L = total length of the rectangle circumscribing the guilloche
r = radius of the eyelet
n = number of complete loops in a guilloche

$$c = \tfrac{1}{2}(a - b)$$

$$c \approx \tfrac{1}{2} b$$

$$c \approx r$$

$L = c + 6a + 6b$ (since $L = c + 12d$ in a guilloche of 12 complete loops)

$L \approx c + \tfrac{1}{2} na + \tfrac{1}{2} nb$ (in a guilloche of n complete loops)

$$L \approx \tfrac{1}{2} b + nb + \tfrac{1}{2} nb$$

$$L \approx \tfrac{1}{2} b\,(1 + 3n) \approx r\,(1 + 3n)$$

In summary, the width of one strand of a Cosmatesque guilloche is approximately equal to the radius of the eyelet:

$$c \approx r$$

and the total length of the rectangle circumscribing a guilloche of n complete loops is approximately equal to $(1 + 3n)$ times the radius of the eyelet:

$$L \approx r\,(1 + 3n)$$

Keeping in mind that the diameter of the eyelet hole must be equal to or greater than the diameter of the large *rota*, it follows that all the principal measurements for the outline of a Cosmatesque guilloche are a function of the dimension of the largest of the available *rotae*, evidence of the importance of the initial phase of collecting spoliated materials in determining the final form of a Cosmatesque design.

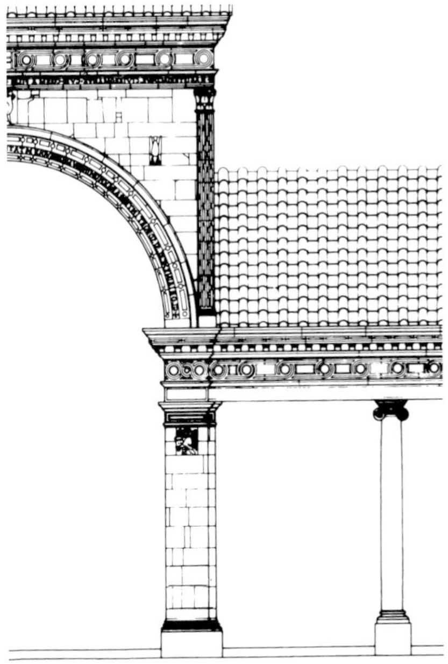

4-35. Mixed guilloche of circles and rectangles. Entablature of the portico, Santa Maria Maggiore, Cività Castellana.

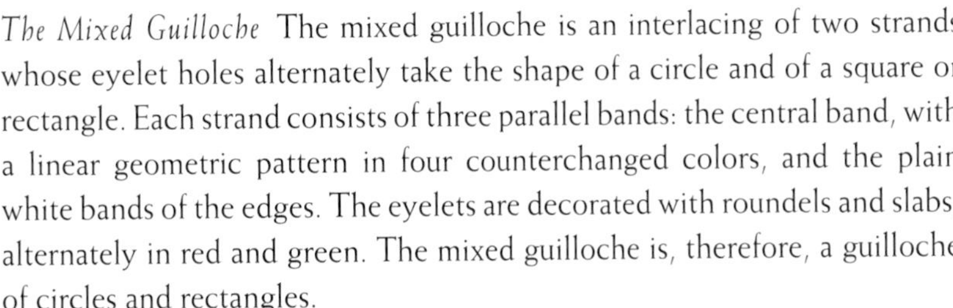

The Mixed Guilloche The mixed guilloche is an interlacing of two strands whose eyelet holes alternately take the shape of a circle and of a square or rectangle. Each strand consists of three parallel bands: the central band, with a linear geometric pattern in four counterchanged colors, and the plain white bands of the edges. The eyelets are decorated with roundels and slabs, alternately in red and green. The mixed guilloche is, therefore, a guilloche of circles and rectangles.

The intervals that result from circumscribing a mixed guilloche with a rectangle drawn with white bands are filled with surface linear geometric patterns in four counterchanged colors.

The guilloche of circles and rectangles is the dominant motif of the pavements executed in northern Latium by the Cosmatesque artists of the Ranucius family.[5] This motif appears in the entablature of the portico of the *duomo* of Cività Castellana (fig. 4-35), in the nave of Sant'Anastasio in Castel Sant'-Elia (fig. 4-36), in the schola cantorum of Sant'Andrea in Flumine in Ponzano Romano (fig. 4-37), and in the schola cantorum of Santa Maria di Castello in Tarquinia.[6] In Rome both the entablature of the cloister of San Giovanni in Laterano (figs. 4-38, 4-39, and 4-40) and the entablature of San Paolo fuori le Mura (fig. 4-41) display designs of mixed guilloche executed with minute tesserae.

4-36. [Above] Mixed guilloche of circles and rectangles. Detail of the pavement of the nave of Sant'Anastasio, Castel Sant'Elia.

4-37. Mixed guilloche of circles and rectangles. Pavement of the schola cantorum, Sant'Andrea in Flumine, Ponzano Romano.

4-38. [*Above*] *Mixed guilloche of circles and rectangles ornamenting an entablature.* (*Drawing, tempera on paper, A. Terzi, 1915–16*)

4-39 [*Left*] *Detail of mixed guilloche of circles and rectangles.* (*Drawing, tempera on paper, A. Terzi, 1915–16*)

4-40. [*Below, left*] *Mixed guilloche. Detail of the entablature in the cloister, San Giovanni in Laterano, Rome.*

4-41. [*Below*] *Mixed guilloche. Detail of the entablature in the cloister, San Paolo fuori le Mura, Rome.*

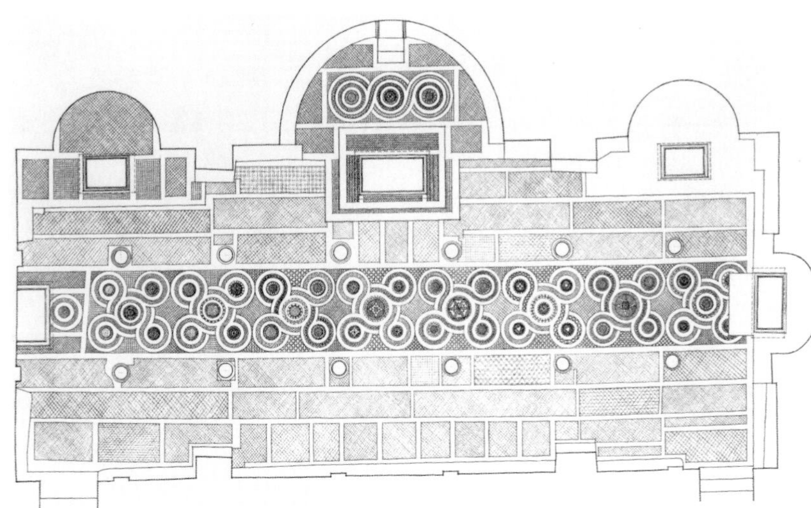

4-42. Series of eight tangent quincunxes that ornaments the nave of the crypt of the Anagni Cathedral.

The Series of Tangent Quincunxes The series of tangent quincunxes is a row of straight quincunxes in which the loops in adjoining angles of consecutive quincunxes touch each other at a point (fig. 4-42).

To compose a row of contiguous quincunxes, the imaginary squares that contain them are arranged adjacently. The placement of the central roundel in each square does not pose a problem since its center coincides with the point on which the two diagonals of the square cross. The position of the four roundels in the angles of each quincunx is determined by a system common in the Middle Ages, *the method of rotating squares.*

The inverted inscribed square is drawn in the square that contains the quincunx, that is, the square whose vertices are the midpoints of the sides of the exterior square (fig. 4-43). The lines forming the sides of the interior square turn until they are parallel to the sides of the square circumscribed to the quincunx (fig. 4-44). The vertices of the interior square, resting upon the diagonals of the exterior square, mark the centers of the roundels in angle.[7]

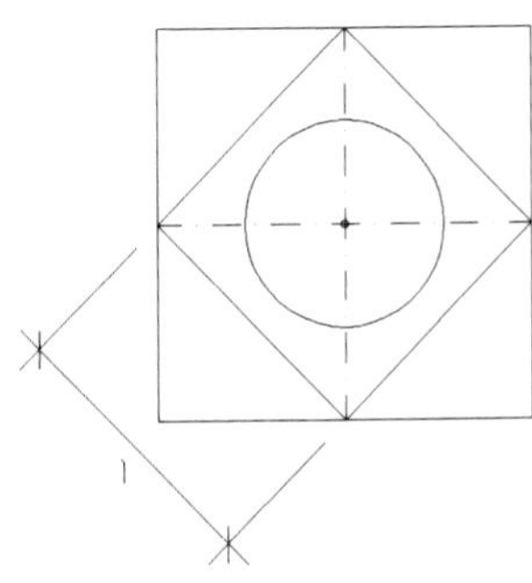

4-43. Method to place the four peripheral roundels of a quincunx. First geometric operation: given the square that will circumscribe the quincunx, draw its inverted inscribed square.

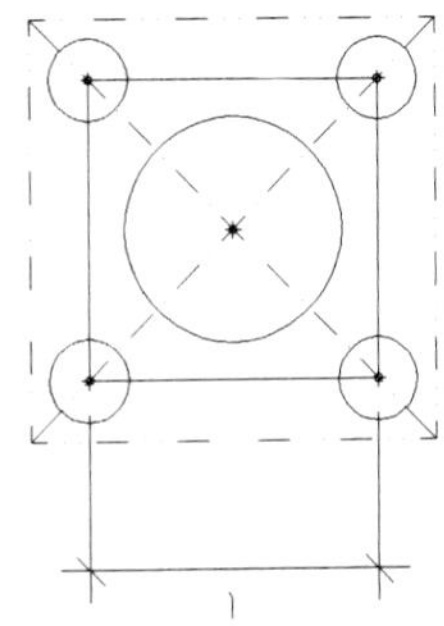

4-44. Method to place the four peripheral roundels of a quincunx. Second geometric operation: rotate the inverted inscribed square, with its center at the center of the exterior square, 45 degrees; its vertices, now resting upon the diagonals of the exterior square, mark the centers of the roundels in angle.

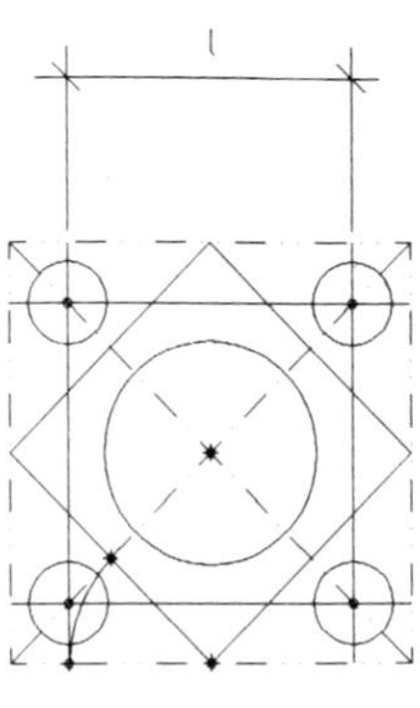

4-45. Method to place the four peripheral roundels of a quincunx. An alternative to the second geometric operation: rotate a line segment half the side of the inverted inscribed square with the center at the vertex of the said square until the line segment is superposed on the side of the exterior square; draw the line perpendicular to that side by the free end of the line segment; the intersection of this line with the diagonal of the exterior square marks the centers of two of the roundels in angle.

4-46. *Series of three tangent quincunxes. Pavement of the schola cantorum, view of the interior of Santa Maria in Cosmedin, Rome.*

4-47. *Pair of tangent quincunxes. Detail of the pavement of the nave, Santa Maria in Trastevere, Rome.*

Another method of rotating the inscribed square consists of turning half the line that delineates one of the sides of the inscribed square, with the center at the midpoint of one of the sides of the exterior square, until it is superposed on the side of the exterior square. Upon drawing a line perpendicular to that side by the free end of the half chord of the inscribed square, one obtains the straight line that contains one of the sides of the rotated square. The straight line, by cutting across the diagonals of the exterior square, determines the placement of the remaining sides of the rotated square and, consequently, the centers of the corner roundels (fig. 4-45).

The series of tangent quincunxes appears frequently in Cosmatesque mosaics. The long series of eight tangent quincunxes that ornaments the nave of the San Magnus crypt in the Cathedral of Santa Maria in Anagni is a remarkable example (see chapter 5).[8] Rome contains several noteworthy examples: the series of three tangent quincunxes that carpets the pavement of the schola cantorum of Santa Maria in Cosmedin (fig. 4-46), the pair of tangent quincunxes that fills each of the compartments of the grid of the nave at Santa Maria in Trastevere (fig. 4-47), and the series of two quincunxes that has survived at the entrance of the small church of San Benedetto in Piscinula (fig. 4-48).

4-48. *Series of two tangent quincunxes. Detail of the pavement, San Benedetto in Piscinula, Rome.*

4-49. Series of linked quincunxes. Detail of the pavement in the western part of the nave, Santi Giovanni e Paolo, Rome.

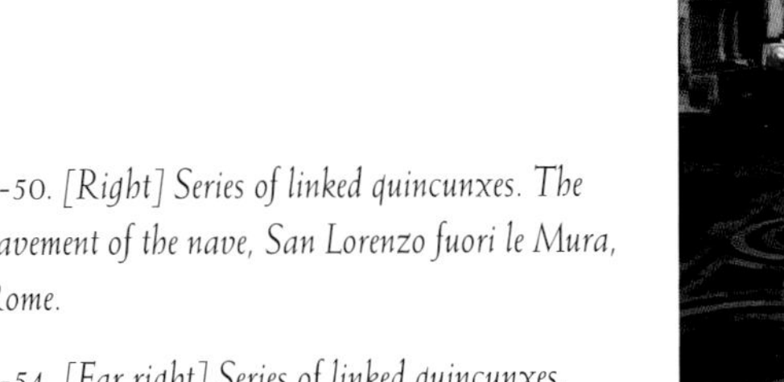

4-50. [Right] Series of linked quincunxes. The pavement of the nave, San Lorenzo fuori le Mura, Rome.

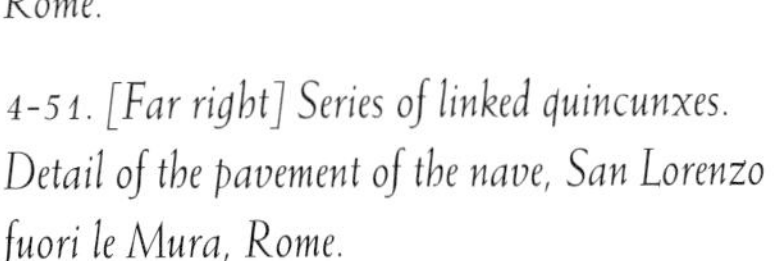

4-51. [Far right] Series of linked quincunxes. Detail of the pavement of the nave, San Lorenzo fuori le Mura, Rome.

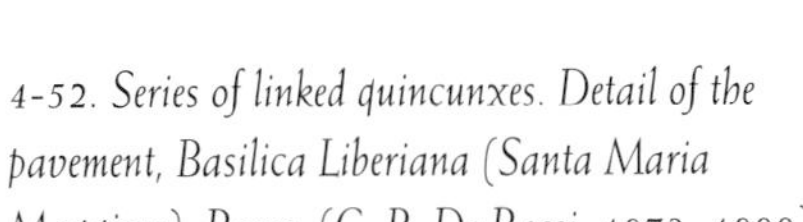

4-52. Series of linked quincunxes. Detail of the pavement, Basilica Liberiana (Santa Maria Maggiore), Rome. (G. B. De Rossi, 1873–1899)

The Series of Linked Quincunxes A series of linked quincunxes is a row of straight quincunxes in which the loops in angle of consecutive quincunxes overlap, because these loops are connected by interlacing.

Designs of this type appear, for example, in the pavement of the nave of Santi Giovanni e Paolo (fig. 4-49), San Lorenzo fuori le Mura (figs. 4-50 and 4-51), and Santa Maria Maggiore (fig. 4-52), all in Rome.

4-53. *Series of linked figures. Detail of the pavement surrounding the altar, San Lorenzo fuori le Mura, Rome. (P. M. Letarouilly)*

The Series of Linked Figures To understand this type of linear interlacing design, first one must understand the meaning of the term *figure* in this context. The term refers as much to pointed interlacing designs (such as the quincunx, quincunx of square center, quincunx of poised-square center, quincunx of rectangular center, decussate quincunx, decussate-quincunx-in-quincunx, and the like, all described earlier in this chapter) as to basic geometric forms (such as the square, circle, lozenge, rectangle) drawn with the typical Cosmatesque band, that is, a band with a tetrachrome mosaic in the center and plain white borders.

A series of linked figures is a row of figures in which the peripheral loops of consecutive figures overlap, since those loops connect in interlacing.

The series of linked quincunxes is simply a series of linked figures, all of which are quincunxes of equal shape and size.

The Cosmatesque artists regale us with numerous beautiful examples of series of linked figures. As a general rule, the geometric complexity of these examples increases the later their date of execution.

The Cosmatesque design in the pavement at San Lorenzo fuori le Mura offers several examples of a series of linked figures (figs. 4-53 through 4-58).[9] Moving from the entrance toward the altar, over the longitudinal axis of the church, it is possible to view three such series. In the first, four quincunxes and a square are linked, the square occupying the center of the row. In the second, rectangles and circles are connected, the rectangles flanked by linked circles; one might also describe the figures that are joined in the second series as decussate quincunxes of rectangular center. The third series, which is composed of three quincunxes of circular center, two quincunxes of poised-square center, and three quincunxes of rectangular center, encloses the altar, forming a square boundary of linked figures.

4-54. *Series of overlapping linked quincunxes of rectangular center from the pavement in the nave of San Lorenzo fuori le Mura, Rome.*

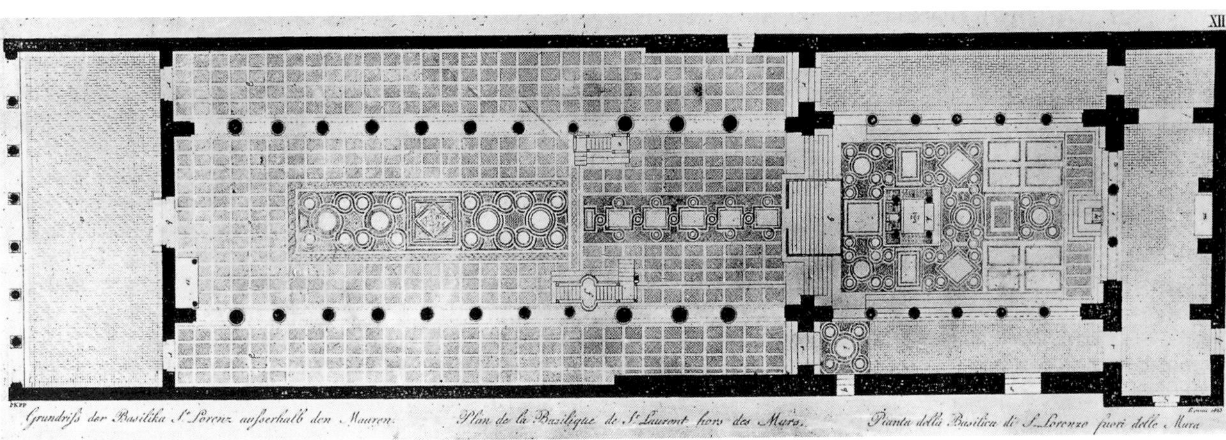

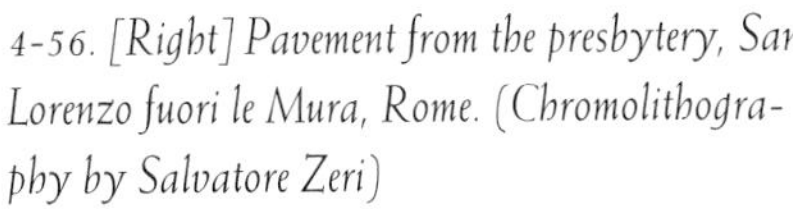
4-55. [Above] Floor plan, San Lorenzo fuori le Mura, Rome. (Engraving by Bunsen: MKPP, Rome, 1823)

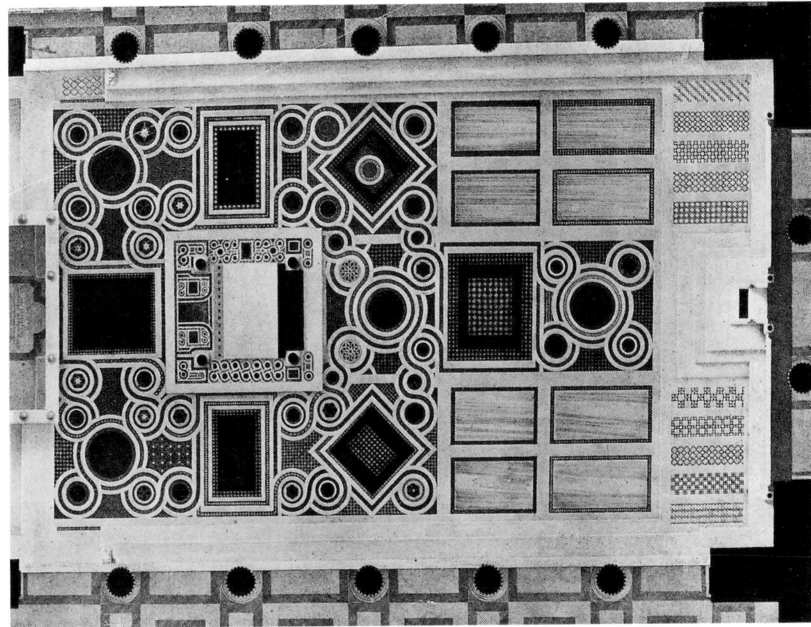
4-56. [Right] Pavement from the presbytery, San Lorenzo fuori le Mura, Rome. (Chromolithography by Salvatore Zeri)

4-57. [Below] Series of three linked figures, consisting of two quincunxes of circular center and a quincunx of rectangular center. Detail of the pavement surrounding the altar, San Lorenzo fuori le Mura, Rome.

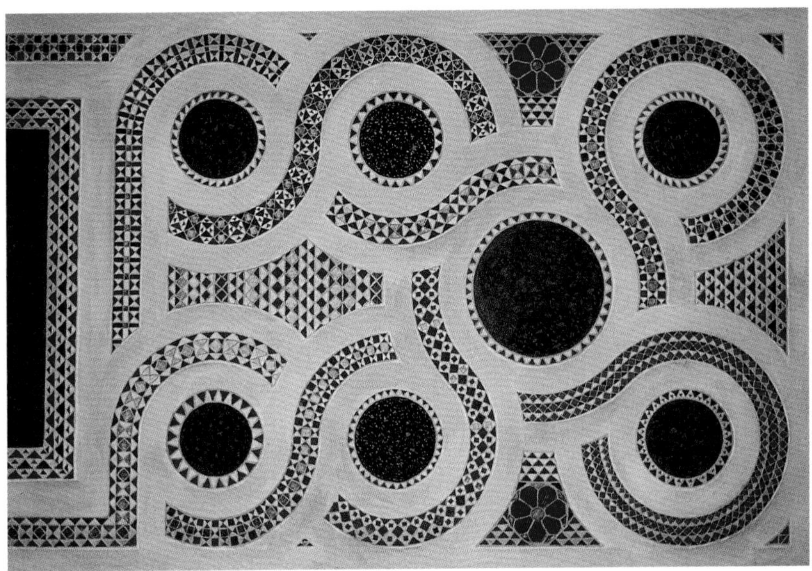
4-58. [Right] Detail of a series of linked figures, one of which is a quincunx. (Drawing, tempera on paper, A. Terzi, 1915–16)

4-59. Detail of a surface pattern of linked roundels. (Drawing, tempera on paper, A. Terzi, 1915–16)

4-60. Pattern of linked roundels; the centered geometric patterns that fill some of the eyelets exhibit clear signs of Arab influence (the design characteristics stemming from this imported influence were explained in chapter 1). Ambo from the Cathedral of Ravello, Campania, Italy.

SURFACE INTERLACING DESIGNS

The Cosmatesque artists used various designs in interlacing when covering a surface. The most noteworthy patterns can be classified as one of two types: the pattern of linked roundels or the grid of guilloches.

The Pattern of Linked Roundels The pattern of linked roundels is a surface pattern of *rotae* joined in interlacing (figs. 4-59 and 4-60).

4-61. *Pattern of linked roundels. Detail of the pavement in the nave, San Gregorio Magno, Rome.*

Among the Byzantine *sectilia* of the eleventh century that are considered predecessors to the Cosmatesque mosaics is an example of a pattern of linked roundels: a fragment from the pavement in the mausoleum of Orhan Gazi in Bursa, in which nine equal *rotae* joined in interlacing uniformly cover a square surface (see chapter 5 for more information about this fragment).

The Cosmatesque pavement in the nave of the church of San Gregorio Magno in Rome contains a composition of twelve linked roundels inscribed in a rectangle (fig. 4-61). In this composition, a square ring formed by eight connected roundels is inscribed in the center of the rectangle; the four remaining roundels are placed in the angles of the rectangle, linked to the roundels located in the angles of the square ring.

The Grid of Guilloches The grid of guilloches is an orthogonal grid drawn by bands consisting of series of linked roundels, forming square or rectangular compartments.

The pavement in the nave of Santa Maria in Trastevere in Rome is carpeted with a grid of guilloches forming rectangular compartments; each compartment bears a series of two tangent quincunxes (fig. 4-62).

4-62. *Grid of guilloches. Detail of the pavement in the nave, Santa Maria in Trastevere, Rome.*

The Interstitial Fabric

The ornamental fabric that covers the intervals created by the framework consists of geometric patterns. These patterns are constructed from elements organized by an underlying regulating design.

The Elements of Composition and the Regulating Design

The elements of composition are coincident to the basic constructive units, the tesserae. The geometry of their forms is simple and includes the circle, semicircle, square, isosceles right triangle (semisquare), rectangle, scalene right triangle (semirectangle), equilateral triangle, short isosceles triangle, long isosceles triangle, trapezoid, lozenge (double equilateral triangle or double isosceles triangle), rhomboid (double semisquare or double semirectangle), pentagon, hexagon, octagon, dart, and spindle (figs. 4-63 and 4-64).

4-63. Cosmatesque geometric patterns; detail showing tesserae in the shape of a square, an isosceles right triangle, and a lozenge. (Detail of drawing, tempera on paper, A. Terzi, 1915–16)

4-64. Cosmatesque panel; detail showing tesserae in the shape of an equilateral triangle, short isosceles triangle, isosceles right triangle, square, rectangle, and a lozenge. (Detail of drawing, tempera on paper, A. Terzi, 1915–16)

The regulating design that underlies an interstitial fabric is a geometric net that can be a centered, linear, or surface structure, depending upon the form of the interval that the fabric is to cover. One might classify into four groups the shapes of the interstitial spaces created by the framework: circular forms; those bound by curved sides; straight-sided ones; and those bound by curved and straight sides. The first are filled with *rotae* or with ornamental patterns of centered structure; the second with patterns of linear structure; and the remaining interspaces, with patterns of surface structure. Therefore, both the rectangular lateral intervals created by the gross framework as well as the interstitial spaces of one or more curved sides associated with the interlacing designs are covered with geometric patterns. The surface compositions that cover the rectangular intervals have modules of greater dimensions than those of the smaller intervals with one or more curved sides.

The Geometric Patterns

The repertoire of geometric patterns used by the Cosmati is very broad. Although it would make an interesting study, a complete and systematic cataloging of that repertoire has yet to be accomplished.[10] Due to its enormous breadth, such a task remains out of reach for this book. This discussion is limited to classifying the geometric patterns into four large groups: the roundels, the centered patterns, the linear patterns, and the surface patterns.

THE ROUNDELS

The roundel (from the Latin *rota,* meaning wheel), that is, the circle, is the chief geometric form in the principal design motifs of the compositions of the Cosmati. The placement of these large monolithic rounds of porphyry and serpentine in the most important areas of the pavement is a consequence of their high symbolic and material value.[11] In fact, the *rotae* might be called the gems of the Cosmatesque mosaics.

All of the determining measurements of the morphology of a Cosmatesque design depend on the diameter of the largest *rota*, as explained earlier in this chapter with regard to the guilloche. To this explanation must be added the conclusions that D. F. Glass reached after measuring the pavement at Santi Quattro Coronati in Rome, in which she affirmed that all the significant dimensions of the design are multiples of a module equal to one-half of the radius of the central *rota* of the principal quincunx (fig. 4-65).[12]

THE CENTERED GEOMETRIC PATTERNS

A centered geometric pattern is a pattern inscribed in a circle or in a polygon of equal sides that can be inscribed in a circle.

The proliferation of centered geometric patterns in the circular intervals of the Cosmatesque interlacings is due, above all, to the scarcity of large dark-colored roundels in one piece. When monolithic rounds of red and green marble were not available, the Cosmati filled the eyelets with a tessellation of small pieces of various geometric forms (fig. 4-66). This occurred frequently in the mosaics of the churches located in small cities of Latium, for example, in Anagni, Santa Maria; in Cività Castellana, Santa Maria Maggiore; in Spoleto, Assunta; in Tivoli, San Pietro (fig. 4-67); in Vetralla, San

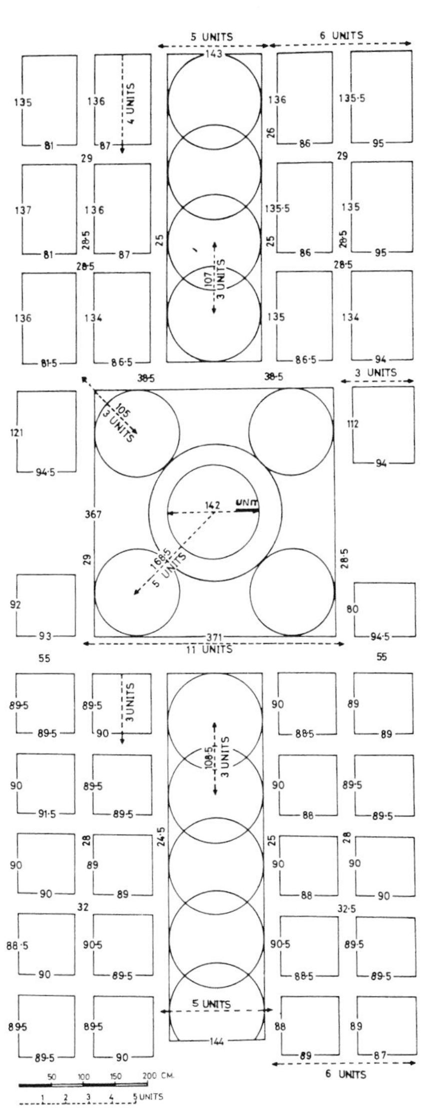

4-65. Measurement of the pavement of Santi Quattro Coronati, Rome. (D. F. Glass)

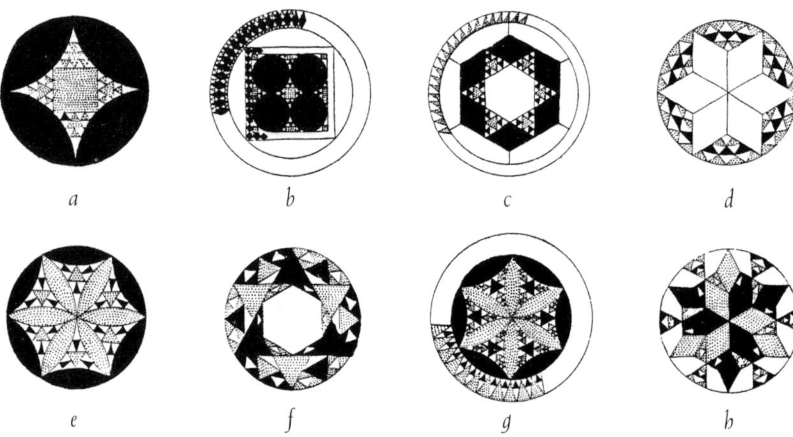

4-66. *Centered geometric patterns (all in Rome).*
a. Santi Quattro Coronati
b. San Giovanni in Laterano
c. Santa Maria Maggiore
d. San Giovanni in Laterano
e. San Marco
f. San Giovanni in Laterano
g. Santa Maria in Trastevere
h. San Giovanni in Laterano

4-67. *[Left] Quincunx whose eyelets (circular intervals) bear centered geometric patterns. Detail of the pavement in the nave, San Pietro, Tivoli.*

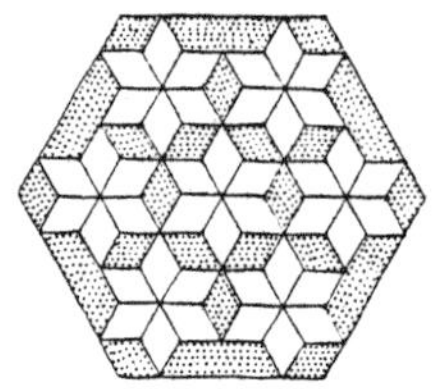

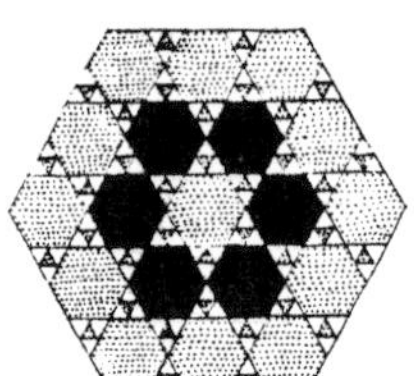

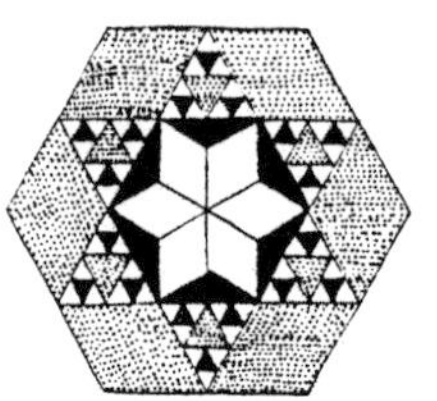

4-68. *[Left] Three examples of centered geometric patterns. Santa Maria in Trastevere, Rome.*

4-69. *[Below] Bishop's throne by Vassallettus (or Vassalletto, one of the families of artists called Cosmatesque), Cathedral of Santa Maria, Anagni.*

Francesco.[13] These parishes could not afford to obtain and transport expensive rounds of porphyry and serpentine from the ruins of Rome.

The centered patterns of the examples cited thus far are contained in a circle. Others are enclosed in a hexagon, as occurs in the pavement of Santa Maria in Trastevere in Rome (fig. 4-68) and in the episcopal throne in the Cathedral of Santa Maria in Anagni, where the center of the star of two triangles that adorns the head of the back of the seat is encrusted with a fractionized triaxial pattern in mosaic (fig. 4-69).

The virtual nonexistence of monolithic *rotae* beginning in the final centuries of the Middle Ages is apparent, in Rome, in the abundance of centered patterns in the neo-Cosmatesque pavements of the fifteenth century, such as those at the Sistine Chapel (fig. 4-70) and, later, in the pavements that have been massively restored, redone, or built in recent centuries, such as that in San Giovanni in Laterano (fig. 4-71).

4-70. Three examples of centered geometric patterns. Details of the pavement, Cappella Sistina (Sistine Chapel), Vatican City.

4-71. Two examples of centered geometric patterns. Details of the pavement, San Giovanni in Laterano, Rome.

4-72. *Eight linear geometric patterns. (Drawing, tempera on paper, A. Terzi. 1915–16)*

4-73. *Six linear geometric patterns. (Drawing, tempera on paper, A. Terzi, 1915–16)*

The Linear Geometric Patterns

The glossary earlier in this chapter defines the basic linear patterns most common in the Cosmatesque mosaics: band of chessboard pattern of *X*; pattern of rows of *X*; rack; sawtooth pattern; dog's-tooth pattern; rectilinear thorns; rows of *X* and *Y*; points. All of these and their combinations offer an inexhaustible repertoire of geometric designs appropriate for covering intervals in the form of a rectilinear band (figs. 4-72 through 4-75) or a curvilinear band (fig. 4-76).

The curvilinear patterns appear frequently in the pavements, as much to fill the central bands in the strands of the interlacing motifs as to extend the diameters of the *rotae*. To enlarge the appearance of the *rotae*, one can border them with an adjoined linear pattern (fig. 4-77) or center them in a set of concentric rings drawn alternately in white marble bands and minute tetrachrome geometric linear patterns (figs. 4-78 and 4-79).

4-74. *[Above] Seven segments of linear geometric patterns. (Drawing, tempera on paper, A. Terzi, 1915–16)*

4-75. *[Below] Six segments of linear geometric patterns. (Drawing, tempera on paper, A. Terzi, 1915–16)*

4-76. *[Right] Two examples of linear geometric patterns filling a curved band. Details of the pavement, San Pietro, Tivoli.*

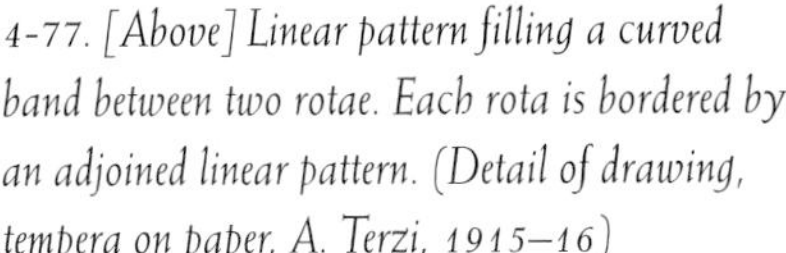

4-77. *[Above] Linear pattern filling a curved band between two rotae. Each rota is bordered by an adjoined linear pattern. (Detail of drawing, tempera on paper, A. Terzi, 1915–16)*

4-78. *[Below] General view of the interior, Cappella Sistina (Sistine Chapel), Vatican City.*

4-79. *[Below, right] Rota centered in an arrangement of concentric rings drawn alternately in white bands and tetrachrome linear patterns. Detail of the pavement, Cappella Sistina (Sistine Chapel), Vatican City.*

4-80. Orthogonal grid of linear geometric patterns. Pavement, Santa Maria in Aracoeli, Rome.

4-81. [Above, left] Orthogonal pattern of rectangular rings of linear geometric patterns. Pavement, Santa Sabina, Rome.

4-82. [Above] General view of the interior, Santa Sabina, Rome.

In exceptional cases linear geometric patterns, rather than the usual bands of white marble, define the gross framework of the pavement. Examples can be found in Santa Maria in Aracoeli (fig. 4-80) and in Santa Sabina (figs. 4-81 and 4-82), both in Rome, where bands of minute polychrome mosaic flank large white paving stones (see chapter 3 for earlier pavements with this type of design).

Linear patterns also embellish the furnishings of churches. Examples can be found in the entablature of the ciborium, in the parallel bands that twist around the shaft of the paschal candlestick, and in the flat geometric designs or the borders thereof that decorate altars, screens, pulpits, ambos, tombs, bishop's chairs, and confessios.

On the exterior of the church, one also finds linear patterns, framing the opening of the main entrance, defining the arch of the tympanum, beneath the cornice of the porticoes and porches, in the entablature and columns of the cloisters, and embellishing the rose window of the façade (figs. 4-83 through 4-90).

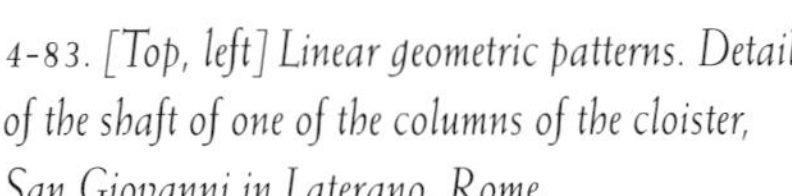

4-83. *[Top, left] Linear geometric patterns. Detail of the shaft of one of the columns of the cloister, San Giovanni in Laterano, Rome.*

4-84. *[Top, center] Linear geometric patterns. Detail of the shaft of one of the columns of the cloister, San Paolo fuori le Mura, Rome.*

4-85. *[Top, right] One of the sides of the cloister, with paired columns encrusted with mosaics, San Paolo fuori le Mura, Rome.*

4-86. *[Above, left] Linear geometric patterns. Tympanum over the door, Duomo, Santa Maria Maggiore, Cività Castellana.*

4-87. *[Above, middle] Linear geometric patterns. Detail of the door jamb, Duomo, Santa Maria Maggiore, Cività Castellana.*

4-88. *[Above, right] Linear geometric patterns. Detail of the base of the central arch of the portico, Duomo, Santa Maria Maggiore, Cività Castellana.*

4-89. *[Right] Linear geometric patterns. Detail of the door frame, San Giovanni a Porta Latina, Rome.*

4-90. *[Far right] Linear geometric patterns. Detail of the rose window of the façade, San Pietro, Tuscania.*

4-91. Four surface geometric patterns. (Drawing, tempera on paper, A. Terzi, 1915–16)

4-92. Four surface geometric patterns. (Drawing, tempera on paper, A. Terzi, 1915–16)

The Surface Geometric Patterns

Surface geometric patterns are those that extend along the plane, providing a homogeneous cover (figs. 4-91 through 4-95).

Patterns of this type whose dimensional module is small generally appear in the vertical panels contained in the furnishings of a church. Those with a large dimensional module are employed in the pavements (fig. 4-96), where they constitute the rectangular panels that tessellate the aisles and a large part of the nave (the rectangular panels that flank the interlacing motifs superposed on the longitudinal axis of the basilica).

As discussed in chapter 3, the fundamental traits of the isotropic patterns used by the Cosmatesque artists stem from the surface patterns that were employed by the Roman mosaicists of antiquity (figs. 4-97 and 4-98).

Two basic underlying elements generate an isotropic pattern: the net and the graph.[14] The net is the underlying mesh of regular geometric design that serves as a guide for the transfer of the graph over the surface. The graph is

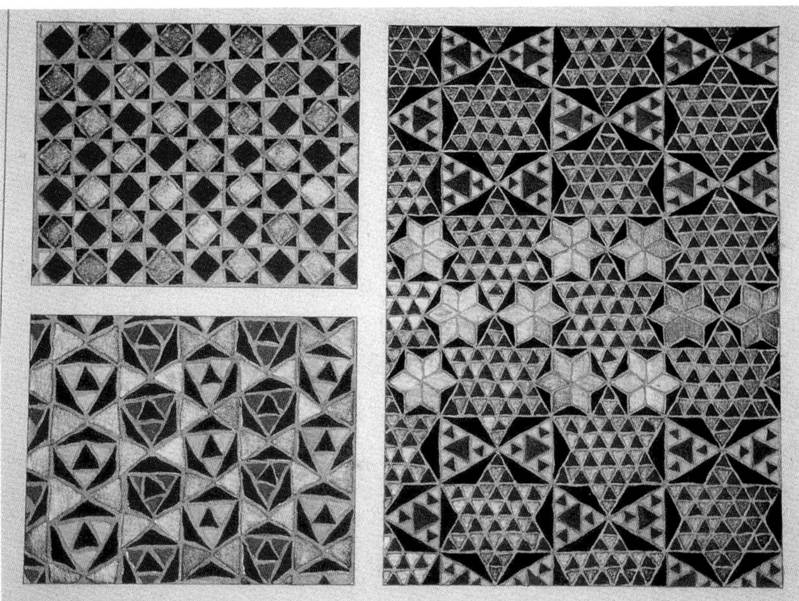

4-93. *Three surface geometric patterns. (Drawing, tempera on paper, A. Terzi, 1915–16)*

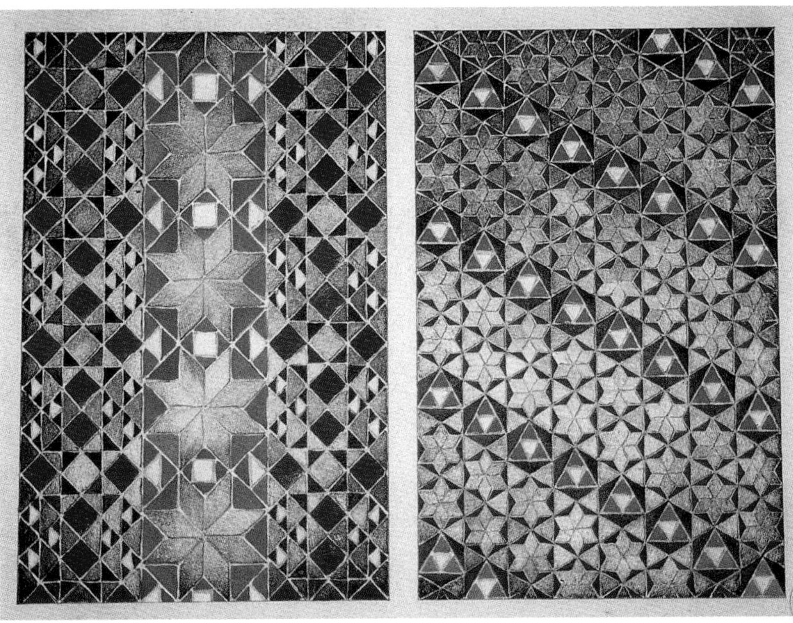

4-94. *Two surface geometric patterns. (Drawing, tempera on paper, A. Terzi, 1915–16)*

4-95. *Two surface geometric patterns. (Drawing, tempera on paper, A. Terzi, 1915–16)*

4-96. Cosmatesque mosaic. Surface geometric patterns. Detail of the pavement, San Clemente, Rome.

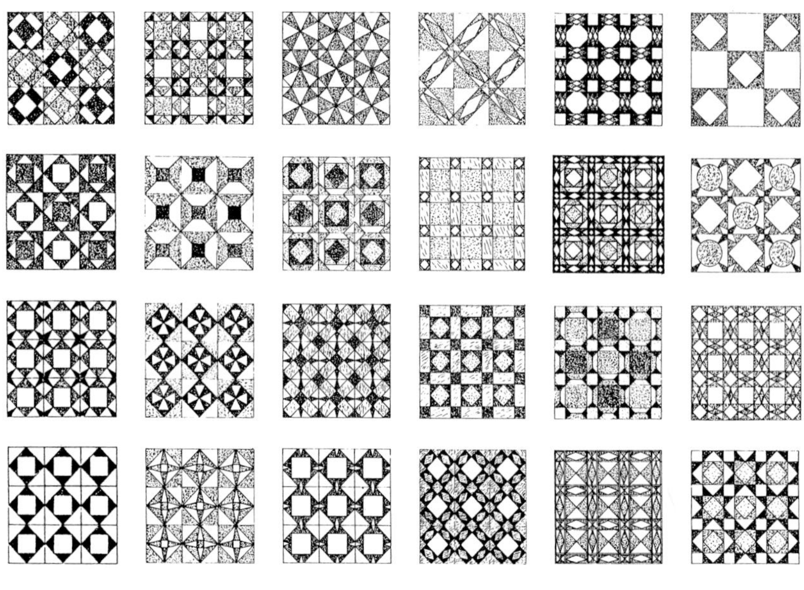

4-97. Roman mosaics: samples of opus sectile pavements with simple motifs that offer some opportunity for chromatic composition. (F. Guidobaldi)

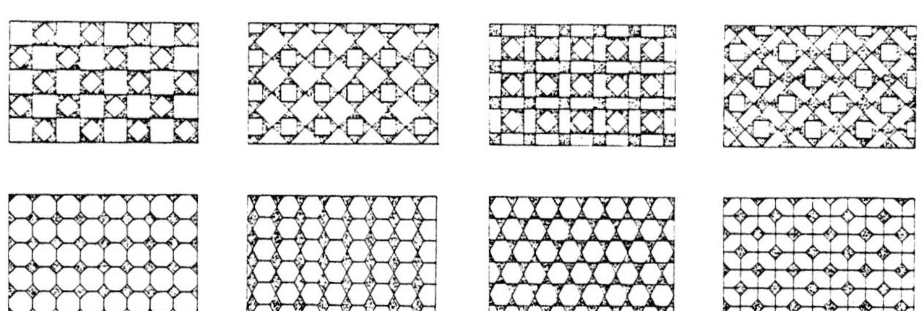

4-98. Roman mosaics: samples of opus sectile pavements with small modules that offer some opportunity for chromatic composition. (F. Guidobaldi)

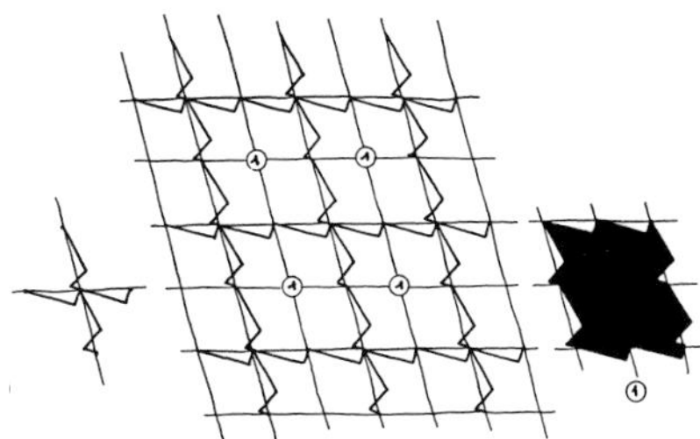

4-99. Mosaic. The generating elements of a regular partition of the plane: the graph, the net, and the tessera. (R. Zoido)

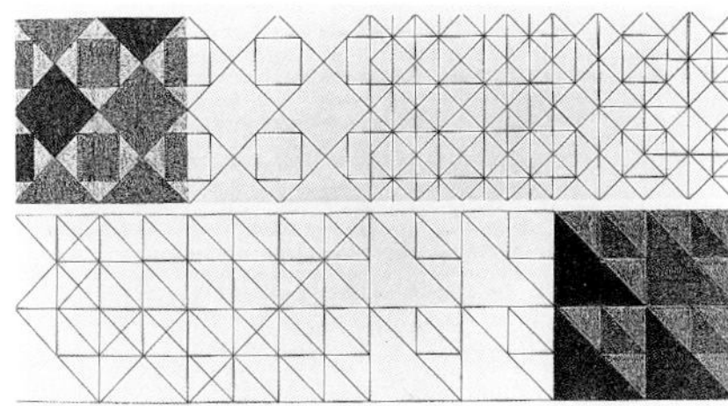

4-100. Analysis of the underlying scheme in biaxial geometric patterns. Detail of two bands of the pavement of the sanctuary, Westminster Abbey, London. (R. Foster, 1991)

4-101. Analysis of the underlying scheme in triaxial geometric patterns. Detail of two bands of the pavement of the sanctuary, Westminster Abbey, London. (R. Foster, 1991)

the motif of repetition, that is, the figure that is systematically repeated over each of the nodes of the net, composing the regular partition of the plane that defines the borders of the tesserae of the mosaic (fig. 4-99).

The net is constructed with straight lines parallel to a system of axes, paired or in a trio. When the system consists of two axes perpendicular to one another, the net that results from drawing the straight lines parallel to those axes is called an *orthogonal biaxial net* or, simply, a *biaxial net*. In the event that the pair of axes form an angle other than 90 degrees, the underlying net is called an *oblique biaxial net*. When the system of reference is composed of three axes intersecting at 120 degrees, the net that results from drawing the lines parallel to those axes is a *triaxial net*.

The surface pattern generated over an orthogonal biaxial net is referred to as a biaxial geometric pattern; the one generated over an oblique biaxial net is called an oblique biaxial geometric pattern; and the one generated over a triaxial net, a triaxial geometric pattern. The triaxial geometric patterns are rich in tesserae in the shape of an equilateral triangle and its derivatives (such as the lozenge with two 60-degree angles, hexagon, star of two triangles, and star of six lozenges). The orthogonal biaxial geometric patterns present an abundance of tesserae in the shape of a right triangle (semisquare and semirectangle) and its derivatives (such as the square, rectangle, lozenge, rhomboid, octagon, star of two squares, and star of eight rhomboids; figs. 4-100 through 4-105).

The geometric patterns classified as linear represent a subgroup of the surface geometric patterns, defined by the surface geometric patterns that carpet figures whose longitudinal component is very dominant. This becomes evident upon considering that a band or row is no more than a markedly long rectangle. When a geometric pattern tessellates a rectangle that is not particularly long, its classification is uncertain; I generally classify as linear those geometric patterns that cover oblong figures whose length is greater than three times their width.[15]

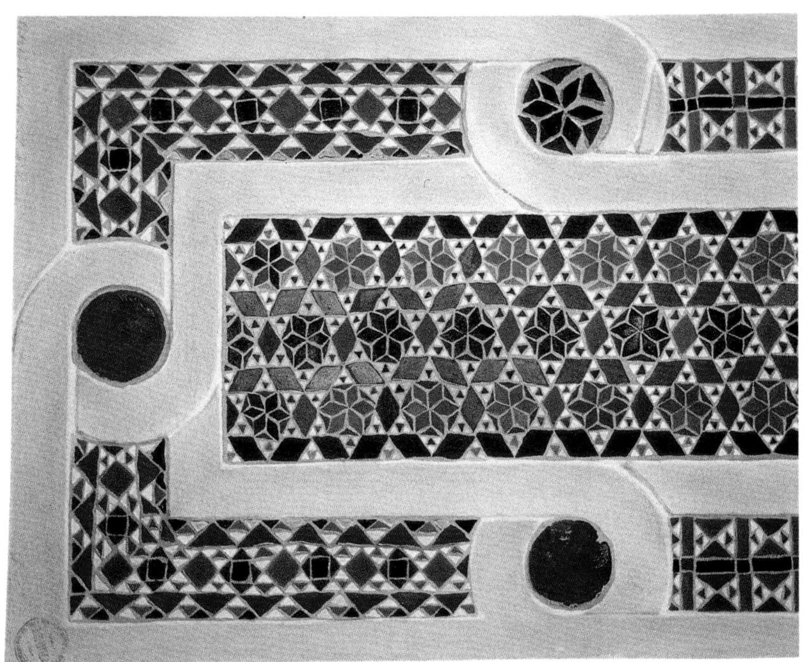

4-102. Detail of a panel showing a biaxial geometric pattern in the bordering band and a triaxial geometric pattern in the central surface. (Drawing, tempera on paper, A. Terzi, 1915–16)

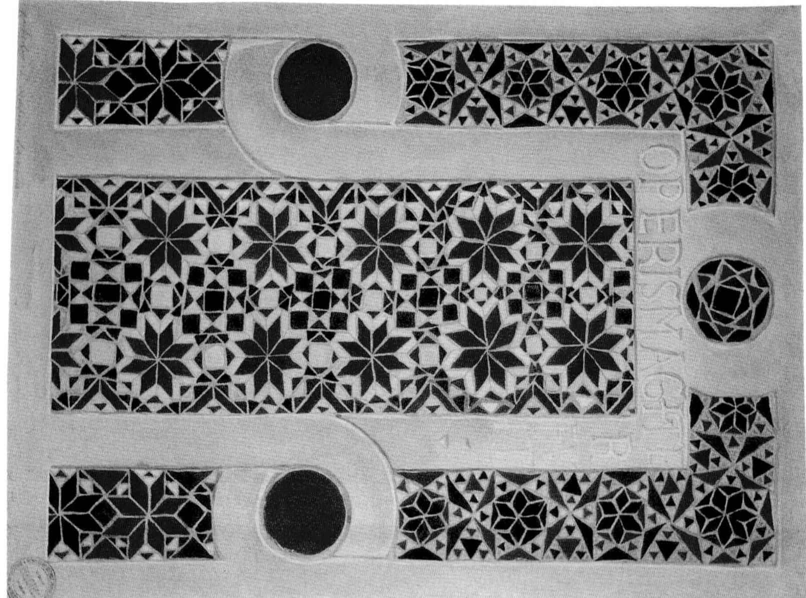

4-103. Detail of a panel showing a triaxial geometric pattern in the bordering band and a biaxial geometric pattern in the central surface. (Drawing, tempera on paper, A. Terzi, 1915–16)

4-104. Detail of a panel showing two perpendicular bands decorated with biaxial geometric patterns which flank surfaces bordered by white bands; a triaxial geometric pattern ornaments one of the surfaces. (Drawing, tempera on paper, A. Terzi, 1915–16)

4-105. Detail of three of the intervals of a mosaic, defined by an orthogonal grid of white bands. Each interval is covered with surface geometric patterns, one of which is triaxial and the other two are biaxial. (Drawing, tempera on paper, A. Terzi, 1915–16)

4-106. Mosaic of riverbed cobble. Pella: area 1, block n.1,A. (From J. Charbonneaux, 1973, fig. 58)

The Cosmatesque Process of Fragmentation Expressed in the Language of Fractals: The Case of the Sierpinski Triangle

In an effort to make the most of available construction materials while still satisfying the traditional local and Byzantine rules of design, the Cosmati fractionized the basic motifs of their patterns through a mechanism of subdivision that involved breaking a figure into small pieces by inscribing its inverse within it.

The oldest sources of mosaics with figures bearing their inscribed inverse seem to be Greece at Delos and Pella (fig. 4-106) and Italy at Pompeii. Surviving pavements from these places date back to the Hellenistic period (338–146 B.C.) and the early Roman period. These examples contain a motif identifiable as a rectangle bearing an inscribed lozenge, which in turn contains an inscribed rectangle, which is laden with an inscribed lozenge, and so on successively (fig. 4-107). Asher Ovadiah, relying on the absence of prior examples of similar design executed in other arts, holds that this motif owes its origin to the inventiveness of the mosaicists.[16] In the Roman mosaics of the second and first centuries B.C., designs of squares laden repeatedly with their inscribed inverse appear frequently, for example, in many of the floor tiles of the triclinium of the Casa dei Cervi in Herculaneum (fig. 4-108) and in the marble pavement in the porticoed building at the corner of the Decumanus and the Via dei Molini in Ostia (fig. 4-109).

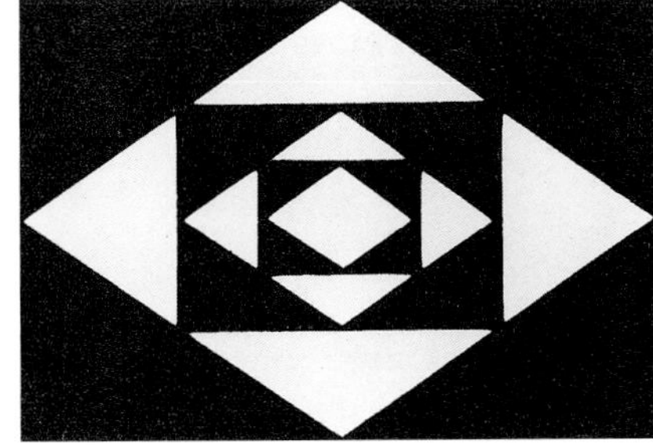

4-107. Lozenges and rectangles, one inscribed within the other.

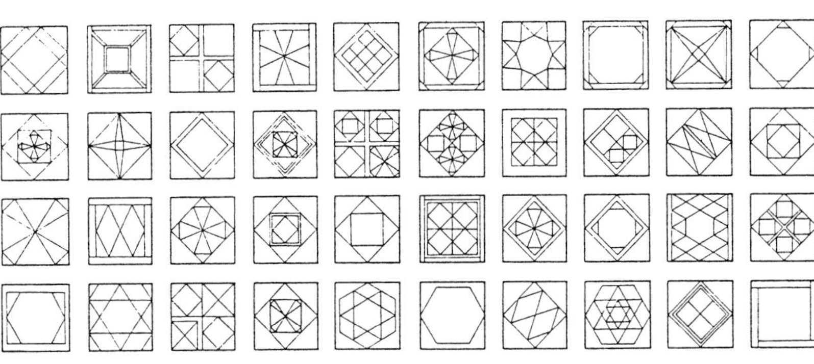

4-108. Tiles composed of various designs and marbles. Pavement of the triclinium, Casa dei Cervi, Herculaneum.

The loading of a figure with its inscribed inverse is a constant in the creation of Cosmatesque designs. In addition to operating in conjunction with the method of rotating squares, which, as explained earlier in this chapter, is used to position the peripheral roundels of a quincunx, this mechanism is the predominant configuration of the vast majority of the geometric patterns employed by the Roman marble artists of the twelfth century. The Cosmatesque patterns are simply the result of inscribing the corresponding inverted figures in the intervals of the patterns used by the Roman mosaicists of antiquity (as is evident in the paired figures illustrated in chapter 3).

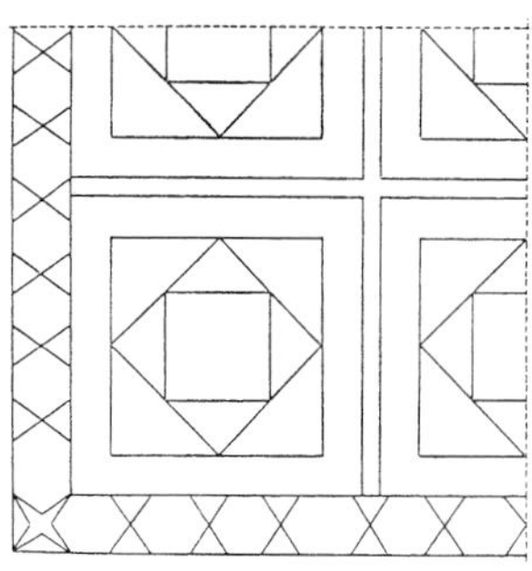

4-109. Marble pavement at the southern end of the portico of the building at the corner of the Decumanus and the Via dei Molini in Ostia.

Loading a figure with its inscribed inverse, immediately repeating that operation in the intervals of the resulting figure, and then continuing the same pattern of operation several times over, was the preferred method of fragmentation for the Cosmati. The geometric patterns created by this iterative mechanism are peculiar to Cosmatesque work. In particular, the designs carried out in this manner that employ only triangles appear very frequently (figs. 4-110, 4-111, and 4-112).

Thus far, the repetitive process of subdivision that the Cosmati employed to fractionize their geometric patterns has been explained in words. Today, thanks to a new language, the language of *fractals,* it is also possible to explain this process mathematically. This language, which stems from the findings of Benoît B. Mandelbrot and of Michael Barnsley, published in the 1980s, allows for precise and appropriate descriptions of structures that appear to have great complexity.[17]

In the language of fractals, the description of a figure relies on rules of calculus and algorithms. Fractals are those structures with a geometric property called *invariability to scale*, which means that if they are analyzed on different scales, the same basic elements appear again and again.[18] The fundamental

4-110. Cosmatesque designs created with triangles.

4-111. Inverted inscribed figures abound in these mosaic pavements. Santa Maria Maggiore, Rome, 431–1750. (Chromolithograph by F. M. Hessemer, 1842)

characteristic of fractals is their unusual dimension. The concept of *fractal dimension* is based on work published by Felix Hausdorf (1868–1942) in 1919. It is calculated by finding the fractal dimension D through the formula $a = s^D$, which provides the dimension as a quotient of two logarithms:

$$D = \log a / \log s$$

where D = dimension of self similarity; a = the number of equal parts into which an object is divided; and s = the factor of scale that converts any of the parts in the whole. The dimension that corresponds to the majority of structures with invariability to scale is *fractional*.[19] Hence the name fractals, which Mandelbrot gave these structures in the 1970s, a name derived from the French *fractale*, from the Latin *fractus*, which means broken.

A fractal has infinitely many elements and in this way is radically different from the objects such as triangles and circles studied in traditional euclidean

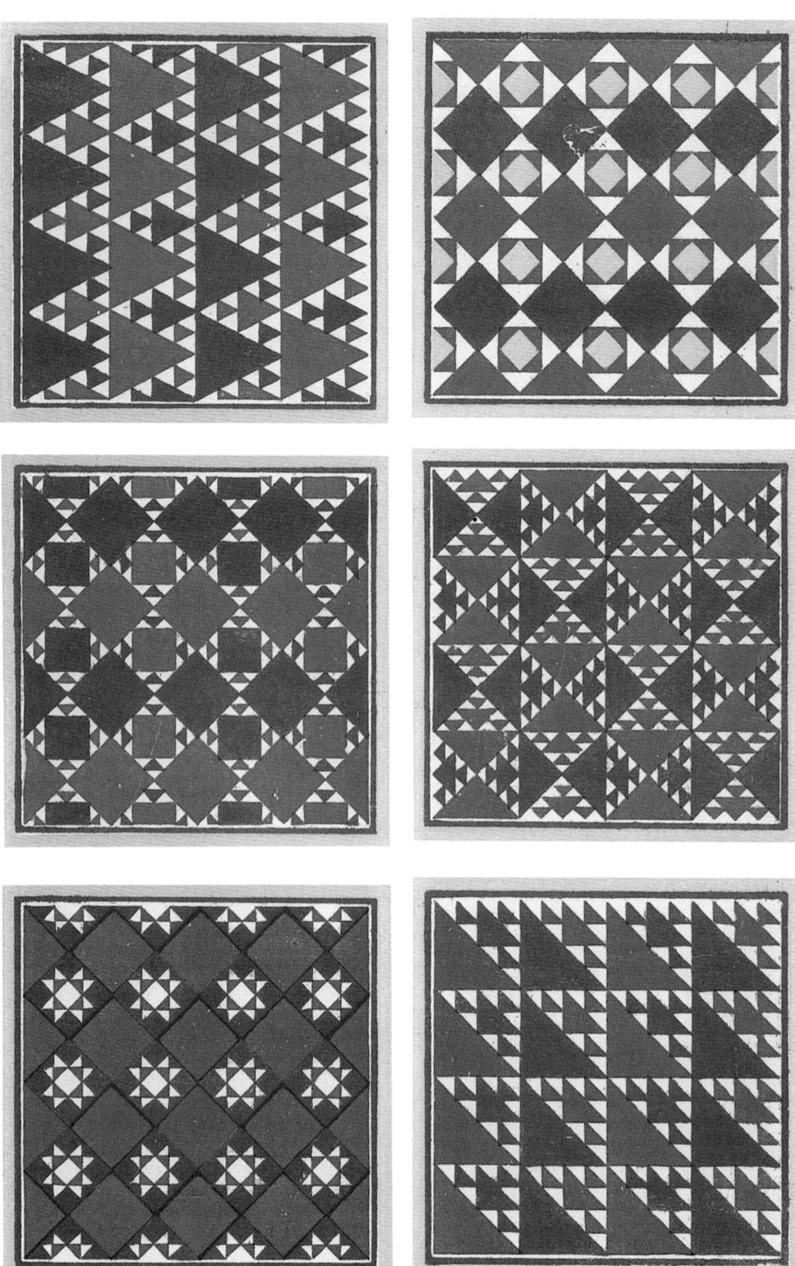

4-112. Inverted inscribed figures abound in these mosaic pavements. Santa Maria in Cosmedin, Rome, sixth through twelfth centuries. (Chromolithograph by F. M. Hessemer, 1842)

gemoetry. The German mathematicians Hartmut Jürgens, Heinz-Otto Peitgen, and Dietmar Saupe commented on these differences in their discussion of the language of fractals:

> Fractal geometry is, above all, a new language. But its elements are not derived from direct intuition, which distinguishes them essentially from the elements of Euclidean geometry, such as the line, the straight line, the circumference, or the sphere.
>
> Fractal geometry is expressed by means of algorithms, which is to say, by means of the rules and instructions of procedure, which require the help of a computer in order to turn into forms and structures. Furthermore, they are available in unlimited quantities.
>
> ... Traditional Euclidean geometry possesses only a few elements, such as the straight line, the circumference, etc. With these few elements more complex objects are constructed.... On the contrary, fractal geometry ... [is] composed of an infinite number of elements, radically different from

Euclidean ones. What are, then, these elements? The simplest manner to describe them consists of identifying them with rules of calculus or algorithms. Such algorithms can be considered directly as the significant units of fractal language.[20]

The problem lies in how to approach the rules of calculus that describe or create a fractal. Different techniques that facilitate this step have gradually been discovered: the Julia set, the Mandelbrot set, Aleatory Fractals, L-Systems, Iterated Function Systems. The explanation of one of these techniques, Iterated Function Systems, follows. It allows for the generation of figures through a process similar to the mechanism of fragmentation assiduously employed by the Cosmati: the cutting in a figure of a similar figure that has at its vertices the midpoints of the sides of the first figure.

Iterated Function Systems, discovered by Michael F. Barnsley, is a general procedure for generating an image by a series of *affine transforms*. The group of most reduced related transformations capable of describing a particular figure receives the name of *Iterated Function System*. How does one know which are the affine transforms that compose the group? Said Roger T. Stevens:

> An affine transform is the combination of a set of rotations, scalings, and linear translations. For a two-dimensional system, the effect of such a transform on a point (x_n, y_n) can be described by the following equations:
>
> $$x_{n+1} = a_i x_n + b_i y_n + e_i$$
>
> $$y_{n+1} = c_i x_n + d_i y_n + f_i$$
>
> Barnsley proved the collage theorem, which shows that a picture can be accurately described by defining the affine transforms that are needed to produce smaller replicas of the picture, positioned to tile the entire picture. The way this process is used is to start with a point and select from the group of affine transforms randomly in accordance with a probability table; where the probability that each transform occurring is usually proportional to the area of the picture that it will cover. The transform is applied to an initial point, another transform is selected and applied to a new point, and the process continues for as long as you want it to. The result is a picture that looks very much like the original.[21]

Therefore, the technique of Iterated Function Systems provides a mechanism for obtaining objects similar to themselves. In the words of A. K. Dewdney, "Upon applying to an object an infinite series of affine transforms, the picture obtained at the limit possesses the property of being self similar; that is, each portion of the result has, when amplified, the same aspect as the whole."[22]

The linear affine transforms of the plane are characterized by the fact of transforming straight lines into straight lines. This occurs in one of the classic fractals, the *Sierpinski Triangle* (figs. 4-113 and 4-114). This self-similar figure is one of the designs that appear most frequently in the geometric compositions of the Cosmati. Although the Sierpinski Triangle can be created by means of various techniques—Barnsley Fractals,[23] L-Systems,[24] and Iterated Function Systems—this discussion will examine only the third, because Iterated Function Systems is the only technique for creating fractals that corresponds with the systems of fractionalization employed by the Cosmati. The Sierpinski Triangle results from applying, to a system that consists of the points that compose a flat triangle, an Iterated Function

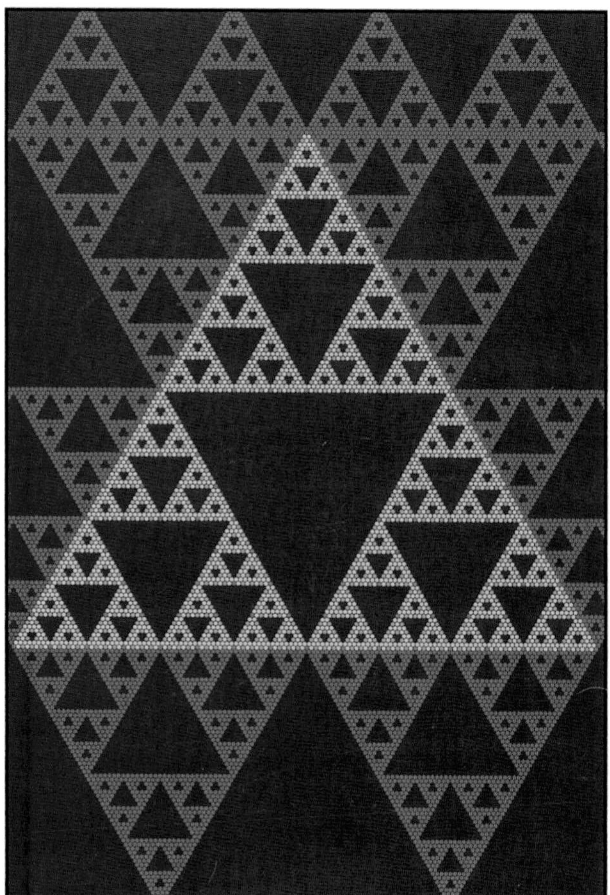

4-113. Equilateral Sierpinski triangle.

4-114. Guilloche of two eyelets; the center of each eyelet is laden with an equilateral Sierpinski triangle. Detail of the pavement in San Gregorio Magno, Rome.

4-115. Table of parameters for an isosceles triangle that has as its base the unequal side and whose height measures half the base. Each set of parameters occurs with a probability of 1/3.

a	b	c	d	e	f
0.50000	0.00000	0.00000	0.50000	0.00000	0.00000
0.50000	0.00000	0.00000	0.50000	1.00000	0.00000
0.50000	0.00000	0.00000	0.50000	0.50000	0.50000

4-116. Table of parameters for a right isosceles triangle, resting on a side adjacent to the right angle.

a	b	c	d	e	f
0.50000	0.00000	0.00000	0.50000	0.00000	0.00000
0.50000	0.00000	0.00000	0.50000	0.00000	1.00000
0.50000	0.00000	0.00000	0.50000	0.50000	0.50000

4-117. Right isosceles Sierpinski triangle, created with the Iterated Function Systems technique. From "Mathematical Recreations" by A. K. Dewdney. Copyright © 1990 by Scientific American, Inc. All rights reserved.

4-118. Table of parameters for an equilateral triangle.

a	b	c	d	e	f
0.50000	0.00000	0.00000	0.50000	0.00000	0.00000
0.50000	0.00000	0.00000	0.50000	0.50000	0.00000
0.50000	0.00000	0.00000	0.50000	0.25000	0.43301

4-119. [Below] Equilateral Sierpinski triangle, created with the Iterated Function Systems technique. From top to bottom, the figure shows the results of one, two, four, and six iterative transformations. Bottom two triangles from "The Language of Fractals," by Harmut Jürgens, Heinz-Otto Peitgen, & Dietmar Saupe. Copyright © 1990 by Scientific American, Inc. All rights reserved.

4-120. [Right, top] Linear chessboard pattern of poised squares in three rows; the intervals are filled with right isosceles Sierpinski triangles. Detail of the pavement, San Crisogono, Rome.

4-121. [Right, bottom] Centered pattern with equilateral Sierpinski triangles. Detail of the pavement, San Crisogono, Rome.

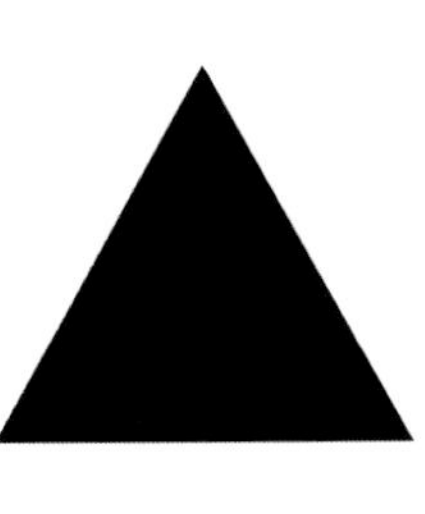

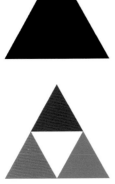

System comprising three affine transforms whose parameters (*a, b, c, d, e, f*) take the following values:

A. In an *isosceles* triangle that has as its base the unequal side and whose height measures half the base (fig. 4-115)[25]

B. In an *isosceles right* triangle, resting on a side adjacent to the right angle (figs. 4-116, 4-117, and 4-120)[26]

C. In an *equilateral* triangle (figs. 4-118, 4-119, and 4-121)

For the three types of triangles, the probability that each of the transformations will occur is equal to 1/3.

The Iterated Function System inherent in the Sierpinski Triangle transforms a triangle into a figure of the same outline composed of three triangles whose sides are half the length of the sides of the initial triangle. In the center of the resulting figure lies a blank space in the shape of an inverted triangle the same size as the other three. The transformation involves cutting into a solid triangle its inscribed inverse, and then repeating this operation in each of the resulting triangles in angle. The Cosmati interrupted the process of fragmentation when the size of the tesserae became so small that it reached the limit of manageability in construction.

Chapter 5

THE SIGNIFICATION

THE COSMATESQUE QUINCUNX: A DOUBLE-CROSS MOTIF

quincunx: [L, *quincunc-*, *quincunx*, lit. five twelfths, from *quinque* five + *uncia* twelfth part—more at FIVE, OUNCE] (1658): an arrangement of five things in a square or rectangle with one at each corner and one in the middle. (*Webster's Collegiate Dictionary*, tenth edition)

What Is a Quincunx?

Although dictionary definitions provide a sense of the shape and origins of the quincunx, understanding its significance requires further explanation, drawing on the meanings that some scholars of medieval and Byzantine art attribute to the term.

Richard Krautheimer, following the example of K. J. Conant, uses the term *quincunx* to designate a *three-dimensional* reality in his studies of Byzantine architecture.[1] He considers a quincunx to be an architectural type, one that, in fact, is the most widespread and characteristic of mid-Byzantine ecclesiastic construction.

To D. F. Glass, in her studies of the Cosmatesque mosaics that cover the floors of medieval churches in Rome, a quincunx designates a *flat* geometric ornament. That is also the meaning used in this book.

Glass used the term *quincunx* in her monograph on Cosmatesque pavements, in which she collected her research in a very advanced stage.[2] In a much earlier study that, slightly modified, would form part of the monograph in which she focused on the iconography of the pavements,[3] she called the quincunx design, less accurately, *quatrefoil* (from the Latin *quatri-*, four, and

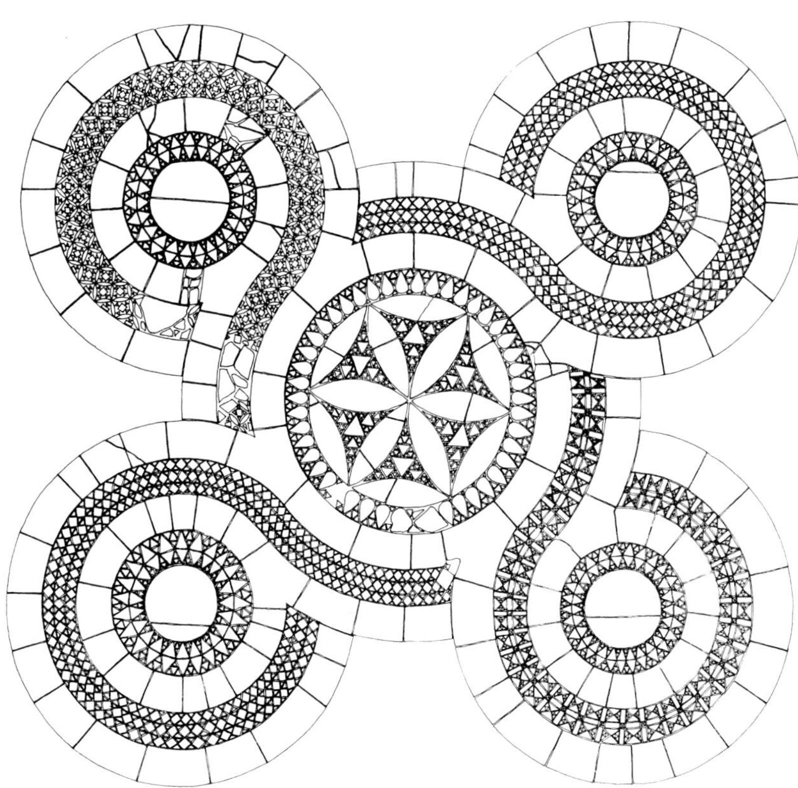

5-1. Example of a Cosmatesque quincunx. Detail of the pavement of the crypt in the cathedral of Anagni (Cosmas, Luca, and Jacopo, 1231); fourth motif from the north in the series of tangential quincunxes that carpet the nave of the crypt.

folium, leaf), a term that she abandoned completely in favor of quincunx in later studies. Glass, unlike Krautheimer, has never definitively explained why she decided to use the term quincunx, even though finding an appropriate name for this Cosmatesque motif apparently was not an easy task for her.

The following pages will focus more thoroughly on both Krautheimer's spatial quincunx and Glass's flat quincunx, as well as the relationship between them.

To study the origins and significance of the quincunx, it is necessary to be familiar with its appearance. The Cosmatesque quincunx, or the flat quincunx, is a flat polychrome geometric ornament composed of five roundels linked by interlacing strands. One of the roundels, larger than the other four, is enclosed within an imaginary square, occupying the motif's center; the four remaining roundels are placed in the residual space left free by the central roundel, one in each angle. The interlacing strands that connect the roundels are generally composed of three bands, two white marble borders and one central strip containing linear geometric patterns. This central band is divided into four curling lines that constitute a graph in the form of a swastika with undulating arms. The round openings, or eyelets, bear roundels of two colors, red and green—one color for the central roundel and the other for the four corner roundels—or contain centered geometric patterns. These patterns, linear and centered, are executed in *opus sectile* of minute pieces, in four counterchanged colors, two dark, red and green, and two light, white and yellow (fig. 5-1).

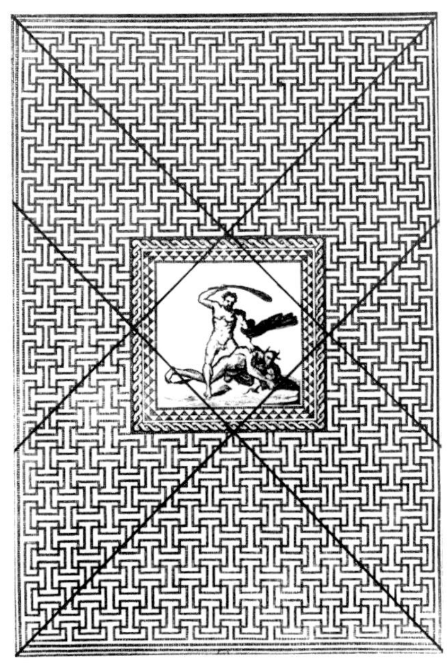

5-2. Roman mosaic with a figurative emblem in the middle of a geometric field. (Aix-en-Provence, France; G. Lafaye, Inv. des mos. de la Gaule, no. 47)

In some of their geometric mosaics in *opus tessellatum*, the Romans of antiquity placed an *emblem*, an elaborate motif, preferably figurative.[4] Inserted into the center of the homogeneous geometric field, it dominated the arrangement of the decorative composition, becoming the visual focus of the mosaic (fig. 5-2).

Inscribing a quincunx in a square of the gross framework, as was normal in Cosmatesque pavements, created residual intervals, or interspaces. These

5-3. *Example of a quincunx-in-square. Detail of the main quincunx of the early-twelfth-century pavement from the church of Santi Quattro Coronati, Rome.*

intervals were filled with surface geometric patterns, also executed in tetrachrome *opus sectile* of minute pieces. A square thus bearing a quincunx is a *quincunx-in-square* (fig. 5-3).

The quincunx-in-square can be considered the emblem of the Cosmatesque mosaics: a geometric emblem, regulated by curved forms (the interlacings), which was inserted into a background, also geometric, regulated by grids drawn with straight lines (the decoration with surface geometric patterns of the rectangular panels).

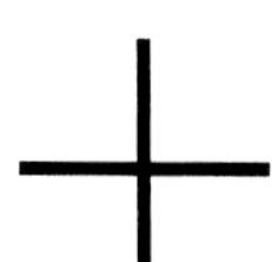

5-4. *Greek cross.*

5-5. *Decussate cross with perpendicular lines.*

The Underlying Geometry of the Cosmatesque Quincunx: The Double Cross

The simplest underlying linear schema in the Cosmatesque quincunx comprises four lines grouped, two by two, in two crosses: one straight and the other poised, both centered at the same point. The straight cross, of equal arms, is a *Greek cross* (fig. 5-4). The poised cross is a *decussate cross* (in the form of an X) of perpendicular lines (fig. 5-5). It is also known as Saint Andrew's cross.

5-6. *Double cross.*

A double cross is a form composed of a decussate cross superimposed on a Greek cross (fig. 5-6). The double cross is the regulating design underlying the geometry of the Cosmatesque quincunx.

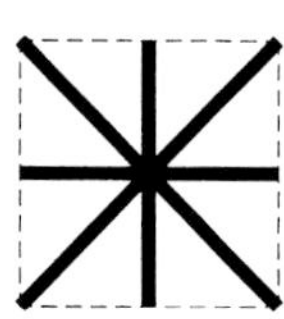

5-7. *Square asterisk.*

When the double cross is inscribed in a square, it is a *square asterisk* (fig. 5-7), because it has the shape of an eight-pointed asterisk whose diagonal lines touch the vertices of the square that circumscribes it. The two diagonal bars are, therefore, longer than the other two. A square asterisk always underlies the Cosmatesque quincunx. A double cross inscribed in an octagon is an *octagonal asterisk* (fig. 5-8), and an asterisk inscribed in a circle is a *circular asterisk* (fig. 5-9). All of these designs are akin to the regulating pattern of the flat quincunx.

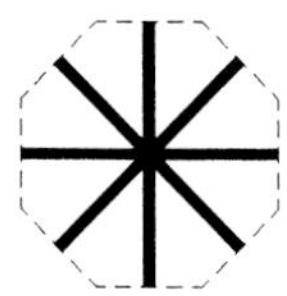

5-8. *Octagonal asterisk.*

A structure is a *quincuncial composition* when the basic regulating diagram underlying it is a square asterisk. Therefore, the Cosmatesque quincunx is always a quincuncial composition, but it is not the only one; an infinite number of structures can receive the same label.

5-9. *Circular asterisk.*

The Origins of the Square Asterisk

A variety of structures, from different places and times, exhibit regulating designs analogous to the square asterisk underlying the flat quincunx. A study of these structures sheds some light on the possible antecedents of the geometry of the Cosmatesque quincunx.

Among the decorative geometric motifs of the primitive mosaics that flourished in various locations in the Mediterranean world (Italy, Sicily, the lands of the Aegean, Asia Minor, Israel, and the area at the mouth of the Nile) from the classical period (500–338 B.C.) until the age of Augustus (27 B.C.–A.D. 14), five cruciform motifs already existed. In Pompeii excavated mosaics that date from the first century B.C. display the motif of the cross contained in a square (fig. 5-10). In Delos, Pompeii, and Rome, the motif of the cross of equal arms formed by squares was used (fig. 5-11); in Delos and Pompeii, the quincunx formed by equal squares (fig. 5-12); in Pompeii, the quincunx formed by equal rhombuses (fig. 5-13); in Olynthus and Pompeii, the gammadion or swastika (fig. 5-14). A. Ovadiah, in studying the origins of these cruciform ornaments, through comparative examples taken from the arts that preceded mosaic pavements (such as weaving, sculpture, architecture, ceramics, metalwork), affirms that the first mosaicists must have copied the cross contained in a square from the numerous metal coins that, from the seventh to the fourth centuries B.C., displayed this motif in Greece and Asia Minor. He found the origin of the rest of the cruciform designs in the decorations painted on Greek ceramic pots in the archaic period (800–500 B.C.). The swastika was an especially popular motif that appeared in all of the arts and extended over a vast area, including Greece, Italy, and Egypt.[5]

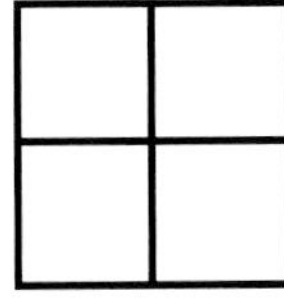

5-10. Cross contained in a square.

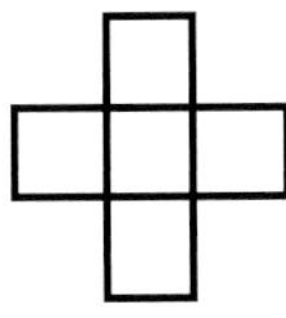

5-11. Cross of equal arms formed by squares.

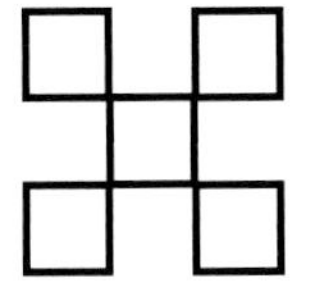

5-12. Quincunx formed by equal squares.

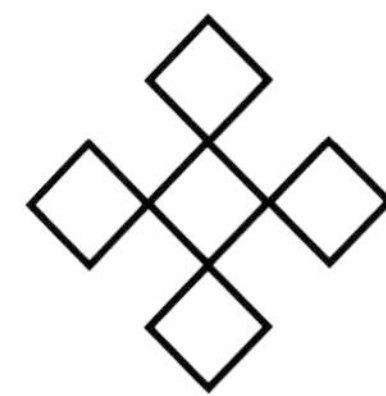

5-13. Quincunx formed by equal rhombuses.

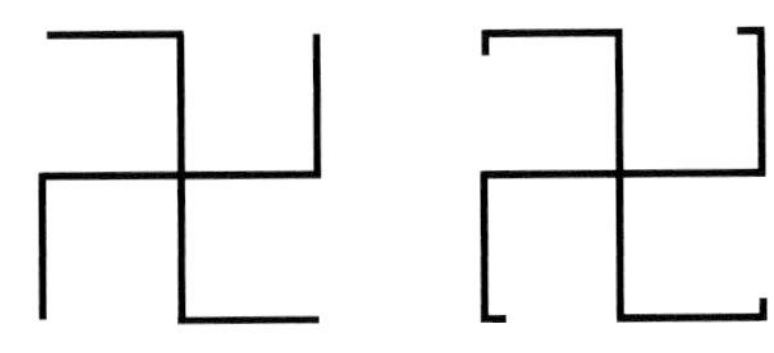

5-14. Gammadion or swastika.

Some of the most significant examples of early quincuncial compositions were executed in porphyry, the most precious marble of the ancient age.[6] Thus, in the apse of the basilica of the tetrarchic villa at Piazza Armerina in Sicily, built in about A.D. 300, lie the remains of an *opus sectile* pavement with porphyry square panels and roundels that very probably marked the place of the throne of the emperor or imperial magistrate.[7] One of the squares is ensconced in the angles between four roundels.

Porphyry was abundant in Constantinople in all of the building activity of late antiquity (in the third and fourth centuries A.D.). In the famous Constantinian imperial palace was a square pavilion, with a view of the ocean and the port, that had a pyramidal roof and a pavement with insertions of porphyry. Its walls were also clad in porphyry. This pavilion, which bore the Greek name for porphyry, was the birthing room of the empress. Hence came the designation *porphyrogenitus* emperors, meaning "born in the purple," from the Greek *porphýreos*, "of purple," and the Latin *genitus*, "generated."[8] The sacred birth of the emperor/god took place under a cross formed by the two diagonals that are the plan projection of the edges of the pyramidal roof.[9]

Under Constantine (306–337) and his successors, porphyry would continue to be associated with the use that had always distinguished it: the glorification of the emperor, especially in the key moments of his life: birth, coronation, and death. At the same time, it would begin to become associated with the architecture and decorations of the ecclesiastic liturgy.

In the pavement in the ancient basilica of San Pietro in Rome were several large porphyry *rotae* for the ceremony of imperial coronation, which during the Middle Ages was celebrated in this Christian church because God presumably named his representative on earth. Sources that state that one of these *rotae*, located at the exterior of the main door, was surrounded by four smaller roundels arranged in the form of a cross attest to the existence of a group of roundels in a quincuncial arrangement.[10]

In the church of Santa Croce in Ravenna were four porphyry *rotae* in front of a poorly identified building (*ante nominatas regias*). The empress Galla Placidia (circa 390–450) spent whole nights praying, kneeling at the center of the four roundels, over which had been placed candles and candelabra.[11] While praying, Galla Placidia joined the four peripheral porphyry *rotae* into a quincuncial group in which she occupied the central point, probably kneeling over a fifth *rota*.[12]

The wave of Eastern influence that swept over the mosaic art of the western Mediterranean during the second half of the fourth century and the fifth century was characterized by a new aesthetic based on interlacing as a decorative norm. Dimas Fernández-Galiano studied various mosaics in *opus tessellatum* on the Iberian peninsula with design directly related to the Byzantine interlacing mosaics.[13] Like their eastern predecessors, the Iberian mosaics display geometric compositions inscribed in a square—or in a circle or in a combination of both—divided into four or eight parts (fig. 5-15). The mosaic of Dulcitius from the villa of the Ramalete (Navarra), from the end of the fourth century or early fifth century (fig. 5-15d), is the most comparable to the Cosmatesque interlacings because of its entirely curved designs. By uniting two by two the diametrically opposed peripheral roundels, a cross and a superposed X-shaped cross are revealed. The asterisk of eight points, drawn by means of four lines at 45-degree angles that pass through the center of the central roundel, underlying the generating geometry of the mosaic of Dulcitius, is a double cross inscribed in a circle: a circular asterisk.

In Rome the sixth-century pavement of the church of Santa Maria Antiqua in the Roman Forum contains mosaics of large tesserae filling the intervals of the orthogonal grid that compartmentalizes the pavement. They display simple designs with an underlying double cross drawn with straight and curved lines in a quatrefoil design; the center of each bears a small porphyry disc (see chapter 3 for a floor plan of this pavement).

Among the examples in his study about the components of the decorative taste of the Cosmati, Guglielmo Matthiae cites the painted panel in the apse of the ancient basilica of San Crisogono in Rome, attributed to the time of Gregory III (731–34). The quincunxes with X-shaped crosses in this fresco offer a fairly evolved example of what would become the essential motif in the Cosmatesque works of the twelfth and thirteenth centuries (fig. 5-16).[14]

The excavations of the church of San Giovanni Evangelista in Ravenna, in a stratum 1.87 meters (6.14 feet) below ground, dating from prior to 1213, have revealed remains of mosaic pavements executed in a spare geometric *opus tessellatum*. The designs are formed by the interlacing of straight lines and arcs that produce double-cross schemata.[15] Particularly noteworthy is a panel consisting of a border decorated with intersecting semicircles that frame a rectangle composed of three adjacent squares containing figures of quincuncial composition (fig. 5-17). Raffaella Olivieri Farioli noted that the figure of the central square could be based on a Byzantine predecessor in

5-15. Interlacing mosaics from the latter half of fourth century to the fifth century A.D.

a. Diagram of the mosaic of La Almunia de Doña Godina (Saragossa, Spain).

b. Diagram of the mosaic of the basilica of Ermione. Predecessor to the mosaic in fig. 5-15a.

c. Diagram of the mosaic of the basilica of Belén. Predecessor to the mosaic in 5-15a.

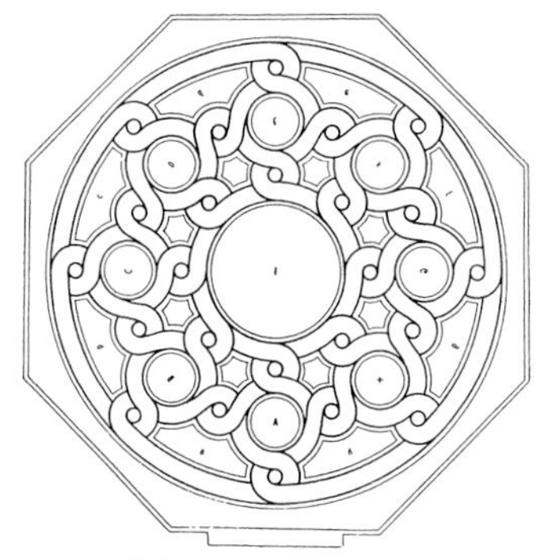

d. Diagram of the mosaic of Dulcitius in the villa of the Ramalete (Navarra, Spain).

5-16. *Painted panel from the lower church, San Crisogono, Rome.*

5-17. *The remains of a mosaic found below ground in the right aisle of the church of San Giovanni Evangelista, Ravenna.*

opus sectile, like the pavement from the eleventh century in the abbey of Pomposa.[16] The designs created by the interlacing of arcs frequently appear in the pavements from the other side of the Alps as of the tenth century and find graphic antecedents in the decorations of Carolingian manuscripts.

To understand thoroughly the deep architectural roots that produced the underlying geometry of the Cosmatesque quincunx, it is necessary to review the architecture of Byzantine churches.[17]

The prolific construction of Byzantine ecclesiastic buildings from the seventh to the thirteenth centuries almost always produced *centralized architectural types*: the principal types are the cross-domed plan, the atrophied Greek-cross plan, the octagon-domed plan, the Greek-cross octagon plan, and the quincunx plan.

In the 250 years after Justinian's rule (600–850), which includes the iconoclastic century (726–843), the cross-domed church was the dominant type. The nucleus of this type of church, surrounded on three sides with aisles and galleries, formed a cross; the center of the nucleus was covered with a dome and its four short arms with barrel vaults resting on four strong corner piers. The buildings most representative of this type are the church of Koimesis in

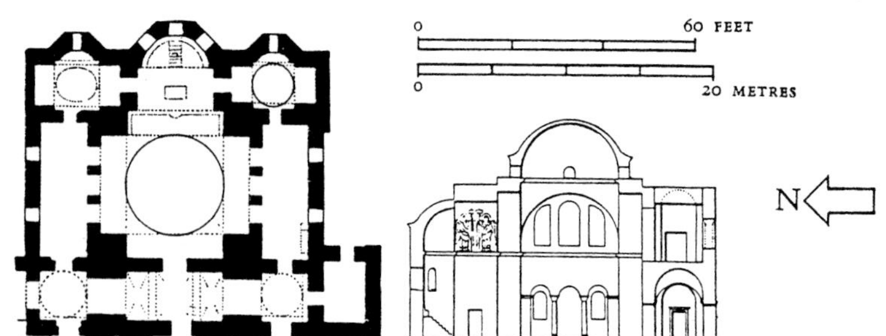

5-18. *Floor plan and cross section of the circa early-eighth-century church of Koimesis, Nicaea (now Iznik).*

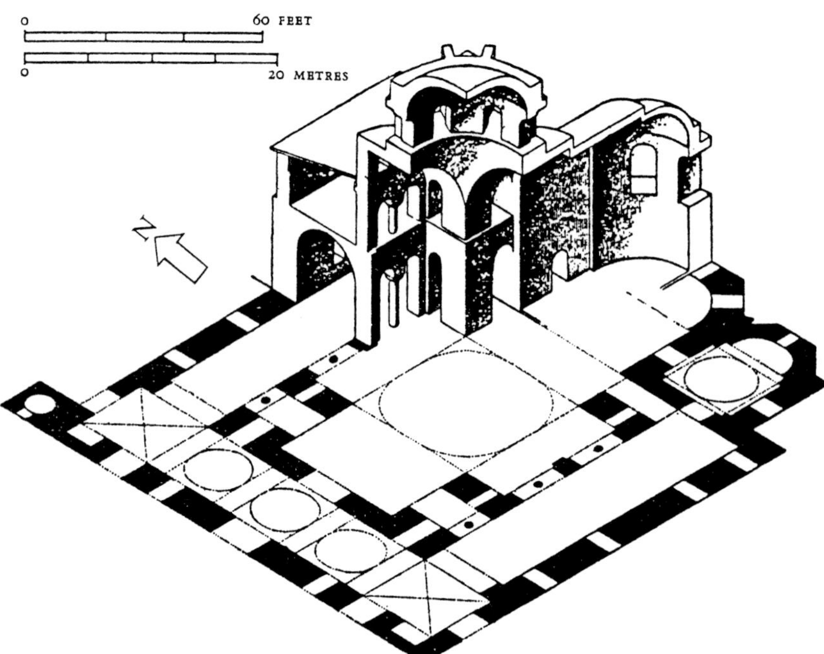

5-19. *Isometric perspective of the circa early-eighth-century church of Hagia Sophia, Salonika.*

Nicaea (fig. 5-18), the church of Hagia Sophia in Salonika (fig. 5-19), and the Kalenderhane Cami (fig. 5-20) and the Gül Cami in Constantinople.[18] Morphological comparisons with other earlier archeological remains imply that the cross-domed plan must have arisen much earlier, possibly in the sixth century, and that it might have been a creation of the Justinian circle, in the final years of his reign. On the southern coast of Turkey, in Antalya (Adalia), are the ruins of the Cumanin Cami from the end of the sixth century (fig. 5-21). This church, although surmounted by a wooden structure, shows a basic floor plan equivalent to those of the eighth-century cross-domed churches of Nicaea and Salonika.

The middle of the ninth century to the beginning of the thirteenth century (864–1204) was a period of cultural resurgence under the Macedonian dynasty, an era that has come to be called the middle-Byzantine age. While a few examples of obsolete architectural types were reborn or survived from earlier eras because of special circumstances or local predilection,[19] during this period new types arose. These types, possibly inspired by buildings in the outlying areas of the empire, may not have been unprecedented, but they transformed the preexisting types so radically that they can be considered new. They were the atrophied Greek-cross plan, the octagon-domed plan, the Greek-cross octagon plan, and the quincunx plan (also called cross-in-square plan). The first three were creations of the middle-Byzantine

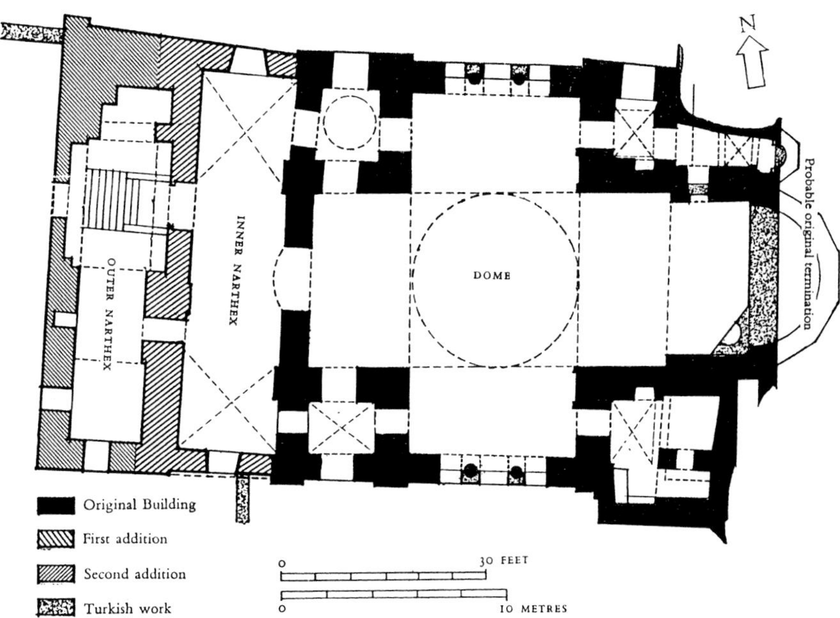

5-20. *Floor plan of the circa mid-ninth-century Kalendarhane Cami (church of Akataleptos), Constantinople.*

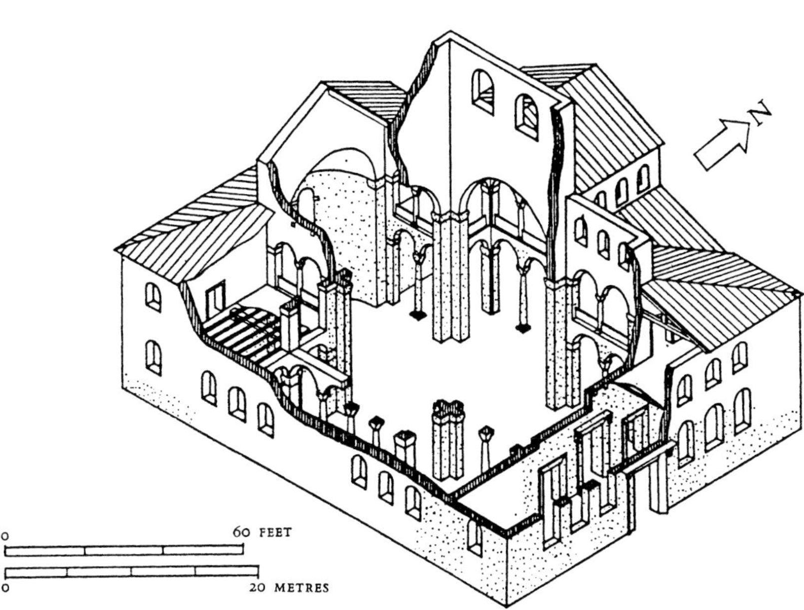

5-21. *Isometric reconstruction of the late-sixth-century Cumanin Cami, Antalya (Adalia). (The dotted areas still exist.)*

age, in the tradition of centralized church designs, uninterrupted and consistent since the sixth century. The quincunx plan appeared, although very rarely (apparently transferred from secular or semireligious buildings of late antiquity), much earlier than the previous three, in preiconoclastic or iconoclastic times, but it consolidated in the middle-Byzantine age.

The atrophied Greek-cross church could be defined as the isolated nucleus of a cross-domed church. It consisted of a central bay with four arms of very little depth and one or three apses; the barrel vaults over the arms were essentially wide arches, and the dome over the central bay was perforated with large windows. Apparently this plan was derived from the Greek-cross churches from the time of Justinian, with deeper arms and corner aisles, or from the cross-domed churches from the period immediately following Justinian. An example of this type is the original core of the Chora church (Kahrie Cami) in Constantinople, from the eleventh and twelfth centuries.

The atrophied Greek-cross buildings do not constitute an important group among the middle-Byzantine churches, whose general character was dominated by octagon-domed, Greek-cross octagon, and quincunx types.

The octagon-domed church is, in essence, a square plan, its corners bridged by squinches, which support a dome over the resulting octagon. This type was carried to the Aegean island of Chios (off the western coast of Turkey) from Constantinople. A handful of examples survive on the island, in particular, the church of Nea Moni. As the floor plan of this church in figure 5-22 indicates, the central area of the interior narthex (esonarthex) is covered by an octagonal pumpkin dome with an opaion (the circular opening at the apex of the dome). Under this dome is found the design in quincunx that ornaments the pavement in *opus sectile* of the esonarthex (see chapter 3 for an illustration of this pavement). As much the quincunx as the dome above it are structures in double-cross design: the one above, an octagonal asterisk; the one below, a square asterisk.

The Greek-cross octagon church can be defined as the fusion of a central nave, in the form of a domed octagon, and a Greek cross of arms covered by

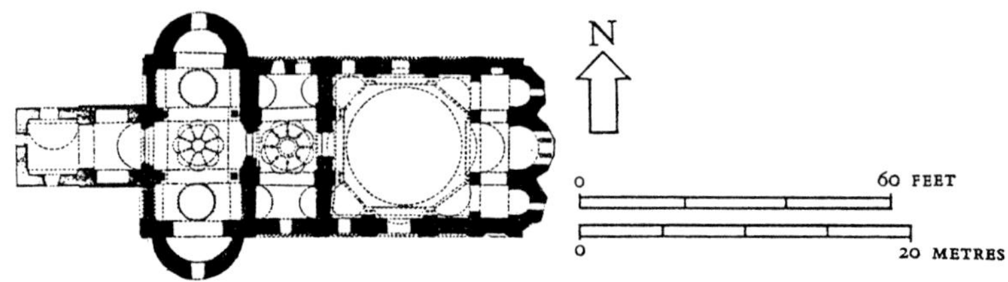

5-22. Floor plan of the church of Nea Moni (1042–56), Chios.

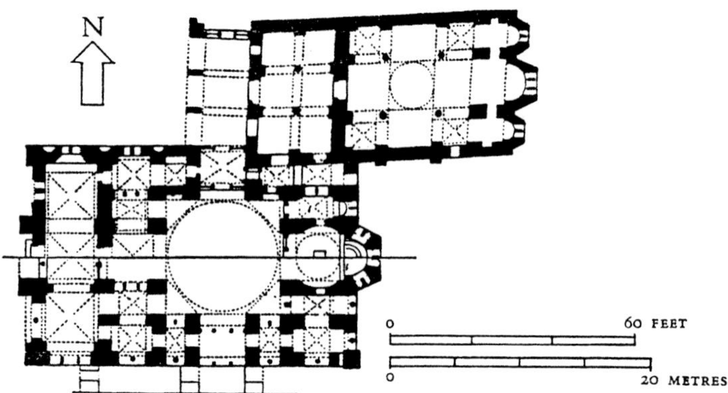

5-23. Floor plan of the eleventh-century church of Katholikon (to the south); floor plan of the mid-tenth-century church of the Theotokos (to the north), both in the monastery of Hosios Lukas, Phocis.

5-24. Isometric of the eleventh-century church of Katholikon (to the right); isometric of the mid-tenth-century church of the Theotokos (to the left), both in the monastery of Hosios Lukas, Phocis.

barrel vaults, encroaching on an outer belt of aisles and sometimes galleries, all of which is enclosed in an exterior square or rectangle; it is also called a church with squinches in the angles. The most representative examples are the eleventh-century church of the Katholikon in the monastery of Hosios Lukas in Phocis (figs. 5-23 and 5-24) and the church in Daphni. Both show a beautiful and complex play of interpenetrating spaces, high and low, light and dark. The Greek-cross octagon is perhaps the most impressive of the middle-Byzantine plans, although, like the octagon-domed type, it is not very widespread. The surviving examples are found in continental Greece. The Greek-cross octagon church seems to arise from the meeting of the spatial conception of purely Byzantine tradition with constructive solutions imported from regions bordering the empire.[20]

The quincunx or the spatial quincunx is the most widespread middle-Byzantine church plan. Richard Krautheimer provides the following definition:

> Quincunx: A structure divided into nine bays, the centre bay a large square, the corner bays small squares, the remaining four bays rectangular; the centre bay, resting on four columns, is domed; the corner bays are either domed or groin-vaulted; the rectangular bays are, as a rule, barrel-vaulted; also referred to as cross-in-square, cross-inscribed, *'croix-inscrite'* [figs. 5-25 and 5-26].[21]

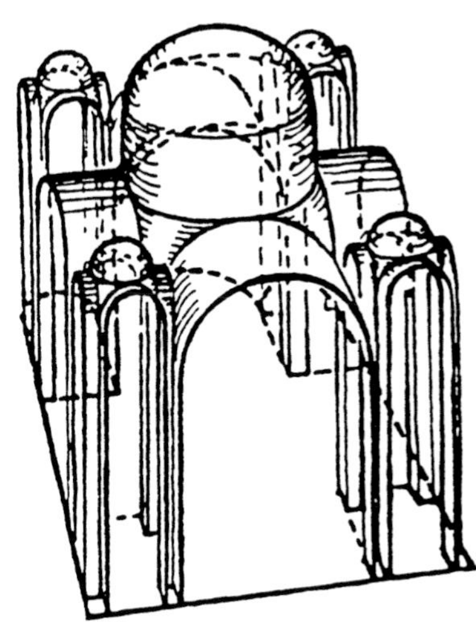

5-25. A three-dimensional, or spatial, quincunx, according to Richard Krautheimer.

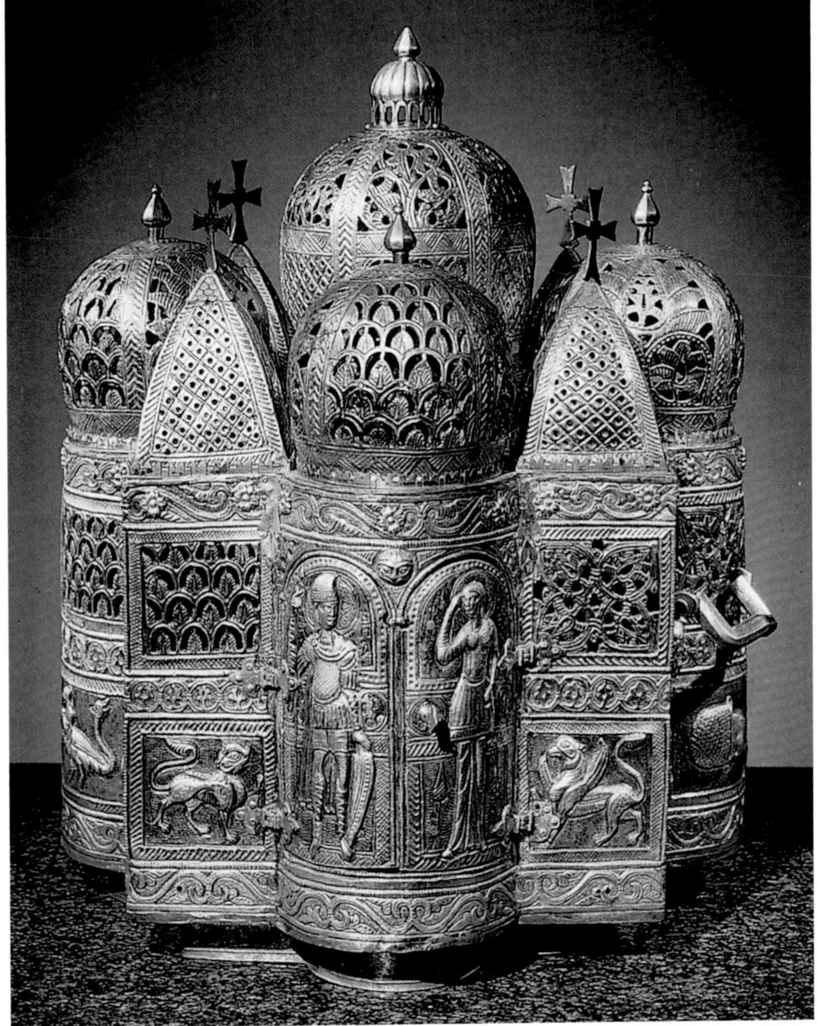

5-26. "Model" of spatial quincunx, a twelfth-century censer of gold and silver (Treasury of S. Marco, Venice).

Structures that may be possible antecedents to the spatial quincunx existed in the ninth century in Constantinople and in the eighth to ninth centuries in the provinces (in the west, France, Spain, Italy; in the east, Asia Minor, Thrace) and in areas bordering the empire (Iran, Armenia). In addition, spatial-quincunx structures had existed in the Roman and Byzantine Near East: in the second century, in Syria, a small building in the Roman camp of Mousmieh, which must have served as a temple (a religious building) or a praetorium (a secular building imbued with religious connotations); in the sixth century, outside the walls of R'safah, a local chieftain, Al-Mundir, had as an audience hall a spatial-quincunx construction executed by Byzantine artists from the provinces. At some point between the sixth and the ninth centuries, the plan of the spatial-quincunx audience hall was apparently transferred to ecclesiastic construction. The cross-domed church (for example, Koimesis in Nicaea, Hagia Sophia in Salonika), the middle-Byzantine type that generally is accepted as the starting point in the evolution that produced the quincuncial plan, very possibly influenced that transfer collaterally.[22]

The spatial quincunx became the almost universally accepted type throughout the Byzantine realm from the tenth century until the fall of Constantinople, surviving in Russia and the Balkans until much later dates. Examples of this type include: the tenth-century church of Theotokos (the Mother of God) in the monastery of Hosios Lukas in Phocis (see figs. 5-23 and 5-24), the church of the monastery of Hosios Meletios, near Megara, from the eleventh century (fig. 5-27), and the church of San Nicola in Olynthus, from the last third of the eleventh century (fig. 5-28).[23]

From the ninth to the fifteenth century, numerous churches arose in the various regions of Byzantine influence that followed centralized architectural plans derived from the principal types (figs. 5-29, 5-30, and 5-31).

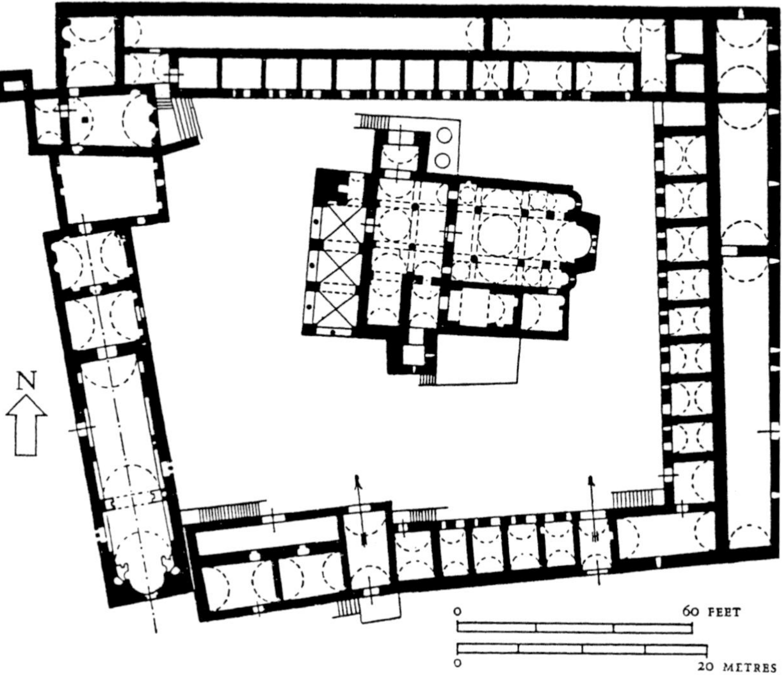

5-27. Floor plan (in the center) of the eleventh-century church of the Monastery of Hosios Meletios, Megara.

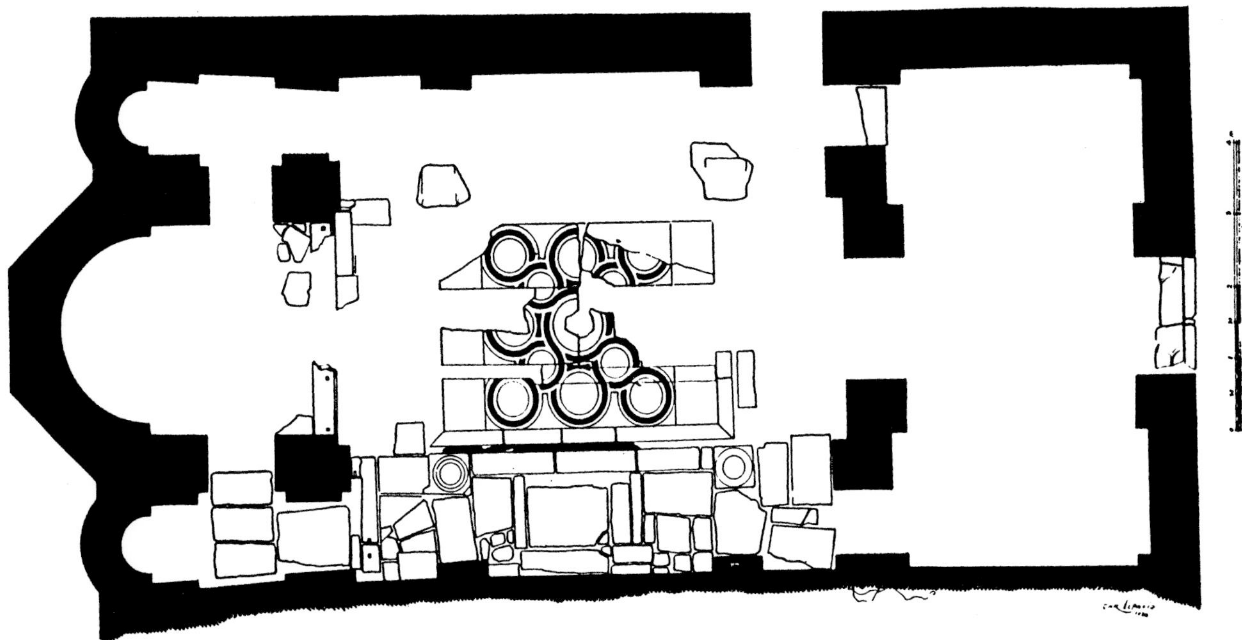

5-28. *Floor plan of the eleventh-century church of San Nicola, Olynthus.*

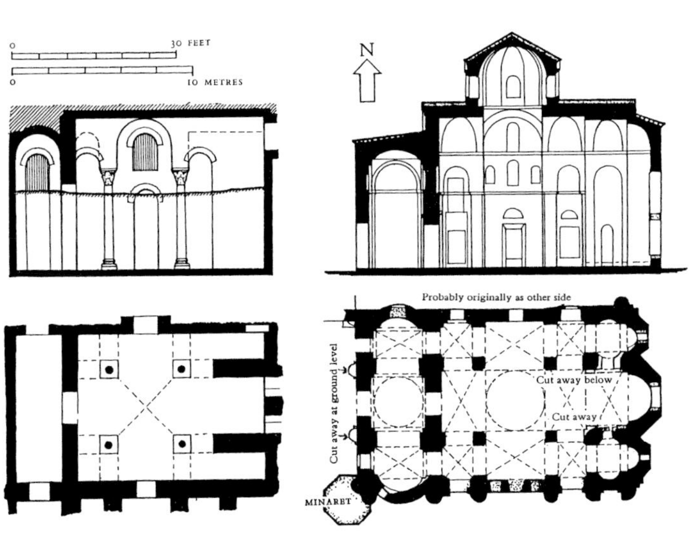

5-29. *Cross sections and floor plans of the upper and lower church of the tenth-century Budrum Cami, Constantinople.*

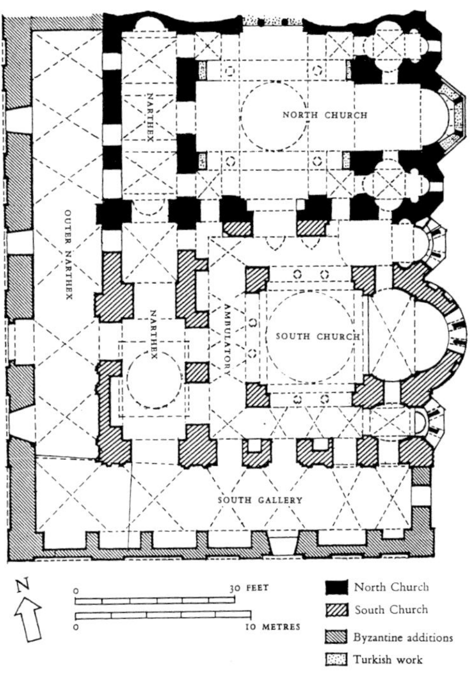

5-30. *Floor plan of the tenth-century Fenari Isa Cami (Church of the Lips of Constantine), Constantinople.*

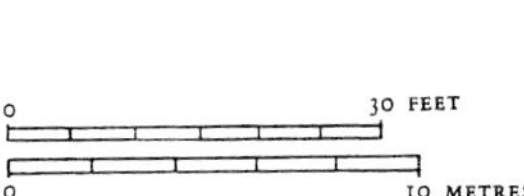

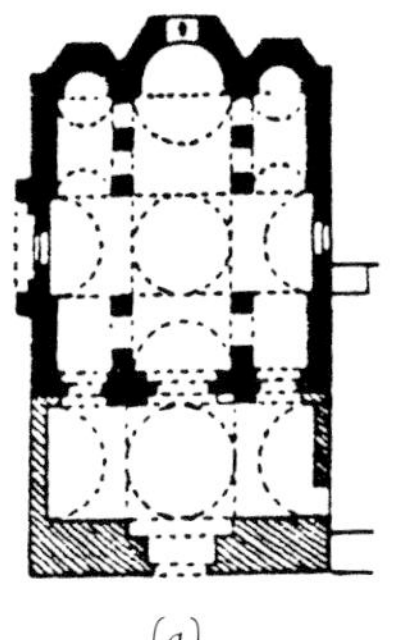

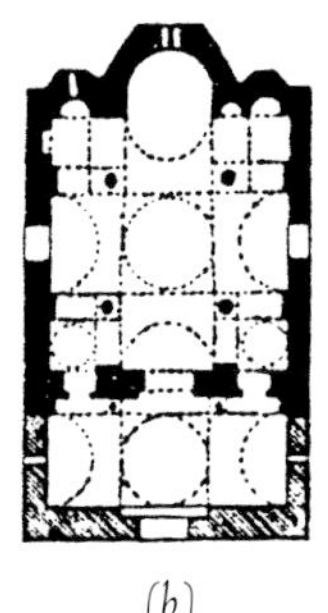

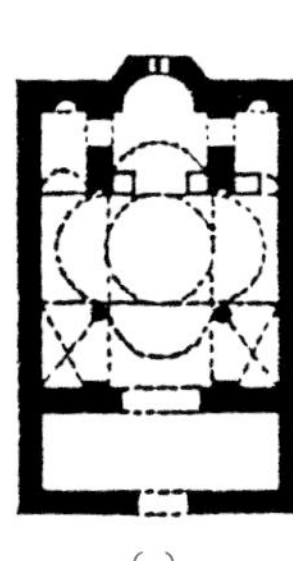

5-31. *Floor plans: (a) late-eleventh-century church, Kaisariani, Hymettos; (b) early-twelfth-century Saint John the Theologian, Hymettos; (c) late-eleventh-century Hagia Yoannis, Ligourio.*

Although the derivative plans and their examples can be examined in more depth,[24] sufficient evidence has already been presented to demonstrate that the plan projections of the spatial structures that constitute those types are regulated by cruciform designs similar to the underlying design of the Cosmatesque quincunx (flat quincunx). The cross-domed plan is regulated by a Greek cross inscribed in a square; the atrophied Greek-cross plan, by a Greek cross; the octagon-domed plan, by an octagonal asterisk; the Greek-cross octagon plan, by a square-octagonal asterisk; and finally, the quincunx plan, by a square asterisk, that is, by a geometric trace identical to that underlying the Cosmatesque quincunx.

What regulating traces control the flat structures that ornament the floor plan of these spatial structures? To respond to this question, it is necessary to study the mosaic remains still visible on the floors of some middle-Byzantine churches.

5-32. Pavement of the arms of the transept, church of Katholikon (Greek-cross octagon) (1020–40), monastery of Hosios Lukas, Phocis. (R. Schultz and S. Barnsley, 1901, plate 31)

The remains of the tenth-century pavement in the narthex of the church of Theotokos provide a fairly exact idea of the type of composition in *opus sectile* that covered the narthex of a quincunx church (see chapter 3 for an illustration of this pavement). The type of composition that ornamented the floor of the central bay of a spatial quincunx can be studied in the mosaic remains in *opus sectile* of the church of San Nicola at Olynthus, discovered in the excavations led by David M. Robinson (see fig. 5-28 and chapter 3).

The pavement in the quincunx church at Olynthus is the latest of numerous examples used by Goffredo Bendinelli to explore the origin of the Cosmatesque pavements. Bendinelli describes the geometric emblem occupying the center of the central bay:

> The mosaic, of a fairly simple geometric design, results from a central roundel flanked by four smaller roundels and by four others slightly larger in the intervals; four others of the same dimensions, arranged diagonally, are in contact with the smaller roundels. The whole design, composed of thirteen roundels with white and dark concentric bands, is inscribed into a square. More than a mosaic pavement, one would say that it is a mosaic emblem of a pavement, since the rest of the paving is made of simple slabs of white marble, except for the remnants of a dark band designed to frame the emblem. The interest of this stellate composition comes from the fact that the roundels are held together by a band or strip that runs around each roundel, forming interlacing.[25]

5-33. Pavement, church of the monastery of Iviron on Mount Athos (976–1025).

The design regulating this mosaic is easily identified as a double cross inscribed in a square, that is, a square asterisk. The emblem of the church of San Nicola is thus regulated by a pattern identical to that underlying the Cosmatesque quincunx.

The church of San Nicola at Olynthus is not the only one with the remains of a pavement with interlacing based on the double cross. In fact, it is one of numerous centralized churches from the eleventh century that contain this sort of pavement. Examples include the church of Katholikon in the monastery of Hosios Lukas at Phocis (fig. 5-32); the church of the monastery of Iviron on Mount Athos (fig. 5-33),[26] the church of Hagia Sophia at Nicaea (fig. 5-34),[27] and the mausoleum of Orhan Gazi at Bursa (figs. 5-35 and 5-36). All these eleventh-century mosaic remains indicate that many, if not all, middle-Byzantine centralized churches display an interlacing of quincuncial composition in the pavement of the central bay beneath the main dome.

5-34. Pavement in the nave, church of Hagia Sophia (circa 1065), Nicaea.

The preceding assertion implies, on the one hand, that the regulating design of the flat composition ornamenting the pavement of a middle-Byzantine centralized church coincides with the design that regulates the spatial composition of the church itself, since both are quincuncial compositions. Moreover, the intimate relationship between the spatial structure of the church and the flat structure of the ornament of the pavement is a constant in middle-Byzantine religious architecture.

This union may have originated in the time of Justinian, since it was during his reign that the first pavements with interlacing motifs executed in *opus sectile* appeared and that centralized architectural types dominated ecclesiastic architecture for the first time (as in the Church of the Holy Apostles). It is very possible that these interlacings developed within the centralized churches in conjunction with the development of the churches themselves, since the interlacings follow the regulating design underlying the churches, the double cross. Thus may have been born the indissoluble, almost congenital union between interlacing ornament and centralized church, which would subsist in the examples from the sixth century and which is equivalent to, in the particular case of the quincunx church, the stable alliance between the flat quincunx and the spatial quincunx.

The models of the centralized plan from the middle-Byzantine age are present not only in the heart of the Byzantine Empire but also in the peripheral regions and in the bordering areas, where they followed their own paths of development.

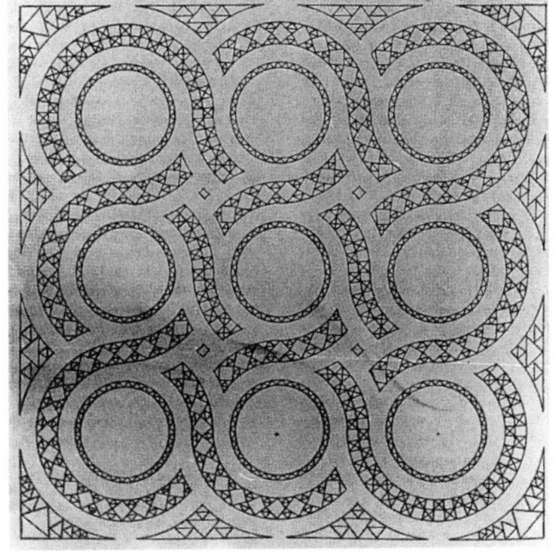

5-35. Drawing of fragment A from the pavement of the mausoleum of Orhan Gazi (circa 1065), Bursa.

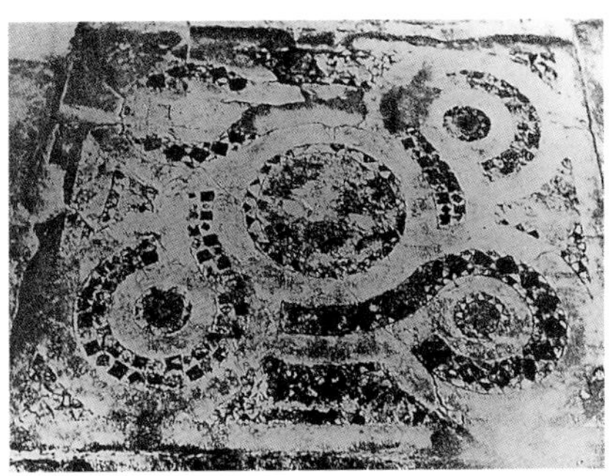

5-36. Fragment C from the pavement of the mausoleum of Orhan Gazi (circa 1065), Bursa.

With the exception of the Chapel of San Zenone in the church of Santa Prassede, Rome does not contain buildings of direct Byzantine heritage. The Chapel of San Zenone is a brilliant example of the integration of architecture and ornamentation. This small chapel of square plan is famous for the splendid mosaics that decorate the vault, examined in numerous studies.[28] The same is not true of the pavement, which seems to go unnoticed despite the impressive round of porphyry of 1.45 meters (4.76 feet) in diameter—perhaps the largest monolithic *rota* in Rome—that occupies its center, and despite being the most remarkable of the very few examples that attest to the resurgence of geometric *opus sectile* in Rome in the Carolingian period.[29]

The two diagonals that constitute the plan projection of the groin-sail vault covering the Chapel of San Zenone create an X-shaped cross (decorated by four angels, one on each arm of the X).[30] At the cross ends are circles that represent, in plan projection, the four supporting columns situated on the vertices of the square that constitutes the floor plan. Beneath the intersecting point of the two diagonal lines, that is, under the keystone of the vault, is the center of the enormous porphyry roundel, the chief ornament of the pavement. In the center of the mosaic that sheathes the vault, a representation of Christ Pantocrator, enclosed in a circular frame, is superposed over the sacred porphyry roundel of the floor.[31] The central entrance door to the chapel is located in the wall of the right aisle of the church. The altar of the chapel faces that door. At each side of the square of the chapel is a small room accessible by means of a side door; therefore, the two side doors are confronted on the axis perpendicular to the one that joins the central door with the altar (figs. 5-37a and 5-37b).

The geometry that determines the volume of the Chapel of San Zenone—and the geometry that orchestrates the flat ornament of the pavement as

5-37a. Plans of ceilings and floor and elevations of the walls of the Chapel of San Zenone in Santa Prassede, Rome. (G. B. De Rossi)

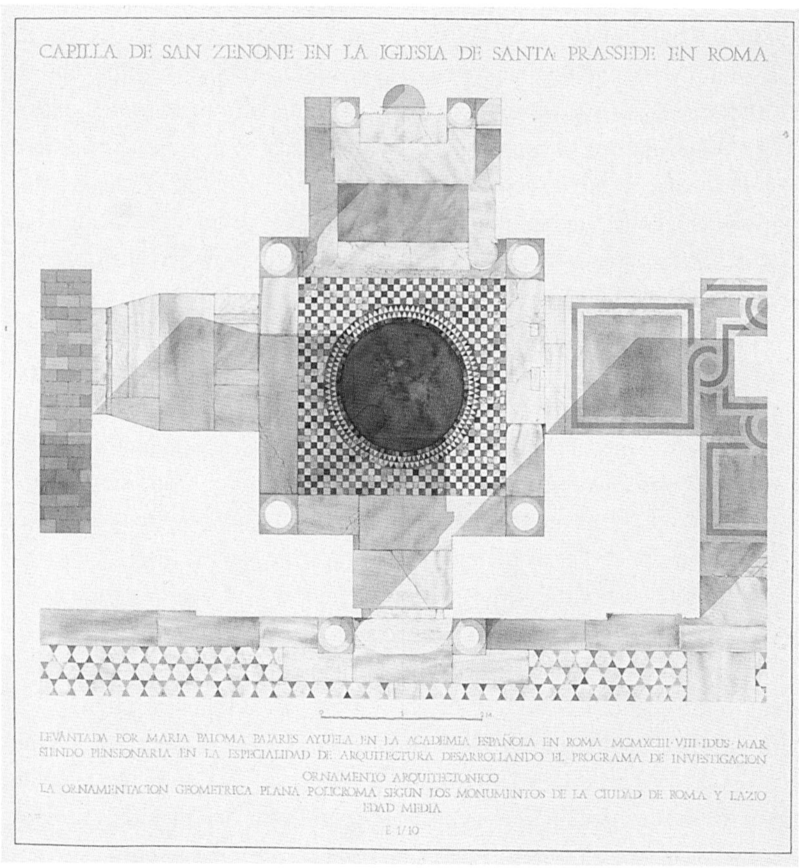

5-37b. Floor plan of the Chapel of San Zenone in Santa Prassede, Rome. (Scale 1:10 meters, watercolor on paper, 104 by 102 cm, P. Pajares, 1993)

well—has for plan projection a schema that can be described as a decussate cross (formed by the edges of a groin-sail vault) superposed over a Greek cross (formed by the axis that joins the central door with the altar and the axis that unites the side doors) inscribed within a square at whose center lies a large roundel (the *rota* of the pavement and the Pantocrator of the mosaic) ensconced in the angles between four roundelets (the four columns in plan projection). The three-dimensional geometry of the Chapel of San Zenone concurs entirely with the flat geometry that regulates the Cosmatesque quincunx, as the square asterisk underlies both.

In the church of Santi Quattro Coronati in Rome survive two chapels of square plan and a groin vault. These two ninth-century chapels, although their original characteristics have not been preserved, are closely related to the Chapel of San Zenone. The Chapel of Santa Barbara is adjoined to the right aisle of the ancient basilica of Leo IV (847–55). The Chapel of San Nicola is adjoined to the left aisle, in correspondence with the other chapel.[32]

In Italy the principal sites of Byzantine influence during the tenth, eleventh, and twelfth centuries were the High Adriatic region (especially Venice), the southern portion of the peninsula, and Sicily.

Venice, which was strongly connected diplomatically, commercially, and culturally to the Eastern Empire, shows a greater Eastern influence than the southern regions. In the eleventh century in Venice, a Byzantine prototype from the sixth century was brilliantly revived in the basilica of San Marco (fig. 5-38): the Greek cross capped by five domes (one over each arm and another over the crossing) from the Apostoleion of Justinian, a composition in square asterisk. Byzantine artists worked on the execution of the splendid pavement of San Marco, which includes numerous quincuncial compositions, three of which are quincunxes.[33] Two are situated in the northern arm of the transept, one at the end and the other in the interior (fig. 5-39), and the remaining one is at the end of the southern arm of the transept (see chapter 1 for more information about San Marco).

5-38. *Aerial view of Venice from San Marco.*

5-39. Pavement in the basilica of San Marco.

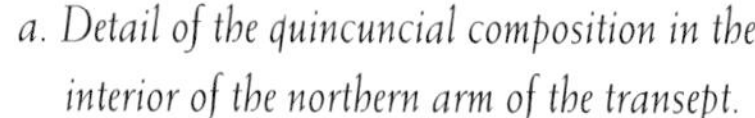

a. Detail of the quincuncial composition in the interior of the northern arm of the transept.

b. Detail of one of the rings of the quincuncial composition in the interior of the northern arm of the transept.

The centralized Byzantine model was transplanted to the south of Italy and Sicily in a complete way, as can be seen in the small quincunx churches in Apulia, Calabria, and Sicily, for example, San Marco in Rossano, Cattolica in Stilo (fig. 5-40),[34] and San Costanzo in Capri. Although of awkward proportions and provincial style, these churches attest to the fluid cultural exchange with the East, in particular Greece, at the end of the tenth century, establishing a hybrid union with Western models. In the case of the buildings in Sicily in the twelfth century, such as the Norman Palace in Palermo (fig. 5-41) or the cloister of the cathedral in Monreale (illustrated in chapter 1), a triple influence, Byzantine-Greek, Arab, and Norman, is evident.

Mid-Byzantine ecclesiastic architecture exhibits a complex and refined ornamental system that Western artists eagerly adopted.[35] They found in it a developed language, rich, sophisticated, of dense symbolic weight, capable of expressing of the spiritual world derived from their religious beliefs. However, in determining the general configuration of the space of the churches, they opted for directional architectural solutions which, in their fundamental traits, followed Western models, especially the church of basil-

5-40. Exterior perspective of the quincunx church of the Cattolica, Stilo, Calabria.

5-41. King Roger's chamber in the twelfth-century Norman Palace, Palermo, Sicily.

ical plan, which was more monumental, spacious, and better adapted for the Roman liturgy than the tiny centralized Byzantine churches.[36] The churches in Montecassino, Salerno, Ravello, Bari, and Monreale were arranged according to or by modifying the Western custom: Roman paleo-Christian basilicas, Norman and Lombard Romanesque churches with galleries, basilicas with segregated crossings crowned by a drum and dome.

The basilical church in the abbey of Montecassino, in which much of the ornament of the pavement shows marked Eastern influence, is a clear example of hybrid construction, blending Byzantine ornament and Western typology (see chapter 3 for additional discussion of the pavement at Montecassino).

The same is true in the abbey of Saint-Benoît-sur-Loire, where the abbot Gauzlin (1004–30) had placed in his church a magnificent marble pavement that he had ordered brought from the *Romania*, a term that would have indicated the Byzantine Empire.[37] Xavier Barral i Altet, in his catalog of this mosaic, noted that this pavement seemed very similar to the Roman pavements of the twelfth century.[38] He also noted the difficulty in dating the pavement with accuracy because three levels of remains of pavement in *opus sectile* had been found superimposed. The upper level, in view today (see chapter 1 for illustrations), is medieval, probably from the eleventh century, with medieval repairs and additions (perhaps from the twelfth century) and

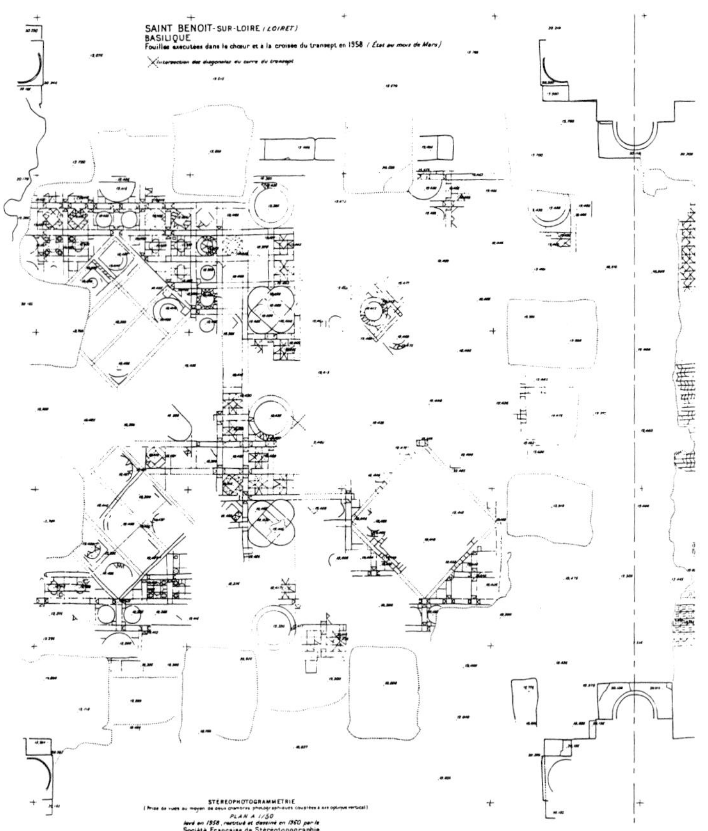

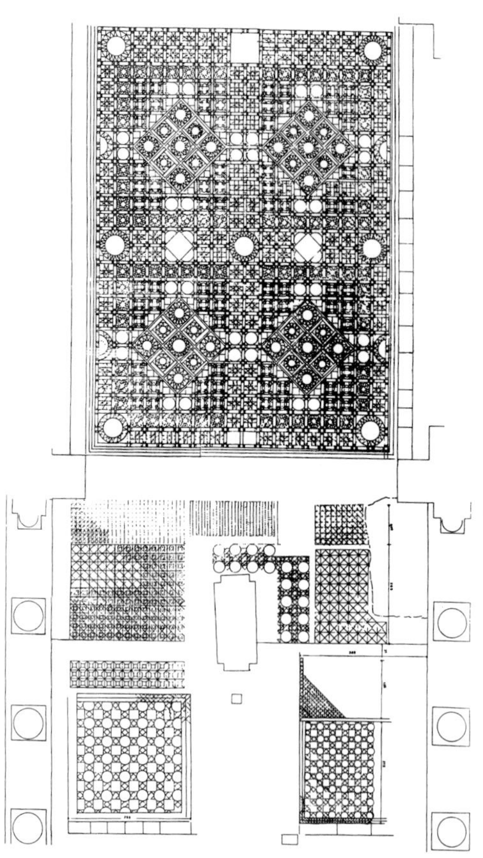

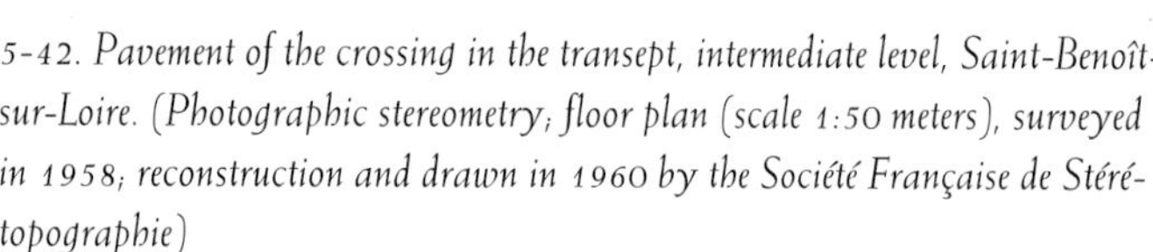
5-42. Pavement of the crossing in the transept, intermediate level, Saint-Benoît-sur-Loire. (Photographic stereometry; floor plan (scale 1:50 meters), surveyed in 1958; reconstruction and drawn in 1960 by the Société Française de Stéré-topographie)

5-43. Pavement of the choir and the crossing in the transept, intermediate level, Saint-Benoît-sur-Loire. (Reconstruction by P. Lablaude, 1959, after a drawing by R. Bauchery, 1958)

Renaissance alterations (the cardinal Duprat, abbot of Saint-Benoît-sur-Loire, imported large porphyry rounds from Rome between 1531 and 1535 to improve the pavement; in 1642 part of the paving was again reformed). Beneath this upper level, remains of another pavement have been found, possibly from the Carolingian era (fig. 5-42). In the next level below are remains from another pavement, which could be pre-Carolingian. The ensemble of the pavement, 7 by 15.40 meters (22.97 by 50.52 feet) is composed of two parts: one covers the choir, and the other the "square" crossing—7 by 7.5 meters (22.97 by 24.61 feet)—in the transept. Although the design of the part situated in the transept is more refined, an analysis of the mortar proves the unity of the ensemble. In the reconstruction of the pavement from the intermediate level or stratum, one observes that the mosaic of the square crossing in the transept displays a geometric design with an underlying double cross; the pavement is thus a quincuncial composition (fig. 5-43). The ends and the center of the cross and the X are marked with circular and square porphyry slabs. The center of this quincuncial composition coincides with the center of the transept. The pavement found below it, that is, in the lower stratum of the square crossing in the transept, is circular, 4.45 meters (14.60 feet) in diameter. It is composed of a central roundel 1.5 meters (4.92 feet) in diameter, outlined with a band of squares forming a sawtooth pattern and surrounded by five concentric bands in which the bands of mosaic and bands of stone alternate. In the central circle of the tessellation were found fragments of columns and of Carolingian screens.

The design and dimensions of this pavement's central roundel are reminiscent of the large porphyry roundel occupying the center of the ninth-century paving in the Chapel of San Zenone, in the church of Santa Prassede in Rome. At Saint-Benoît-sur-Loire, the intersecting point of the diagonals of the square crossing in the transept lies at the center of the circle, which is 1.5 meters (4.92 feet) in diameter. Outlined by a row of squares in a sawtooth design, it dominates the paving of the church. Similarly, in the square Chapel of San Zenone, the diagonals intersect at the center of the porphyry *rota* (1.54 meters [5.05 feet] in diameter) that dominates the paving of the small chapel. The *rota* is bordered by a design of three concentric bands (the interior, a row of squares; the central and exterior bands, sawtooth pattern) and lies over a chessboard-pattern background of squares.

Thus, in Saint-Benoît-sur-Loire, a quincuncial mosaic paves the center of the transept of the church. This mosaic is an early example of how a centralized Byzantine ornamental composition is integrated into a directional basilical design typical of the West.

Other elements characteristic of the centralized Byzantine models appear in structures whose fundamental traits are Western, as in the hybrid basilica with a domed crossing. In this case, the church with a typical Western basilical plan receives a dome that, like the main dome of the small Byzantine churches, covers and emphasizes its center.

Hypothetically, then, it is reasonable to assert that the flat quincunx, occupying the pavement beneath the central dome of the spatial quincunx, accompanied the latter in its incursions into southern Italy. Once there, the flat quincunx became gradually integrated, shifting residence from the centralized Byzantine plan to the directional Western plan and progressively adapting its symbolism and function, inherited from the Byzantine liturgy, to meet the not-so-different demands of the Roman liturgy. Initially, the flat quincunx found shelter in the hybrid basilica, resting as an emblem beneath the dome that covered the crossing, and from there moved to the entirely basilical church. The shift of the flat quincunx through the hybrid basilica to the basilica with a timber roof was not a difficult transition since the quincunx maintained not only its status of emblem,[39] laden with the symbolism and function attributed to it in the Roman liturgy, but also its position at the center of the pavement in the nave, with the difference that, for the first time, a flat or double-eaved roof, rather than a dome, covered it.

Regardless of whether this hypothesis offers a correct interpretation of the process by which the quincunx passed from the Byzantine centralized church to the Western directional church, there is no doubt that by the eleventh century the quincunx had settled in the nave of the Western directional churches. Examples include, in the High Adriatic region, the pavement of the church of the abbey in Pomposa inscribed 1026 (fig. 5-44),[40] and in central Italy, the pavement of the church of the abbey in Montecassino.

The quincunx, once transplanted to the center of the church of basilical plan, became the visual and symbolic focal point of the pavement. The resolution of the background of the composition remains to be seen. The pavement of the church of the abbey in Montecassino is the oldest whose

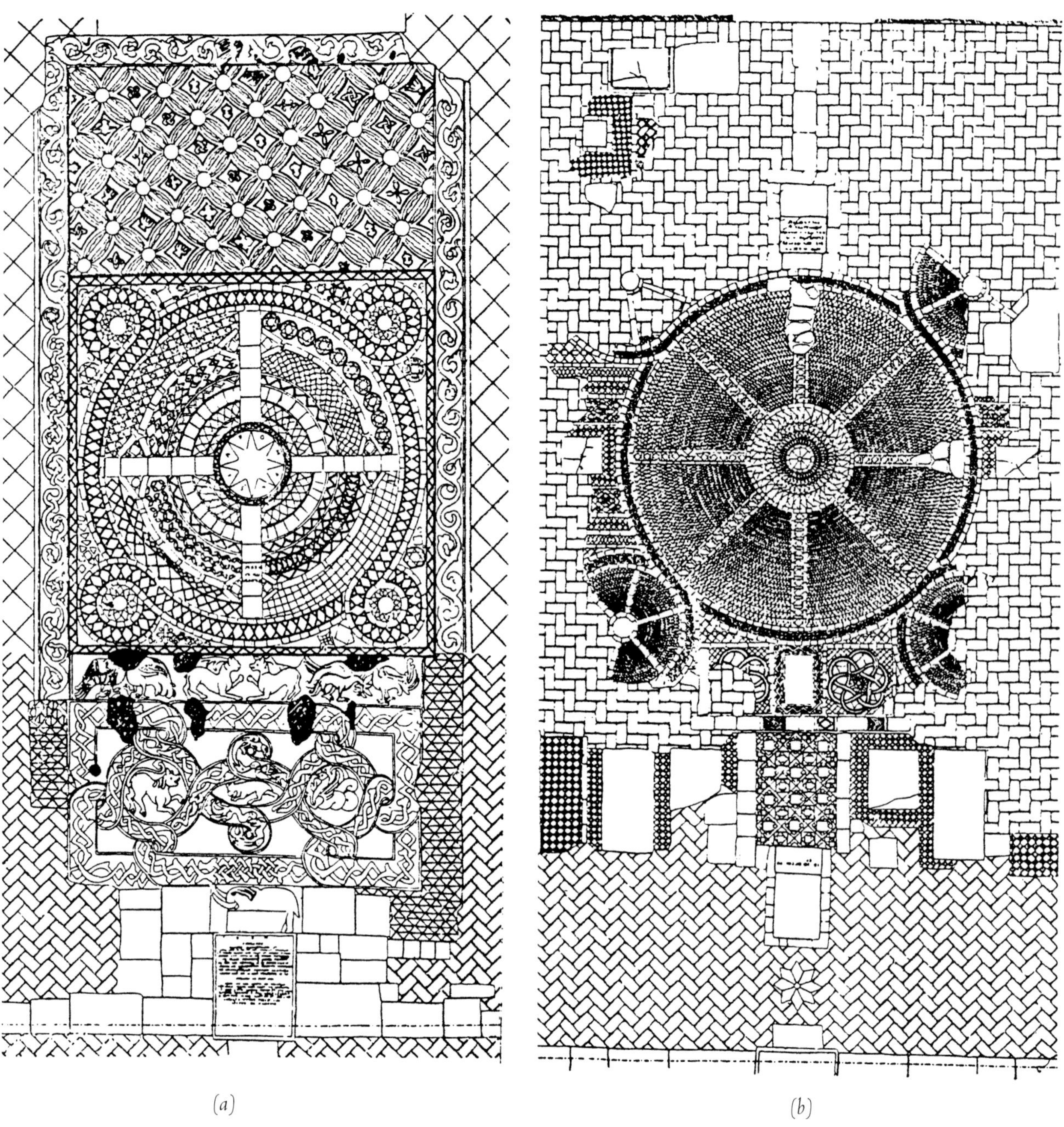

(a) (b)

5-44. Pavement of the abbey of Pomposa.
a. Eleventh-century pavement. (M. Salmi, 1966, fig. 256)
b. Eleventh-century pavement.

background is similar to that of the Cosmatesque pavements. In the pavement in Montecassino, the quincuncial compositions of Byzantine origin act as emblems. The background displays surface geometric patterns of Western origin, given their heritage in the geometric patterns of the Roman mosaics of late antiquity.

The pavement in Montecassino anticipated the hybrid nature of the Cosmatesque pavements. Because of the clever integration of imported and local elements, these pavements successfully created a consistent ornamental language in which the quincunx, accompanied by other background geometric patterns, acted as the emblem or the visual, functional, and symbolic center of a directional composition, capable of fully satisfying the material and spiritual requirements associated with the staging of the Roman liturgy.

The Signification of the Underlying Geometry of the Cosmatesque Quincunx

Artistic production in the Middle Ages was full of designs whose regulating schema was the double cross. The persistent and frequent appearance of quincuncial compositions, as much in the East as in the West, during the Middle Ages allows one to speak of a medieval "quincunx mania."

The abundance of quincuncial compositions in every manifestation of Christian art (architecture, sculpture, painting, metalwork, miniatures, calligraphy) leads one to think that they all share a basic common meaning, linked to concepts or ideas that form an essential part of Christian beliefs, fundamental to the mentality of medieval society. If one assumes that a correspondence between the shapes of the two signifiers correlates to a correspondence, total or partial, between their meanings, one can then begin to understand at least the essential signification of the Cosmatesque quincunx by studying the symbolic content of other structures, two- or three-dimensional, whose regulating geometry is akin to that underlying the flat quincunx.

Thus, the symbolic content of a series of structures regulated by the double cross may illuminate the search for the meaning of the Cosmatesque quincunx. This series includes both flat and spatial structures. The group of flat structures consists of a repertoire of images, familiar to the eyes of the medieval observer, that were akin to that of the Cosmatesque quincunx. The meanings of these images provide an overview of the connotations of the quincuncial forms in the Middle Ages. The contemporary observer can study and understand the forms and meanings of the principal quincuncial images that populated the medieval mind, which in turn will help to capture the meaning of the Cosmatesque quincunx.

The first structure is architectural, the centralized Byzantine church, with the first interlacings in *opus sectile* comparable to the Cosmatesque quincunx. The meaning of the flat quincunx must have developed jointly with the spatial structure that housed it. The intimate correspondence between interlacing ornament and the centralized church and, in particular, between the flat quincunx and the spatial quincunx, resulted from their common origin: both sprang from the "living" geometry, material and immaterial, associated with the Byzantine liturgy. Material "living" geometry reflects the human movements necessary to stage the liturgy. Immaterial "living" geometry regulates the placement of the symbolic representations associated with the Christian spiritual world. The "living" geometry, in the form of a double cross, as explained below, determines the "nonliving" geometry, which is the arrangement of the material used in construction of the building, two- and three-dimensional.

Keys to the spatial configuration of the church can be found in the ornament of the paving, since the flat quincunx is both a part and, simultaneously, the synthesis of the spatial quincunx. In other words, the ornament of the pavement can be considered as a coded representation of the architecture that houses it. Both—the ornamentation and the architecture—find their origin in the staging of the Byzantine liturgy.

The layout of the centralized Byzantine churches was integrated with the Byzantine liturgy to perfection, as much in the functional arena (material living geometry) as in the symbolic (immaterial living geometry).

That the functional/liturgical aspects—the actions of the faithful and of the officiating clergy who together staged the many rites comprising the liturgical celebration in the Byzantine age—remained integrated is due as much to the general spatial design of the centralized church as to the particular position of each of the areas that constitute it. The location of these areas was established with the objective of completely satisfying the multitude of requirements of the program of a church. For example, an exterior enclosure was needed to receive the faithful before and during religious ceremonies. An entrance vestibule was used for reception and deposit of the offerings of the faithful. Areas were reserved for participation, static and dynamic, by the faithful or visitors comprising the audience of the religious ceremonies. A ceremonial stage was needed for the officiants, seated or standing. A barrier was needed to separate the spaces designated for the faithful and those exclusively for the clergy. Space was required for processions of the clergy, a dressing room for the officiants, the exposition and storage of the Gospels, the reading of the Gospels, the storage of the species and utensils of the Eucharist, the preparation of the Eucharistic species before the services, the table for celebration of the Eucharistic sacrifice, the display of the Eucharistic species after services, the burial of martyrs, the display and custody of relics, an archive, and a library.[41]

During Byzantine times, the relationship of the symbolic/liturgical aspects and construction was not irrelevant to the considerations of intellectuals, who interpreted the structures of the churches through an elaborate system of symbols. The writings in which the theologians of the eighth century collected these interpretations do not contain symbolic relationships of their own invention. Quite the contrary, they attest to the symbolic readings common in that period which, inherited from earlier eras, were the fruit of centuries of evolution and would continue until the fourteenth century. Each part of the church was thus symbolically linked to one or several of the integrating aspects of the material and spiritual world associated with the life of Christ and his doctrine. For example, for Germanus I, patriarch of Constantinople in the eighth century, the building of the church represented the temple of the Lord. The sacred precinct represented heaven where God resided and the sacred cave where Christ was buried and resurrected. He associated the presbytery and the altar with the manger, the table of the Last Supper, and the tomb of Christ; they were also seen as the celestial altar where the angels offered the eternal sacrifice. The apse was the symbol of the cross. The seats of the clergy represented the elevated place and throne in which Christ sat among his disciples; the columns of the templon (chancel), the division between this world and the celestial world. The architrave over those columns represented the cross. The baldachin was the place of the crucifixion. And the dome was heaven.[42]

Another type of symbolic association assigned each part of the church to a corresponding part of the body of Christ. This type of association is not unrelated to the vision of man as a microcosm, that is, as a symbol and compendium of the cosmos. Inherited from Greek thought, this view survived in the early Middle Ages with the adjustments necessary to make it acceptable to Christian eyes. The pictures expressing this vision were abundant in medieval times. They took the form of a circle divided into a number of parts

5-45. Twelfth-century miniature belonging to the Latin codex of Saint Hildegarde.

equal to a multiple of four (four, eight, or twelve), in which the elements perceived by the medieval observer to shape man, the year, the world, and the cosmos appeared interrelated: the four seasons, the twelve signs of the zodiac, the four elements (air, fire, earth, water), the four primordial and essential elemental properties (heat, cold, humidity, drought), the four cardinal points, the four humors of the human body (blood, phlegm, black bile, and yellow bile), the four virtues of the Christian religious man (prudence, strength, temperance, justice), the four stages of human life (childhood, adolescence, adulthood, old age), the twelve winds, and more.[43]

Medieval manuscripts show figures that weave together these components on images of an underlying double cross. A circular asterisk regulates a twelfth-century miniature belonging to the Latin codex of Saint Hildegarde in which a human figure occupies the center of a roundel with an X surrounded by the twelve winds (fig. 5-45). A square asterisk underlies an image from an Italian medical treatise of the early eleventh century that portrays the influence of the stars on the different parts of the human body: the sun/God appears at the center, the signs of the zodiac, in the twelve divisions of the central roundel; the four seasons, in the roundelets in the angles (fig. 5-46).[44] An octagonal asterisk regulates a figure from the mid-ninth century that represents the circular nature of the cosmos in the treatise

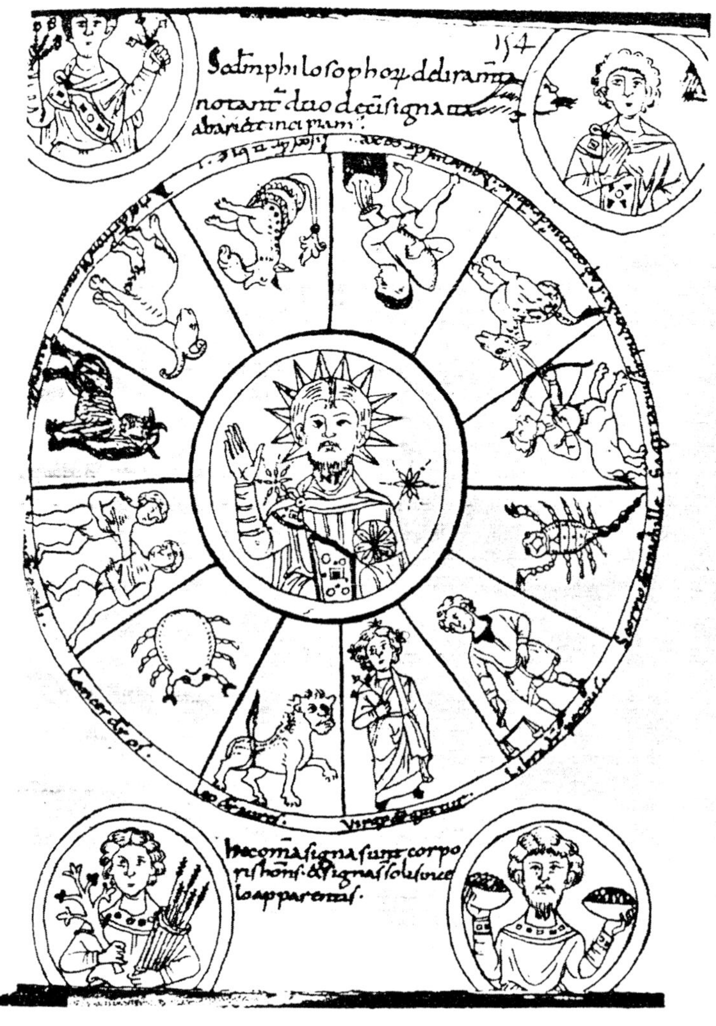

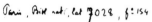

5-46. *Early-eleventh-century manuscript lat. 7028, f. 154.*

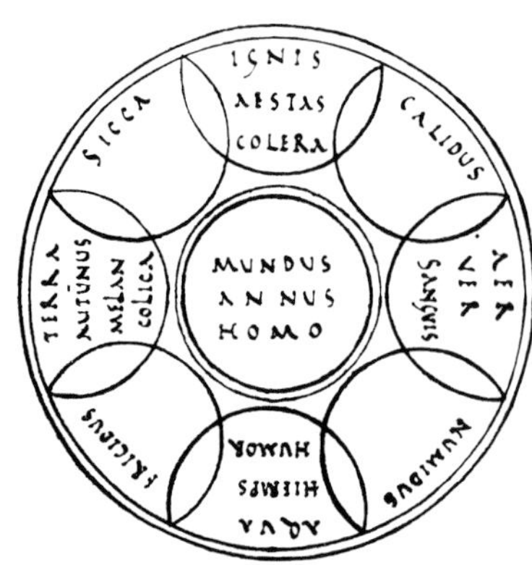

5-47. *Mid-eleventh-century manuscript lat. 5543, f. 136.*

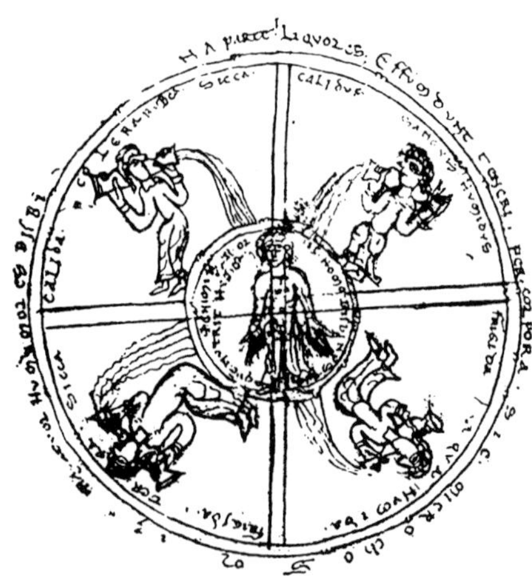

5-48. *Figure designed in England in the eleventh century.*

De natura rerum by Isidore of Seville; this diagram relates man, the world, and the year through the four essential properties, the four elements, the four seasons, and the four humors of the human body (fig. 5-47).[45] A circular asterisk underlies a figure designed in England in the eleventh century in which the fundamental humors, personified, surround the small man who occupies the central circle; the figure interrelates the same elements that appear in the abstract diagram of the previous example (fig. 5-48).[46] A design in double cross regulates the dense diagram that appears in an English manuscript, a copy from the twelfth century of an original from the early eleventh century (fig. 5-49). This remarkable and clever design interrelates the four elements, the four essential properties, the four cardinal points, the four ages of human life, the twelve winds, and a calendar that indicates the twelve signs of the zodiac, the months with the names of their days, the equinoxes, and the solstices. The name of Adam is represented by its letters at the ends of a cross.[47] A quincuncial composition dictates the design of the twelfth-century miniature belonging to the sacramentarian of Marmoutier, which presents, in the central roundel, the abbot Reinaud blessing his parishioners and, in the corner roundelets, the four virtues of the practicing Christian (fig. 5-50).

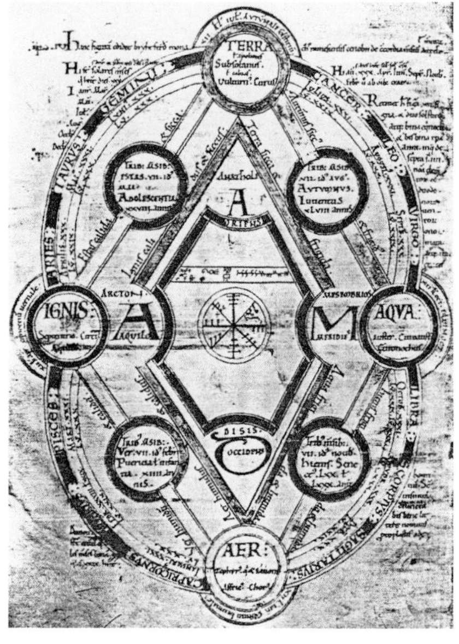

5-49. *English manuscript, a twelfth-century copy of an early eleventh-century original.*

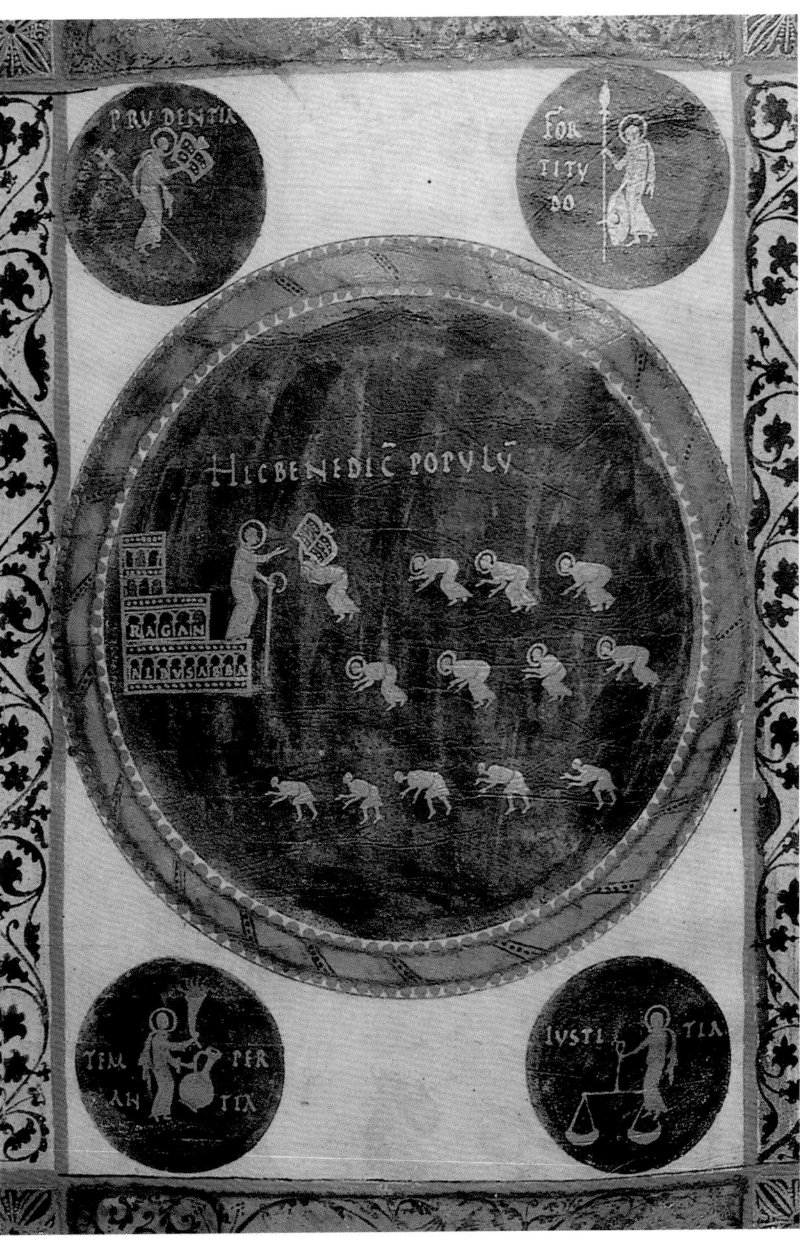

5-50. The abbot Reinaud blessing his parishioners in a twelfth-century miniature belonging to the sacramentarian of Marmoutier. (Bibliothèque Municipale, Autun)

The use of the quincuncial composition to represent man as a microcosm also appears in architecture, as exemplified in a painting from the vault of the crypt in the cathedral of Anagni (fig. 5-51). In the center of this concentric design, divided into four sections, appears a naked person with the inscription HOMO enclosed in a circle reading *Microcosmus, id est minor mundus*. The image establishes relationships among the ages of life, the humors of man, the four seasons, the elemental properties, and the four elements. At the four ends, large letters form the word MU-N-D-US.[48] The floor of the crypt is carpeted with a Cosmatesque mosaic in which a series of quincunxes covers the nave. Consequently, the ornament of the ceiling as much as that of the floor are regulated by compositions in square asterisk (fig. 5-52).

A miniature of a late-thirteenth-century copy from the encyclopedia by Thomas Cantimpratensis (MS Munich, Clm 2655 fol.105^{r}) is one of the images with which Steven H. Wander illustrates his studies of the Cosmatesque pavement in the sanctuary at Westminster Abbey. The miniature portrays the cosmos as the joining of the universe existing in the divine

5-51. Painting in a vault of the crypt of the cathedral of Anagni.

5-52. Crypt of the cathedral of Anagni.

5-53. *Miniature of a late-thirteenth-century copy of an encyclopedia.*

mind, which appears described along the edge of the figure, and its materialization in the tangible world, located at its center (fig. 5-53). Wander attributes a cosmological meaning to the quincuncial composition that ornaments the pavement of the sanctuary, interpreting each of the geometric elements that compose the Cosmatesque mosaic and the relationship among them, in accordance with the structure of the universe reflected in the miniature.[49] The pavement from the sanctuary is, according to Wander, a schematic description or symbolic compendium of the whole universe. Wander is not the only author to attribute a cosmic symbolism to the quincuncial composition at Westminster. R. Foster also does so, basing the assertion as much on a detailed analysis of the inscription on the pavement as on the study of the symbolism of the overall geometry regulating the composition (figs. 5-54 through 5-57).

5-54. *Pavement of the sanctuary of Westminster Abbey. (Watercolor produced for History of the Abbey of Rudolph Ackermann, published in 1812)*

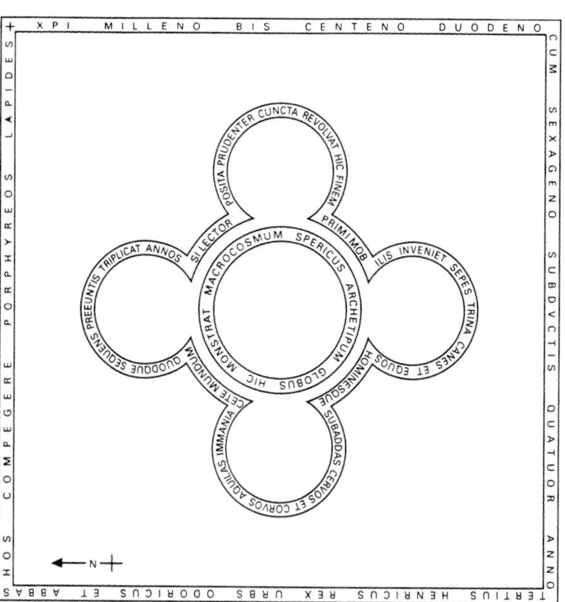

5-55. *The inscription, in three sections, that appears in the pavement of the sanctuary of Westminster Abbey. (R. Foster)*

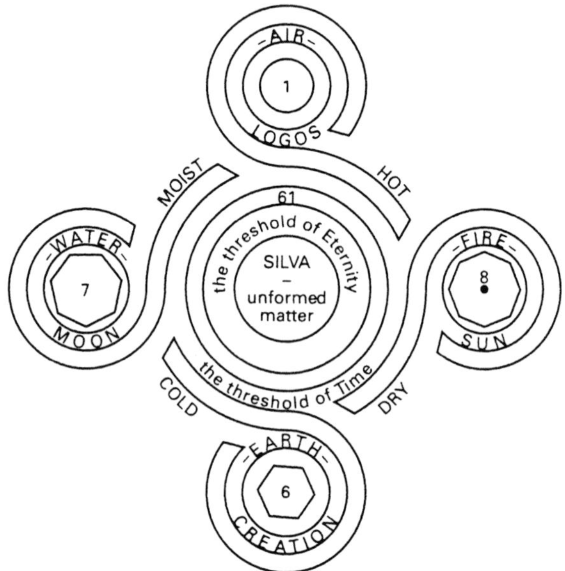

5-56. *A symbolic diagram of the central quincunx of the pavement of the sanctuary of Westminster Abbey. (R. Foster)*

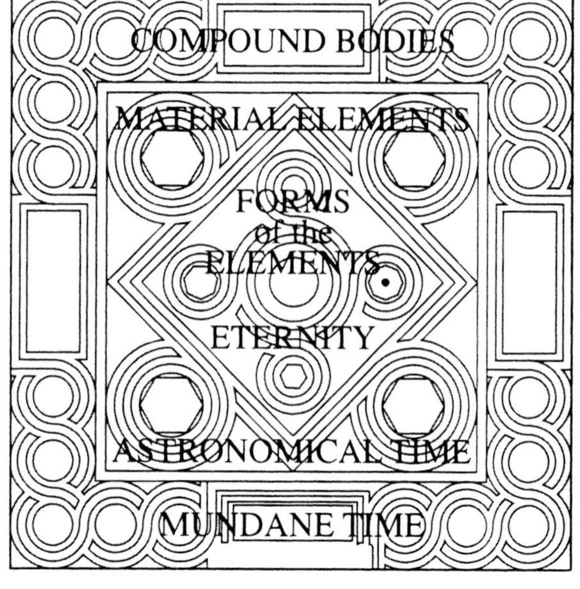

5-57. *Symbolism in the pavement of the sanctuary of Westminster Abbey, depicting the three material states and the three scales of time. (R. Foster)*

The cross inscribed in a circle regulates the miniature from heavenly Jerusalem that Carol Heitz includes in her studies on the symbolism of numbers in the religious architecture of the early Middle Ages (fig. 5-58).[50] Heitz relates this flat representation of the celestial city to a spatial structure, the rotunda of the Holy Sepulchre, built by Constantine in Jerusalem (fig. 5-59). She sees in this building the source of the spatial geometry of the Palatine Chapel in Aachen (796–805), whose proportions she explains in detail, emphasizing the symbolic content of the numbers that define them (figs. 5-60 and 5-61).[51]

5-58. *The ninth-century apocalypse of Saint-Amand, heavenly Jerusalem.*

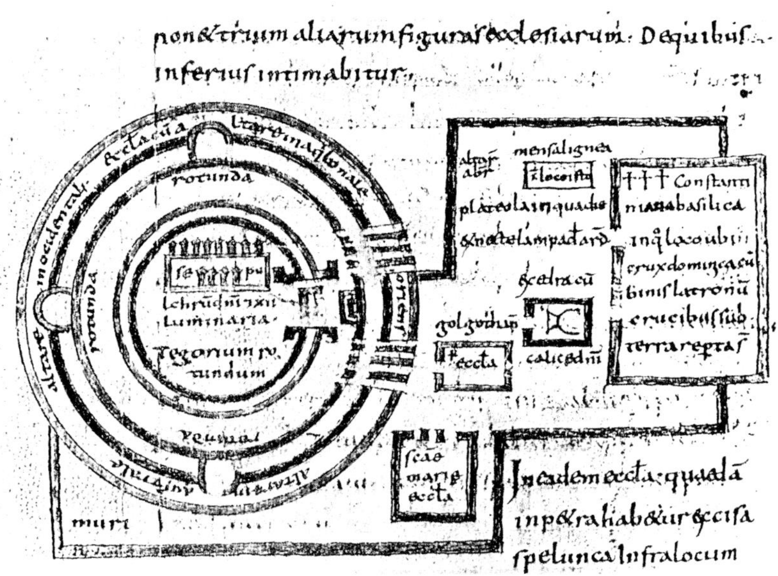

5-59. *The Holy Sepulchre of Jerusalem.*

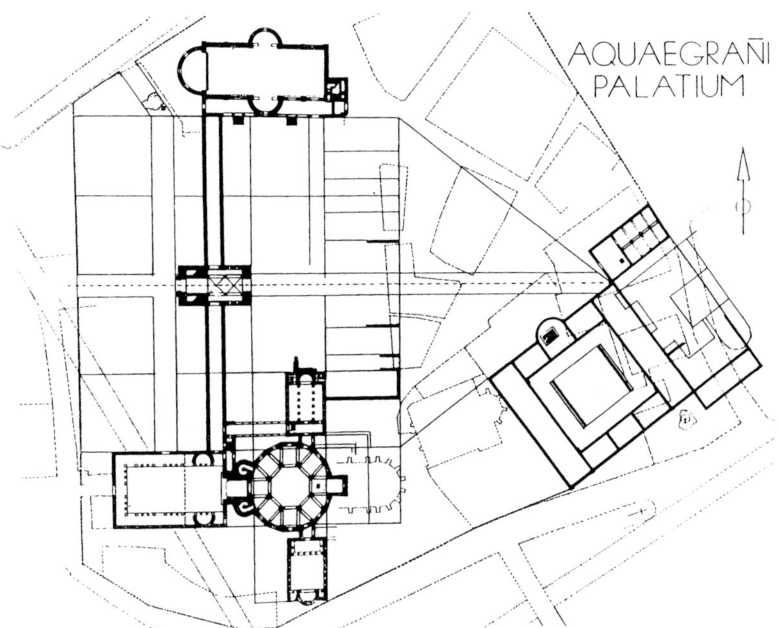

5-60. *General floor plan with square modules of the eighth-century Palatine Chapel, Aachen, Germany.*

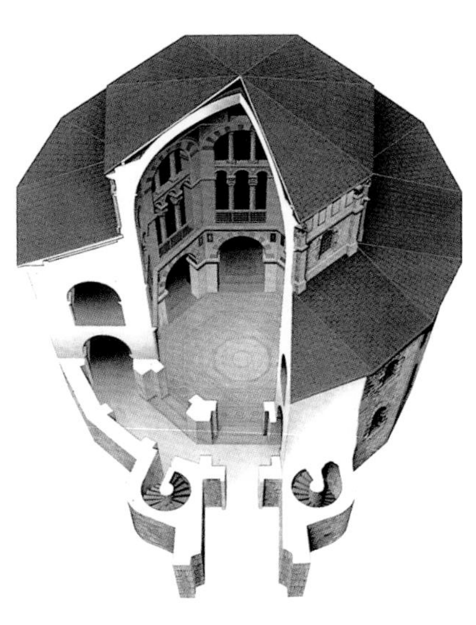

5-61. *Sectional perspective of the Palatine Chapel of Aachen (796–805).*

The Palatine Chapel of Aachen, by virtue of its octagonal design, is regulated by the double cross. The same is true of many other earlier important medieval centralized constructions, including the fifth-century baptistery of Constantine at San Giovanni in Laterano in Rome (fig. 5-62), Santo Stefano Rotondo in Rome, 468–483 (fig. 5-63), the mausoleum of Theodoric I in Ravenna, 530 (fig. 5-64), San Vitale of Ravenna, 547, and the mosque at the Dome of the Rock in Jerusalem, 691.[52]

All the functional and symbolic aspects examined thus far must have contributed, through intimate and prolonged contact with the aspects of

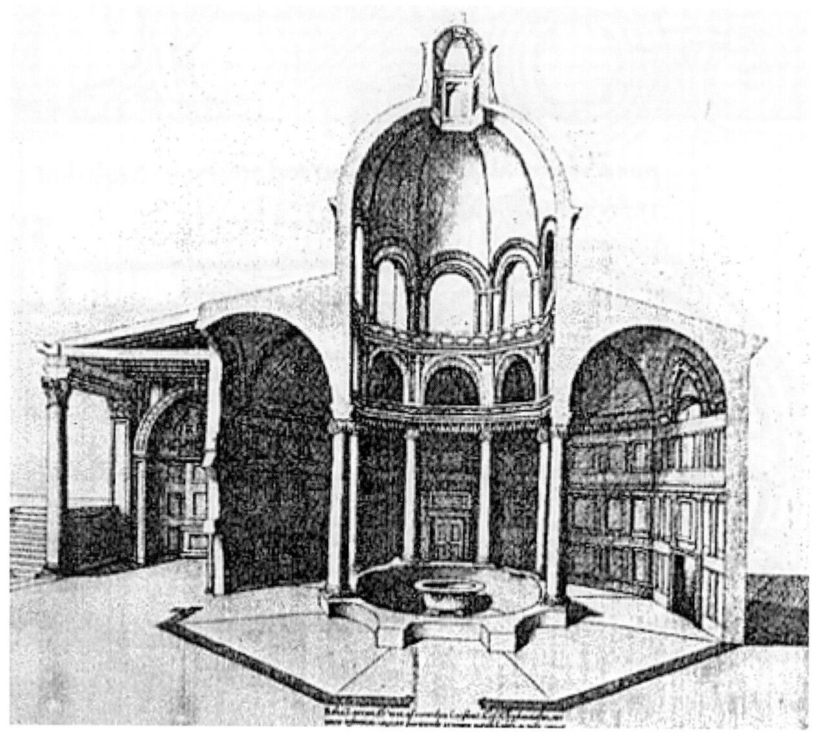

5-62. Elevation with sectional perspective of the fifth-century baptistery of the basilica of San Giovanni in Laterano, Rome. (Engraving by Antoine Lafreri, 1575)

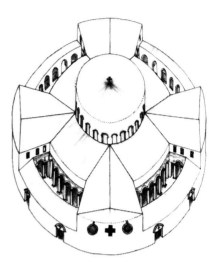

5-63. Isometric reconstruction of the exterior of Santo Stefano Rotondo, Rome (468–83). (S. Corbett, revised by J. B. Lloyd)

construction, to the development of not only the buildings cited but the centralized architectural types of the middle-Byzantine churches, whose underlying design is the double cross. Furthermore, they must have affected the appearance and consolidation of the interlacing ornament in quincuncial composition that paved the floors in the nucleus of these churches. Possibly following the process explained on the preceding pages, the quincuncial motif reached western lands, where it was firmly established as of the eleventh century, appearing frequently, as an emblem, at the center of the pavement in the nave of directional churches.

The studies by D. F. Glass of the iconography of the Cosmatesque pavements explain in detail a fundamental aspect of the correspondence between the living geometry and the nonliving geometry in the Western medieval basilicas: the concrete relation between the Roman liturgy and the flat quincunx.[53]

One of the rites involved in the ceremony of consecration or dedication of a basilica consisted of the chrismation of the central quincunx. According to Glass, first a decussate cross was drawn with ashes: the first line, from the left eastern angle to the right western one; the second line, from the right eastern angle to the left western one. The Greek alphabet was then drawn over the first line, beginning from the left eastern angle and ending on the right western one, and the Latin alphabet was drawn over the second line, beginning from the right eastern angle and ending at the left western one. Next was executed an upright cross, centered on the decussate cross.[54] The double crossing of the central quincunx resulted in a double-cross monogram drawn with ashes, over which the Greek and Latin alphabets were written (fig. 5-65).[55]

In the High Adriatic region, two pavements from the eleventh century, created immediately prior to the first Cosmatesque pavements, contain designs that can be directly related to this ceremony. The pavement in the

5-64. Mausoleum of Theodoric I, Ravenna (530).

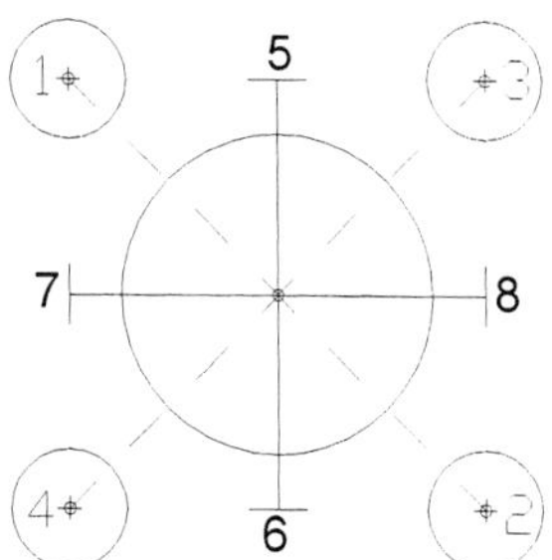

5-65. Diagram of the double cross that was drawn with ashes over the principal quincunx during the ceremony dedicating the church.

church of the abbey in Pomposa, shaped or dissected, literally, the ephemeral trace that was created with ashes during the dedication ceremony of the church. In the pavement, inscribed in a quincunx, is a double cross executed in mosaic, forming a permanent part of the composition (illustrated earlier in this chapter). In Venice, in the pavement in the basilica of San Marco, is an X-shaped cross, executed in mosaic, that unites the diagonally opposed roundels of the quincunx situated at the end of the northern arm of the transept.[56]

In Rome the square asterisk composition in the Chapel of San Zenone in the church of Santa Prassede leads to the hypothesis that its ninth-century pavement may be the oldest one appropriate for the ceremony of double crossing at the central point. The Cosmatesque pavements of Santa Maria in Cosmedin, Santi Quattro Coronati, and Santa Croce in Gerusalemme, all from the twelfth century, are the clearest cases in which a principal quincunx appears intended for the drawing of the double cross during the dedication ceremony.

5-66. The Return of the Crusader, a twelfth-century bas-relief belonging to the abbey of Salival, France.

The design executed with ashes in the chrismation of the main quincunx of a Cosmatesque pavement is akin to the diagrammatic symbolic forms that dominated the representation of the spiritual world in early Christianity. Paleo-Christian decorative art is full of allegories and symbols (lamb, fish, anchor, chrismon, cross, and the like) that would continue in use during the Middle Ages. The cross and the chrismon are two omnipresent symbols in the medieval Christian and Byzantine world; both are contemporaries of the double cross drawn with ashes over the Cosmatesque quincunx and share, partially or totally, their formal characteristics.

The formal relationship of the double cross and the cross is evident, since the first contains the second. The cross, fundamental emblem of Jesus Christ and his doctrine, was the most important and repeated symbol in the Middle Ages, an era dominated by Christian religiousness. The necessity of including the cross, in an overt or indirect way, in any Christian ornamental design caused the field of design to be divided from the start into a number of parts equal to a multiple of four. For that reason, the vast majority of medieval symbols have an underlying "quadruped" grid, with four arms or a multiple thereof. The double cross is a "quadruped" graph, and the Cosmatesque quincunx is one of an infinite number of ornaments and symbols regulated by it.

The cross, insignia and sign of Christianity, was drawn by the gesture of the sign of the cross in all Christian ceremonies (baptism, communion, confirmation, marriage, consecration, blessing, dedication, extreme unction). The Crusaders fought in the Holy Land in the name of the cross, using it as an emblem on their chests, capes, and banners (fig. 5-66). A multitude of religious, civil, and military orders made the cross their badge (fig. 5-67).

5-67. Members of military orders of the Iberian peninsula: Santiago (1170), Alcántara (1156), and Calatrava (1158).

5-68. *Medieval coins.*
a. Thirteenth-century Genovino.
b. Dinar minted in Barcelona in 1134.
c. Twelfth-century money of Alfonso VI.
d. Twelfth-century óbolo.
e. Twelfth-century óbolo.
f. Thirteenth-century diner de tern of Jaime I, reverse.

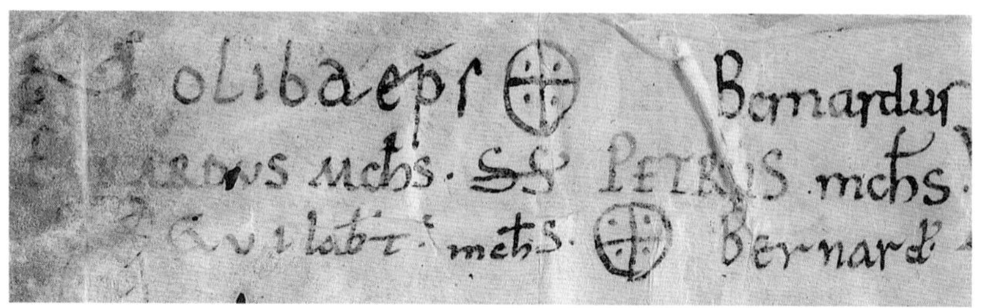

5-69. *The signature and monogram of the abbot Oliba on an eleventh-century parchment documenting the donation of lands to the monastery of Santa Maria de Ripoll.*

The symbol of the cross also appeared on coins.[57] The emperor Constantine, for example, marked numerous coins with the cross, both to show himself to be a follower of the new evangelical law and to familiarize his people with the concept. Even today in Spain, the reverse side of a coin is called the cross, an expression stemming from medieval times when the reverse of coins was decorated with a coat of arms, generally arranged in a cross (fig. 5-68). The sign of the cross also appeared in medieval documents, an example of which is the monogram formed by a cross inscribed in a circle, accompanied by four dots, one in the middle of each quarter-circle, with which the abbot Oliba crowned his signature in a parchment from the eleventh century (fig. 5-69).

The first Christians, persecuted for their religious beliefs, believed they were destined to live their faith in secrecy. They thus had the custom of encoding the name of Christ by means of figured graphics, such as the fish,[58] or alphabetical emblems, such as the chrismon. The chrismon, sometimes called the trophy of the cross, was the monogram of Jesus Christ, formed by the superposition of the first two letters, chi, X, and rho, P, of Christ's name in Greek (fig. 5-70 and 5-71). Other Christograms were formed by the superposition of X and I (fig. 5-72), or of X and + (fig. 5-73 and 5-74) and were usually accompanied by alpha (α) and omega (ω), the first and last letters of the Greek alphabet.

The chrismon is also referred to as the Constantinian monogram. After his celestial vision at the battle of the Milvian Bridge in 312, where he defeated Maxentius, Constantine replaced the Roman eagle with the monogram on the labarum, helmet, shield, and arms of his troops. The term *labarum* refers

5-70. A fourth- or fifth-century example of a chrismon, formed by X and P, on a brick stamped with a Constantinian monogram.

5-71. A late-eleventh-century example of a chrismon, formed by X and P, on the tympanum of San Pedro el Viejo, Huesca.

5-72. A seventh-century example of a Christogram, formed by X *and* I, *on a Visigothic decorative piece.*

5-73. A thirteenth-century example of a Christogram, formed by X *and* +, *in a detail of the door surround of the annunciation of the Catedral Vieja de Lérida.*

5-74. Late-eleventh-century example of a Christogram, formed by X *and* +, *on the tympanum of San Pedro el Viejo, Huesca.*

5-75. An early-twelfth-century trinitarian Christogram on the tympanum of the cathedral of Jaca.

to the imperial banner whose red squared cloth, hanging from a bar transverse to the flagpole, was embroidered with a chi-rho. The labarum was an example of a square asterisk, displaying a double cross inscribed within a square.

As much in the East as in the West, the monogram of Christ appeared on sarcophagi, stamped bricks, decorative plaques, doorways, porticoes, sepulchral mosaics, screens, niches, and more. Examples of Christograms in their three forms, the chi-rho,[59] the X and I,[60] and the X and +,[61] have survived on the Iberian peninsula. The monogram containing X and + found in the tympanum of the cathedral of Jaca can be defined as a true circular asterisk (fig. 5-75). Joaquín Yarza offers the following interpretation of its signification:

> The chrismon has changed its christological meaning by substituting the rho for the *P* of Pater. It becomes a trinitarian sign. The *P* corresponds to the Father; very possibly, the alpha and omega to Christ; and the *S* to the Holy Spirit. The circle is, therefore, not just a sign of God, but also a wheel. More than one text indicates that the trinity is symbolized in it (the wheel). However, perhaps it would be convenient not to put aside completely the memory of Christ when talking about the chrismon.[62]

Of the many examples of Christograms in Rome, noteworthy instances that appear in Cosmatesque churches include those at San Clemente (fig. 5-76) and Santa Maria in Trastevere (fig. 5-77), both executed in mosaic at the key of the arch of the apse; that painted at Santa Maria in Cosmedin; and the one executed in brick on the external right wall of Santi Giovanni e Paolo (fig. 5-78).

The geometry of the Christogram is akin, when not identical, to the double cross underlying the Cosmatesque quincunx. The double cross materialized in the design drawn with ashes during the chrismation of the principal quincunx of the pavement during the ceremony of consecration of the church. The undeniable formal similarity between the Christogram and the double cross drawn with ashes seems even more evident upon recalling that on the ends of one of the lines that constituted the cross, the diagonal line over which was written the Greek alphabet, were drawn the letters α and ω.

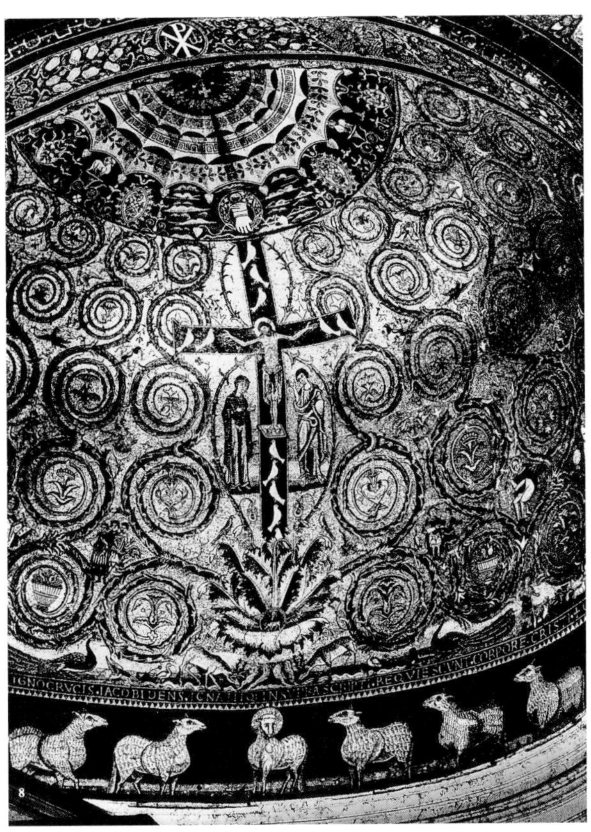

5-76. *A Christogram in mosaic in the keystone of the arch of the apse, San Clemente.* (PHOTO ZODIAQUE)

5-77. *A Christogram in mosaic in the keystone of the arch of the apse, Santa Maria in Trastevere.* (PHOTO ZODIAQUE)

5-78. *A Christogram in the external right wall, Santi Giovanni e Paolo.*

If one accepts that the formal affinity of two signifiers implies some correspondence in their signification, it is reasonable to affirm that the chrismon and the double cross drawn over the Cosmatesque quincunx in the dedication ceremony of a church share, at the very least, the objective of summoning Jesus Christ.

To conclude, I would like to present some examples that, when added to all those cited thus far, confirm both the constant presence of the double cross as an emblematic design in the Middle Ages and its direct affiliation with power.

Earlier in this chapter, in discussions of the origins of the underlying geometry in the Cosmatesque quincunx, several cases were cited in which the double cross appears connected to temporal power: its relationship to the birthplace of the porphyrogenitus emperors, the ceremony of imperial coronation in the ancient basilica of San Pietro in Rome, the place of prayer of the empress Galla Placidia, and the audience halls of late antiquity that preceded the middle-Byzantine quincunx church. To these examples must be added the adornment associated with Byzantine and medieval emperors. In these ornaments, true symbols of imperial power, frequently appear designs in double cross.

The ornaments of the Iron Crown of Lombardy, a sixth-century piece from a metalworks in Constantinople, are of quincuncial design (fig. 5-79). This crown was worn by the Lombard kings, by Charlemagne and his successors in the Holy Empire, by Charles V, and by Napoleon I. In the gold votive crown of the king Recesvinto, a work of the seventh century inspired by models from the imperial Byzantine court, the gems appear set on the ends of square asterisks arranged in a series (fig. 5-80).

5-79. The sixth-century Iron Crown of Lombardy.

5-80. The seventh-century gold votive crown of King Recesvinto, belonging to the treasury of Guarrazar, Toledo.

Many of the Byzantine imperial scepters were crowned by emblems in the form of an X-shaped cross, a cross, or a double cross. The scepter was one of the imperial insignia, like the cloak and crown. This essential symbol of sovereign power took on different forms according to the period. From the fifth to the tenth century, scepters crowned by forms based on the cross, the pommel, and their derivatives predominated. As of the ninth century, the scepters that harked back to the Constantinian labarum, with all of its essential characteristics, were imposed. Thus appeared scepters crowned by quincuncial compositions, for example, a cross at the center of a plaque (from Theophilus, 829–42, to Romanus I Lecapenus, 920–44), a decussate cross dotted with gems at the angles (from Constantine VII, 913–59, to Nicephorus II Phocus, 963–69), or five gems arranged over the diagonals in the shape of a cross (from Constantine VIII, 1025–28, to John II Comnenus, 1118–43). Theophilus was the first emperor to revive the use of the Constantinian sign of triumph when, after defeating the Arabs in Tarsus and Massina in 831, he returned to Constantinople victorious, displaying, among other ornaments, a military insignia or banner, a labarum. The nonfigurative nature of the labarum might have favored the return of this insignia by Theophilus, given his iconoclastic tendencies. After Theophilus, the double cross, heiress to the Constantinian monogram, would underlie the quincuncial compositions that crowned the scepters of the Byzantine emperors until the twelfth century (fig. 5-81).[63]

Before turning to gem-studded objects of liturgical use, a brief note concerning the struggle for temporal power that entangled the emperors and the popes during the Middle Ages is useful. This struggle, which was most evident in the Controversy of Investitures, was possibly one of the last factors to establish the systematic use of designs in double cross by medieval Christian artists and, in particular, the employment of the quincunx by Cosmatesque artists. The Cosmati worked under the guidance of the ecclesiastic power which, after long conflicts, had managed to reach the apex of temporal and spiritual power in the twelfth century. The ecclesiastic authority employed the churches as vehicles of propaganda of its new preponderance, loading them with the ornaments and the symbols traditionally associated with the temporal power customarily reserved for the exclusive use of the

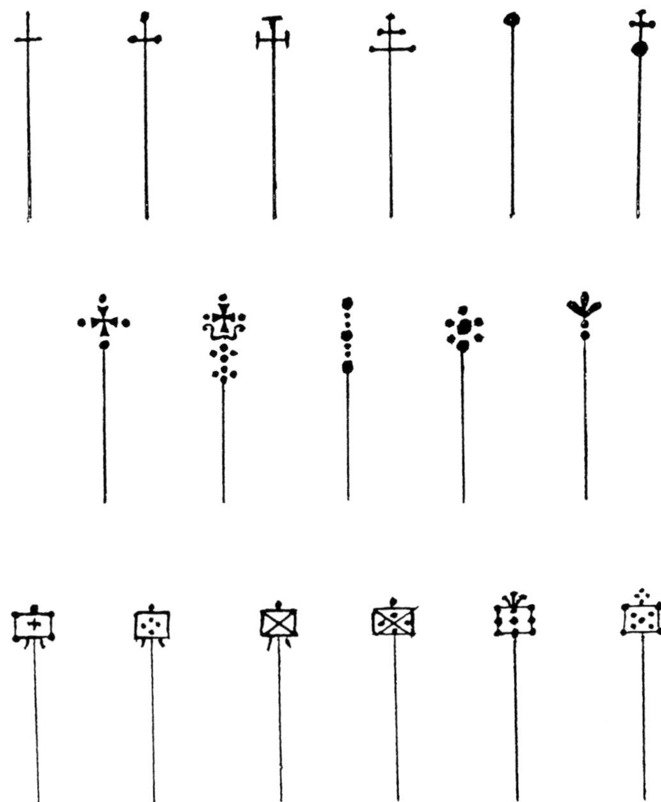

5-81. Top: fifth- to tenth-century imperial scepters; center: tenth- to twelfth-century imperial scepters; bottom: labarums, ninth- to twelfth-century Byzantine imperial scepters.

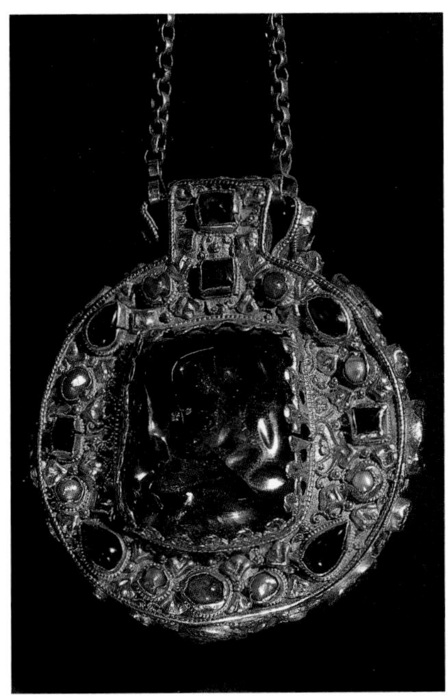

5-82. The eighth-century talisman of Charlemagne.

emperor. These ornaments frequently had an underlying double-cross schema, the Cosmatesque quincunx being only one example.

Objects ornamented with gems in a quincuncial arrangement frequently appeared as early as the Carolingian era. The spare geometry (five points forming a quincunx) to which the monogram of Christ was reduced as of the ninth century possibly resulted from the phobia of images that dominated the iconoclastic century (726–843), carried to the extreme. In addition to the Byzantine scepters of the ninth century, many works reflected the Constantinian monogram in the simplified form of a group of gems dotting an underlying double cross. These gem-studded anagrams, which symbolized the Christogram X and +, were symbols of a symbol.

Throughout his life, Charlemagne wore a talisman that contained several relics, among them, a fragment of Christ's cross (fig. 5-82). Eight gems adorned the talisman, placed at the ends of a double cross: four sapphires at the ends of the X-shaped cross and four emeralds at the ends of the upright cross, with eight pearls in the intervals between them. The double cross was also part of the regulating geometry of another German piece of gemmed metalwork: the flabellum (liturgical fan) from the thirteenth century, which today is in the Cloisters Collection of the Metropolitan Museum of Art in New York (fig. 5-83).[64] The Cross of the Angels, 808 (fig. 5-84), and the Cross of the Victory, 908 (fig. 5-85), both in the Holy Chamber of the cathedral in Oviedo, display gems dotting the center and the eight ends of a circular asterisk on the face of their central disc. An eleventh-century icon of Saint Michael Archangel, originally from Constantinople, is preserved in the treasury of San Marco in Venice; the border of this piece alternates figurative ornamental motifs with groups of gems in quincunx (see chapter 3 for an illustration of this icon). The liturgical paten from the eleventh and

5-83. A thirteenth-century flabellum, or liturgical fan, from Germany (the Rhine Valley, possibly Cologne). Gilded bronze, champlevé enamel, silver, semiprecious stones, glass gems; diameter 29.2 cm. (The Metropolitan Museum of Art, The Cloisters Collection, 1947. [47.101.32] Photograph ©1985 The Metropolitan Museum of Art)

5-84. Face of the Cross of the Angels (808). (Holy Chamber, Cathedral of Oviedo)

5-85. Face of the Cross of the Victory (908). (Holy Chamber, Cathedral of Oviedo)

5-86. Eleventh- to twelfth-century liturgical paten of gilded silver and jewels.

twelfth centuries that is preserved in the Museo Monástico Medieval in Santo Domingo de Silos exhibits a border with gems dotting the extremes and intervals of a circular asterisk, and a deep-set octolobate center in whose lobes were placed the fragments of the Eucharistic form, surrounding the large circular gem that occupies the middle of the paten (fig. 5-86).[65]

The evangelistary of Lindau, Carolingian metalwork that served as a cover for the gospel books, shows a quincuncial composition integrated by a cross and four gems arranged in the middle of the quadrants; the gems of the central motif of the cross form a quincunx (fig. 5-87). A quincunx formed by five gems ornaments the cover of the books that accompany Saint Augustine as he is portrayed in an anonymous fifteenth-century retable (fig. 5-88); the four peripheral gems of the quincunx possibly symbolize the four Evangelists. Quincuncial compositions also ornament the cover of books that Saint Stephen and Saint Lawrence carry in images created by Giotto. In the Box of Agates, given by Fruela II of Spain to the cathedral of Oviedo in 910 (fig. 5-89), the gems set in the center of the cover form a quincuncial composition (fig. 5-90), a reflection of the design that appears on the bottom of the reliquary box (fig. 5-91), where the symbols of the Evangelists are grouped around a cross of equal arms, each occupying one of the four quadrants created by the cross.[66]

Quincuncial compositions abound in the interior of medieval churches. They appear not only on liturgical metalwork, but also on the marble works,

5-87. *The evangelistary of Lindau, Carolingian metalwork.*

5-88. *An anonymous fifteenth-century retable depicting Saint Augustine (354–430).*

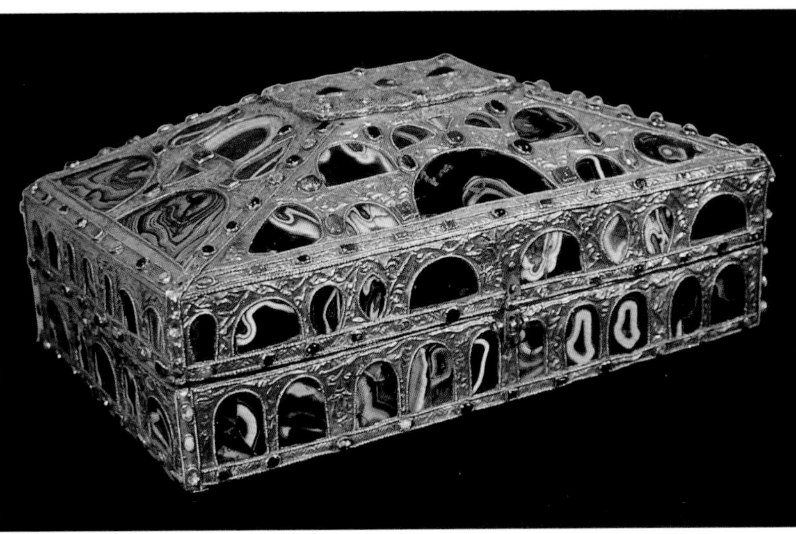

5-89. *The Box of Agates, a gift from Fruela II to the cathedral of Oviedo in 910.*

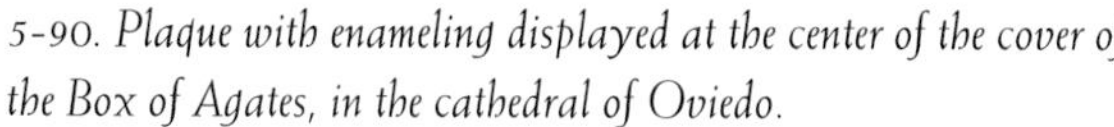

5-90. *Plaque with enameling displayed at the center of the cover of the Box of Agates, in the cathedral of Oviedo.*

5-91. *The bottom of the Box of Agates, with the symbols of the Evangelists, in the cathedral of Oviedo.*

such as the pavement and fixed furnishings (such as the ambo, pulpit, altar, tomb, and episcopal throne), where rounds of porphyry and serpentine took the place of the gems used in metalwork. Although rarer, it is also possible to find quincuncial compositions ornamenting the exterior of the church. The thirteenth-century façade of the church of San Pietro in Tuscania includes symbols of the Evangelists on the four peripheral points of a quincunx whose center is occupied by a beautiful Cosmatesque rose window (figs. 5-92, 5-93, and 5-94).[67]

The preceding pages have focused on the search for the meaning of the Cosmatesque quincunx through the study of examples of structures in double-cross design that belong to the formal and symbolic context in which the medieval observer perceived the quincunx.

The definitive loss of the signification of a signifier leads to a shift, when the signifier is an ornamental design, from *ornament* to *decoration*. Therefore, to consider the Cosmatesque quincunx as a simple decoration may be the most natural and immediate response for the average contemporary observer, since the quincunx today lacks function or symbolic content in the modern liturgy. The difficult task of seeking the forgotten signification of the Cosmatesque quincunx contributes to the reaffirmation of the marked ornamental nature of the motif. In the Cosmatesque churches, the central

5-92. The thirteenth-century rose window of the façade in the church of San Pietro in Tuscania.

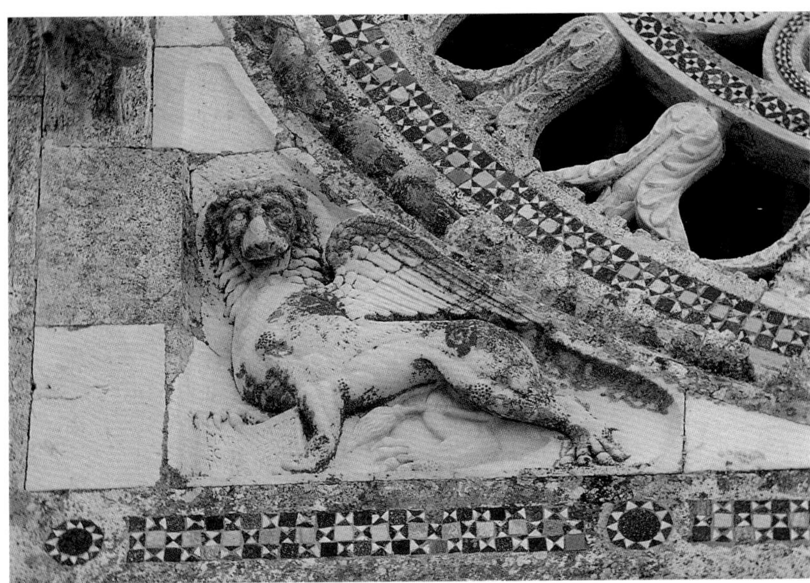

5-93. Detail of the lower left angle of the rose window in the façade of the church of San Pietro in Tuscania, which depicts a winged lion, symbol of Saint Mark.

5-94. Detail of the upper right angle of the rose window in the façade of the church of San Pietro in Tuscania, which depicts a man-angel, symbol of Saint Matthew.

quincunx is the ornament in which both the function and symbolism of the pavement are concentrated, and so the meaning of a Cosmatesque pavement is virtually equivalent to the meaning of its principal quincunx. Thus, restoring the signification of the quincunx reaffirms the decidedly ornamental—not merely decorative—character of the pavement as a whole.

Understanding the meaning associated with the geometry of the Cosmatesque quincunx and remembering the intimate relationship between the flat quincunx and the spatial configuration of the church, one can define the Cosmatesque quincunx as *a two-dimensional abstract representation, that is, the monogram or coded representation, that signifies the three-dimensional reality associated with the medieval Christian cult.* This reality includes as much the living spatial geometry derived from the beliefs and ceremonies associated with the Roman liturgy as it does the nonliving spatial geometry—which shapes and reshapes itself in continuous interaction with the living geometry—defined by the material used in the construction of the church.

The Quincunx as a Cosmic Symbol

The previous sections included numerous examples of quincuncial compositions, flat and spatial. All of them are associated with buildings, objects, or people linked to sacredness or to a supreme authority, temporal or spiritual. One might wonder about the final reason for asserting a connection between the quincunx and sacredness, between the quincunx and supreme power. The key to this question is found in the essential symbolic nature of the quincunx, because it encompasses the four fundamental cosmic symbols: the center, the cross, the circle, and the square.

The center symbolizes the beginning, the origin, the starting point, the pure being, the absolute, the transcendent; in three dimensions, the center corresponds to the axis, which unites a point with the zenith (the North Star), indicating verticality. The circle—in space, the sphere—represents the infinite, transcendent, and complete, in sum, the divine, God. The square—in space, the cube—is the symbol of the material, of the finite, nontranscendent, limited, solid; it is the symbol of the earth, connected in its order to the four cardinal points. The cross marks the four points of the compass; it stems from joining the center with each one of the points, establishing the orientation of the point in space and in time (solstices and equinoxes; change of seasons). The cross is the mediating symbol that connects heaven and earth.

These four fundamental symbols are inseparably joined with the help of a simple chord, or a compass, the attribute of the Creator. Given a point, a circle is drawn whose center is that point; thus the circle is no more than an extension of a point. By uniting the point with each of the four cardinal points, the cross appears and in turn divides the circle into four parts. At each of the intersections of the cross and the circle, an arc whose radius is the same as that of the initial circle is drawn, providing the two diagonals of an oriented square. This simple succession of geometric operations symbolizes the sacred rite of the genesis of the universe. The resulting composition, which is synthesis of the four fundamental or universal symbols, is a quincuncial composition. The quincunx is therefore a universal symbol that satisfies the need to make evident the four-pointed structure of the cosmos.

The four fundamental symbols are as ancient as man, since they are related to the immediate perception of the universe, the perception of the universe when observed from earth. Today we know that the perception of the "world" from earth is no more than one among an infinite number of possible interpretations and, thanks to space exploration, we have had the opportunity to see images of the universe taken from some nonterrestrial points of view. However, humans for the most part continue to perceive the world and its order, day after day, in the same way as people of the most ancient civilizations and of the Middle Ages: from Earth. For that reason, not only is the system of fundamental symbols that dominated the representation of the cosmos in the ancient and medieval civilizations not foreign to us, but it forms part of our own existence.

Their attentive perception and observation of the immediate universe led the ancients to conceive of the world as a space delineated by a hemisphere above, the celestial vault, crowned by the immobile North Star, around which, like a great paddle wheel, rotated all the stars (figs. 5-95 and 5-96). The vault rested on four points, the four principal constellations (Taurus, Leo, Scorpio, and Aquarius), which marked the solstices (June 21 and December 21) and the equinoxes (March 21 and September 21) and, consequently, the change of seasons throughout the year. The earth was a plane, in square shape, anchored or hanging from those four points of support of the celestial vault, and surrounded by seas. The seas occupied the space between the square of the earth and the circle that circumscribed it, a horizontal projection of the celestial vault. Beneath the earth were the lower waters, the abyss, the kingdom of the dead. Above the celestial vault were the upper waters, which fell to earth through the holes that opened in the hard, transparent dome. On top of the celestial vault, over its zenith, sat the

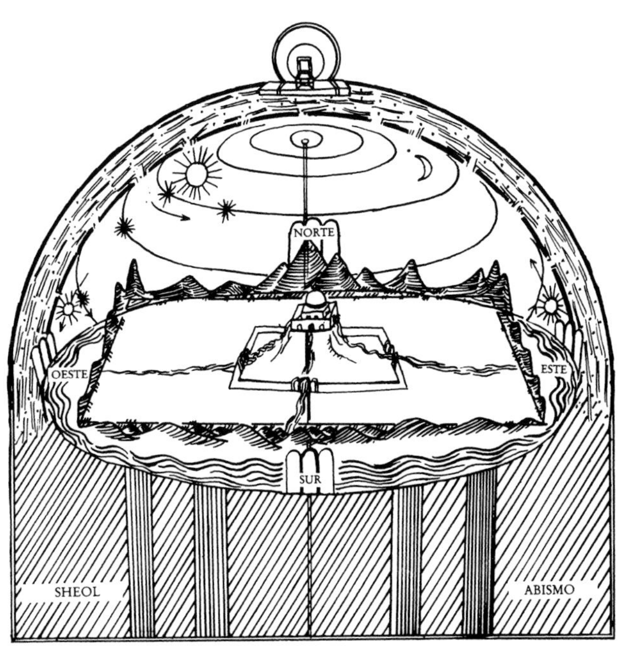

5-95. *The cosmography of the people of antiquity.*

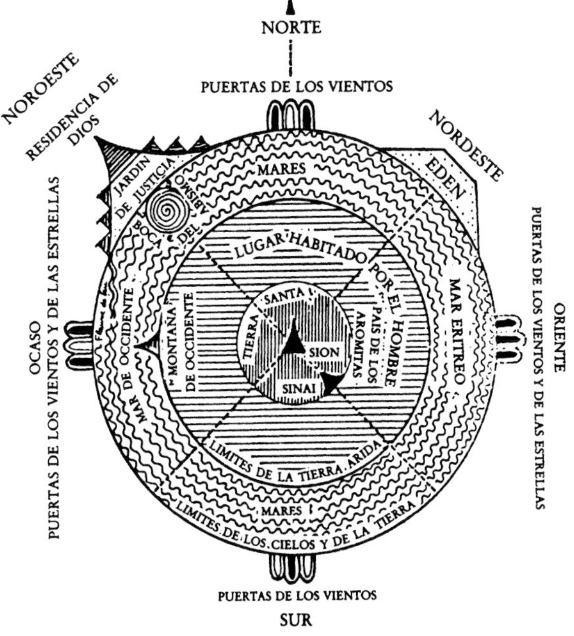

5-96. *Mythical map from the Book of Henoc. (P. Grelot)*

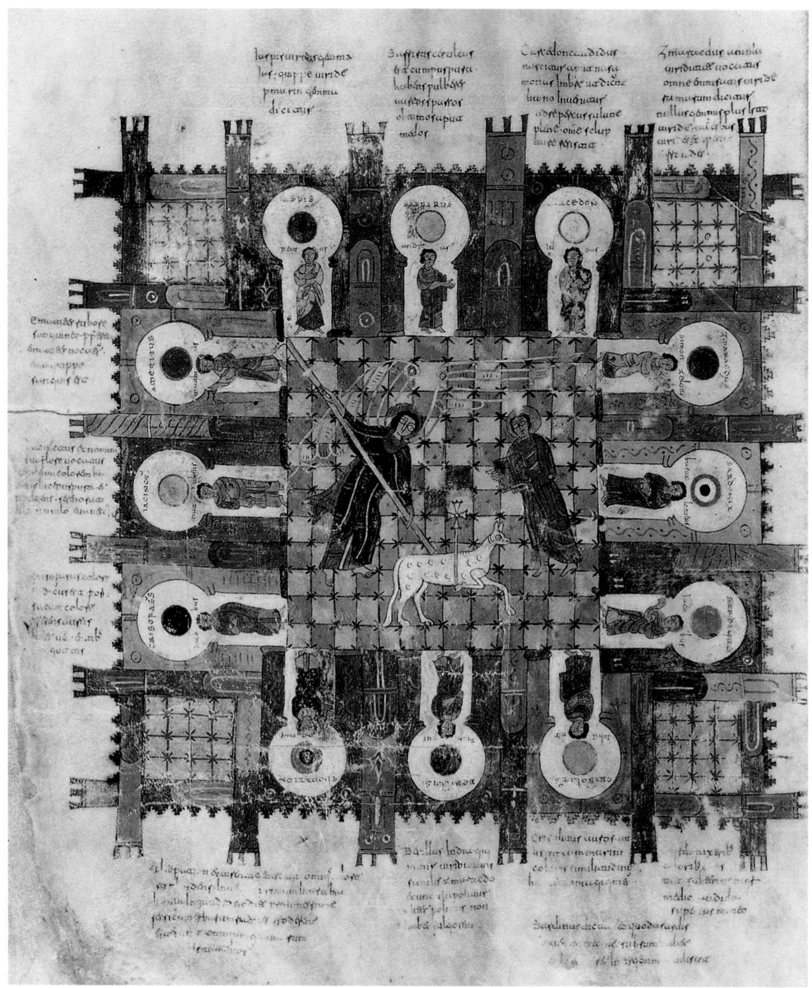

5-97. Heavenly Jerusalem. (The Pierpont Morgan Library, New York. M. 644, f. 222v.)

creator, God, on a throne over the North Star. Thus, three vertical levels were distinguished, from below upward: the subterranean abyss (turbulent waters over which rested the earth, held by an aquatic monster, a fish or a bull; the dwelling place of the dead), earth (the space between the horizontal plane of the terrestrial square and the celestial vault, the dwelling place of the living), and sky (the space above the celestial dome where the upper waters flowed; the dwelling place of the divine). This conception of the world would fundamentally prevail in the Middle Ages, passed through the evangelical sieve. The three levels of the world cited correspond to the Christian hell, earth, and heaven.

Quincuncial symbols proliferated in the Middle Ages, the era in which the fundamental symbols of antiquity were translated completely to the Christian idiom. Such a task depended on a universal vocabulary to express the mysteries of the Creator and of the world created by him. For the translation or adaptation of the symbols, of fundamental importance were the descriptions of the cosmos in one of the most divulged texts of the early Middle Ages, the Revelation According to Saint John, which incorporated numerous aspects of the visions of Ezekiel and Isaiah. The beautiful symbolic images elaborated upon by the medieval monks in illustrating this text are, for the scholars of today, the principal keys for interpretation of the rich iconographic repertoire of Romanesque art, images that exist not only in the miniature illustrations of the manuscripts, but also in works of sculpture,

5-98. *Heaven ajar. (The Pierpont Morgan Library, New York. M. 644, f. 87.)*

architecture, painting, mosaic, tapestry, vestments, and metalwork.[68] The visions of Saint John, Ezekiel, and Isaiah contained the symbolic elements most characteristic of Romanesque iconography, including the twenty-four Ancients; the four Living; the four tetramorphic cherubim; the four horsemen, riding four horses whose trappings displayed the four traditional colors of the four cardinal points (white, red, black, and green); the twelve tribes of Israel grouped by three, in four camps around a square tent; and heavenly Jerusalem (fig. 5-97).[69]

The tetramorph, which in the Middle Ages replaced the ancient cosmic quaternary, is perhaps the star among the symbols from the Christian language of the Romanesque period. The tetramorph is composed of four hybrid figures, half man, half beast: Saint Matthew, the man-angel; Saint Mark, the lion; Saint Luke, the bull; and Saint John, the eagle. Each of the figures occupied one of the angles of a square. Each figure possessed two or more (four, six) angel wings—which were an inheritance from the cherubim who also appeared sometimes in analogous quaternary disposition—and was accompanied by a wheel with a multitude of eyes (fig. 5-98). The spirit of the being was in the wheels which symbolized the displacement, the mutation of the condition of place, and the correlative spiritual state. The star-eyes symbolized the omnipresence of the celestial divinity. The tetramorph formed, together with a central figure, a quincuncial composition that symbolized heaven, sacredness, the place of the chosen. This central figure was,

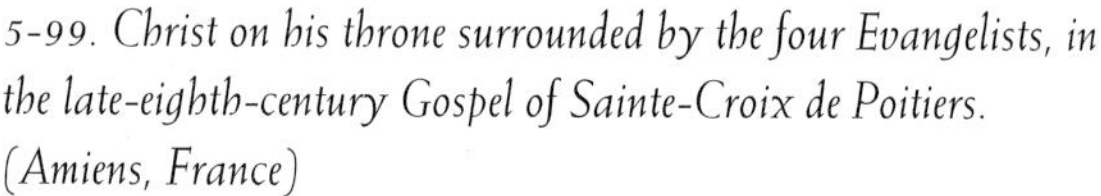

5-99. Christ on his throne surrounded by the four Evangelists, in the late-eighth-century Gospel of Sainte-Croix de Poitiers. (Amiens, France)

5-100. Christ Pantocrator, at the center of a tetramorph with angels, in a Beato in the Treasury of the Cathedral, Gerona.

almost always, a Christ figure (figs. 5-99 and 5-100), or one of the symbols that represented him, such as the lamb or the cross.[70] On occasion the central motif was, instead of Christ, a figure of the Virgin and Child or, simply, a circular opening, symbol of heaven (fig. 5-101).

5-101. Circular opening symbolizing heaven in the façade of Saint-Gabriel. (B.-du-Rh.)

The tetramorph with Christ in the center appeared with great frequency in the door surrounds of Romanesque churches, indicating that the church was a sacred place, a place of the chosen, the path toward heaven. On the façade of the church of San Pietro in Tuscania, the Cosmati executed a quincuncial composition consisting of the tetramorph with a rose window at the center. The rose window, whose central area was divided radially into twelve parts by means of colonnettes and small arches decorated with polychrome mosaics, appeared as a great wheel, symbol of the celestial dome that rotated around the North Star (fig. 5-102).

The quincuncial composition consisting of the tetramorph with Christ in the center was a figurative symbol, one comprising only figures. When the center of the tetramorph held, instead of a figure, a geometric element (such as a cross, a chrismon, a wheel), the symbol was no longer only figurative but mixed, that is, composed of figurative and geometric elements, as seen in the façade of San Pietro in Tuscania. In the case of the quincunx that appears in the Cosmatesque pavements, the symbol came to be purely geometric, since the figures in the angles, the figurative and mixed quincuncial compositions, here were replaced by four roundels: the peripheral *rotae*. These *rotae* were linked to the central roundel by means of curved bands

5-102. Detail of the rose window in the façade of San Pietro in Tuscania.

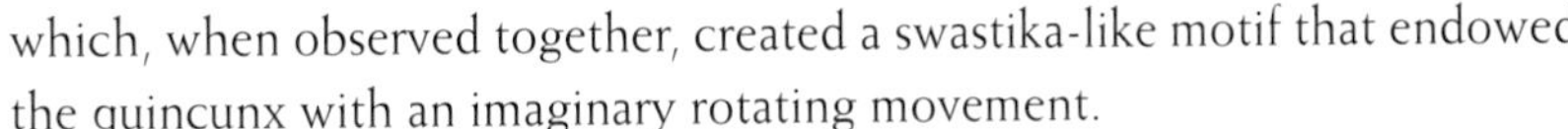

which, when observed together, created a swastika-like motif that endowed the quincunx with an imaginary rotating movement.

The Cosmatesque quincunx is the geometric translation of the figurative symbol composed of the tetramorph with Christ in the center. Therefore, it is the geometric abstraction of a figurative symbol, the symbol of a symbol. The red porphyry *rota* that occupied the great central eyelet hole of a Cosmatesque quincunx symbolized Christ, who saved the world with the spilling of his blood; the center of that *rota* was the bloody axis of the great cosmic wheel. The peripheral *rotae* of green serpentine represented the hope of salvation disseminated by the four Evangelists. Each Evangelist was symbolized by one of the rotating roundels or "wheels"—which represented the being, the spirit—linked to the central roundel by the mosaic bands that formed a pseudo-swastika. The ensemble represented heaven, the revelation, the incarnation.

5-103. Quincuncial composition with a chrismon at the center.

The degree of symbolic abstraction achieved in the Cosmatesque quincunx through geometrization was enormous, surpassed only by the chrismon (fig. 5-103),[71] or by the spare quincunxes composed solely of five gems that appeared in some works of Byzantine (such as the scepters of the emperors) and Carolingian (such as the Gospel book covers) metalwork, where each of the circles of the quincunx was reduced to its minimum expression: a point. Possibly, the geometrization of Christian symbols with their consequent abstraction, taken to the limit, might have had its origin in the ideas that dominated Byzantine religious thought during the iconoclastic century (725–842).

Aside from the symbolism of the quincunx, derived from its own geometric composition, the related symbolism derived from its location or situation in the medieval church, of which it formed part, must also be considered. To do so, one must understand the fundamental symbolism associated with a church in the Middle Ages.

The church was a sacred, and therefore cosmic, building, and as such it reproduced symbolically the structures of the world. All construction of a sacred building was a cosmogenesis, a holy creation, an imitation of God the

Creator. In the church God and man met. The church was the place where religion was practiced, where the relation of heaven and earth was relinked and renewed. The Christian of the Middle Ages conceived of the church above all as a place of assumption, of elevation of the spirit; as the ladder or path of salvation that led the sinner from earthly hell to the glory of heaven. The volumetric and spatial composition of the medieval churches was dominated by this perception. The church was thus a representation of the cosmos and, at the same time, a representation of man, insofar as man was a symbol of the cosmos, a microcosm.[72] Man was the temple of God, just as the cosmos was God's temple.

The centralized medieval church celebrated the ritual passing from the center to the circle and from the circle to the square. In its volume materialized the transition from the cube to the sphere, from the earthly to the celestial, from the imperfect to the perfect in an elevating movement that traveled the vertical axis passing through the center of the building. The centralized medieval churches were, in general, laid out on a quincuncial plan (that is, a square divided into nine equal squares; each side of the square divided into three parts; twelve parts in all, a four-by-three design that followed the description of heavenly Jerusalem according to the Revelation of Saint John) and covered by a main hemispherical dome that represented the ceiling of the celestial tent. This dome often was accompanied by four peripheral domes that completed the quincunx (fig. 5-104). The designs of the mosaic pavements of these churches reinforced the centered quincuncial composition.

5-104. *Reliquary church from the treasury of the Guelphs; originally from Cologne, circa 1175.*

In the case of the directional medieval church, the ascendant movement of the spirit was produced along the longitudinal axis of the floor plan, advancing toward the east, from the nave to the apse. The symbolic correspondences, in simplified terms, linked: the portico and the exterior of the church in general with hell; in the interior, the sancta (enclosure where the faithful congregated) with earth; and the sancta sanctorum (enclosed area to which only the officiants had access) with heaven. The choir, situated between the sancta and the sancta sanctorum, symbolized purgatory or the door of heaven. There was a marked partition that separated the created from the eternal. The messianic message revealed the way to pass from one area to another.

In the classical Cosmatesque designs of the twelfth century (for example, Santa Maria in Cosmedin, San Clemente, Santa Croce in Gerusalemme), the main quincunx of the pavements was found in the center of the area reserved for the faithful, or the sancta. Here the principal part of the ceremony of consecration of a church was conducted, with the chrismation of the quincunx, as explained previously.

The Cosmatesque quincunx was the geometric emblem of the tetramorph with Christ at the center, which was the symbol of heaven, of sacredness, of the revelation. The covers of the Gospel books, called evangelistaries, were ornamented with works of gemmed metalwork, with the gems placed in a quincuncial arrangement. In the medieval miniatures, each time that the book of the Gospels, that is, the book of the divine revelation of the path to salvation, was depicted in the hands of a holy person, the drawing was of a square in which the five points of the gems of the cover were sometimes also included. All this confirms the quincunx as a symbol of the revelation of the path to salvation through the message of Christ collected by the Evangelists.

Therefore, the quincunx, symbol of the revelation, was the logical center of the space reserved for the faithful, the sancta, symbol of the earthly world, since Christ came to earth and revealed the path toward heaven. The quincunx centered in the pavement of the sancta was connected with the entrance to the church and with the schola cantorum by means of guilloches superposed over the longitudinal axis of the church, marking the path for redemption. The schola cantorum was elevated one or several steps above the rest of the pavement and was enclosed by panels or screens. These partitions, together with the ones that enclosed the presbytery, symbolized the celestial dome that separated heaven from earth. The schola cantorum symbolized the saints or angels who praised God at the entrance to his celestial abode; it might also be considered a symbol of the place in which the pious souls completed their purification before reaching the height of heavens, or purgatory. The pavement of the schola cantorum was frequently directional, composed of a single guilloche or several parallel ones that marked the path toward the presbytery. To access the presbytery, again it was necessary to climb steps, since the house of God was found at the highest point of heaven, in the sancta sanctorum of the church. In the presbytery lay the altar, a cube or pseudo-cube, located beneath the ciborium or the baldachin. The altar was in turn elevated over several steps. In the ritual of consecration of the altar, the consecrating pontiff drew five crosses twice—in quincunx, a cross in each angle and one in the center—over the table of the altar (fig. 5-105); the crosses were first drawn with holy water, symbolizing purification, and then with oil of catechumens.[73] The ciborium was composed of four porphyry columns over which rested a hemispherical dome, often decorated with gold stars on a blue background. Beneath the altar lay the crypt where the remains of martyrs and relics were kept. The crypt symbolized the abyss, hell. On occasion, the altar itself served as a tomb/reliquary. The trio of crypt/altar/ciborium was a symbol of the evangelized cosmos, where the Christian spirit was freed from death, from hell, in an ascending movement that passed from the cube to the sphere, from the earthly to the celestial. This ascendant trio was reinforced in some continental European churches by a fourth element, the dome/tower over the crossing under which was found the altar (fig. 5-106).[74] Behind the altar, normally at the back of the eastern apse, sat the episcopal throne, elevated a few steps. The throne symbolized the place God occupied in heaven, the holiest place. At the feet of the episcopal throne, in the paving over the longitudinal axis of the church, frequently appeared a Cosmatesque quincunx which, with its roundels of red porphyry and green serpentine, emphasized the very holy place in which God sat over colored precious stones, as the visions of the prophets recounted. The throne, composed of a cubic seat and circular back, was located in the apse, covered by a quarter-sphere dome that was decorated with glowing golden mosaics, corresponding to the divine dwelling at the summit of heaven.

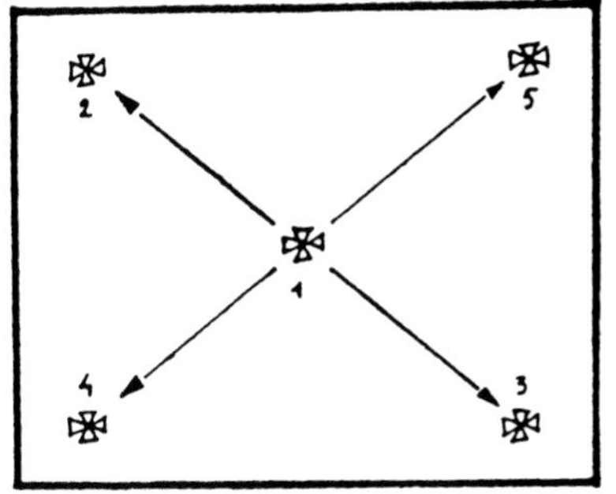

5-105. *The ritual of consecration of the altar.*

5-106. *Kalundborg, Denmark.*

The church as much as each of the elements that compose it were symbols of the evangelized cosmos, which permits the assertion of further symbolic correspondences virtually indefinitely and with growing detail. Knowing these general interpretive guidelines, the reader can continue independently without difficulty to analyze the symbolism of each of the remaining elements of the church and of each of the details contained in them. I would add only a few brief words about some of the noteworthy symbolic relationships not yet explained, although they are present in some Cosmatesque churches.

The atrium, where a fountain was often located, symbolized the lower waters or seas of the abyss, in other words, hell. The well, which on occasion appeared in the patio preceding the entrance to the church, was another cosmic symbol that alluded to the ladder to salvation, connecting hell, earth, and heaven, just as the deep hole of the well reached subterranean waters from its seat on earth, and heaven was reflected in its water. The ambos, from which the prayers were directed and the Epistles and Gospels were read, were an echo of one of the most universal symbols, the sacred mountain, which was a symbol of reunion. On the mountain, an elevated place where heaven and earth met, the meeting between God and man occurred with greater ease and frequency (for example, Moses on Mount Sinai, Christ on the Mount of Olives, and Christ at Golgotha). The lion, which often appeared on the entrance door to the Cosmatesque churches, one at the foot of each jamb, symbolized the guardian of sacredness; his mere presence announced the proximity of holiness. A lion with a small animal or human figure held in his claws acted as the guardian who kept vigil over the tranquillity of the congregation gathered within the temple. When the lion appeared with an animal or human figure in its mouth, he represented a variation of the man-eating monster that gobbled up its victim and then spit it out (for example, the whale that swallowed Jonah); hence, this lion is a symbol of resurrection, of regeneration, of the transition from one world to another. The eagle, which appeared frequently sculpted on the lectern of the ambones of the Cosmatesque churches, was another universal symbol signifying the spirit, elevation, ascension. The cloister, which often presented a quadripartite division of the floor plan, was another cosmic symbol. The quaternary division of the floor plan of the cloister was often accompanied by the tripartite division of the elevation of each of its four sides, based on the holy design of heavenly Jerusalem, ordered by twelve, a perfect number.

Romanesque architecture in general, and in particular its symbolic/ornamental compositions, was dominated by the law of subordination to the imperatives of the square, allied to its inseparable companion, the circle. The rule was due to the medieval cosmological conception that manifested itself insistently in the vast majority of the images that constituted the symbolic repertoire of Christianity at the time.

Here concludes this abbreviated introduction to the symbols of the Middle Ages that were linked to the most characteristic elements of the Cosmatesque churches and their pavements, the quincunx being the preeminent symbolic element.[75] The medieval "quincunx mania," and in particular the Cosmatesque "quincunx mania," is explained by the universal nature of the quincunx as a cosmic symbol that unites in its design the four fundamental cosmic symbols: the center, the cross, the circle, and the square. Christian piety made medieval art a strongly symbolic art; it is not surprising that the quincunx took on an indisputable lead role given its nature as an essential cosmic symbol that represented in multiple forms the diverse aspects of the admirably organized whole.

Chapter 6

ANALYSIS OF A MOSAIC

THE PAVEMENT OF THE SCHOLA CANTORUM OF SAN CLEMENTE

This chapter studies the pavement that ornaments the floor within the enclosure of the schola cantorum in the church of San Clemente in Rome (figs. 6-1 through 6-6). A thorough description of the mosaic is followed by an analysis of the regulating geometry, noting the associated aspects of construction, such as the characteristics of the basic units of construction and the possible order in which the work proceeded. The geometric nonconformities observable in the built work are analyzed in detail, and finally, the factors that determined the degree of decorum in the different parts of the pavement are noted.

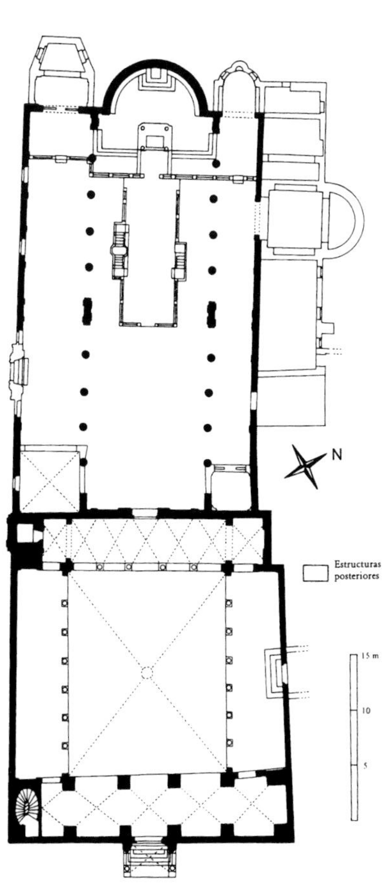

6-1. Floor plan of San Clemente, Rome. (Barclay Lloyd, 1986)

Description

The general design of the pavement that covers the rectangle of the schola cantorum of San Clemente (13.05 by 4.90 meters, or 42.81 by 16.08 feet, along the inside of the screen) is an orthogonal composition of straight-edged rectangles, having edges drawn with bands of adjacent rectangular slabs of white marble in different lengths.

The principal axis is the longitudinal axis of the church, in this case, the east/west axis, with the altar to the west and the entrance façade to the east. The transverse axis (in this case, the north/south axis) is thus the one perpendicular to the principal axis. A long horizontal rectangle of straight white edges, superposed on the principal axis, circumscribes the linear interlacing design that dominates the pavement: a guilloche of two sinusoidal strands,

6-2. *View of the interior taken from the entrance, San Clemente, Rome. (Engraving by P. M. Letarouilly, 1840)*

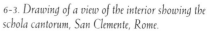

6-3. *Drawing of a view of the interior showing the schola cantorum, San Clemente, Rome.*

6-4. *View of the schola cantorum, San Clemente, Rome.*

6-5. *General view of the interior from the entrance, San Clemente, Rome.*

6-6. View of the schola cantorum from above, San Clemente, Rome.

forming twelve circular eyelets, in three counterchanged colors, red, green, and white. This rectangle constitutes the long line of a recumbent T. Each of the two short arms of the T is defined by a vertical rectangle, also of straight borders in white, filled with an isotropic surface pattern in three contrasting colors. The arms, like the sinusoidal guilloche, are heavily laden with red and green, unlike the rest of the pavement enclosed in the schola cantorum, where white predominates (fig. 6-7, 6-8, and 6-9).

The recumbent T represents the dynamic zone of the pavement. This portion of the pavement carpets the area of circulation in the schola cantorum, connecting the three entrances of the precinct, which are located at the three ends of the T. The static zones are the two lateral rectangular intervals, where benches are arranged for seating the members of the choir. These benches and their users conceal the pavement in the lateral areas, whose mosaics exhibit greater decorative austerity than the tessellation covering the far more visible T of access.

The decorative splendor of the T is derived not only from the richness of the materials used—an abundance of fine marbles (porphyry and serpentine) and large monolithic pieces (large roundels, or *rotae*, in the eyelets)—but also from the quality of the human labor, as evidenced by the atomized mosaic pattern that the Roman marble artists laid with great precision and delicacy.

The two rectangular intervals formed on either side of the T display a pattern of two contiguous bands of straight edges in white. Each of the bands that flank the rectangle circumscribing the sinusoidal guilloche contains five adjacent horizontal rectangles, filled with their respective isotropic patterns, with a correspondence between the motifs on both sides of the principal axis. The remaining two bands (adjacent to the screens in which the ambos are inserted) are covered with two long horizontal rectangles, filled with isotropic patterns with no correspondence between the motifs on either side of the principal axis.

6-7. Floor plan of the schola cantorum of San Clemente. (Watercolor on paper; dimensions of original drawing 178 by 110 cm., P. Pajares, 1993)

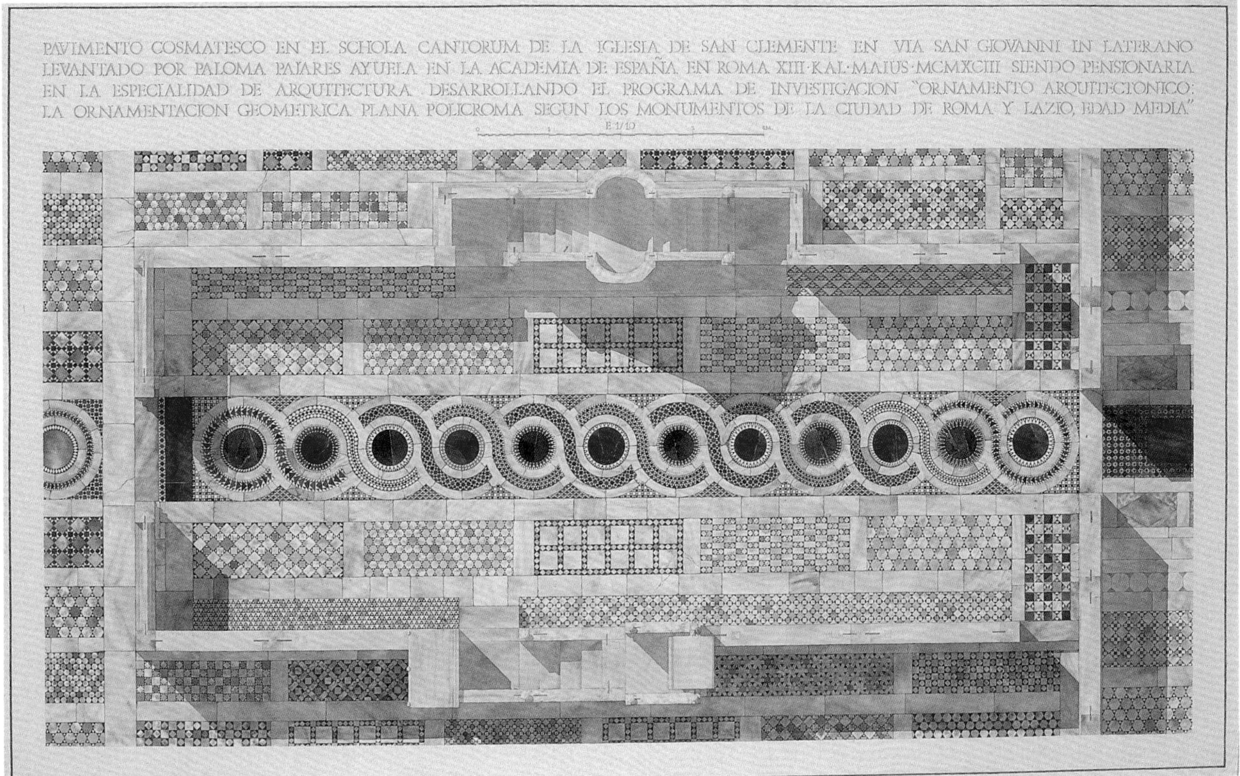

6-8. *Detail, floor plan of the schola cantorum of San Clemente. (Watercolor on paper; P. Pajares, 1993)*

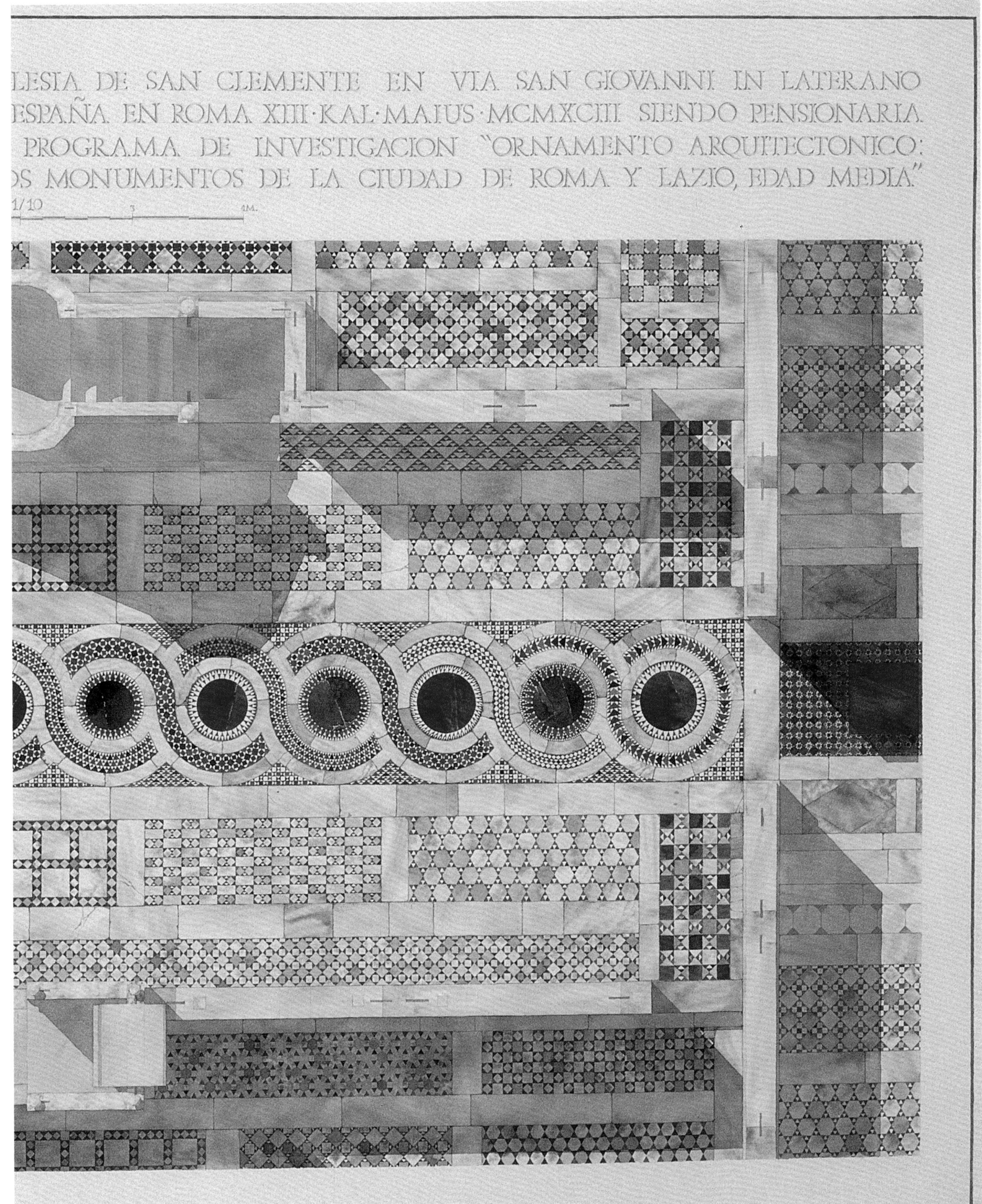

LESIA DE SAN CLEMENTE EN VIA SAN GIOVANNI IN LATERANO
ESPAÑA EN ROMA XIII·KAL·MAIUS·MCMXCIII SIENDO PENSIONARIA
PROGRAMA DE INVESTIGACION "ORNAMENTO ARQUITECTONICO:
OS MONUMENTOS DE LA CIUDAD DE ROMA Y LAZIO, EDAD MEDIA"

6-9. *Detail, floor plan of the schola cantorum of San Clemente. (Watercolor on paper; P. Pajares, 1993)*

The Linear and Surface Patterns

The long line of the T is a rectangle, superposed to the longitudinal axis of the church. It circumscribes a guilloche formed by a pair of crossed sinusoids, opposed, which create twelve circular eyelets in three counterchanged colors (red, green, and white), with interlacing straight-edged bands, here in white.

The borders of the circumscribed rectangle are drawn with white bands on the long sides, south and north, and on the short side, west. One band in red closes the short side to the east, resulting in a rectangle of 12.50 by 1.40 meters, or 41.01 by 4.59 feet (measurements to the interior edges of the bands on the border). Contiguous to the red vertical band of the eastern side is a linear geometric pattern: a row of tangent poised squares, forming hourglasses, in three counterchanged colors. The squares alternate red and green, and the intervals bear pairs of inverted inscribed triangles (each member of the pair to one side of the axis of the band), alternately red and green, forming triangles in white (fig. 6-10).

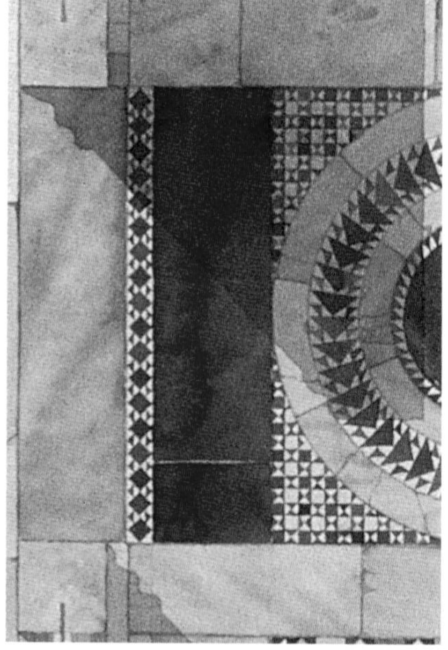

6-10. Porphyry band that encloses the eastern side of the rectangle circumscribing the sinusoidal guilloche.

In the eyelet holes of the sinusoidal guilloche are inserted roundels (alternately in green and red), bordered with linear patterns. Each border has a different pattern, as described below, moving from east to west:

1. Eyelet bearing a serpentine roundel bordered by a band of rack pattern, in three counterchanged colors. The triangles adjacent to the eyelet here are white. The intervals are alternately red and green (fig. 6-11).
2. Eyelet laden with a porphyry *rota* bordered by a band of darts, forming triangles, in three counterchanged colors. The darts are juxtaposed, tangent, here in green, of long isosceles point and semihexagonal base contiguous to the circle of the roundel. The triangles, in white, are of two types: equilateral (with the base adjacent to the circle of the roundel) and isosceles (each bearing an inverted inscribed triangle in red), creating the effect of a band composed of two imbricated rows of dog's-tooth pattern; the more fractionized the row, the closer it lies to the exterior edge of the band (fig. 6-12).
3. Eyelet containing a round of serpentine bordered by a band of dog's-tooth pattern in three counterchanged colors. The base of the triangles, here in white, rests adjacent to the circle of the roundel. Each interval bears an inverted inscribed triangle in white, forming three triangles in red and green, creating the effect of a band composed of two imbricated rows of dog's-tooth pattern. The more minute the piecing, the closer it lies to the exterior edge of the band (fig. 6-13).
4. Eyelet bearing a porphyry *rota* bordered by a band of chessboard pattern of isosceles right triangles, in two rows, in three counterchanged colors, red, green, and white. The compartments adjacent to the circle of the roundel are white. Every other compartment is laden with an inscribed inverted triangle, here in white, forming triangles in red and green, thus creating the effect of a band composed of two rows of contiguous, concordant rack pattern. Each row, in turn, is composed of two imbricated rows of rack pattern, with piecing more minute in the row nearer to the exterior edge of the band (fig. 6-14).
5. Eyelet laden with a serpentine roundel bordered by a band of darts, forming triangles in three counterchanged colors. The juxtaposed, tan-

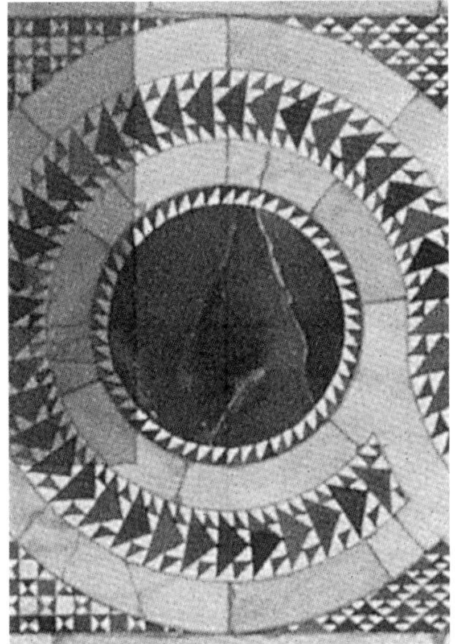

6-11. *Eyelet 1.*

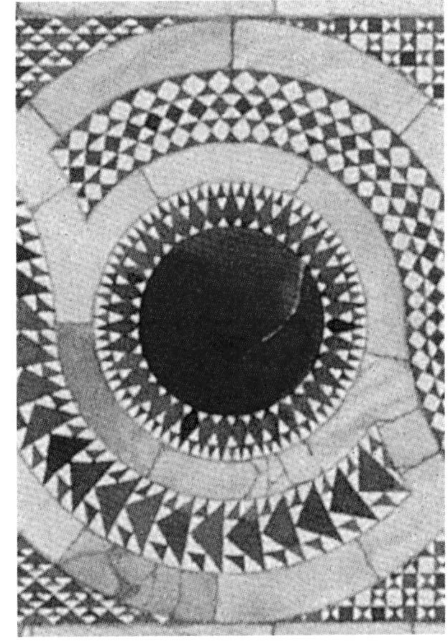

6-12. *Eyelet 2.*

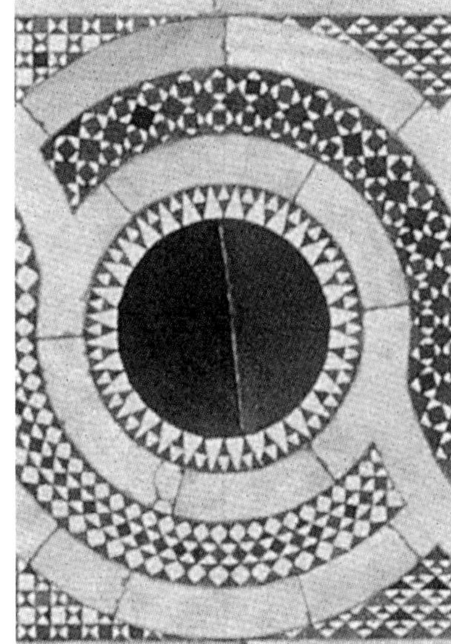

6-13. *Eyelet 3.*

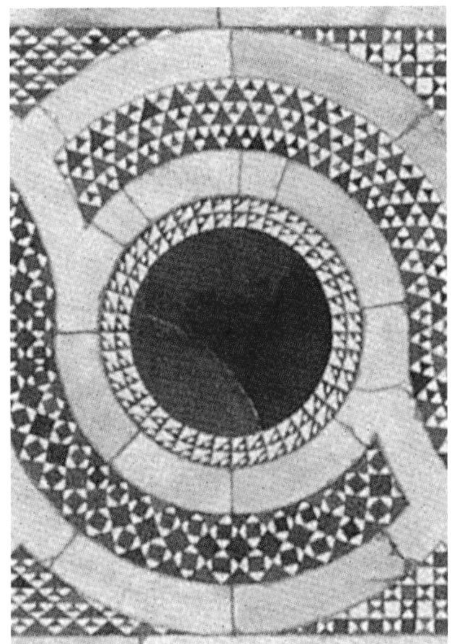

6-14. *Eyelet 4.*

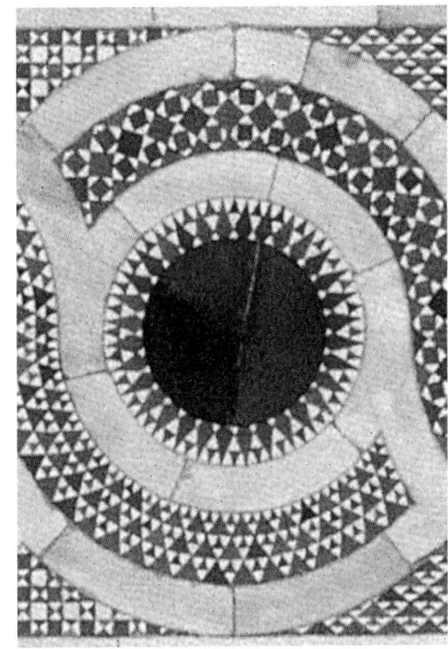

6-15. *Eyelet 5.*

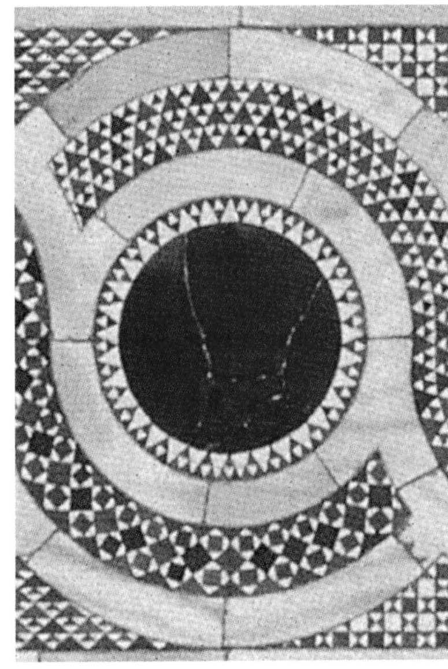

6-16. *Eyelet 6.*

gent darts, here in red, are of long isosceles point and semihexagonal base contiguous to the circle of the roundel. The triangles, in white, are of two types: equilateral (with the base adjacent to the circle of the roundel) and isosceles (each bearing an inverted inscribed triangle in green), creating the effect of a band composed of two imbricated rows of dog's-tooth pattern. The row closer to the exterior edge of the band contains more minute tesserae (fig. 6-15).

6. Eyelet containing a porphyry *rota* bordered by a band of sawtooth pattern, in three counterchanged colors. The triangles are equilateral, here in white, with the base adjacent to the circle of the roundel. Each interval bears an inverted inscribed triangle in white, forming three triangles in red and green, creating the effect of a band composed of two imbricated rows of sawtooth pattern. The row closer to the exterior edge of the band contains more minute tesserae (fig. 6-16).

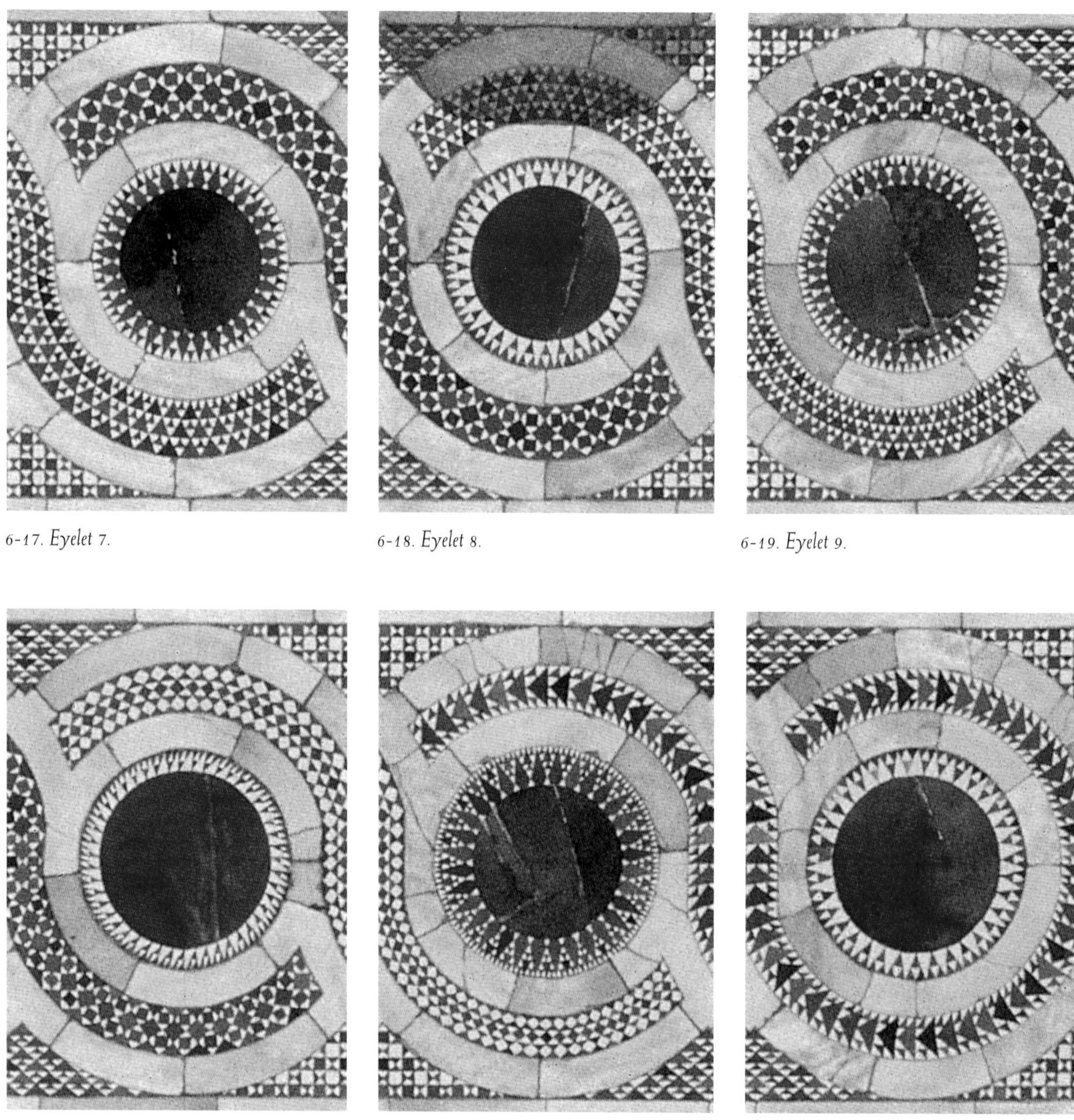

6-17. *Eyelet 7.*

6-18. *Eyelet 8.*

6-19. *Eyelet 9.*

6-20. *Eyelet 10.*

6-21. *Eyelet 11.*

6-22. *Eyelet 12.*

7. Eyelet bearing a roundel of serpentine bordered by a band like that of roundel 5 (fig. 6-17).
8. Eyelet laden with a porphyry *rota* bordered by a band like that of roundel 3 (fig. 6-18).
9. Eyelet containing a round of serpentine bordered by a band like that of roundels 5 and 7 (fig. 6-19).
10. Eyelet bearing a round of porphyry bordered by a band of rack pattern in three counterchanged colors. The base of the triangles, in white, lies adjacent to the circle of the roundel. Each interval is laden with an inverted inscribed triangle, in white, forming three triangles, in red and green, creating the effect of a band composed of two imbricated rows of rack pattern. The row closer to the exterior edge of the band contains more minute tesserae (fig. 6-20).

11. Eyelet containing a serpentine roundel bordered by a band of darts, forming triangles in three counterchanged colors. The darts are juxtaposed and tangent, here in red, of long isosceles point and semihexagonal base contiguous to the circle of the roundel. The triangles, in white, are of two types: equilateral, with the base adjacent to the circle of the roundel, and isosceles. Each isosceles triangle is laden with an inverted inscribed triangle (alternately in green and in red), that forms three triangles, each bearing, in turn, an inscribed triangle in red and green, creating the effect of a band composed of four imbricated rows of dog's-tooth pattern. The closer to the exterior edge the band is, the more minute the tesserae (fig. 6-21).
12. Eyelet laden with a round of porphyry bordered by a band like that of the roundels 3 and 8 (fig. 6-22).

The diameter of the *rotae* that fill the openings is not constant. Remember that the Cosmatesque artists obtained these roundels by cutting slices from the columns that they retrieved from ancient Roman ruins. The sizes of the *rotae* vary because the roundels came from columns of similar, but not identical, girth. Furthermore, the entasis of the shaft of a single column generated equally slight variations in the diameters of its slices, depending upon the height at which each cut was made.

Moving from the eyelets of the guilloche to the interlacing strands, these sinusoidal threads are composed of monochrome straight edges (defined by plain white slabs) and a central polychrome band, filled with linear geometric patterns of minute tesserae in three colors.

The central band contains eleven sections, most in the shape of an S, except for the two at the end, which close the circle. They are filled with four types of linear patterns, identified as *a*, *b*, *c*, and *d*.

Starting at the eastern end of the guilloche, at the first point of tangency (between roundels 1 and 2), is a band of type *a* (fig. 6-23). It consists of a band of short rectilinear thorns in three counterchanged colors. The triangles (here, isosceles right triangles, alternately red and green) rest on a white background. Each of the intervals bears an inverted inscribed triangle, in green or red, creating the effect of a rack pattern on each edge of the band.

At the second point of tangency (between roundels 2 and 3) is a band of type *b* (fig. 6-24). It consists of a chessboard pattern of poised squares, in three rows and three counterchanged colors, creating the effect of a pattern of three contiguous rows of poised squares forming hourglasses. The squares superposed on the axis of the band, here in two colors (alternately red and green), lie over a white background. The squares of the lateral rows, here in white, form hourglasses, alternately in red and green.

At the third point of tangency (between roundels 3 and 4) is a band of the type *c* (fig. 6-25). It consists of a chessboard pattern of poised squares, in two rows and three counterchanged colors. One row is superposed over the axis of the band and two half rows appear along the edge, composed of triangles. The squares alternate two colors, red and green. The triangles alternate red and green, chromatically out of synchrony with respect to the row of superposed squares. The background is white. The compartments of the background bear inverted inscribed squares, in red and green, in chromatic concordance by pairs (each member of the pair to one side of the axis of the band).

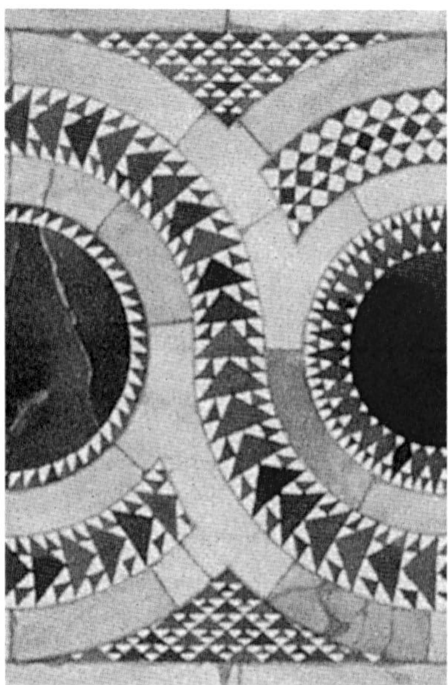

6-23. *Section 1 (passes between roundels 1 and 2) of the central band of the strand, a band of type a.*

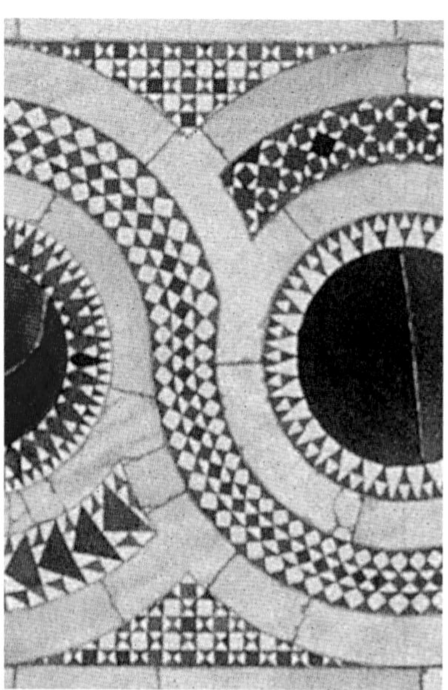

6-24. *Section 2 (passes between roundels 2 and 3) of the central band of the strand, a band of type b.*

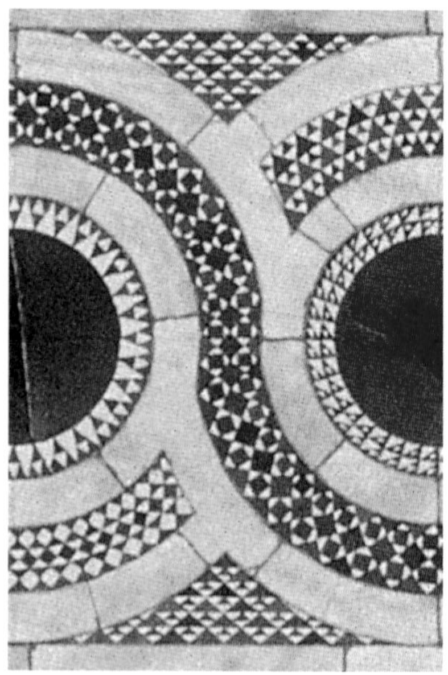

6-25. *Section 3 (passes between roundels 3 and 4) of the central band of the strand, a band of type c.*

At the fourth point of tangency (between roundels 4 and 5) is a band of the type *d* (fig. 6-26). It consists of a chessboard pattern of equilateral triangles, in three rows and three counterchanged colors, creating the effect of a pattern of three contiguous rows of sawtooth pattern over a white background. Red triangles occupy the central row; green triangles occupy the outer rows. Each compartment in the background bears an inverted inscribed triangle in red and green.

At the fifth point of tangency (between roundels 5 and 6) is a band of the type *c*.

At the sixth point of tangency (between roundels 6 and 7) is a band of type *d*.

In studying the five remaining points of tangency, which complete the eleven points at which the twelve circles are tangent, two by two, the decorative series becomes apparent:

a - b - c - d - c - d - c - d - c - b - a.

It is symmetrical with respect to the vertical axis drawn by the sixth point of tangency (the midpoint of the linear interlacing design, situated between roundels 6 and 7), through which passes a band of type *d*.

The strands in each roundel have different widths, since the line of their interior edge circumscribes the eyelets, which are of different diameters, while at the same time, the line of the exterior edge must be drawn tangent to the circumscribed rectangle, which has a constant width of 1.40 meters (4.59 feet).

Figure 6-27 notes the diameters, in centimeters (inches), of the eyelets and of the roundels with which they are laden, advancing from east to west, as well as the total widths, in centimeters (inches) of the strands encompassing each *rota* and the partial widths of their three components (exterior edge, central band, and interior edge).

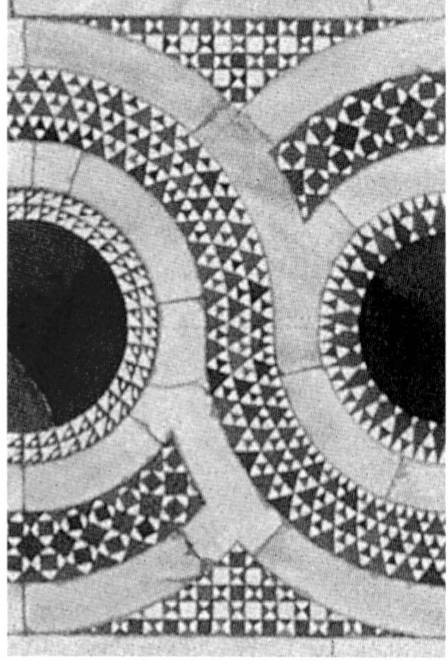

6-26. *Section 4 (passes between roundels 4 and 5) of the central band of the strand, a band of type d.*

Numbered, from east to west	Diameter of eyelet cm. (in.)	Diameter of roundel cm. (in.)	Width of strand cm. (in.)	Width of exterior edge cm. (in.)	Width of central band cm. (in.)	Width of interior edge cm. (in.)
1	64.00 (25.20)	56.50 (22.24)	38.00 (14.96)	10.50 (4.13)	16.50 (6.50)	11.00 (4.33)
2	60.50 (23.82)	45.00 (17.72)	39.75 (15.65)	10.50 (4.13)	17.50 (6.89)	11.75 (4.63)
3	65.50 (25.79)	50.00 (19.69)	37.25 (14.67)	10.50 (4.13)	15.25 (6.00)	11.50 (4.53)
4	63.00 (24.80)	45.00 (17.72)	38.50 (15.16)	11.00 (4.33)	16.00 (6.30)	11.50 (4.53)
5	62.00 (24.41)	44.00 (17.32)	39.00 (15.35)	12.00 (4.72)	15.50 (6.10)	11.50 (4.53)
6	64.00 (25.20)	53.00 (20.87)	38.00 (14.96)	11.00 (4.33)	15.50 (6.10)	11.50 (4.53)
7	60.00 (23.62)	43.00 (16.93)	40.00 (15.75)	11.50 (4.53)	16.75 (6.59)	11.75 (4.63)
8	63.00 (24.80)	47.00 (18.50)	38.50 (15.16)	11.00 (4.33)	16.00 (6.30)	11.50 (4.53)
9	64.50 (25.39)	47.50 (18.70)	37.75 (14.86)	11.00 (4.33)	15.25 (6.00)	11.50 (4.53)
10	66.00 (25.98)	53.50 (21.06)	37.00 (14.57)	11.00 (4.33)	14.50 (5.71)	11.50 (4.53)
11	69.50 (27.36)	46.50 (18.31)	35.25 (13.88)	11.00 (4.33)	12.75 (5.02)	11.50 (4.53)
12	69.50 (27.36)	53.00 (20.87)	35.25 (13.88)	11.00 (4.33)	12.50 (4.92)	11.75 (4.63)
Average cm. (in.)	64.29 (25.31)	48.66 (19.16)	37.85 (14.90)	11.00 (4.33)	15.33 (6.04)	11.52 (4.54)

6-27. The principal dimensions of the components of the loops (roundels and strands).

Isotropic patterns are arranged in *écoincon* (triangular residual spaces with one or two concave sides), in two alternating designs, 1E and 2E (fig. 6-28):

1E. A grid of bands of adjacent squares in three counterchanged colors, with a square at the intersections and a square at each box. The squares of the bands are in white; every other one bears an inscribed horizontal hourglass in red and green, creating the effect of a pattern of horizontal monochrome rows of square boxes (except in the four corner *écoincons*, where the rows are vertical), in two colors, alternating red and green.

2E. A chessboard pattern of isosceles right triangles in three counterchanged colors, creating the effect of a pattern of monochrome horizontal rows of sawtooth pattern, in two colors (alternately red and green) over a white background. Each interval is laden with an inverted inscribed triangle, in red and green, forming three triangles in white.

6-28. Isotropic patterns in écoincon. The center of the image has a type 2E pattern; the ends, type 1E.

Having examined all the geometric patterns contained in the rectangle that constitutes the long line of the T, let us now continue with the study of the vertical rectangles (of proportion 11:5) that define the two short lines of the T, each of which is filled with an isotropic pattern, 1T or 2T (fig. 6-29):

1T. A grid of bands of adjacent squares in three counterchanged colors, with a square at the intersections and a square as each box. The squares of the bands are in white, every other one containing an inscribed horizontal hourglass whose triangles in turn bear an inverted inscribed triangle, in white, thus forming three triangles, in red and green. The square boxes, in two colors, create the effect of three rows of monochrome squares, which are horizontal (parallel to the longitudinal axis of the rectangle) and of alternating colors (red, green, red).

2T. A grid of bands equivalent to that covering the first rectangle, 1T.

Having explored in detail the mosaics that carpet the dynamic zone of the pavement, let us now proceed to the study of the isotropic patterns that decorate the areas not covered by the recumbent T, the static rectangular lateral intervals, each formed by two contiguous bands of adjacent rectangles.

The five adjacent horizontal rectangles—of proportion 11:4 that is, approx. 25:9 (208 by 75 centimeters, or 81.89 by 29.53 inches)—that constitute the two bands, to the south and north, that flank the guilloche superposed on the principal axis, are filled, from east to west, with the following isotropic patterns:

1F. A chessboard pattern of poised squares in three counterchanged colors. Every other compartment bears an inscribed straight square, in white, which creates four corner triangles. Each of these triangles contains, in turn, an inverted inscribed triangle, in white, which forms three triangles, in red and green, creating the effect of an orthogonal pattern of eight-point stellate squares that form squares (fig. 6-30).

6-29. Isotropic pattern 1T and 2T in the short arms of the T.

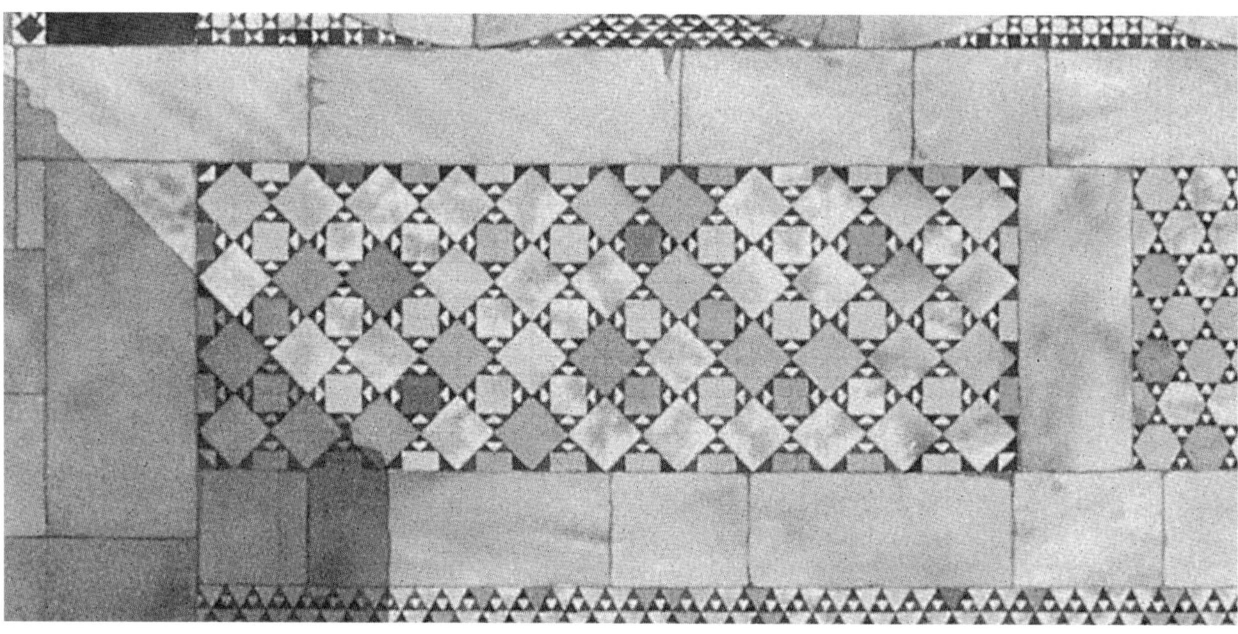

6-30. Isotropic pattern 1F in the rectangle flanking the guilloche.

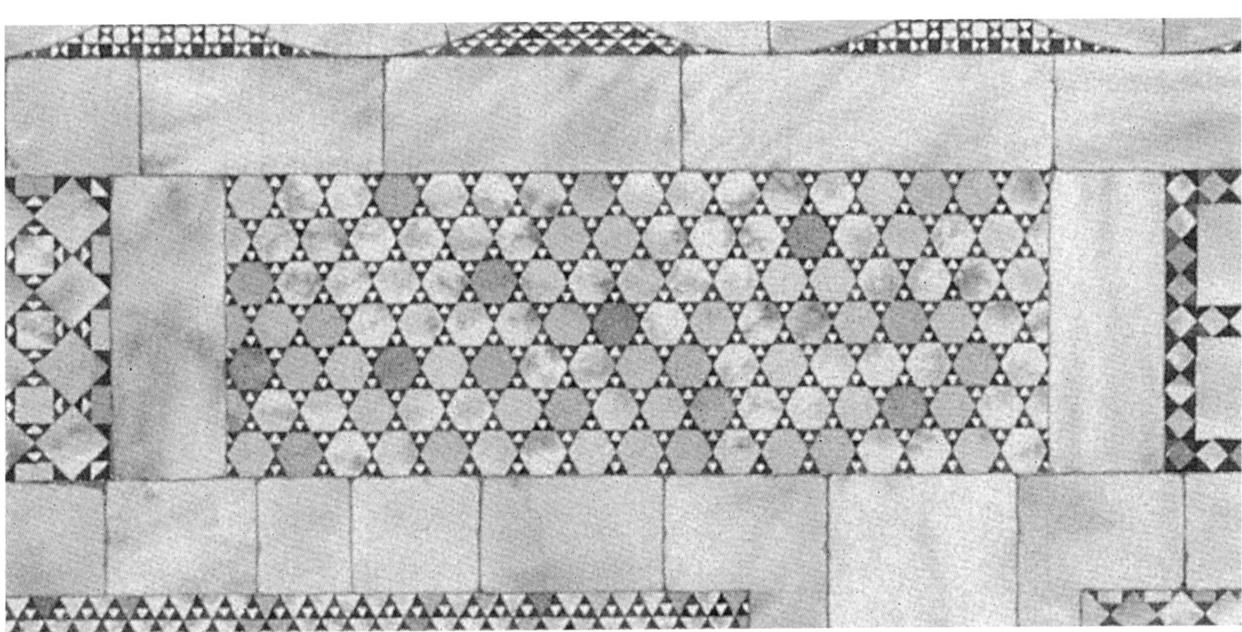

6-31. Isotropic pattern 2F in the rectangle flanking the guilloche.

2F. A triaxial pattern of tangent hexagons, forming triangles, in three counterchanged colors. The hexagons are white. Each triangle bears an inverted inscribed triangle, in white, which forms three triangles, in red and green, creating the effect of six-point stars (created by the intersection of two triangles), the points of which are laden with inscribed triangles (fig. 6-31).

3F. A grid of bands of tangent poised squares, forming hourglasses, in three counterchanged colors (the squares in white, the intervals in red and green) with a poised square at the intersections and each square box flanked by three poised squares (fig. 6-32).

4F. A chessboard pattern of rectangles in three counterchanged colors. Every other compartment is laden with an inscribed pair of tangent poised squares that form four triangles in the corners (in red and green) and an hourglass in the center. Each triangle of the hourglasses in turn

6-32. Isotropic pattern 3F in the rectangle flanking the guilloche.

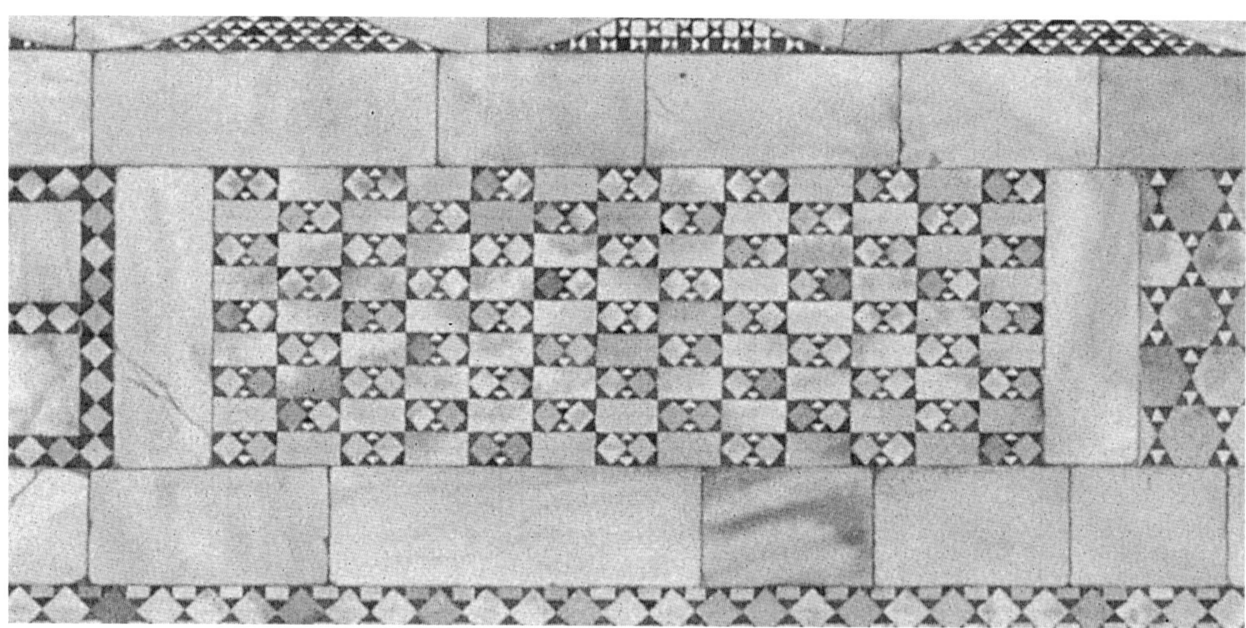

6-33. *Isotropic pattern 4F in the rectangle flanking the guilloche.*

bears an inverted inscribed triangle, in white, forming three triangles, in red and green (fig. 6-33).

5F. A triaxial pattern analogous to that covering the rectangle in 2F, above.

The two long horizontal rectangles that cover the band adjacent to the southern enclosure screen display, from east to west, the following isotropic patterns:

1S. A chessboard pattern of rectangles analogous to that covering the rectangle in 4F, above.

2S. A chessboard pattern of short isosceles triangles in three counterchanged colors. Every other compartment is laden with an inverted inscribed triangle, in white, forming three triangular intervals. Each interval bears, in turn, an inscribed triangle, forming three triangles in red and green (fig. 6-34).

6-34. *Isotropic pattern 2S in the rectangle adjacent to the southern enclosure screen.*

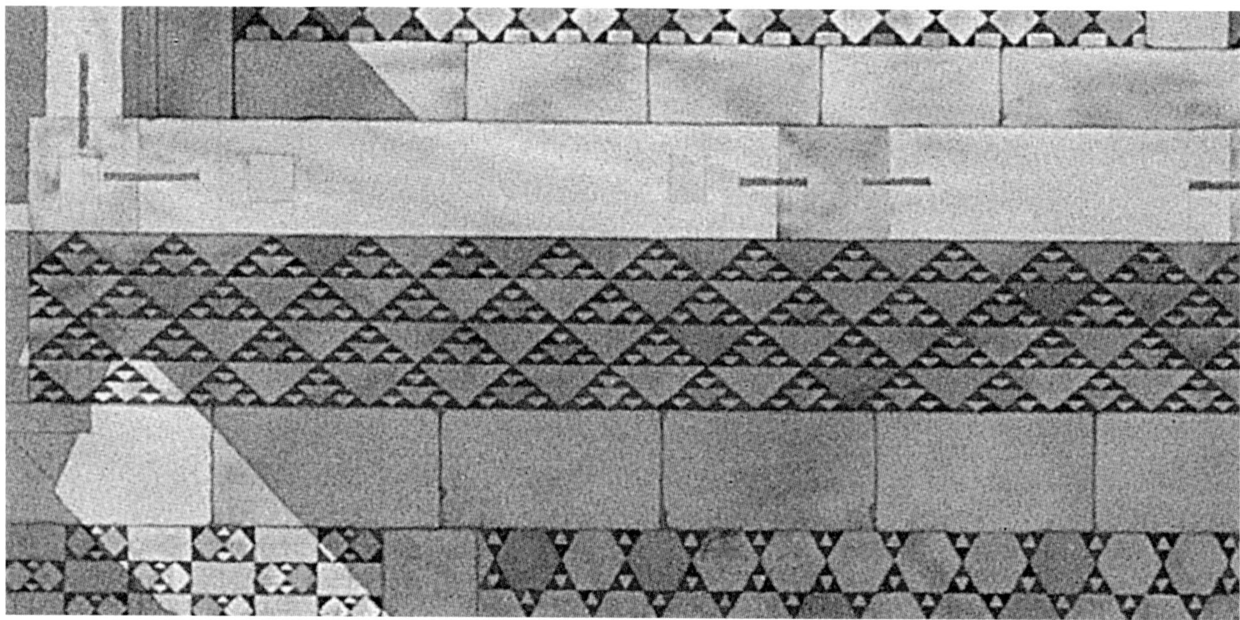

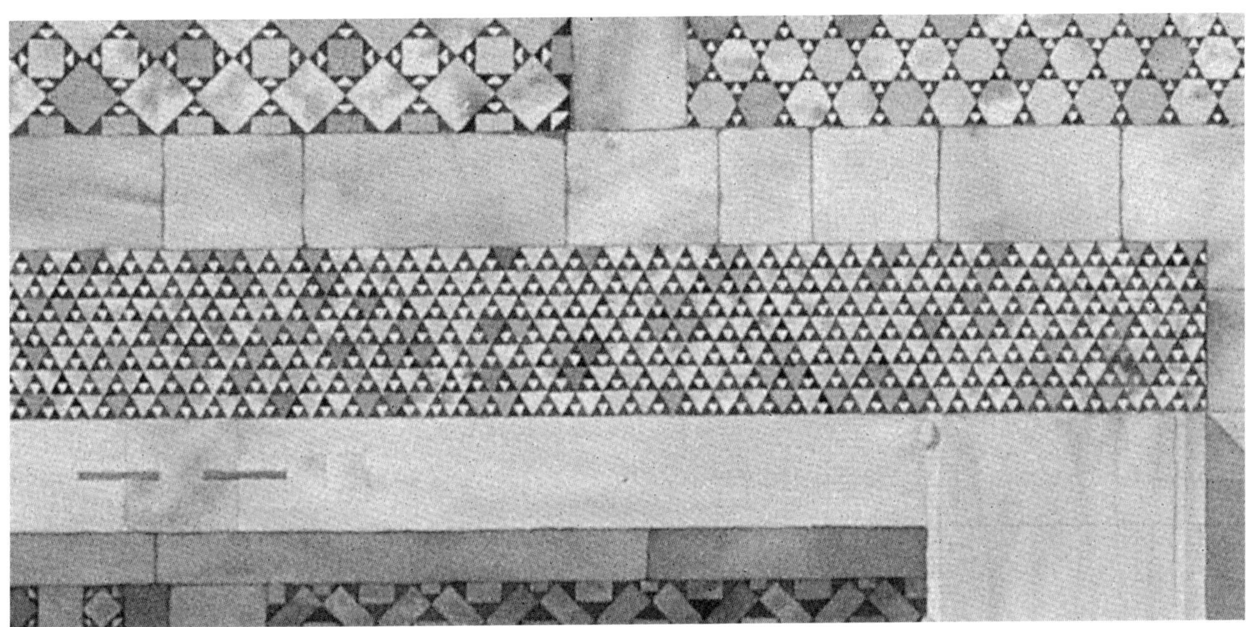

6-35. Isotropic pattern 1N in the rectangle adjacent to the northern enclosure screen.

The two long horizontal rectangles that cover the band adjacent to the northern enclosure screen display, from east to west, the following isotropic patterns:

1N. A chessboard pattern of equilateral triangles in three counterchanged colors. Every other compartment contains an inverted inscribed triangle, in white, forming three triangles in red and green (fig. 6-35).

2N. A chessboard pattern of poised squares in three counterchanged colors. Every other compartment bears an inscribed square, in white, forming four corner triangles in red and green (fig. 6-36).

6-36. Isotropic pattern 2N in the rectangle adjacent to the northern enclosure screen.

The Regulating Geometry

This study of the geometry that regulates the pavement of the schola cantorum of San Clemente is divided into three sections, covering the basic geometric relations, the basic units of construction, and the order of tasks.

THE BASIC GEOMETRIC RELATIONS

Within the geometric simplicity that dominates the composition, the motif that exhibits the greatest complexity is the sinusoidal guilloche. The whole schema of the guilloche can be determined once two initial dimensions have been established:

a = width of the rectangle circumscribing the guilloche
b = diameter of the eyelet (average value)

The width of the strands, c, as well as the total length of the rectangle circumscribed on the guilloche, L, are proportioned as a function of these two initial facts:

$$c = 1/2\,(a - b)$$

$$L = c + b + a + b + a + b + a + b + a + b + a + b + a$$

$$L = 1/2\,(a - b) + 6b + 6a$$

$$L = 1/2\,(a - b) + 6(a + b)$$

The measurements taken in situ are as follows:

L = 1,250.00 cm., or 492.13 in.

a = 140 cm., or 55.12 in.

b = 64.29 cm., or 25.31 in. (average value)
$\geq$ diameter of the largest *rota* (56.5 cm., or 22.24 in.)

c = 37.85 cm., or 14.90 in. (average value)

The calculations expressed above demonstrate that the theoretical value of c corresponds to the actual value found in construction:

$c = 1/2\,(a - b) = 1/2\,(140 - 64.29) = 37.85$ cm., or

$c = 1/2\,(a - b) = 1/2\,(55.12 - 25.31) = 14.90$ in.

In the case of the total length of the guilloche, there is a small discrepancy. The actual guilloche is shorter than the one indicated by the theoretical formula:

$$L = 1/2\,(a - b) + 6(a + b)$$

$L = 1/2\,(140 - 64.29) + 6(140 + 64.29)$, or

$$L = 1/2\,(55.12 - 25.31) + 6(55.12 + 25.31)$$

$L = 1{,}263.59 \geq 1{,}250.00$ cm., or

$L = 497.48 \geq 492.13$ in.

Later in the text, the execution of the regulating schemata of the general geometry of the guilloche is explained.

The Basic Units of Construction

The general geometry of the composition is clearly not complex; even less so is the geometry of the pieces used in the pavement, which approaches the elementary.

The pavement contains tesserae of small dimensions of side p, such that $1.50 \le p \le 17.50$ centimeters, or $0.59 \le p \le 6.89$ inches. They are in the form of squares, rectangles, equilateral triangles, isosceles right triangles, scalene right triangles, long isosceles triangles, short isosceles triangles, darts, and hexagons.

The roundels that fill the openings are of circular form, of diameter r, such that $43.00 \le r \le 56.50$ centimeters, or $16.93 \le r \le 22.24$ inches.

The pieces that border the rectangles into which the pavement is compartmentalized are rectangular, of width g, such that $13.00 \le g \le 38.00$ centimeters, or $5.12 \le g \le 14.96$ inches, and of length h, such that $25.00 \le h \le 140.00$ centimeters, or $9.84 \le h \le 55.12$ inches.

The pieces that form the edges of the strands have the shape of an arc of a circle, of width u, such that $10.50 \le u \le 12.00$ centimeters, or $4.13 \le u \le 4.72$ inches, and of length v, such that $23.00 \le v \le 70.00$ centimeters, or $9.06 \le v \le 27.56$ inches..

The smaller pieces were obtained by cutting up marble fillets, which in turn were obtained by breaking up slabs taken from the horizontal or vertical sheathing of buildings in ruins.

The squares resulted from cutting slices from straight parallelepipeds of square base. These squares could in turn be split along one or two of their diagonals, which created, respectively, two or four isosceles right triangles (figs. 6-37 and 6-38).

The rectangles were obtained by cutting slices from straight parallelepipeds of rectangular base. One rectangle split along its diagonal resulted in two scalene right triangles.

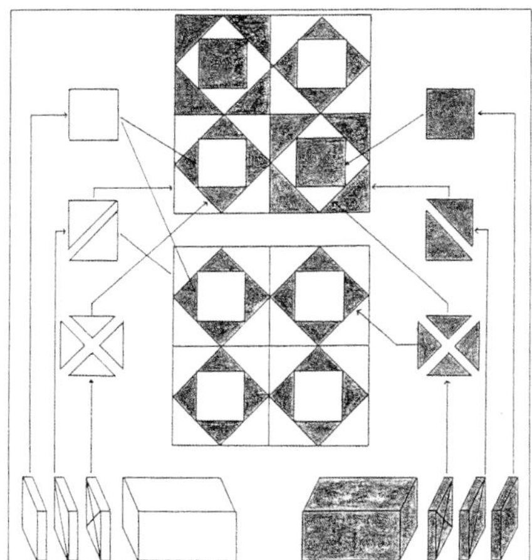

6-37. *The use of quadrature (application of the ratio 1:√2) when cutting the stone, for two different designs. (F. Guidobaldi)*

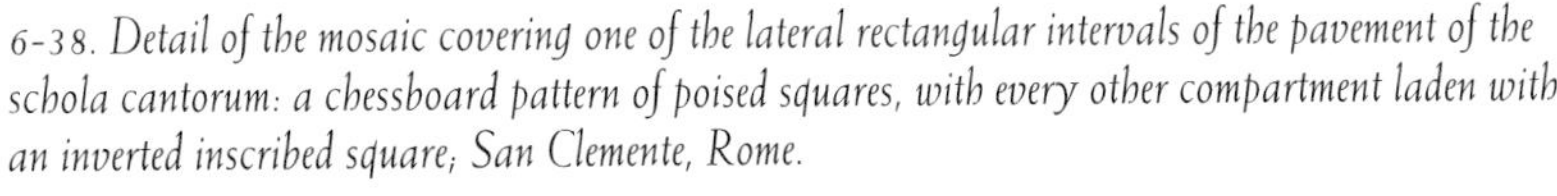

6-38. *Detail of the mosaic covering one of the lateral rectangular intervals of the pavement of the schola cantorum: a chessboard pattern of poised squares, with every other compartment laden with an inverted inscribed square; San Clemente, Rome.*

The equilateral triangles could be obtained either by cutting up straight prisms of triangular or rhomboidal base (in this case, the resulting lozenges would then be split in two), or by cutting slices from a fillet of rectangular base such that it circumscribed an hourglass formed by two diagonals crossed at 60 degrees. Each rectangle cut on two diagonals would result in four pieces: two equilateral triangles and two short isosceles triangles.

Similarly, one can easily imagine the multiple types of straight prisms that could generate slices whose forms belong to the geometric repertoire of a Cosmatesque pavement.

The Order of Tasks

One might wonder about the succession of the tasks that the Roman marble cutters followed to execute a pavement. The first step must have been to search for and collect the construction materials. Since the materials were spoliated, their availability as well as the formal and dimensional characteristics would determine the fundamental traits of the design.

The materials can be classified into various groups with regard to their dimensions and chromatic characteristics. One group consists of the colored pieces, where two subgroups are evident: one includes the pieces of small dimensions (tesserae), and the other includes the pieces of large dimensions (*rotae*). Another group consists of the white pieces, which also are of two types: wide (slabs used to define the bands bordering the rectangles) and narrow (slabs used to define the bands bordering the strands).

The most difficult step must have been to obtain the colored marbles, especially large monolithic pieces, since the stock of these materials depended upon their survival among the ruins of ancient Rome. The imperial quarries of Greece and North Africa from which these materials were extracted in Roman times were out of service by the late Middle Ages. The white marble was easier to obtain given the abundant existence of spolia in this color, in addition to the white marble that was extracted from the contemporary quarries.

The Cosmati searched not only for large colored pieces for the *rotae*; they also gathered and cut others of smaller dimensions for the small pieces of elementary geometric forms, the tesserae.

My observations, derived from a thorough formal analysis of the pavement, inform the following explanation of the execution of the pavement.

Once the twelve roundels destined to fill the eyelets had been collected, the dimension was set for the diameter of the eyelet, *b*, a dimension that must always be greater than the diameter of the largest *rota*. Next was determined the width, *a*, of the "carpet of circles." With these two initial measurements, the regulating schema of the general geometry of the guilloche could then be drawn:

First placed was the white rectangular slab, of length *a*, which served as the western border of the rectangle that would circumscribe the guilloche. Advancing eastward along the axis of the church a distance $\frac{1}{2}(a - b)$, a circle was drawn of diameter *b* (the eyelet for roundel 12); continuing in the same direction, this time distance *a*, a second circle was drawn of diameter *b* (the eyelet for roundel 10); and so on for the four remaining circles, all of diameter *b* (the eyelets for roundels 8, 6, 4, and 2), separated, two by two,

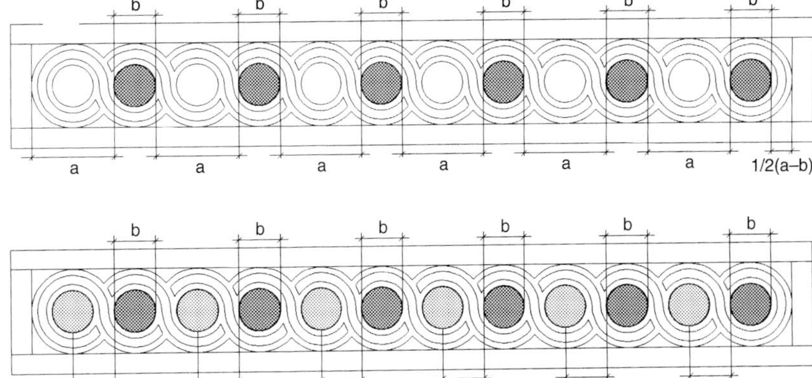

6-39. The placement of the eyelets bearing rounds of porphyry.

6-40. The placement of the eyelets bearing rounds of serpentine.

by distance *a*. Thus were laid the six eyelets that would bear rounds of porphyry.

At a distance *a* from the edge of the last eyelet drawn so far (that of roundel 2), a band of porphyry was placed. It enclosed, to the east, the rectangle that would circumscribe the guilloche, thus determining the total length of the rectangle. The southern and northern sides of the rectangle were then closed with bands drawn with rectangular slabs of white marble (fig. 6-39).

Next, at the midpoint of each of the five free areas situated between each pair of porphyry *rotae* was placed a serpentine *rota* (roundels 11, 9, 7, 5, and 3). The last green *rota* (roundel 1) would have as its center the point situated at the middle of the free space between the contour of the last porphyry *rota* (roundel 2) and the interior edge of the band of porphyry, already placed, that closed the rectangle on the eastern side. Thus the six rounds of serpentine were positioned (fig. 6-40).

Next were laid the white edges of the strands: the interior edge, contouring the circles of the eyelets that had already been drawn, and the exterior edge, tangent to the bands previously set, that defined the rectangle circumscribing the guilloche.

Once the general layout of the guilloche was completed, the lateral regions of the pavement were divided into rectangles. Separating lines were drawn with bands composed of rectangular slabs of white marble.

After all the pavement had been sectioned, the "filling operation" began, which involved covering all the intervals created by the pieces placed up to this point.

The interstices, in the shape of a circular ring, that remained between the *rotae* and the interior edge of the strands that surrounded them were filled with very fractionated linear patterns.

The curvilinear intervals situated between the interior edge and the exterior edge of the strands were filled with equally minute linear patterns.

Also of delicate piecing were the surface patterns that cover the triangles of one or two concave sides situated between the exterior edge of the strands and the defining bands of the rectangle circumscribed around the guilloche.

Isotropic surface patterns were used to fill the rectangles of the lateral zones.

One can suppose that once the general layout of the pavement was completed, using white marble bands, various artists could work simultaneously on the "filling operation," each occupied with a concrete area or a type of geometric pattern whose execution the artist had mastered. In this way, the total time of execution of the pavement was enormously reduced.

Therefore, the succession of tasks that led to the construction of the pavement of San Clemente followed an order that began by establishing the whole in order to address the parts, going from the general to the particular, in a process regulated principally by subdivision.

However, one must not forget that the subdivisions that the Cosmatesque artists created in the general sectioning of the floor of the church were rectangles of proportions inherited from the consolidated geometric legacy of the ancient Roman mosaic, proportions that facilitated the subdivision of those rectangles into whole numbers of constructive pieces of elementary geometry.

Nonconformities

A number of discrepancies or nonconformities are apparent in the executed pavement, each of which has a possible explanation.

Each *rota* lies within a circular ring composed of four contiguous concentric bands: from the inside out, (1) linear pattern bordering the *rota*; (2) interior border of the strand; (3) central band of the strand; and (4) exterior border of the strand.

We know that the size of the *rotae* varies, from a diameter of 43.00 to 56.50 centimeters, or 16.93 to 22.24 inches. However, the loops of the guilloche (circles shaped by each *rota* and the ring circumscribing it) must be of a *constant* diameter equal to the width of the rectangle circumscribing the guilloche (140 centimeters, or 55.12 inches).

The concentric bands, because of their different widths, mitigate the dimensional variations of the diameters of the roundels, even completely absorbing those variations by imposing a constant diameter for the loops.

At the point of junction of the sections of the concentric bands drawn from the centers of two consecutive roundels appear defects in the connection due to the different dimensions of the widths of the bands. These discrepancies are especially apparent at the junctures of the curves that form each of the S-shaped sections of the central bands of the strands.

Figure 6-41 shows, from east to west, the value of the error, in centimeters (inches) at each of the junctions of the eleven sections that make up the central band. The average value of the error is 0.90 centimeter, or 0.35 inch. Given that the average width of the central band is 15.33 centimeters, or 6.04 inches, the average value of the error is consequently nearly 6 percent (5.87 percent) of the width of the connected band.

The maximum absolute value of the executed dimensional error is found at the junction of the curves whose center lies in roundels 2 and 3. Here the width of the central band changes abruptly from 17.50 to 12.25 centimeters, or 6.89 to 4.82 inches, producing a discrepancy of 2.25 centimeters, or 0.89 inch. Given that, in this section, the average width of the **S** curve is 16.37 centimeters, or 6.44 inches, the resulting error approaches 14 percent (13.74 percent) of the width of the connected band.

Thus, the last zones to be executed, the "filling" zones, must absorb the dimensional errors of greatest caliber. They can do so because of their very

6-41. The value of the error at each of the junctions in each section of the central band.

Junction	Error cm. (in.)
1–2	1.00 (0.30)
2–3	2.25 (0.89)
3–4	0.75 (0.30)
4–5	0.50 (0.20)
5–6	0.00 (0.00)
6–7	1.25 (0.49)
7–8	0.75 (0.30)
8–9	0.75 (0.30)
9–10	0.75 (0.30)
10–11	1.75 (0.69)
11–12	0.25 (0.10)

fractionated geometric piecing, capable of squeezing or expanding without difficulty, by means of minimal variations in the dimensions of the tesserae and/or of the seams that separate them.

The majority of the **S**-shaped sections are pinched, more or less clearly, in the area of the juncture of the curves that shape them. This narrowing is resolved by jamming together the minute units of construction (tesserae). In like manner, the meeting of nontangent curves in the juncture area results in the appearance of angular points. These variations are particularly obvious given the color contrast between the darkness of the central band of the strands (green and red) and the white of the bands of the edges.

The nonconformities described thus far result from the dimensional variations of the diameters of the *rotae.* Another nonconformity observable in the pavement is the fractional modulation of the piecing of the sections of the central band.

The dimensions of the basic geometric figures that cover the central band are obtained by the subdivision of its width. Thus, for example, in the section of the band that passes between roundels 1 and 2, the hypotenuse of the isosceles right triangles that shape the band of rectilinear thorns is equal to the width of the band. In the section between roundels 2 and 3, however, the diagonal of the poised squares measures one-third of the width of the band. In the case of the section between roundels 3 and 4, the diagonal of the poised squares measures one-half of the width of the band; and in the section between roundels 4 and 5, the height of the equilateral triangles measures one-third of the width of the band.

Having determined the dimensions of the basic geometric figures, they were then used to fill the eleven sections of the central band. To fill each section, the basic figures were arranged beginning at one end of the section, advancing along the longitudinal axis of the band toward the other extreme of the section. At the initial end of each band, the first figure was placed, *whole,* tangent to the white edge of the strand (fig. 6-42). In each section, the figure placed in the last position runs into the end of the section and is

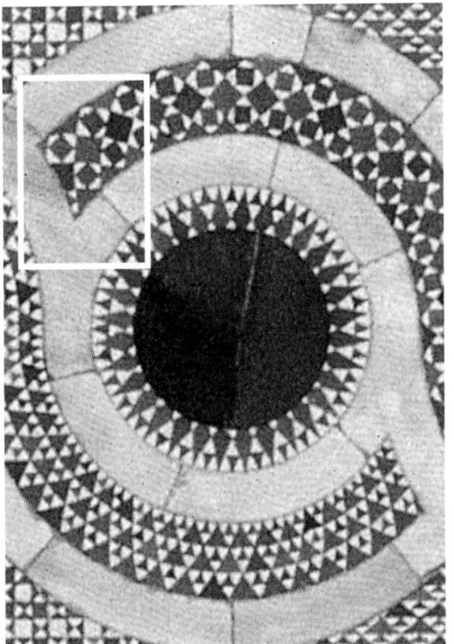

6-42. *Detail of the northern end of section 5 of the central band of the strand, with a whole initial figure (a white poised square).*

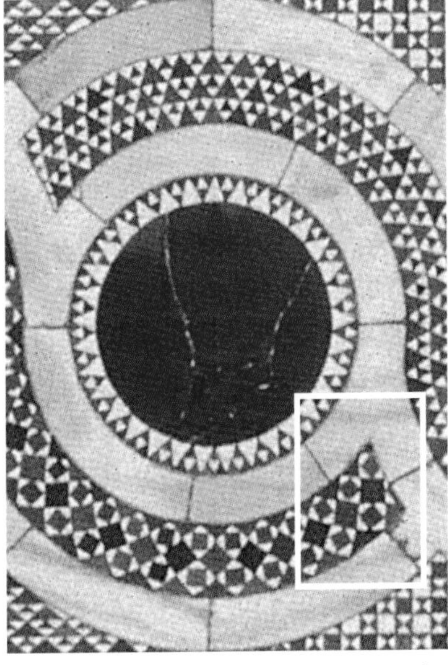

6-43. *Detail of the southern end of section 5 of the central band of the strand, with a cut final figure (a white poised square).*

always fractional, cut by the white border of the strand (fig. 6-43). This nonconformity occurred because the total length of the section being filled had not previously been calculated as a whole multiple of the dimension of the basic geometric figures used in the filling process. Therefore, the nonconformity arose from the initial lack of dimensional coordination between the process of *modulation* by *subdivision* and the process of *filling* by *multiplication*.

The linear patterns that border the roundels do not exhibit this type of nonconformity. In the linear patterns, all the figures (tesserae in the shape of triangles and darts) are entire, because their dimensions are determined by dividing the length of the circumference of each eyelet into a whole number of parts. This number varies from 53 to 32, with the division into 32 parts (eight tesserae per 90 degrees) being the most frequent; four eyelets are divided in this way. Two eyelets show a division into 40 parts (ten tesserae per 90 degrees). Figure 6-44 notes the number of parts into which each eyelet is divided.

Another "error" or maladjustment is the lack of coincidence between the length of the guilloche and the length of the rectangle enclosed by the screens of the schola cantorum.

The general sectioning of the pavement of the church determined the length of the rectangle of the schola cantorum. The length of the guilloche, as already explained, is a function of two factors: the diameter of the eyelet and the width of the rectangle circumscribing it.

The initial lack of dimensional coordination between these two lengths is evident in the extension of the guilloche, insufficient at its eastern end for a tangent contact with the interior line of the screen of the schola cantorum. The interstice of 38 by 490 centimeters, or 14.96 by 192.91 inches, perpendicular to the longitudinal axis of the church and adjacent to the eastern enclosure screen of the schola cantorum, which lies uncovered due to the difference of lengths, is filled with three plain bands: the two bands at the extremes in white, and the central band in red (38 by 140 centimeters, or 14.96 by 515.12 inches), tangent to the guilloche (fig. 6-45).

This discrepancy implies that the guilloche was initiated at its western end, where it is tangent to the screen of the schola cantorum. In advancing the construction work toward the east, the residual strip, whose center is filled with the porphyry slab, remains free.

That the Cosmatesque artists, always clever, initiated the construction of the guilloche at its western end was not a casual decision. In doing so, they succeeded in leaving the residual stripe at the eastern end of the rectangle of the schola cantorum, thus unnoticed by the spectator, who advances through the church from the entrance toward the altar. Looking therefore toward the altar, situated to the west, the spectator is unaware of the lateral zones of the residual border, since they remain out of sight, hidden behind the eastern enclosure screens of the schola cantorum.

Other nonconformities can be observed in the general composition of the pavement. The southern ambo is symmetrical with respect to the transversal axis that passes through the central point of the rectangle contained in the screens of the schola cantorum. The ambo is the only element split entirely in half by that axis. The center of the geometric design that paves the rectangle appears to be in the center of the sixth *rota* (counting from the east), but the center of that *rota* in fact lies to the east of the center of the rectangle contained by the enclosure screens. An imaginary transversal axis

Numbered eyelets, east to west	Number of parts
1	53
2	39
3	32
4	40
5	32
6	33
7	32
8	33
9	40
10	47
11	32
12	35

6-44. The number of parts into which each eyelet is divided.

6-45. The residual stripe adjacent to the screen at the eastern end of the schola cantorum, filled with white bands at the extremes and a porphyry band at the center.

6-46. *The central zone of the pavement.*

drawn through the center of the sixth *rota* would indicate another slight nonconformity: the axis would fall somewhat to the east of the transversal axis, which would divide into two truly equal parts the rectangles that flank the central zone of the guilloche (covered by a grid of bands forming twelve boxes arranged in two rows of six boxes each; isotropic pattern 3F; fig. 6-46).

The impression that an overall view of the Cosmatesque pavement of the schola cantorum of San Clemente conveys is one of a composition organized with tyrannical geometric rigor. However, a conscientious analysis of the pavement reveals that, in reality, such rigor cannot be qualified as hard or inflexible, but rather as gentle and adaptable. Studying the pavement carefully, with the help of a measuring tape, we see that almost every aspect of it is "slightly misplaced." The controlled lack of scrupulousness, the subtle freedom from care with which the Cosmatesque artists approached and resolved on-site the discrepancies of their geometric arrangement leads to the adaptability of their composing solutions. This capacity for adaptation guaranteed the success of the labor of integration, needed when embarking upon the rehabilitation or ornamentation of a building, to initiate the indispensable dialogue between the geometry of the preexisting structure (the geometry of the church, the geometry of the pieces made from spoliated materials) and the geometry of the new (the geometry imposed by the master marble workers in their ornamental designs).

Degrees of Importance

The Cosmatesque artists invested different parts of a pavement with different degrees of importance. The propriety or decorum of each part of the pavement, that is, the degree of richness or elaboration appropriate for its distinction, was achieved through a combination of factors, namely: the sectioning of the pavement in accordance with its use, the degree of detail of the piecing, and the chromatic characteristics of each area.

The different zones of the pavement of the schola cantorum tend to be more distinguished the greater their visibility, the greater their association with uses of circulatory or processional character, the greater their delicacy of execution, and the greater the amount of dark-colored materials employed.

As noted previously, the sectioning of this mosaic gave rise to a spatial division of the enclosure stemming from two types of use: dynamic and static. The dynamic zone is the recumbent T, which functions as a circulatory space connecting the three entrances to the precinct and, through its long line, allowing for processional transit toward the altar. The static zone is composed of the two rectangular lateral intervals that function as an area of rest.

Also noted, the piecing is most minute in the zones of filling that constitute the sinusoidal guilloche.

With the coloring of the different parts of the pavement also taken into consideration, four different zones of importance can be distinguished. From most to least important, they are: (1) the long section of the T; (2) the two short sections of the T; (3) the two rectangles flanking the central part of the guilloche (laden with the isotropic pattern of type 3F); and (4) the remainder of the pavement.

In the first three zones, the tesserae of dark colors (red and green) abound, exhibiting the most expensive and esteemed materials. Zone 1 is the darkest, closely followed by Zone 2 and, at a certain distance, by Zone 3. Zone 4 is the most humble, dominated by light colors (ranging from white to gray; some pieces in ancient yellow). Zone 1 is the richest because, in addition to the tesserae, the eyelets of the guilloche bear porphyry and serpentine monolithic *rotae* of respectable size, that is, pieces of great value.

As for the delicacy of execution (value added by human labor), the gradual increase in the size of the piecing is evident, ranging from the minute dark tesserae that cover the central band of the strands of the guilloche in the sophisticated Zone 1 to the white tesserae of medium size that fill the rectangles of the more humble Zone 4.

NOTES

Chapter 1: Panorama

1. Notable titles about the Cosmatesque artists, their work, or both include: A. M. Bessone-Aurelj, 1935; C. Boito, 1860; C. Boito, 1880; G. Clausse, 1897a; P.C. Claussen, 1987; P. C. Claussen, 1989; G. Giovannoni, 1914–15; G. Giovannoni, 1936; D. F. Glass, 1969; D. F. Glass, 1980; E. Hutton, 1950; R. E. Malmstrom, 1981; G. Matthiae, 1952; A. Melani, 1899.

2. The city of Rome, founded in 753 B.C., would become the center of a great territorial empire that would dominate the Mediterranean. Its history is divided into three stages: the monarchy (eighth to sixth centuries B.C.), the republic (sixth to first centuries B.C.), and the empire (first century B.C. to fourth century A.D.). The empire is further divided into the high empire (first century B.C. to third century A.D.) and the low empire (third to fourth centuries A.D.).

3. Three stages in the history of the Byzantine Empire are distinguishable: Latin (fifth to sixth centuries), Hellenistic (sixth to eighth centuries), and a final period of decline (thirteenth to fifteenth centuries).

4. In its period of maximum expansion, Islam would come to occupy the south of Italy, Sardinia, and Sicily.

5. In the sixth century, during the reign of Justinian I (527–65), the Byzantine Empire would reach its maximum expansion in an attempt to restore the unity, first territorial and later political, of the Roman Empire. Under Justinian, Italy and Rome would be under Byzantine rule, with Ravenna the capital of the western Byzantine territory.

6. About the iconoclastic dispute, see L. Bréhier, 1904.

7. The Carolingian empire would extend its dominance to the Italian peninsula, conquering the northern half, including Rome, and leaving the southern half (the dukedom of Benevento) as a dependent territory.

8. The resurgence of the Eastern Empire during the Macedonian era (867–1058) allowed it to realize its maximum territorial expansion around the year 1025. At that time, the Byzantine Empire only held the southern portion of the Italian peninsula, the territory that today corresponds to Calabria, Basilicata, and Puglia (D. Matthew, 1989, 66, 67).

9. Regarding the revival of classical influence in the Carolingian period, see R. Krautheimer, 1942a; C. B. McClendon, 1980; M. Salmi, 1954.

10. Regarding the reform of the Church and the political ideas of the Papacy in the Middle Ages, see G. B. Ladner, 1954; G. B. Ladner, 1967; W. Ullmann, 1976.

11. Regarding the terms *Renaissance, renewal, renovatio, renouveau,* and *new rebirth* used in reference to the resurgence of classical influences in Rome during the twelfth century, see H. Bloch, 1982; C. N. L. Brooke, 1969; E. Kitzinger, 1982; K. Noehles, 1966; A. E. Priester, 1990; H. Toubert, 1970.

12. Sicily in the twelfth century has been deservedly described by the Arab geographer ash-Sharif al-Idrisi, for example, as the "pearl of the century" (P. Martínez Montávez and C. Ruíz Bravo-Villasante, 1991, 23).

13. About the Normans and their artistic production, see E. Calandra, 1941; A. di Montecassino, 1935; F. Valenti, 1932.

14. The disputes between the emperor and the pope were not continuous. In 1075 the controversy began; in 1122 the Concordat of Worms marked the beginning of a period of relative peace, which would last until 1159, at which time another period of dispute began, which would last until 1177.

15. The five Crusades signaled the unstable presence of the West in the Middle East from the eleventh to the thirteenth centuries. The Crusades produced the Christian principalities of the Middle East—the kingdom of Armenia, the county of Edessa, the principality of Antioch, the county of Tripoli, the kingdom of Jerusalem, and the kingdom of Cyprus—and the Latin empire of Constantinople, the result of the Christian attack on Constantinople during the fourth Crusade. Jerusalem would be lost definitively for the Christians in the year 1244. The last base for the Crusaders was abandoned in 1291.

16. Three commercial centers stand out: the cities of the north, the Hanseatic League; the Italian cities on the banks of the Ligurian Sea and the high region of the Adriatic Sea, whose commercial dealings with the Orient supplied Europe with exotic products; and the Byzantine Empire, commercial intermediary between East and West.

17. For additional information about the geography and history of Europe and the Mediterranean in the Middle Ages, see P. Brezzi, 1947; C. Fradejas et al., 1979, 158–86; R. Guilland, 1956; D. Matthew, 1989; Michelin, 1985, 11–12, 17–18, 21–24; Michelin, 1987, 18–22.

18. The chromolithographic plate reproduced in figure 3-2, entitled "Byzantine Ornamentation #3" by its author, Owen Jones, is composed of ornamental details taken from several Italian buildings: the Cathedral of Monreale, San Marco (Venice), Santa Maria in Aracoeli (Rome), San Lorenzo fuori le Mura (Rome), Santa Maria Maggiore (Rome), San Vitale (Ravenna), Santa Maria in Cosmedin (Rome), San Giovanni in Laterano (Rome), the *duomo* of Cività Castellana, and the baptistery of San Marco (Venice).

19. About works in the region of Latium, see S. Aurigemma, A. Bianchini, and A. DeSantis, 1966; R. Lancini, 1940; A. Serafini, 1927. For more about the Abbey of Montecassino, see H. Bloch, 1946; B. Cartei, 1964; E. Gattola, 1733; G. Nuti, 1964; A. Pantoni, 1973.

About works in the region of Umbria, see G. Giovannoni, 1942; about Orvieto in particular, see D. Matthew, 1989, 169; Michelin, 1987, 135.

About works in the region of Abruzzi, see C. Carobara, 1979; G. de Angelis d'Ossat, 1942.

20. About paleo-Christian and medieval works and pavements in Friuli-Venezia Giulia, see X. Barral i Altet, 1975; G. Brusin, 1960; G. Brusin and P. Zovatto, 1957; P. L. Zovatto, 1963. About Aquileia in particular, see C. Cecchelli, 1933; O. Fasiolo, 1915; about Grado in particular, see P. Zovatto, 1947–48; P. Zovatto, 1952.

About works in the region of Veneto, see G. Brusin, 1950; P. Zovatto, 1950; P. Zovatto, 1957; P. Zovatto, 1962. About San Marco of Venice in particular, see P. Angelo and M. Maccin, 1962; A. Bruyère, 1990; O. Demus, 1960; P. Gascar, 1964; G. Matthiae, 1952, 259–60 and fig. 12; G. Urbani de Gheltof, 1888.

About works in the region of Emilia-Romagna, in particular about Pompona, see H. Stern, 1968; in particular about Ravenna (ancient and medieval pavements), see F. Berti, 1976; G. Bovini, 1953; G. Bovini, 1954; G. Buonamici, 1748; G. Cortesi, 1964; E. Dyggve, 1941; R. Farioli, 1965; R. Olivieri Farioli, 1969; R. Olivieri Farioli, 1970; R. Farioli, 1975; R. Farioli, 1984.

About works in the region of Lombardy, in particular about Como (works by the Comacini masters), see F. Frigerio and B. Nogara, 1912; G. Merzario, 1967; U. Monneret de Villard, 1912; U. Monneret de Villard, 1914; U. Monneret de Villard, 1916.

About works in the region of Tuscany, in particular about Florence, see E. W. Anthony, 1927; H. Beenken, 1926–27; W. Horn, 1943; E. Madoni, 1914; in particular about Pisa (Islamic influence), see R. Meoli Toulmin, 1977; in particular about Lucca (San Frediano), see O. Puccinelli, 1950.

21. About works in Sicily, see G. Arata, 1914; I. Beck, 1975; S. Bottari, 1955; E. Calandra, 1941; J. Deér, 1959; G. Di Stefano, 1955; M. Ecochard, 1977; H. G. Franz, 1957; G. Giovannoni, 1921–22; W. Krönig, 1965; G. Marçais, 1954; P. Martínez Montávez and C. Ruíz Bravo-Villasante, 1991; D. Serradifalco, 1838; Touring Club Italiano (Sicilia), 1989; F. Valenti, 1932.

About works in the region of Campania, see X. Barral i Altet, 1982; E. Bertaux, 1904; G. Bertelli, 1978; S. Bottari, 1955; A. Capone, 1927–29; C. Carobara, 1979; D. Salazaro, 1871–77; F. Valenti, 1932; A. Venditti, 1967.

About works in the region of Apulia, see C. Bargellini, 1974. In particular, about Bari, see P. Martínez Montávez and C. Ruíz Bravo-Villasante, 1991, 49; Michelin (Italia), 1987, 51, 52. Otranto, the last Byzantine territory in Italy, resisted first the Lombards and then the Normans; the pavement of the cathedral has figures and was executed in 1165 by Pantaleone, a local artist (Michelin (Italia), 1987, 138); for more information about Otranto, see A. Antonaci, 1955; G. Garufi, 1906–7; G. Gianfreda, 1970; W. Haug, 1975; W. Haug, 1977; C. Settis Frugoni, 1968.

22. About works in France, see W. Krönig, 1962–63; E. Mâle, 1922; V. Mortet, 1911. In particular, about Saint-Benoît-sur-Loire, see X. Barral i Altet, 1991; R.-H. Bautier, 1968; J.-M. Berland, 1968; M. Blanchard-Lemée, 1991; E. Vergnolle, 1980.

About works in England, in particular, about London (Westminster Abbey), see P. Binski, 1990; C. Formilli, 1910; R. Foster, 1991; W. R. Lethaby, 1906; W. R. Lethaby, 1925; G. A. Sartorio, 1896; S. H. Wander, 1978; about Canterbury, see E. Hutton, 1950.

23. Some of the Italian centers of flat polychrome geometric ornament correspond to the five styles traditionally identified in Italian Romanesque art: *Lombard-Romanesque*, the style created by the Comacini masters, which spread

throughout northern and central Italy, with important examples in Como, Pavia, and Verona; *Pisan-Romanesque*, Pisa's own style in which primarily Lombard architectural structure and orientalizing decorative motifs merge; *Florentine-Romanesque*, a style unique to Florence characterized by the use of white and green marble; *Cosmati*, the style peculiar to central Italy, primarily in Latium and Campania, characterized by multicolored mosaics of marble and glazed ceramic tiles; and *Sicilian-Norman*, the style present in southern Italy and Sicily in which Lombard, Arab, and Norman influences converge; the first two influences are reflected above all in the decoration and the third in the floor plan of the buildings (Michelin, 1987, 29).

24. Giotto (1266–1337) had direct contact with the marble workers of the Roman school. It is known that Giotto was called to Rome in 1298 to execute the mosaic of the *Navicella* in the portico of San Pietro, and that Pietro Cavallini, one of the best-known masters of the late-Cosmatesque school, worked under the direction of Giotto on this mosaic (W. R. Lethaby, 1904, 286). On the other hand, in the church of San Francesco in Assisi, the work of Giotto coexists with the work of the Cosmatesque artists. Regarding the work of the Cosmati in Assisi, see G. Giovannoni, 1942.

25. About the transition of mosaic pavement from ancient to medieval, see X. Barral i Altet, 1973.

26. Regarding the architecture of the medieval Christian world influenced by Islamic art, see I. Beck, 1975; M. Ecochard, 1977; G. Marçais, 1954.

27. About the pavement at Saint-Benoît-sur-Loire (east of Orleans), see J. M. Berland, 1968; M. Blanchard-Lemée, 1991, 13, 125–27, and plates LII to LVII. This pavement is discussed and illustrated further in chapter 5.

28. A. M. Bessone-Aurelj studied this monument in detail, calling it the "master work of the Cosmati" (1935, 81–86).

29. About these mosaics, see C. B. McClendon, 1980.

30. This influence could have arisen from the Muslim invasions that, at times, razed the city or from the commercial relations the Pisans maintained with Islamic peoples.

31. G. Bendinelli, 1951, 827–828.

32. W. R. Lethaby, 1904, 72, 115, 116.

33. A. M. Bessone-Aurelj, 1935, 58.

34. *"Impronte Cosmatesche nell' Italia Meridionale"* is the title of the chapter in which Bessone-Aurelj discusses these works (1935, 149–59).

35. For more detailed information about these artists and their works (inscriptions, dates, and places), see A. M. Bessone-Aurelj, 1935; G. Clausse, 1897; P. C. Claussen, 1987; D. F. Glass, 1980; F. Hermanin, 1945; E. Hutton, 1950; W. R. Lethaby, 1904; R. E. Malmstrom, 1981; A. Melani, 1899; and A. Muñoz, 1954.

36. Edward Hutton also includes Canterbury as an English center of Cosmatesque art, declaring that the pavement in the Trinity Chapel of Saint Thomas à Becket in Canterbury Cathedral is Cosmatesque (E. Hutton, 1950, 52 and fig. 64). I am not in agreement with this declaration, given that the pavement, although a work of flat polychrome geometric ornament, does not have the fundamental geometric characteristics proper to the works executed by the Cosmati.

37. This list of Cosmatesque works in Westminster is based on E. Hutton, 1950, 55; and P. Binski, 1990, 8. In Westminster, in addition to the Cosmatesque works cited, there is a recent neo-Cosmatesque work, an adaptation of one of the pavements of the Cappella Palatina in Palermo, which was carried out under the direction of Edward Hutton in Saint Paul's Chapel in Westminster Cathedral (E. Hutton, 1950, 28n1).

38. In the late Middle Ages, the Normans dominated a broad territory, which included the south of England and the western portion of the continent (Normandy and western France to the Pyrenees), and the kingdom of Sicily (Sicily and the southern half of the Italian peninsula).

39. In the Middle Ages, Rome became the "world" center for exportation of large pieces of precious marbles, obtained from the ruins of its ancient buildings. The marble quarries located in Greece and North Africa, which the Roman Empire had exploited, were the original source of these materials, but by the Middle Ages, these quarries were closed. Thus, the ruins of ancient Rome were the only "quarry" in use in medieval times. The Cosmati commercially exploited that source, demolishing buildings and recovering materials for local consumption or for export.

40. One might wonder how Petrus traveled from Rome to London. Did he follow the traditional Roman route, to Provence and then up through the Loire? Did he see Saint-Benoît-sur-Loire? Did he see the cities that hosted the great markets of France? Did he see works of French Gothic art, such as the Cathédrale de Notre Dame at Chartres (1194–1220)? Or did he take a medieval alpine route, crossing the Alps and then continuing up along the Rhine? Or perhaps, given the heavy weight of the stones that accompanied him from Rome, he traveled by sea, from Italy to Gibraltar to the Gulf of Biscay to London, following the customary route of the merchants from northern Italy (Genoa, Venice) when they did business with the Hanseatic League. Perhaps Petrus traveled by land and the materials by sea; this option is another possibility, given that the Cosmati engaged in the export of spoliated marble. About the commercial routes of the Roman Empire, see M. P. Charlesworth, 1926. About the medieval alpine routes, see D. Matthew, 1989, 78, 79.

41. For a list of the principal studies of the Cosmatesque work in Westminster, see note 22.

42. For a schematic map of Latium with the locations of Romanesque churches, see E. Parlato and S. Romano, 1992, 34, 35.

43. The Synod of Sutri in 1046 initiated the reform of the Roman Catholic Church (D. Matthew, 1989, 8).

44. With regard to these acts of restoration and/or guardianship, see E. Parlato and S. Romano, 1992, 18, 19.

Chapter 2: Rome

1. For schematic maps of Rome showing the location of the medieval churches, see E. Parlato and S. Romano, 1992, 36; and R. Krautheimer, 1983, fig. 90, 160 and fig. 97, 171.

2. Regarding the churches of this period in Rome and Latium, see. E. Parlato and S. Romano, 1992.

3. Regarding nineteenth-century neo-Cosmatesque works in Italy, see A. M. Bessone-Aurelj, 1935, 174–75. There are also some neo-Cosmatesque works in England, from the mid-twentieth century, by Edward Hutton. In 1943 he executed a pavement in the sanctuary at Buckfast Abbey, inspired by one of the designs from the pavement in the nave of San Giovanni in Laterano (Hutton, 1950, 26n2). In Saint Paul's Chapel in Westminster Cathedral, he executed an adaptation of one of the pavements in the Cappella Palatina in Palermo (Hutton, 1950, 28n1).

4. Regarding the history of Rome in the Middle Ages, including the destruction of ancient Rome, see P. Brezzi, 1947; F. Gregorovius, 1925; R. Krautheimer, 1980; R. Lanciani, 1892; R. Lanciani, 1897; R. Lanciani, 1899; E. Parlato and S. Romano, 1992; A. M. Romanini, 1991; D. Waley, 1961.

5. Ancient Rome was a great quarry throughout the Middle Ages. R. Lanciani conducted a thorough study of the process of destruction that ancient Rome underwent from imperial times to the nineteenth century. In the study, an entire chapter (R. Lanciani, 1899, 180–97) is devoted to exploring the damage caused by the Cosmati, referred to as "marble cutters" (*Marmorarii*) and "lime burners" (*Calcararii*).

6. About the origins, development, and morphological characteristics of the Christian basilicas of medieval Rome, see A. M. Bessone-Aurelj, 1935, 9; M. Cagiano de Azevedo, 1970, 244; G. Clausse, 1897b; L. Crema, 1942; A. L. Frothingham, 1908; F. Hermanin, 1945; R. Krautheimer, 1965, 125–30; R. Krautheimer, 1980, 3–202; R. Krautheimer, 1983, 155, fig. 86; G. Matthiae, 1962, 287; E. Parlato and S. Romano, 1992.

7. The polychromy was achieved by combining a variety of materials, as was done in Rome during late antiquity. In the Middle Ages, the preference for polychromy produced from the use of several materials in a single work prevailed. Regarding the relation between the use of multiple colors and multiple materials in works of art dating from late antiquity and from the early Middle Ages, see M. Cagiano de Azevedo, 1970.

8. R. Krautheimer, 1965, 129 and fig. 52, 54A.

9. Regarding the survival of the Cosmatesque pavements, see E. Hutton, 1950, 29.

10. The column from San Paolo fuori le Mura is studied in great detail in A. M. Bessone-Aurelj, 1935, 117–25.

11. A *fluted column* displays vertical grooves on its shaft, with or without fillets between them. A *geminated* (or *paired*) *column* displays twin parallel or juxtaposed shafts (the name is both singular and plural). An *ophidian column,* so named for the resemblance of the shaft to ophidians, or snakes, is formed by two long narrow cylinders that interlace in a spiral. A *wreathed* (or *braided*) *column* has a shaft with several grooves superposed around a single vertical axis. A *turned column* has a shaft decorated with moldings or other motifs in a helix arrangement around a central cylinder (J.-R. Paniagua, 1993, 103, 104).

Chapter 3: Antecedents

1. Regarding pavements in Rome from the Carolingian age, see F. Guidobaldi and A. Guiglia Guidobaldi, 1983, 315–19, 418–35.

2. A. Guiglia Guidobaldi, 1984, 57–72.

3. G. Bendinelli, 1951, 828.

4. A. L. Frothingham, Jr., 1895, 192–200.

5. D. F. Glass, 1980, 29–32. A. Guiglia Guidobaldi disagrees with Glass's opinion on Venetian pavements, believing that the Upper Adriatic medieval pavements in, for example, Aquileia, Venice, Torcello, and Pomposa are the result of a completely local decorative heritage that assimilated Eastern influences with a flair all its own for design and color, totally independent of the Roman tradition. Regarding High Adriatic pavements, see X. Barral i Altet, 1975, 275–85; H. Stern, 1968, 157–69.

6. G. Matthiae, 1952, 252–54.

7. As stated by León Ostiense and repeated by Amato di Montecassino (1935, 175), according to D. F. Glass (1980, 33): *"Et pour ce qu'il non trova in Ytalie homes de cert art, manda en Costentinnoble et en Alixandre pour homes grex et sarrazines; pour aorner lo pavement de la eglize de marmoire entaillie et diverses paintures; laquelle nous clamons 'opere de mosy'; ovre de pierre de diverses colors."*

8. A. Pantoni, 1973, 101–37, 180–93.

9. A. Guiglia Guidobaldi cites as an example of a miniature an articulated composition based on the quincunx: the frontispiece of the *Dioscoride* of Vienna, illustrated in K. Weitzmann, 1977, plate 15.

10. A. Guiglia Guidobaldi cites examples distributed throughout the Byzantine realm, among them some in the High Adriatic (Ravenna, Grado), Jordan, Greece (insular and continental), Crete, and Asia Minor (Ephesus, Nicaea). They appear illustrated in P. Asimakopoulou and P. Atzaka, 1984, 67–72; F. Berti, 1976, plate XXIV; R. Farioli, 1975, fig. 4; H. Kier, 1970, 32; S. Pelekanidis and P. Atzaka, 1974, plate 25; M. Spiro, 1975, fig. 334; P. L. Zovatto, 1963, fig. 144.

11. For example, in painting, in the frescoes in Santa Maria Antiqua (P. J. Nord-Hagen, 1962, 53–72, plate III), in those of San Crisogono (M. Mesnard, 1935, fig. 32, 34, 35, 36; G. Matthiae, 1962, fig. 192), and in those of Santa Maria Egiziaca, which was once the Tempio della Fortuna Virile in the Foro Boario (G. Bendinelli, 1951, 824); in sculpture, in the ninth-century plutei (L. Pani Ermini, 1974, plate XVI; A. Melucco Vaccaro, 1974, plates II, III; M. Trinci Castelli, 1976, 232, plate LXXIII) and in the *opus tessellatum* in the vault of Santa Costanza (G. Matthiae, 1967, plate I, fig. 3).

12. F. Guidobaldi, 1985.

13. An example of the latter is the icon of Saint Michael Archangel, shown in figure 3-6, in which various interlacings of the quincunx family can be discerned. The interlacing bands of each quincunx are drawn with enamels; five precious stones enrich each quincunx (one at its center and one at each corner, forming an X).

14. Regarding *opus sectile* in Bithynia, see U. Peschlow, 1983, 435–47.

15. G. Bendinelli, 1951, 827.

16. G. Bendinelli, 1951, 824–25.

17. For examples of and a bibliography concerning pavements in *sectile* from the middle and late Byzantine age, see U. Peschlow, 1983; S. Eyice, 1963.

18. G. Bendinelli, 1951, 827–28.

19. Pavements in *sectile* from the Campania region are numerous. Regarding the

one in the basilica of San Vincenzo al Volturno, see A. Pantoni, 1980, 45–46; regarding that in Sant'Angelo in Formis, see X. Barral i Altet, 1982, 55–60.

20. About large roundels that they probably obtained from the remains of pavements in *opus sectile* from the early and late imperial age or pavements from the Carolingian age in which large roundels from the imperial age had already been reused, see F. Guidobaldi and A. Guiglia Guidobaldi, 1983, 17–58 (pavements of the imperial age), 460–85 (pavements from the Carolingian age).

21. For descriptions and illustrations of the cited examples, see F. Guidobaldi and A. Guiglia Guidobaldi, 1983, 262–319. To those pavements must be added others, also in panels but with intervals not filled with *opus sectile* but rather with *opus sectile/tessellatum*, that is, with marble mosaic of large tesserae with elements in *opus sectile* (ibid., 349–459).

22. The reticular partition in the pavements of the sixth and seventh centuries differs from that in the later Cosmatesque pavements in the proportions of the mesh: the earlier pavements have a square grid, as can be seen in Santa Maria Antiqua, whereas those of the twelfth century are decidedly rectangular. The pavement from Santi Quattro Coronati, one of the oldest Cosmatesque pavements, displays very short rectangles, of proportions approaching those of a square.

23. Such a transfer could have happened in the case of the primitive oratory of San Saba, from which were taken all of the mosaics, to transplant them in the pavement of the upper church.

24. P. Srbinovski, 1983, 128, 129.

25. The central area of *opus sectile* that paves the small basilica is compartmentalized into three parallel bands of adjacent rectangles, whose outlines are defined by bands of white marble slabs. The rectangles are filled with surface isotropic patterns from the geometric repertoire of the classic Roman mosaic (chessboard of poised squares, every other square laden with an inverted inscribed square). The central band is narrower than the two side bands, creating the impression of a directional band superposed over the longitudinal axis of the basilica.

26. D. F. Glass, 1980, 30. For illustration of the two pavements, see P. L. Zovatto, 1963, fig. 99 (Theodoran basilica of Aquileia), fig. 147 (San Eufemia of Grado).

27. The change in the design is linked to a change in the order of the steps of execution of the pavement. In the case of the bands in *opus sectile* bordering the marble slabs, first the slabs were set, and then the interstitial bands were filled with mosaic in *opus sectile*. In the case of the marble bands that compartmentalized the field of mosaic in *opus sectile*, first the marble bands were set and then the rectangular intervals were filled with *opus sectile*. The *opus sectile* is always executed at the end because, with its diminutive size, it needs the existence of "barriers of contention" that guide its execution.

28. *Sectilia* from the sixth century in Santa Maria Antiqua are identical in dimensional module and design to those of the twelfth century in San Clemente and Santi Quattro Coronati, as illustrated in comparison photographs in A. Guiglia Guidobaldi, 1984, 69, figs. 17, 18; plate V, figs. 1, 2, 3, 4.

29. These works in *sectile* from the imperial age were familiar to the Roman marble workers of the twelfth century; the Cosmati knew the imperial ruins very well, since these constituted the "wreckage" from which they obtained the majority of the materials that they used in their pavements.

30. Evolution studied in detail in F. Guidobaldi, 1983.

31. These isotropic surface patterns are systematically described and illustrated in C. Balmelle et al., 1985.

32. Regarding the characteristics of the black-white mosaic in Italy, see G. Becatti, 1965.

33. If one accepts this hypothesis of gradual transition, it follows that the appearance of interlacing in *sectile* can be considered as the result of an evolution in continuity not necessarily supported by a single Eastern influence (as implied by the epithet of true Byzantine "invention" which it receives in A. Guiglia Guidobaldi, 1984, 57) but also by the evolution of local pavements in porphyry marble mosaic.

34. The fractionation of the motifs was clearly present in the east as early as the sixth century, as works in *sectile* in Syria (J. C. Balty, 1969, plate XXVII) and in Cyprus (A. H. S. Megaw, 1976, 4–9, plate V), among others, attest.

35. For an early attempt at graphically cataloging Cosmatesque motifs in the Roman pavements, see A. Piazzesi, V. Mancini, and L. Benevolo, 1954, 15–19. Although the motifs are classified in various groups defined by their formal characteristics, this study does not study their antecedents. See D. F. Glass, 1980, 29, and its Appendix, pp. 140–151, for a brief catalog of the most frequent motifs in the Cosmatesque mosaics, grouped according to the families who produced them and identifying a group of eleven motifs of the Roman mosaics that continue to appear in the Cosmatesque mosaics but not in the Byzantine mosaics of the Macedonian age. This work remains unbalanced, given that a study equivalent to the one completed on the eleven Roman motifs is not in turn carried out for an analogous group of mid-Byzantine motifs. See also H. Kier, 1970, 147–201n10, which selects a hundred of geometric motifs and verifies their presence, from the Roman era to the late Middle Ages, throughout the Mediterranean and continental Europe.

36. Because the intervals of the second group are smaller and have curved sides or sides that frequently are nonperpendicular, creating sharp and obtuse angles, it became essential that the tesserae covering those intervals also be very small; only in this way could the tesserae of regular geometric form (square, isosceles triangle, right triangle, and the like) typical of the Cosmatesque repertoire continue to be used whole. Both the curved forms and the most minute and irregular parts of the intervals are resolved with the help of the joints between the tesserae, which because of their high number and variety of forms, can absorb and cushion all irregularities.

37. M. L. Morricone Matini, 1967, plates XXIX, XXX.

38. The fourth-century building discovered on the outside of the Porta Marina in the excavations of Ostia contains works in *sectile,* both geometric and figurative, with the tetrachromy (red, green, yellow, and white) typical of Rome and its environs. Of special interest in establishing comparisons with the Cosmatesque mosaics are the parietal works in geometric sectile from the interior of the exedra: the lower part is decorated in chessboard and the upper part imitates the *opus mixtum*. G. Becatti, 1969, 102–3; plate XXXIII, fig 2; plates LXXV, LXXVI, LXXVII, LXXVIII, XC.

39. F. Guidobaldi and A. Guiglia Guidobaldi, 1983, color plates I, II, preceding page 504.

40. The ninth-century pavement from the Chapel of San Zenone shows a chessboard pattern surrounding a porphyry roundel of enormous diameter (see chapter 5 for further discussion and illustrations).

Chapter 4: The Regulating Geometry

1. C. Balmelle et al., 1985. Of special interest: 3–18 *(Préface)*, 19–24 *(Lexique française)*, 421–24 *(Lexique espagnol-française)*.

2. Illustrated in D. F. Glass, 1980, plate 5.

3. For commentary and tables comparing the remains of guilloches with two sinusoidal strands found in Chania, Olbia, Pella, Pergamon, Pompeii, Rabat (Malta), Reggio Emilia, Tarsus, and Teramo (indicating place, date, artistic technique, and bibliography for each example), see A. Ovadiah, 1980, 110–11. For an illustration of the example in Nimrud, see A. Speltz, 1915, plate 10(3).

4. D. F. Glass, 1980, 40–41.

5. Regarding the Ranucius family and other families of Cosmatesque artists, see A. M. Bessone-Aurelj, 1935.

6. An illustration of the nave of Santa Maria di Castello in Tarquinia is in D. F. Glass, 1980, plate 47.

7. As explained in D. F. Glass, 1980, 42, 43.

8. In addition to illustrations in chapter 5 of this book, the crypt is illustrated in D. F. Glass, 1980, plates 1 and 2.

9. See P. M. Letarouilly, 1840 (reprint 1982) for a similar, though not identical, floor plan to that in fig. 4-55.

10. The few scholars who have attempted to catalog the geometric Cosmatesque patterns have done so only partially or incompletely: A. Piazzesi, V. Mancini, and L. Benevolo, 1954, 15–19; D. F. Glass, 1980, 29, 140–51; H. Kier, 1970, 147–201n10.

11. These two materials were the most prized hard stones from Roman times. Regarding these materials used by the Romans, see R. Gnoli, 1971, 1988.

12. D. F. Glass, 1980, 42–46.

13. For illustrations of these pavements, see D. F. Glass, 1980, plates, 2, 6, 46, 48, and 49 respectively. The pavement at Assunta in Spoleto appears whitish because it was executed with tesserae of marble in clear tones, from white to gray. The accentuated poverty of means is apparent not only in the complete lack of dark pieces (green and red) of large size (roundels or slabs), but also in the virtual absence of small dark pieces (tesserae).

14. The nomenclature (net and graph) follows that used by Ramón Zoido in studying the geometry of the unimodular and bimodular partitions of the plane that M. C. Escher created for his well-known engravings. See R. Zoido, n.d., 8ff.; and B. Ernst, 1978, 20, 35–41.

15. Consequently, figure 4-75 could also be called "three linear geometric patterns and three surface patterns"; similarly, the foot of figure 4-74 could be "six surface geometric patterns and one linear pattern."

16. A. Ovadiah, 1980, 160.

17. B. B. Mandelbrot, 1983; M. Barnsley, 1988.

18. This definition of fractals is based on that in H. Jürgens, H.-O. Peitgen, and D. Saupe, 1990, 46.

19. This brief explanation of the fractal dimension is a summary of the more detailed one in H. Jürgens, H.-O. Peitgen, and D. Saupe, 1990, 55, 56, 57, figs. 9, 10, 11.

20. H. Jürgens, H.-O. Peitgen, and D. Saupe, 1990, 46, 47, 48. These three mathematicians from the University of Bremen have researched fractals and computer graphics; among their publications are H.-O. Peitgen and P. Richter, 1986; H.-O. Peitgen and D. Saupe, 1988; H.-O. Peitgen, H. Jürgens, and D. Saupe, 1989; H. Jürgens, H.-O. Peitgen, and D. Saupe, 1990.

21. R. T. Stevens, 1990, 273–274. Roger T. Stevens is the author of numerous publications about the programming of images by computer in which he explains techniques for creating fractals; see the bibliography for titles published in 1988, 1989, and 1990.

22. A. K. Dewdney, 1990, 89. Other authors prefer to use the word *sibisimilar* rather than self-similar to allude to the same property: "The Sierpinski triangle, known since 1916, [was named for] the Polish mathematician Waclaw Sierpinski (1882–1969).... It is a typical example of a whole class of sibisimilar objects ...which are characterized by possessing the following property: upon taking a portion of the object, no matter how small it may be, it always contains a figure—a triangle in this case—which, sufficiently amplified, offers us anew the original figure" (H. Jürgens, H.-O. Peitgen, and D. Saupe, 1990, 48).

23. R. T. Stevens, 1990a, 157–59

24. R. T. Stevens, 1990a, 229–30.

25. R. T. Stevens, 1990a, 284–86.

26. A. K. Dewdney, 1990, 89–91.

Chapter 5: The Signification

1. Krautheimer takes the term from K. J. Conant, 1942, 15, as noted in R. Krautheimer, 1965, 362.

2. D. F. Glass, 1980.

3. D. F. Glass, 1969.

4. The emblems were, generally, portable mosaics, executed with embedded tesserae in a stone panel (*opus interassile*) that could be inserted into any preexisting background.

5. A. Ovadiah, 1980, 127, 128, 129, 140, 150, 151, 152, and figs. D1, D3, D4, 117, 118.

6. Regarding the characteristics of porphyry, see M. L. Lucci, 1964.

7. C. B. McClendon, 1980, 162 and plate XXXIV.

8. M. L. Lucci, 1964, 265 and n139, 140.

9. The morphology of this illustrious room seems to foreshadow another, also associated with a divinity, but this time Christian, that was constructed in the ninth century, attached to the right aisle of the church of Santa Prassede in Rome: the Chapel of San Zenone. It is discussed later in chapter 5.

10. M. L. Lucci, 1964, 266, 267, and n145; D. F. Glass, 1980, 48, 49, 52n9, 10, 11.

11. M. L. Lucci, 1964, 267, and n146; C. B. McClendon, 1980, 163, and n27, 28. As Agnellus reported: "*Quod ipsa Galla Placidia augusta super quatuor rotas rubeas marmoreas, quae sunt ante nominatas regias, iubebat ponere cereostatos cum manualia ad mesuram, et iactabat se noctu in medio pavimento, Deo fundere preces, et tamdiu pernoctabat in lacrimis orans, quamdiu ipsa lumina perdurabant*" (1878 [reprint]), 306).

12. D. F. Glass, 1980, 49, 53n16.

13. D. Fernández Galiano, 1983, 419–28, figs. 6, 7, 8.1, 8.2, 9.1, 9.2.

14. G. Matthiae, 1952, 252, 253, and fig. 5.

15. R. Farioli, 1970, 212–15 and figs. 33, 34.

16. R. Farioli, 1970, 215 and n62.

17. This review is based principally on R. Krautheimer, 1965, 201–13, 237–90, 359–63.

18. These and other examples from this period are studied in detail in R. Krautheimer, 1965, 201–13.

19. For example, the basilica with galleries and a wooden roof, the cross-domed church, the Justinian church of five domes, the small basilica with barrel vault, the tri- and tetra-shell church.

20. The dome over squinches was a common architectural solution in Armenian churches, appearing at least since the seventh century. It was also used extensively in Islamic architecture during the tenth and eleventh centuries. The mid-Byzantine architects must have borrowed this solution from those lands bordering the empire. Blending it with the spatial concept of purely Byzantine tradition, apparent—from the final years of Justinian—in the interconnected spaces of the cross-domed churches, they devised the Greek-cross octagon church plan.

21. R. Krautheimer, 1965, 362.

22. With regard to the antecedents of the spatial quincunx, see R. Krautheimer, 1965, 245–47.

23. Regarding this church, see G. Bendinelli, 1951, 814–15, 825, and plates 107, 108.

24. For a detailed study about the development of mid-Byzantine architecture and its diverse regional styles, see R. Krautheimer, 1965, 258–90; particularly 258–83 and figs. 98, 99, 101, 103.

25. *Il mosaico, di un disegno geometrico abbastanza semplice, risulta di un tondo centrale fiancheggiato da quattro tondi minori e da quattro altri poco più grandi negli intervalli; con altri quattro delle medesime dimensioni posti diagonalmente a contatto dei tondi menori. Tutto quanto il disegno, composto di tredici tondi a cerchi concentrici bianchi e scuri, si iscribe in un quadrato. Più che di un pavimento musivo, si direbbe trattarsi di un emblema musivo di pavimento, poichè questo è fatto per il rimanente di semplici lastre di marmo bianco, salvo avanzi di una fascia scura addetta a incorniciare l'emblema. L'interesse de la composizione stellare è dato dal fatto che i tondi sono tenuti insieme da una fascia o nastro, che corre intorno all'uno e all'altro tondo, formando un intreccio* (G. Bendinelli, 1951, 814).

26. About the Great Lavra of Mount Athos, see A. K. Orlandos, 1939–51; v (1939–40) 34ff; ibid vii (1951), 250, 72ff.

27. In the church of Hagia Sophia in Nicaea remains a great square in the eastern part of the nave, over the longitudinal axis of the church, which is perhaps the first of a series that carpeted the main aisle. For a floor plan of the pavement, see S. Eyice, 1963, 375, fig. 1.

28. See, for example, N. Baldoria, 1891; G. Matthiae, 1967, 418, 419, and figs. 196, 197.

29. This resurgence is studied in detail in C. B. McClendon, 1980.

30. A *groin-sail vault* is a groin vault with arrises so gentle or rounded that it takes on the appearance of a sail vault. A *groin* or *arris vault* is one whose two semicircular barrels cut into one another. A *sail vault* is one formed by a hemisphere cut by four vertical planes, each pair of which is parallel.

31. The same can be observed in the Chapel of the Sancta Sanctorum in Rome, where a Pantocrator enclosed in a circle, also supported by four angles, is found in the center of the mosaic of the vault, over the central *rota* of the quincunx that ornaments the pavement of the chapel (P. C. Claussen, 1987, plate 136, figs. 272, 273).

32. F. Hermanin, 1945, 27. For a floor plan of the basilica at the time of Leo IV, see M. G. Barberini, 1989, 16, fig. 6.

33. Regarding the pavement of the basilica of San Marco, see A. Bruyère, 1990; P. Gascar, 1964; G. Matthiae, 1952, 259–60 and fig. 12.

34. Regarding the Catholic church in Stilo, see W. R. Lethaby, 1904, 117.

35. For example, mosaics or murals in the vaulted areas, veneers of marble plaques, elaborate tapestries on the walls, pavements in geometric *opus sectile*, moldings, capitals, ornamental brickwork on the exterior side of walls, icons, and reliquaries of gold, enamel, and glass.

36. The reasons for the small size, the precise and scrupulous execution, and the subtle, refined, and dense symbolism of Byzantine churches are multiple and interrelated. Above all, consider the reduced size of the monastic congregations (in the eleventh century, a monastery with more than eight monks was considered large) that those churches that were taken as models served. The models were the churches of the most important monasteries, all patronized and erected under the direction of the learned and sophisticated rectors of those congregations which, belonging, the vast majority of them, to the most privileged social stratum linked to the aristocracy, knew and established the canons for symbolic-ornamental representation. Regarding these congregations, see R. Krautheimer, 1965, 247–48.

37. According to Xavier Barral i Altet in M. Blanchard-Lemée, 1991, 125, 126, based on R.-H. Bautier, 1968, 67, 44b; and R.-H. Bautier, 1986, 265–66.

38. M. Blanchard-Lemée, 1991, 13, 125–27, and plates II, LII–LVII. Page 126 contains an extensive bibliography about the church and its pavement.

39. The term *emblem* is defined in note 4 for this chapter.

40. Regarding the pavement from the Abbey of Pomposa, see G. Galassi, 1930, 261, 262, and figs. 156, 157, 158; D. F. Glass, 1980, 31, 32, and plate 76; M. Salmi, 1966, 125ff.; H. Stern, 1968, 157–69.

41. For the names and the exact locations of the various spaces that house these functions, including such details as the change of position they undergo in cross-domed churches, see R. Krautheimer, 1965, 210–12, 359–63.

42. R. Krautheimer, 1965, 212–13.

43. For a detailed study of man as a symbol of the cosmos in medieval thought, see M.-T. D'Alverny, 1975.

44. M.-T. D'Alverny, 1975, 135, 136.

45. M.-T. D'Alverny, 1975, 173–76.

46. M.-T. D'Alverny, 1975, 177.

47. M.-T. D'Alverny, 1975, 177, 178.

48. M.-T. D'Alverny, 1975, 182, 183.

49. S. H. Wander, 1978; in particular, 149–51 and figs. 1, 3, 4, 7.

50. C. Heitz, 1975.

51. C. Heitz, 1975, 400–403.

52. The baptistery of Constantine at San Giovanni in Laterano is one of the products of the Sistine renaissance, the period of resurgence of classical models that occurred in Rome under Pope Sixtus III (432–440). Its octagonal floor plan and details recall those of Santa Costanza, built a century before. Santo Stefano Rotondo is another fifth-century construction that attests to the return to classical models. These three buildings with centralized floor plans are regulated by the double cross. For a brief description of them, see R. Krautheimer, 1965, 64, 65; R. Krautheimer, 1983, 167–69, 179–81.

53. D. F. Glass, 1969; D. F. Glass, 1980, 48–54.

54. As D. F. Glass (1980, 50, 51) explains: "After the bishops and clerics had circled the exterior of the church three times, all the while blessing it with holy water, they entered the church and *'interim unus e ministris aspergat cinerem per pavimentum ecclesiae in modum crucis, ita ut de sinistro angulo orientali pergat ad dextrum occidentalem, rursusque de dextro orientali vadat in sinistrum occidentale'* (M. Andrieu, 1938 [vol. 1], 180, XVII, 18).

"One of the priests drew a cross with ashes on the diagonal axes of the church. The place where the two arms of the cross met, the center of the church, is also the spot decorated by a large porphyry quincunx.... Such designs appear, for example, in ... Ss. Quattro Coronati and S. Croce in Gerusalemme, both in Rome.

"The center of the church is again emphasized a few lines later in the dedication ceremony, when the pope *'incipiat...de sinistro angulo ecclessiae ab oreinte scribere per pavimentum cum cambuta sua totum alfabetum graecum, usque in dextrum angulum occidentalem ... Incipiens similiter de dextro angulo orientali totum alfabetum latinum scribat usque in sinistrum angulum occidentalem'* (ibid., 180–81, XVII, 20).

"The pope, in writing the Latin and Greek alphabets on the same diagonal axes on which the sign of the cross was made with ashes, again emphasized the center of the church.

"After the exorcism of the salt, water, and ashes, and the consecration of the altar, the center of the nave was singled out for attention still a third time: *'Diende aspergat in modum crucis per medium ecclesiae in longum et in latum per pavimentum ...'* (ibid., 183, XVII, 36). The making of the cross on the longitudinal and latitudinal axes of the church, ...is significant for its relationship to S. Clemente in Rome .... The shape of the cross made during the dedication ceremony thus appears in the design of the floor.

"Finally, as the consecration ceremony drew to a close, the bishop stood in the middle of the church and commanded *'Oremus.'* The conjugal relationship between the design of early twelfth century Cosmatesque pavements and the coeval ceremony for the dedication of churches is evident...."

For a general discussion of the ceremony of consecration, see L. Duchesne, 1908, 405–25. Reproduction of the above text from the Glass book, courtesy of BAR.

55. The double cross was drawn by sprinkling ashes over the axes of the principal quincunx. The design, according to figure 5-65, resulted from joining the points in the following order: ([1-2]–[3-4]–[5-6]–[7-8]). The alphabets were written in the decussate cross ([1-2]–[3-4]): along the arm [1-2], the Greek alphabet; along the arm [3-4], the Latin alphabet.

56. Illustrated in G. Matthiae, 1952, 259, fig. 12.

57. Regarding Christian iconography on eastern coins from the fourth to the twelfth century, see. G. Carrelli, 1934.

58. In Greek idiom, the fish was called ictis, a term that contained the initials of the words *Jesus Christus teu ios soter,* that is, "Jesus, son of God, the Savior" (G. Carrelli, 1934, 44–45.).

59. In addition to figures 5-70 and 5-71, examples of the chi-rho can be seen on the fourth-century sarcophagus with the symbol of the triumph of Christ, Museo de Valencia (B. Taracena, P. Batlle Huguet, and H. Schlunk, 1947, 203, fig. 203); the fifth-century marble plaque from the church of Quiroga, Museo Diocesano de Lugo (ibid., 238, fig. 236); a detail of the lateral design of the fifth-century sarcophagus of Ithacius, Panteón de los Reyes, Catedral de Oviedo (ibid., 241, fig. 242); the doorway of the mid-twelfth-century church of San Miguel de Uncastillo, Zaragoza, in the Museum of Fine Arts, Boston (J. Gudiol Ricart and J. A. Gaya Nuño, 1948, 150, fig. 249); a detail from the door surround of the thirteenth-century church of Cirauqui, Navarra (ibid., 179, fig. 302).

60. In addition to figure 5-72, the Christogram of X and I can be seen in a fragment of a seventh-century screen originally from Mérida (B. Taracena, P. Batlle Huguet, and H. Schlunk, 1947, 250, fig. 260); and in a seventh-century niche originally from Mérida in the Museo de Mérida (ibid., 251, fig. 262).

61. In addition to figures 5-73, 5-74, and 5-75, the Christogram of X and + can be seen in a detail of the twelfth-century portico of the church of San Andrés de Armentia, Alava (J. Gudiol Ricart and J. A. Gaya Nuño, 1948, 335, fig. 498), and in the twelfth-century door surround of the Platerías in the Catedral de Santiago de Compostela (ibid., 215, fig. 348).

62. J. Yarza, 1980, 131.

63. For a detailed explanation of the different types of scepters, their meaning, and their origins, with references to the Christian appropriation of pagan symbols of power, see A. Pertusi, 1975, 497–516.

64. The liturgical fan served to shoo the flies from the Eucharist. The central part of the fan in figure 5-83 is a small hinged door, which opens to reveal an opening in which a relic was placed.

65. Each of the fragments of the host bore the name of the symbol it represented: West, Birth; East, Passion; South, Ascension; North, Resurrection (C. Heitz, 1975, 393, 394, and n17).

66. Two other beautiful works of medieval metalwork that include quincuncial compositions are in Ambazac, an enameled box from Saint Stephen of Muret (T.-H. Newman, R. Oursel, and L. Moulin, 1987, fig. 143), and in Conques, France, in the treasury of the Abbey of Sainte-Foy, an enameled altar (ibid., fig. 147).

67. Regarding the façade of San Pietro in Tuscania, see Phaidon, 1987, 294, 295 ("the rose window fell in the earthquake of 1971, but it has been reconstructed and reset"); K. Noehles, 1961 (on studying the antecedents of this quincuncial

composition, the author cites, among other examples, mosaics from the Baptistery of Florence; one from the pavement [65, fig. 64] and another from the ceiling [65, fig. 65]); H. Thümmler, 1938; P. Verdier, 1940.

68. Among these images, those that appear in the Beatos stand out. The Beatos are copies that were made in Spain from the tenth to the thirteenth century from an original manuscript by a monk named Beatus, from the monastery of Liébana, in which he commented on and illustrated the Revelation of Saint John.

69. The underlying geometry in all of these symbols is quincuncial. The numbers 4 and 24 (3 x 2 x 4) are associated with the fundamental rhythms of the cycles of nature (four seasons of the year, twenty-four hours in a day). The diagram of heavenly Jerusalem is a square divided into nine equal squares, which result from dividing each side of the square into three parts; this diagram is associated with the perfect number, 12 (3 x 4 =12).

70. In the bottom of the Box of Agates of the cathedral of Oviedo (fig. 5-100), the central figure is a cross.

71. The chrismon, an ancient versatile symbol, was, in antiquity, the symbolic diagram for ritual observation of the sun. For Christians, the chrismon became the monogram of Christ, the symbol uniting the letters X and P (the first two letters of the name of Christ in Greek) or the Christogram X and I (X and the I of Iesous), and therefore the symbol of universal salvation granted by the crucifixion of Jesus.

72. Demonstrating this belief are the words of Saint Cipriano (d. circa 258) about Adam, the biblical first man created by God: "Adam was created with earth taken from the four extremes of the globe. Thus, in the name of Adam, God appears to perpetuate this origin, putting a star at each of the cardinal points: to the east: the one called Anatolé, Dusis to the west, Arctos to the north, Mezenobris at the midday point. Combining the first letters of these four stars, one obtains the name Adam" (the names of the four stars are those of the four cardinal points in Greek) (G. de Champeaux and D. S. Sterckx, 1984, 294).

73. The rite of consecration of the churches repeats, in another format, the principal ceremony of the rite of consecration of the altars. The purification with holy water precedes, in both rites, the unction with oil. The fundamental acts of the ceremony of consecration of a church are the double crossing of the principal quincunx—first the straight cross was drawn (by sprinkling holy water along the longitudinal axis of the church and over the perpendicular axis that passes through the center of the quincunx situated in the middle of the area reserved for the faithful) and then the decussate cross (drawn with ashes, scattered over the diagonals of the quincunx, on which were drawn the Greek and Latin alphabets)—and the unction of the twelve points of support of the church.

74. This plan occurs, for example, in Kalundborg, Denmark, where the altar is found at the crossing, over which rises a square/octagonal tower, covered with a hemispherical dome, above which is found the slender pyramidal roof of four/eight sides. The Latin cross floor plan of this type of church also included other towers, arranged at points of greatest symbolism: one located at the start of the nave, in the entrance; and three others on the upper part of the floorplan: one in the eastern apse and two in the transept, one at the end of each arm.

75. For greater depth and detail about the world of ancient and medieval symbols, see G. de Champeaux and D. S. Sterckx, 1984; O. Beigbeder, 1989.

BIBLIOGRAPHY

Agazzi, A. 1926. *Il musaico in Italia.* Milan.

Agnellus. 1878 (reprint). "Liber Pontificalis Ecclesiae Ravennatis." In *Monumenta Germaniae Historica: Scriptores Rerum langobardicarum et Italicarum saec. 6–9,* edited by O. Holder-Egger, 306.

Ainalov, D. V. 1961. *The Hellenistic Origins of Byzantine Art.* New Brunswick, NJ.

Andarolo, M. 1984. *Il sogno di Innocenzo III all'Aracoeli, Niccolò IV e la basilica di San Giovanni in Laterano* (13 C., Mosaico Aracoeli).

Andrieu, M. 1938–41. *Le pontifical romain au moyen-age.* 4 vols. Vatican City. (Reprint, 1965, Studi e Testi, vol. 86, 87, 88, 89). In particular, see *Le pontifical romain au XIIe siècle,* vol. 1 (Studi e Testi 86).

———. 1954. "La Rota Porphyretica de la Basilique Vaticane." *Mélanges D'Archéologie et D'Histoire* (Rome: Ecole Française de Rome) 66: 189–218.

Angeli, D. 1907. *Le chiese di Roma.* Rome: Società Ed. Dante Alighieri.

———. 1914. "Arti Grafiche," part 1 in *Roma.* Bergamo, Italy.

———. n.d. *Le chiese di Roma.* Rome: Albrighi, Segati e C.

Angelo, P., and M. Caccin. 1962. *Saint-Marc.* Venice.

Angiolini Martinelli, P. 1968. "Altari, amboni, cibori, cornici, plutei con figure di animali e con intrecci, transenne e frammenti vari." In *Corpus della scultura paleocristiana bizantina ed altomedioevale di Ravenna* vol. 1. Rome.

Anthony, E. W. 1927. *Early Florentine Architecture and Decoration.* Cambridge, Mass.

Antonaci, A. 1955. "Otranto (testi e monumenti)." *Studi sulla civiltà Salentina* (Galatina, Italy) 2. Galatina.

Apollonj Ghetti, B. M. 1947–48. "La Chiesa di Santa Maria di Vescovio." *Rivista d'Archeologia cristiana.*

———. 1964. *I Santi Quattro Coronati.* Rome.

———. 1966. *San Crisogono.* Monograph 92 in the series *Le Chiese di Roma illustrate.* Rome: Casa Ed. Roma.

Arata, G. 1914. *L'architettura arabo-normanna e il rinascimento in Sicilia.* Milan.

Argan, G. C. 1937. *L'architettura italiana del '200 e '300.* Florence.

Armellini, M. 1942. *Le chiese di Roma dal secolo IV al XIX.* Edited by C. Cecchelli. 2 vols. Rome.

Asimakopoulou, P. and P. Atzaka, 1984. "I mosaici pavimentali paleocristiani in Grecia: Contributo allo estudio ed alle relazioni tra i laboratori." *Corsi di Cultura sull'Arte Ravennate e Bizantina* 31: 13–75.

Astley, S. 1990. *Border Designs: A Treasury of Decorative Designs in Colour and Black and White.* London: plates 18, 19, and 21.

Aubert, M. 1961. "La construction au Moyen Âge." *Bulletin Monumental* 119: 181–209, 297–323.

Aurigemma, S., A. Bianchini, and A. DeSantis. 1966. *Circeo, Terracina, Fondi: Itinerari dei musei, gallerie e monumenti d'Italia*, 97, 2d ed. Rome.

Avagnina, M. E., V. Garibaldi, and C. Salterini. 1976–77. "Strutture murarie degli edifici religiosi di Roma nel XII secolo." *Rivista dell'Istituto Nazionale d'Archeologia e Storia dell'Arte* 23–24: 173–255.

Baccini Leotardi, P. 1979. *Marmi di cava rinvenuti ad Ostia e considerazioni sul commercio dei marmi in età Romana, Scavi di Ostia.*Vol. 10. Ministerio della Pubblica Istruzione, Sovraintendenza agli scavi di Ostia Antica, Istituto Poligrafico e Zecca dello Stato, Rome.

Baldoria, N. 1891. "La Capella de San Zenone a Santa Prassede in Roma." *Archivio Storico dell'Arte* 4: 256–73.

Balmelle, C., M. Blanchard-Lemée, J. Christophe, J.-P. Darmon, A.-M. Gumier-Sorbets, H. Lavagne, R. Prudhomme, and H. Stern. 1985. *Le Décor Géométrique de la Mosaïque Romaine: Répertoire Graphique et Descriptif des Compositions Linéaires et Isotropes.* Paris: Ed. C N. R. S. de l'Université de Paris X—Nanterre and C. National des Lettres, Picard.

Ballance, S. 1960. "The Bizantine Churches of Trebizond." *Anatolian Studies* 10: 141–175.

Ballerio, C. 1942. "La basilica romana dei Santi Giovanni e Paolo al Celio." *Palladio* 6 (3–5). Casa Editrice Carlo Colombo, Roma: 81–89.

Balty, J. C. 1969. *L'eglise a atrium de la Grande Colonnade, Fouilles d'Apamée de Syrie*, 1, Brussels.

Barberini, M. G. 1989. "I Santi Quattro Coronati a Roma." In *Itinerari d'arte e di culture—Basiliche.* Rome: Fratelli Palombi Ed.

Barbier de Montault, X. 1858. "Généalogie d'artistes italiens du XIIIe siècle." *Annales archéologiques* 18: 265–72.

Barclay Lloyd, J. E. 1985. "Masonry Techniques in Medieval Rome, 1080–1300." *Papers of the British School at Rome* 53: 225–27.

———. 1986. "The Building History of the Medieval Church of San Clemente in Roma." *Journal of the Society of Architectural Historians* 45: 197–223.

———. 1989. *The Medieval Church and Canony of San Clemente in Rome.* Rome.

Bargellini, C. 1974. "Studies in Medieval Apulian Floor Mosaics." Ph.D. diss., Harvard University.

Barnsley, M. 1988. *Fractals Everywhere.* New York: Academic Press.

Barral i Altet, X. 1973. "Le passage de la mosaïque de pavement antique a la mosaïque de pavement médiévale en occident, travaux récents et nouveaux problèmes." *Bulletin D'information de L'Association Internationale pour L'Etude de la mosaïque antique* (Paris) 5: 189–96.

———. 1975. "Note sui mosaici pavimentali dell'Alto Medioevo nell'Italia del Nord." *Mosaici in Aquileia e nell'Alto Adriatico, Antichità Altoadriatiche* (Udine, Italy) 8: 275–83.

———. 1982. "Le pavement médiéval de l'eglise Sant'Angelo in Formis (Campanie)." In *Mosaïque: Recueil d'hommages à Henri Stern.* Paris: 55–60.

Bartoccini, R. 1930. "Il mosaico pavimentale di San Michele in Africisco." *Felix Ravenna* n.s. 8, 3: 11–13.

Bartoli, G. 1907. "Il figlio di Pietro Vassalletto a Cività Lavinia." *Bolletino d'Arte* 9: 22ff.

Battisti, E. 1960. "Simbolo e classicismo." In *Rinascimento e Barroco*. Turin, Italy: 22–23.

Bautier, R.-H. 1986. *Artistes, artisans et production artistique au Moyen Age,* 1, Paris: 265–266.

Bautier, R.-H., and G. Labory, ed. 1968. *Vita Gauzlini, abbatis Floriacensis*. Paris: 67, 44b.

Becatti, G. 1948. "Case Ostiensi del tardo impero-II." *Bollettino d'Arte* 4th series, 33: 197–224, esp. 206ff.

———. 1961. *Mosaici e pavimenti marmorei, Scavi di Ostia*. Vol 4 (testo & tarole), Ministero della Pubblica Istruzione, Sovraintendenza agli scavi di Ostia Antica, Istituto Poligrafico dello Stato. Rome.

———. 1965. "Alcune caratteristiche del mosaico bianco-nero in Italia." In *La mosaïque gréco-romaine: Colloques internationaux du centre national de la recherche scientifique, Paris 1963*. Paris: 15–26.

———. 1969. *Edificio con opus sectile fuori Porta Marina, Scavi di Ostia*. Vol 6, Ministero della Pubblica Istruzione, Sovraintendenza agli scavi di Ostia Antica, Istituto Poligrafico dello Stato, Rome.

Beck, I. 1975. *The Sicilian Dilemma: The Clash between Byzantine Mosaic Decoration and Arab Architectural Tradition*: 285–287; illustrations 1, 2, 3.

Becker, M. 1981. *Medieval Italy*. Bloomington, Indiana.

Beenken, H. 1926–27. "Die Florentiner Inkrustationsarchitektur des XI. Jahrhunderts." *Zeitschrift für Bildende Kunst* 60: 221–30, 245–55.

Beigbeder, O. 1989. *Léxico de los símbolos*. Vol. 15 of *Europa Románica*. Madrid: Ed. Encuentro. Originally published as *Lexique des symboles* (Saint Léger Vauban: Ed. Zodiaque, 1979).

Bella, I. 1956. *La chiesa romanica de San Frediano a Lucca*. Lucca, Italy.

Bellosi, L. 1981. *Giotto: la obra completa*. Florence and New York: Scala/Riverside. Reprint in Italy, 1992.

Bendinelli, G. 1951. "Intorno all'orinine e per una nuova denominazione dei mosaici 'cosmateschi.' " In *Studies Presented to David Moore Robinson*, Vol. 1, 813–28, plates 107–111. George E. Mylonas, Washington University, Saint Louis, Mo.

Berland, J.-M. 1968. "Le pavement du chœur de Saint-Benoît-sur-Loire." *Cahiers de Civilisation Médiévale* 2: 211–19.

Bertaux, E. 1904. *L'art dans l'Italie méridionale*. Paris.

Bertelli, G. 1974. "Una pianta inedita della chiesa alto-medioevale di Santa Maria in Trastevere." *Bollettino d'Arte* 5 (59): 157–60.

———. 1978. *Aggiornamento dell' opera di E. Bertaux*. Vol. 4 of *L'art dans l'Italie méridionale*. Rome.

Berti, F. 1976. *Mosaici Antichi in Italia: Aemilia: Ravenna*. Rome.

Bessone-Aurelj, A. M. 1935. *I marmorari romani*. Milan: Società Anonima Editrice Dante Alighieri, Albrighi, Segati, and C.

Betsch, E. W. 1977. "The History, Production, and Distribution of the Late Antique Capital in Constantinople." Ph.D. diss., University of Pennsylvania, Fine Arts.

Bettini, S. 1937. *L'architettura bizantina*. Florence.

Bianchi Bandinelli, R. 1970. *Roma: La fine dell'arte antica*. Milan.

Biblioteca Apost. Vaticana. 1941. "Tesoro della Cappella Sancta Sanctorum." *Museo Sacro-Guida* 55. Vatican City.

Binski, P. 1990. "The Cosmati at Westminster and the English Court Style." *The Art Bulletin* 72 (1): 6–34.

Blake, M. E. 1930. "The Pavements of the Roman Buildings of the Republic and Early Empire." In *Memoirs of the American Academy in Rome*, vol 8, 7–160. New York: American Academy in Rome.

———. 1940. "Mosaics of the Late Empire in Rome and Vicinity." In *Memoirs of the American Academy in Rome*, vol 17, 81–130, plates 11–34. New York: American Academy in Rome.

Blanchard-Lemée, M. 1991. *Recueil Géneral des Mosaïques de la Gaulle.* 10th supplément à Gallia; 2: Province de Lyonnaise, 4. Partie occidentale. With J.-P. Darmon and X. Barral i Altet. Paris: Editions du Centre National de la Recherche Scientifique.

Bloch, H. 1946. "Montecassino, Byzantium, and the West in the Earlier Middle Ages." *Dumbarton Oaks Papers* 3.

———. 1982. "The New Fascination with Ancient Rome." In *Renaissance and Renewal in the Twelfth Century*, edited by G. Constable and R. L. Benson., 615–36. Cambridge, Mass.

Bloch, M. 1962. *La società feudale.* Turin, Italy.

Blumenthal, U. 1978. "Paschal II and the Roman Primacy." *Archivium Historiae Pontificiae* 16: 67–92.

Boaga, G. n.d. "Cenni sulla viabilità nel Lazio dal Medio Evo alla fine dell'Ottocento." In *Quaderni di ricerca urbanologica e tecnica della pianificazione*, 271–307.

Boito, C. 1860. *Architettura cosmatesca.* Milan.

———. 1880. *Architettura del medio evo in Italia: I Cosmati.* Milan.

Boni, G. 1893. *The Roman Marmorarii.* Rome.

Borghini, G., ed. 1992. *Marmi antichi.* Ministero per I Beni Culturale e Ambientali. Istituto Centrale per il Catalogo e la Documentacione. Rome: Leonardo-De Luca Editori.

Bottari, S. 1955. "I rapporti tra l'architettura siciliana e quella campana del Medioevo." *Palladio* 5: 7–28.

Bouras, C. 1982. "Nea Moni on Chios." In *History of Architecture*, 67–69, figs. 44, 71, 141, and 142. Athens.

Bourea, A. 1990. "Vel sedens vel trasiens: la création d'un espace pontifical aux XI et XII siècles." In *Luoghi sacri e spazi della santità*, edited by S. Boesch Gajano and L. Scaraffia, 367–79. Turin, Italy.

Bovini, G. 1953. "Un'antica chiesa Ravennate: San Michele in Africisco. *Felix Ravenna* 3d series, 11:5–37.

———. 1954. "Sugli avanzi del mosaico pavimentale della chiesa di San Severo conservati nella Torretta del Giardino del Palazzo della Provincia de Ravenna." *Felix Ravenna* 3d series, 15: 38–51.

———. 1966. "Roma: Basilica di Santa Maria Maggiore." *Tesori d'arte cristiana: 100 Chiese in Europa.* No. 2. Bologna.

Boyle, L. 1991. *Pequeña Guía de San Clemente.* Rome.

Boyle, L., F. Guidobaldi, P. Lawlor, and V. Cosentino. 1990. *La Basilica e L'Area Archeologica di San Clemente in Roma: Guida Grafica ai Tre Livelli.* Rome.

Boyle, L. E. 1894. *Brevi cenni storici con illustrazioni della basilica de San Lorenzo extramuros.* Rome.

Bréhier, L. 1904. *La querélle des images.* Paris.

Brezzi, P. 1947. *Roma e l'Imperio medievale (774–1252).* Bologna.

Brooke, C. N. L. 1969. *The Twelfth-Century Renaissance.* London.

Brounov, N. 1927–28. "La Sainte-Sophie de Trébizonde." *Byzantion* 4: 393–405.

Brusin, G. 1950. "Il mosaico antico nel Veneto." *Arte Veneta* 4: 95–104.

———. 1960. "Tessellati di Cividale del Friuli." *Memorie Storiche Forogiuliesi* 44: 1–23.

Brusin, G., and P. Zovatto. 1957. *Monumenti paleocristiani di Aquileia e di Grado.* Udine, Italy.

Bruyère, A. 1990. *Sols, Saint-Marc, Venice.* Paris: Imprimerie Nationale Éditions.

Budde, L. 1972. "Antike Mosaiken in Kilikien, II." In *Die Heidnischen Mosaiken*, 212, and fig. 259. Recklinghausen, Germany.

Bunsen, C., J. G. Gutensohn, and J. M. Knapp. 1872. *Les Basiliques Chrétiennes de Rome Relevées et dessinées par Gutensohn et Knapp*. Paris: H. Sotheran, J. Baer and Cie. Originally published as *Die Basiliken des Christlichen Roms, nach ihrem Zusammenhange mit Idee und Geschichte der Kirchenbaukunst* (Munich, 1842).

Buonamici, G. 1748. *La metropolitana di Ravenna*. Bologna.

Buren, A. W. van. 1953. *A Bibliographical Guide to Latium and Southern Etruria*. Rome.

Cagiano de Azevedo, M. 1970. "Policromia e polimateria nelle opere d'arte della tarda Antichità e dell'Alto Medioevo." *Felix Ravenna* 4th series, 1: 223–59.

Calandra, E. 1941. "Chiese siciliane del periodo normanno." *Palladio* 5: 232–89.

Capone, A. 1927–29. *Il duomo di Salerno*. 2 vol. Salerno, Italy.

Caprino, C. 1972. "Mosaico con spartizione modulare e sinopia nella villa Adriana a Tivoli." *Bollettino d'Arte* 1: 44–45. Ministero della Publica Istruzione.

Carducci, G. 1866. *Sul grade musaico recentemente scoperto in Pesaro*. Pesaro, Italy.

Carli, F. 1936. *Storia del Commercio italiano: Il mercato nell'Alto Medioevo*. Padua.

Carobara, C. 1979. *Iussu Desiderii: Montecassino e l'architettura campano-abruzzese nell'undicesimo secolo*. Rome.

Carocci, G. 1897. "Il pavimento nel battisterio di Firenze." In *Arte italiana decorativa e industriale*, 34–36.

Carrelli, G. 1934. "In tema di iconografia monetale cristiana dell'Oriente (secoli IV a XII)." *Boll. del Circolo Numism. Napoletano* (Naples) 15 (2): 42–46.

Cartei, B. 1964. "Il restauro delle tarsie marmoree di Montecassino. "In *Marmo* 3, 96–111. Milan and Lucca: Editoriale Metro, S.p.A.

Cattaneo, R. 1888–89. *L'architettura in Italia del secolo VI all mille circa*. Venice.

Cecchelli, C. 1933. *Gli edifici ed I mosaici paleocristiana nella zona della basilica: La Basilica di Aquileia*. Bologna: D. Zanichelli. 109ff.

———. 1958–60. *Vita di Roma nel Medioevo*. 2 vol. Rome.

Cecchetti, C. 1930. *San Clemente*. Rome.

Champeaux, G. de, and D. S. Sterckx. 1984. *Introducción a los símbolos*. Vol. 7 of *Europa Románica*. Madrid: Ed. Encuentro. Originally published as *Le monde des Symboles* (Saint Léger Vauban: Ed. Zodiaque, 1972).

Charbonneaux, J., et al. 1973. *Hellenistic Art*. London.

Charlesworth, M. P. 1926. *Trade Routes and Commerce of the Roman Empire*. 2nd ed. Cambridge, England.

Chehab, M. H. 1957, 1959. "Mosaïques du Liban." *Buletin de Musée de Beyrouth* 14, 1957 (text); 15, 1959 (illustrations), plate LXV, I.

Clausse, G. 1897a. "Les Cosmati et l'église de Sainte-Marie à Cività Castellana." *Revue de l'Art Chrétien* 23: 271–79.

———. 1897b. *Les marbriers romains et le mobilier presbytéral*. Paris: Ernest Leroux, Éditeur.

Claussen, P. C. 1987. "Magistri Doctissimi Romani: Die Römischen Marmorskünstler des Mittelalters (Corpus Cosmatorum I)." In *Forschungen zur Kunstgeschichte und christlichen Archäologie*. Stuttgart: Franz Steiner Verlag.

———. 1989. "Marmi antichi nel Medioevo romano: L'arte dei cosmati." In *Marmi antichi*, edited by G. Borghini, 65–79. Rome: Leonardo-De Luca Editori.

———. n.d. *Die Kirchen Roms in Mittelalter 1050–1308: Liturgische Ausstattung und Architektur (Corpus Cosmatorum II)*.

Collini, A. 1944. "Storia e topografia del Celio nell'antichità." In *Atti della Pontificia Accademia Romana d'Archeologia* 3d series, 7: 238ff., 255ff., 360ff.

Colosanti, A. 1923. *Santa Maria in Aracoeli*. Monograph in the series *Le Chiese di Roma illustrate*. Rome: Casa Ed. Roma.

Conant, K. J. 1942. *A Brief Commentary on Early Medieval Church Architecture*. Baltimore, Md.

Corsi, F. 1845. *Delle pietre antiche*. 3d ed. Rome.

Cortesi, G. 1964. *La zona e la basilica di San Severo nel territorio di Classe*. Ravenna.

Crema, L. 1942. "Le origini e lo sviluppo della basilica cristiana." *Palladio* 6 (5–6): 203–8. Roma, Casa Editrice Carlo Colombo.

———. 1953. "Il pavimento di Santa Maria di Castelseprio." In *Arte del primo millennio: Atti del II° Convegno per lo studio dell'arte dell'alto medioevo, Pavia 1950*, 194–98. Turin, Italy.

———. 1958. "Genesi e sviluppo della cripta dall' VIII all' XI secolo." In *Architettura (L') religiosa del medioevo occidentale: L'alto medioevo*, 80–85. Milan.

Creswell, K. A. C. 1952–59. *The Muslim Architecture of Egypt*. Oxford.

Dalton, O. M. 1911. *Byzantine Art and Archeology*. Oxford.

D'Alverny, M.-T. 1975. "L'homme comme symbole: Le microcosme." *Simboli e simbologia nell'Alto Medioevo* (Spoleto: Centro Italiano di Studi sull'Alto Medioevo) 23 (1, 2): 123–96.

Dami, L. 1915. "La basilica de San Miniato al Monte." *Bollettino de'Arte* 9: 216–44.

Daniele, G. 1873. *Il duomo de Caserta Vecchia*. Caserta, Italy.

Dasti, L. 1878. *Notizie storiche archeologiche di Tarquinia o Corneto*. Rome.

de Angelis, M. 1936. *Il duomo di Salerno, nella sua storia, nelle sue vicende e nei suoi monumenti*. Salerno, Italy.

de Angelis d'Ossat, G. 1942a. *Le influenze bizantine nell'architettura romanica*. Rome.

———. 1942b. " 'Magister Gualterius' marmorario e costruttore abruzzese." *Palladio* 6 (3–4): 97–101. Roma, Casa Editrice Carlo Colombo.

DeBenedictis, E. 1984. "The 'Schola Cantorum' in Rome during the High Middle Ages." Ph.D. diss., Bryn Mawr College. Ann Arbor, Mich.: University Microfilms International.

de Blaauw, S. 1987. *Cultus et Decor: Liturgie en architectur in laattantiek en middleeuws Rome*. Slochteren, Netherlands.

Deér, J. 1959. "The Dynastic Porphyry Tombs of the Norman Period in Sicily." *Dumbarton Oaks Studies* 5. Cambridge, Mass.

de Magistris, A. 1747. *Storia della città di Anagni*. Rome.

Demangel, R. 1945. "Contribution à la topographie de l'Hebdomon." *Recherches françaises en Turquie* 3:21–23. Paris.

Demus, O. 1947. *Byzantine Mosaic Decoration*. London.

———. 1960. *The Church of San Marco in Venice*. Washington, DC.

De Rossi, G. B. 1873–99. *Musaici cristiani e saggi dei pavimenti delle Chiese di Roma anteriori al secolo XV*. 2 vols. (testo & tavole). Rome: Libreria Spithöver di Guglielmo Haass.

———. 1875. "Del cosidetto Opus Alexandrinum dei Marmorari Romanini in Santa Maria di Castello, Tarquinia." *Bollettino d'Archeologia Cristiana* 2 (6): 85–131.

———. 1889. "Tabernacolo altare e sua capsella reliquaria in San Stefano presso Fiano Romano." *Bollettino d'Archaeologia Cristiana*. 1888–9, Roma, 154ff.

———. 1891. "Raccolta di iscrizioni romane relative ad artisti ed all loro opere nel Medio Evo compilata alla fine del secolo XVI." *Bollettino d' Archeologia Cristiana* 5: 73–100.

De Rossi, G. M. 1969. *Torri e castelli medioevali della campagna romana*. Rome.

De Ruggiero, G. 1946. *La filosofia del Cristianesimo*. II, Bari, Italy.

Dewdney, A. K. 1990. "Juegos de Ordenador." *Investigación y Ciencia* (Spanish edition of *Scientific American*) 166 (July 1990): 88–92.

Diamare, G. 1906–7. *Memorie critico-storiche della chiesa di Sessa Aurunca*. 2 vol. Naples.

Diehl, C. 1889. *L'eglise et les mosaïques du convent de Saint-Luc en Phocide*. Paris.

———. 1925. *Manuel d'Art Byzantin*. Paris.

———. 1959. *L'Afrique byzantine*. New York.

Di Re, P. 1986. *Basilica di Santa Prassede; The Basilica of Santa Prassede; Die Basilika Sankt Prassede; Basilique Sainte-Praxède*. Bologna.

Di Stefano, G. 1955. *Monumenti della Sicilia Normanna.* Palermo, Italy.

Dolci, E., ed. 1989. "Il marmo nella civiltà romana: la produzione e il commercio." Proceedings of the seminar Internazionale Marmi e Macchine, Museo del Marmo, Carrara, San Marco Litotipo—Lucca, Carrara.

Dolci, E. and L. Nista, ed. 1992. "La Raccolta Grassi del Museo Nazionale Romano: Marmi Antichi da Collezione." Ministero Beni Culturali e Ambientali, Soprintendenza Archeologica di Roma. Carrara: Museo Civico del Marmo; Pisa: Pacini Editore; Carrara: Museo del Marmo.

Dolmetsch, H. (Heinrich), trans. 1898. *The Treasury of Ornament.* Originally published as *Der Ornamentenschatz,* 1st ed., 1883; 2d ed., 1887. Reissued as *Tesoros de la Ornamentación* (Madrid: Edit. Libsa, 1990).

D'Onofrio, M. 1974. *Le cattedrale di Caserta Vecchia.* Rome.

Dubois, C. 1908. *Etude sur l'administration et l'exploitation des carrières . . . marbres, porphyre, granit, etc. . . . dans le monde romain.* Paris.

Duchesne, L. 1908. *Origines du culte chrétien.* 4th ed. Paris.

Duchesne, L. 1947. *I primi tempi dello Stato Pontificio.* Milan.

———, ed. 1886–92. *Le Liber Pontificalis.* Paris.

Dunbabin, K. 1978. *The Mosaics of Roman North Africa.* Oxford.

Dussaud, R., P. Deschamps, and H. Seyrig. 1931. *La Syrie antique et médiévale illustrée.* Paris.

Dyggve, E. 1941. "Ravennatum Palatium Sacrum: La basilica ipetrale per ceremonie. Studii sull'architettura dei palazzi nella tarda antichità." *Det Kgl. Danske Videnskabernes Sleskab. Archaeologiskkunst-historiske Meddelelser* 3 (2), Copenhagen.

Eclissi, A. 1639. *Pitture della basilica di San Lorenzo.*

Eco, U. 1986. *Art and Beauty in the Middle Ages.* Translated by Hugh Bredin. New Haven, Conn.: Yale University.

Ecochard, M. 1977. *Filiation de Monuments Grecs, Byzantins et Islamiques: une question de géométrie.* Paris.

Ernst, B. 1978. *El espejo mágico de Maurits Cornelis Escher.* Reissued, Berlin: TACO, 1989.

Eroli, G. 1903. *Lugnano, Teverina.* Narni, Italy.

———. 1905. *Descrizione delle Chiese di Narni.* Narni, Italy.

Esch, A. 1969. "Spolien: Zur Wiedereverwendung antiker Baustücke und Skulpturen im mittelalterlichen Italien." *Archiv für Kulturgeschichte* 51: 1–64.

Eyice, S. 1955. *Istanbul: Petit guide a travers les monuments byzantins et turcs.* Istanbul.

———. 1963. "Two Mosaic Pavements from Bythnia." *Dumbarton Oaks Papers* 17: 373–83.

Faldi Guglielmi, C. n.d. *Roma: Basilica di San Lorenzo al Verano,* 12. Bologna, Italy.

Faloci Pulignani, M. 1907. *Foligno.* Bergamo, Italy.

———. 1915. "I marmorari romani a Sassovino." *Archivio della Storia Ecc. dell'Umbria* (Perugia, Italy) 2: 561ff.

Farioli, R. 1965. "Mosaici pavimentali d'età paleocristiana degli edifici di culto di Ravenna." In *XII corso di cultura sull'arte Ravennate e Bizantina,* 335–73. Ravenna.

———. 1969. "La scultura architettonica: Basi, capitelli, pietre d'imposta, pilastri e pilastrini, plutei, pulvini." In *Corpus della scultura paleocristiana bizantina ed altomedioevale di Ravenna,* Vol. 3. Rome.

———. 1970. "I mosaici pavimentali della chiesa di San Giovanni Evangelista in Ravenna." *Felix Ravenna,* 4th ser., 1: 169–259.

———. 1975. *Pavimenti musivi di Ravenna paleocristiana.* Ravenna.

———. 1984. *Pavimenti musivi inediti di Ravenna.* Chiesa di San Vitale.

Fasiolo, O. 1915. *I mosaici di Aquileia.* Rome.

Fedele, P. 1920. "Sul commercio delle antichità in Roma nel XII secolo." *Archivio della Società Romana di Storia Patria* 43: 465–70.

———. 1921. "L'iscrizione del Chiostro di San Paolo." *Archivio della R. Società Romana di Storia Patria* 44: 269–76. Rome.

Felici, M. n.d. *Casertavecchia e l'antica sua cattedrale.* Caserta, Italy.

Fernández, A., M. Llorens, R. Ortega, and J. Roig, 1987. *Historia de las Civilizaciones y del Arte: Occidente.* Barcelona.

Fernández Galiano, D. 1982. *New Light on the Origins of Floor Mosaics.*

———. 1983. "Influencias orientales en la musiva hispánica." In *III Colloquio Internazionale sul Mosaico,* Antico, Ravrena, 1980. Vol 2., 411–30. Ravenna: Edizioni del Girasole.

Ferraro, S. 1903. *Memorie religiose e civili della città di Gaeta.* Naples.

———. 1904. *Il candelabro di Gaeta.* Naples: Giannini.

Focillion, H. 1938. *Art d'occident: Le Moyen Âge roman et gothique.* Paris.

Forcella, V. 1869–84. *Iscrizione delle chiese e d'altri edifizi di Roma dal secolo XI fino ai giorni nostri.* 14 vols. Rome.

Forlati, F. 1949. "Le tecnica dei primi mosaici marciani." *Arte Veneta* a3.

———. 1965. "Storia e restauri del San Marco di Venezia." *Palladio* n.s. 15: 71–85.

Formilli, C. 1910. "The Monumental Work of the Cosmati at Westminster Abbey." *Journal of the Royal Institute of British Architects,* series 3, 18 (3): 69–83.

Foster, R. 1991. *Patterns of Thought: The Hidden Meaning of the Great Pavement of Westminster Abbey.* London.

Fradejas, C., et al. 1979. *Atlas: Geografia e Historia.* Madrid: Ediciones Salma.

Franz, H. G. 1957. "Les fenêtres circulaires de la cathédrale de Cefalù et le problème de l'origine de la 'Rose' du moyen âge." *Cahiers archéologiques* 9: 253–70.

Frey, D. 1914. "Der Dom in Pola." *Jahrbuch des Kunsthistorischen Institutes der K.K. Zentralkommission für Denkmalpflege* 8: 11–26.

Frey, K. 1885. "Genealogie der Cosmati." *Jarhbuch der K. Preuss, Kunstsammlungen* 6: 125–27.

Frigerio, F. and B. Nogara. 1912. "Antichità romane di Como." *Rivista Archeologica di Provincia e Antica Diocesi di Como* 63–64: 60–96.

Frothingham, A. L. 1890. "Notes on Roman Artists of the Middle Age." *American Journal of Archeology* 182, 307 ff., 350. Boston.

———. 1892. "Scoperta dell'epoca precisa della costruzione del chiostro Lateranense." *Bollettino d'Archeologia Cristiana* 6: 45ff. Rome.

———. 1895. "Notes on Byzantine Art and Culture in Italy and especially in Rome." *American Journal of Archeology* 10: 152–208.

———. 1908. *The Monuments of Christian Rome from Constantine to the Renaissance.* New York.

Galassi, G. 1930. *Roma o Bisanzio.* Rome.

Gandolfo, F. 1974–75. "Reimpiego di sculture antiche nei troni papali del XII secolo." *Atti della Pontificia Accademia Romana di Archeologia, Rendiconti* s. 3, 47: 203–18.

Garufi, G. 1906–7. "Il pavimento a mosaico della cattedrale di Otranto." *Studi Medievale* 2: 505–14.

Gascar, P. 1964. "Saint-Marc." In the *"Le génie du lieu"* collection. Zurich: Delpire Editeur.

Gattola, E. 1733. *Historia Abbatiae Cassinensis per saeculorum seriem distributa.* Venice, pages xi–xii, plate VI.

Geertman, H. 1975. *More Veterum: Il Liber Pontificalis e gli edifici ecclesiastici di Roma nella tarda antichità e nell alto Medioevo.* Groningen, Netherlands.

Gentili, E. 1889. "San Pietro in Toscanella." *Archivio storico dell'Arte* 361ff.

Gerola, G. 1909. "Santa Maria di Gazzo." *L'Arte* 12: 313–16.

———. 1913. "Il sacello primitivo di San Vitale." *Felix Ravenna* 10: 427–32; 11: 459–70.

Giacchero, M. 1970. "Prezzi e salari dell'antica Roma." *Studi Romani* 18.

———. 1974. *Edictum Diocletiani et Collegarum de pretiis rerum venalium.* Geneva.

Gianfreda, G. 1963. "Il mosaico pavimentale della cattedrale di Otranto." *Fede e Arte* 11: 386–93.

———. 1970. *Il mosaico pavimentale della basilica cattedrale di Otranto.* 3d ed. Otranto.

Gianfrotta, P. 1975. "Un Giovanni Vassalletto ignoto." *Bollettino dell'Istituto di Storia ed Arte del Lazio meridionale* 8 (1): 63–70.

Gioseffi, D. 1975. 'Terminologia dei sistemi di pavimentazione nell'antichità." In *Mosaici in Aquileia e nell'Alto Adriatico,* 23–28. Udine, Italy.

Giovannoni, G. 1904a. "Drudus de Trivio: marmorario romano. In *Miscellanea per Nozze Hermain-Hausmann,* 23. Rome, pages 313 and following.

———. 1904b. *I monasteri di Subiaco.* Vol 1. Rome.

———. 1904c. "Note sui marmorari romani. *Archivio della Società Romana di Storia Patria* 27: 5–26. Rome, Biblioteca Vaticana.

———. 1908. "Opere dei Vassalletti: marmorari romani." *L'Arte* 11:262–83.

———. 1914–15. "I Cosmati." *Archivio della Società Romana di Storia Patria.*

———. 1921–22. "Un quesito architettonico nel chiostro di Monreale." *Architettura e Arti Decorative* 1: 242–62.

———. 1936. "Il ciborio cosmatesco di Sant'Agata dei Goti a Roma." *Rassegna di Architettura* (Milan) 5: 166–67.

———. 1939. "Campanili medioevali romani." In *Atti del IV Convegno Naz. di Storia dell'architettura,* 65ff. Milan.

———. 1940. "Le basiliche cristiane di Roma." In *Atti del IV congresso Int. di Archeologia cristiana,* 1. Rome.

———. 1942. "Assisi: Chiesa superiore di San Franceso." *Palladio* 6 (1): 36–38. Rome, Casa Editrice Carlo Colombo.

———. 1943. "La chiusura presbiteriale di San Saba." *Palladio* 7 (2–3): 83–84. Rome, Casa Editrice Carlo Colombo.

Giovenale, G. B. 1895. "Santa Maria in Cosmedin." *Annuario cultori architettura.*

———. 1917. "Il chiostro medioevale di San Paolo fuori le Mura." *Bollettino della Commissione Archeologica Comunale di Roma* 45: 125–67.

———. 1927. *La Basilica di Santa Maria in Cosmedin.* Rome.

Glass, D. F. 1969. "Papal Patronage in the Early Twelfth Century: Notes on the Iconography of Cosmatesque Pavements." *Journal of the Warburg and Courtauld Institutes* (The Warburg Institute, University of London) 32: 386–90.

———. 1980. *Studies on Cosmatesque Pavements.* BAR International Series 82. Oxford.

Gnoli, R. 1966. "Marmi e pietre da decorazione usate nell'Antichità." *La Parola del Passato* (Naples: Fascicle 106 (January–February), Gaetano Macchiaroli Editore) 106: 41–55.

———. 1971. *Marmora Romana.* Rome: Edizioni dell'Elefante. Reissued 1988.

Gnoli, R., and P. Pensabene. 1972. "Considerazioni sul trasporto di manufatti marmorei in eta' imperiale a Roma e in altri centri occidentali." *Dialoghi di Archeologia* 6: 357–62.

Gnoli, U. 1939. *Topografia e toponomastica di Roma medioevale e moderna.* Rome.

Gobbo, A. 1903. "La tecnica dei mosaici antichi." *Rassegna d'Arte* (Milan) 6.

Grabar, A. 1958. *La peinture romane du onzième au treizième siècle.* Geneva.

Gray, N. 1948. "The Paleography of Latin Inscriptions in Italy." *Papers of the British School at Rome* 16: 38–167, and plates XII to XXIV.

Gregorovius, F. 1925. *Storia della città di Roma nel Medioevo* 1, 1 and 2. Turin, Italy.

Grekow, B. 1947. *Die Russische Kultur der Kiever Periode.* Moscow.

Grierson, P. 1962. "The Tombs and Obits of the Bizantine Emperors." *Dumbarton Oaks Papers* 16.

Grisar, H. 1909. *Die römische Kapelle Sancta Sanctorum und ihre Schatz.* Freiburg, Switzerland.

Grosso-Gondi, F, 1913. "La confessio dell'altare maggiore e la cattedra papale a San Lorenzo in Lucina: un opera di Magister Paulus?" *Studi Romani* 1: 53–62.

Gudiol Ricart, J., and J. A. Gaya Nuño. 1948. *Ars Hispaniae: Historia Universal del Arte Hispánico.* Vol 5: *Arquitectura y Escultura Románicas.* Madrid.

Guidobaldi, F. 1978. *Il complesso Archeologico di San Clemente.* Rome.

———.1983. "Mosaici con tessere porfiretiche a Roma tra il III e IV secolo." In *III Colloquio Internazionale sul Mosaico Antico,* vol. 2: 491–503. Ravenna: Edizioni del Girasole.

———. 1985. "Pavimenti in opus sectile di Roma e dell'area Romana: proposte per una classificazione e criteri di datazione." In *Marmi Antichi: Problemi di impegno, di restauro e di identificazione,* edited by P. Pensabene. *Studi Miscellanei* (Rome: Seminario di Archeologia e Storia Dell'Arte Greca e Romana dell'Università di Roma) 26: 172–233.

Guidobaldi, F., and A. Guiglia Guidobaldi. 1983. "Pavimenti marmorei di Roma dal IV al IX secolo." *Studi di Antichità Cristiana* (Vatican City: Pontificio Istituto di Archeologia Cristiana) 36: 315–19, 418–35.

Guiglia Guidobaldi, A. 1981. "Note preliminari per una definizione dell'arte pavimentale costantinopolitana dei primi secoli." In *XVI Internationaler Byzantinistenkongress, Akten II/4, Jahrbuch der Österreichischen Byzantinistik* 32/4 (Vienna): 403–13.

———. 1983. "I pavimenti in opus sectile delle tabernae delle Basilica Emilia: Testimonianze Bizantine a Roma nel VI secolo." In *III Colloquio Internazionale sul Mosaico Antico,* vol. 2, 505–13. Ravenna: Edizioni del Girasole.

———. 1984. "Tradizione locale e influenze Bizantine nei pavimenti Cosmateschi." *Bollettino D'Arte* (Rome: Ministeri per i beni Culturali e Ambientali) 26 (July–August): 57–72.

Guilland, R. 1956. *L'Empire d'Orient: Histoire universelle.* Paris.

Hamilton, A. 1933. *Byzantine Architecture and Decoration.* London.

Haug, W. 1975. "Artussage und Heilsgeschichte: Zum Programm des Fussbodenmosaiks von Otranto." *Deutsche Vierteljahrschrift für Literaturwissenschaft und Geistesgeschichte* 49: 577–606.

———. 1977. *Das Mosaik von Otranto: Darstellung, Deutung, und Bilddokumentation.* Wiesbaden.

Heitz, C. 1985. "Symbolisme et architecture: Les nombres et L'architecture religieuse du haut moyen âge." *Simboli e simbologia nell'Alto Medioevo* (Spoleto: Centro Italiano di Studi sull'Alto Medioevo) 23 (1, 2): 387–428.

Herklotz, I. 1985. *"Sepulcra" e "Monumenta" del Medioevo: Studi sull'arte sepolcrale in Italia.* Rome.

Hermanin, F. 1945. "L'arte in Roma dal secolo VIII al XIV." *Storia di Roma* (Bologna): 27: 59ff.

Hessemer, F. M. 1842. *Arabische und Alt-Italienische Bau-Verzierungen.* Berlin: Dietrich Reimer. Reissued as *Historic Designs and Patterns in Color from Arabic and Italian Sources* (Mineola, NY: Dover, 1990).

Heyd, W. 1909–13. *Storia del commercio del Levante nel medioevo.* Turin, Italy.

———. 1959. *Histoire du Commerce du Levant au Moyen-Age.* Amsterdam.

Hoddinot, R. F. 1963. *Early Byzantine Churches in Macedonia and Southern Serbia: A Study of the Origins and the Initial Development of East Christian Art.* London and New York.

Horn, W. 1943. "Romanesque Churches in Florence: A Study of Their Chronology and Stylistic Development." *Art Bulletin* 25: 112–131.

Huetter, L., and E. Lavagnino. 1931. *San Lorenzo in Lucina.* Rome.

Hülsen, C. 1927. *Le chiese di Roma nel Medio Evo.* Rome: Olschki.

Hutton, E. 1934. "An Unknown Victorian." In *The Nineteenth Century and After.* London.

———. 1943 "The New Pavement in the Sanctuary of Buckfast Abbey." *Chronicle* 13: 107–13.

———. 1950. *The Cosmati: The Roman Marble Workers of the Twelfth and Thirteenth Centuries*. London.

Istituto Centrale del Restauro. 1978. *Tecniche d'esecuzione e materiali costitutivi*. Rome.

Jarawan, E. 1987. *Santa Maria in Cosmedin*. Rome.

Jones, O. 1856. *The Grammar of Ornament*. London: Messers Day and Son. Reissued, London: Studio Editions, 1986.

Junyent, E. 1932. *Il titolo di San Clemente in Roma*. Rome.

Jürgens, H., H.-O. Peitgen, and D. Saupe. 1990. "El lenguaje de los fractales." *Investigación y Ciencia* (Spanish edition of *Scientific American*): 169 (October 1990): 46–57.

Kapitän, G. 1980. "Elementi architettonici per una basilica dal relitto navale del VI secolo di Marzamemi (Siracusa)." *Corsi Ravennate* 27: 71–136.

Kidson, P. 1956. "Systems of Measurement and Proportion in Early Medieval Architecture." Ph.D. diss., Courtauld Institute.

Kier, H. 1970. "Der mittelalterliche Schmuckfuszboden." *Die Kunstdenkmäler des Rheinlandes* (Düsseldorf) 14: 24–33.

Kinney, D. 1975a. "Excavations in Santa Maria in Trastevere, 1865–1869: A Drawing by Vespignani." *Römische Quartalschrift für christliche Altertumskunde und Kirchengeschichte* 70 (1–2): 42–53.

———. 1975b. "Santa Maria in Trastevere from its Founding to 1215." Ph.D. diss., New York University, Institute of Fine Arts.

———. 1986. "Spolia from the Baths of Caracalla in Santa Maria in Trastevere." *Art Bulletin* 68: 379–97.

Kitzinger, E. 1965. "Stylistic Developments in Pavement Mosaics in the Greek East from the Age of Constantine to the Age of Justinian." In *La mosaïque gréco-romaine: Colloques internationaux du centre national de la recherche scientifique, Paris 1963*, 41–355. Paris. Reprinted in *The Art of Byzantium and the Medieval West: Selected Studies*, edited by W. E. Kleinbauer, 64–88. Bloomington, Ind.: Indiana University Press, 1976.

———. 1973. "World Map and Fortune's Wheel: A Medieval Mosaic Floor in Turin." *Proceedings of the American Philosophical Society* 117 (5): 344–73.

———. 1976. "Mosaic Pavements in the Greek East and the Question of a Renaissance under Justinian." In *Actes de VI congr. Internat. d'études byzantines, Paris 1951*, 209–23. Reprinted in *The Art of Byzantium and the Medieval West: Selected Studies*, edited by W. E. Kleinbauer, 32–48. Bloomington, Ind.: Indiana Unversity Press, 1976.

——— 1982. "The Arts as Aspects of a Renaissance." In *Renaissance and Renewal in the Twelfth Century*, edited by G. Constable and R. L. Benson, 637–70. Cambridge, Mass.

Klauser, T. 1952. *The Western Liturgy and its History*. Translated by F. L. Cross. New York.

Kraft, J. D. A. 1987. *Die Krypta in Latium*. Munich.

Krautheimer, R. 1942a. "The Carolingian Revival of Early Christian Architecture." *Art Bulletin*: 1–38.

———. 1942b. "Introduction to an Iconography of Medieval Architecture." *Journal of the Warburg and Courtauld Institutes* 5: 1–33.

———. 1965. *Early Christian and Byzantine Architecture*. Pelican History of Art, ed. N. Pevsner. Penguin Books.

———. 1980. *Rome: Profile of a City, 312–1308*. Princeton, NJ: Princeton University Press.

———. 1983. *Three Christian Capitals: Topography and Politics*. Berkeley, Calif.: University of California Press.

Krautheimer, R., S. Corbett, and W. Frankl. 1937–77. *Corpus Basilicarum Christianarum Romae.* 5 vols. Vatican City.

Krönig, W. 1962–63. "La Francia e l'architettura romanica dell'Italia meridionale." *Napoli Nobilissima* 1–2: 203ff.

———. 1965. *Il Duomo dei Monreale e l'architettura normanna di Sicilia.* Palermo, Italy.

Ladner, G. B. 1954. "The Concept of 'Ecclesia' and 'Christianitas' and Their Relation to the Idea of Papal 'Plenitudo Potestatis' from Gregory VII to Boniface VIII." *Sacerdozio e Regno da Gregorio VII a Bonifacio VIII.* Miscellanea Historiae Pontificiae 18: 49–77.

———. 1967. *The Idea of Reform: Its Impact on Christian Thought and Action in the Age of Fathers.* New York.

Lanciani, R. 1892. *Pagan and Christian Rome.*

———. 1897. *The Ruins and Excavations of Ancient Rome.* London.

———. 1899. *The Destruction of Ancient Rome: A Sketch of the History of the Monuments.* New York: Macmillan.

———. 1940. *Lazio e suburbio di Roma.* Vol. 3 of *Architettura minore in Italia.* Rome: Colombo.

———. n.d. "Storia a 1200: Marmorarii." Biblioteca Nazionale di Archeologia e Storia dell'Arte, ms Lanciani 24/V Rome.

Langé, S. 1965. *Architettura dei Crociati in Palestina.* Como, Italy.

Lavagnino, E. 1924. *San Paolo sulla via Ostiense.* Rome.

———. 1936. *Storia dell'arte medioevale.* Turin, Italy.

Lavagnino, E., and V. Moschini. 1923. *Santa Maria Maggiore.* Rome.

Lavin, I. 1963. "The Hunting Mosaics of Antioch and Their Sources." *Dumbarton Oaks Papers* 17: 179–286.

Lee, A. 1888. *Marble and Marble Workers.* London.

Lefèvre-Pontalis, E. 1922. "L'origine des taillors ronds et octogones au XIIe siècle." *Bulletin Monumental,* LXXXI: 198–99.

Letarouilly, P. M. 1840. *Les édifices de Rome moderne, ou, Recueil des palais, maisons, églises, couvents et autres monuments publics et particuliers: les plus remarquables de la ville de Rome.* Paris: Typographie de Firmin Didot Frères. Reissued, Princeton, NJ: Princeton University Press, 1982, plates 103, 104, 105, 247, 248, 249, 268, 269, 270, 271, 272, 304, 305, 306, 322, 323, 337.

Lethaby, W. R. 1904. *Mediaeval Art: From the Peace of the Church to the Eve of the Renaissance, 312–1350.* London: Duckworth and Company.

———. 1906. *Westminster Abbey and the King's Craftsmen.* London.

———. 1925. *Westminster Abbey Reexamined.* London.

Levi, D. 1947. *Antioch Mosaic Pavements.* 2 vols. Princeton, NJ.

Lipinsky, A. 1933. "L'antica cattedrale di Terracina." *L'illustrazione Vaticana* 4: 801–4.

Little, C. T., T. B. Husband, M. Shepard, et al. 1987. *Europe in the Middle Ages.* New York: Metropolitan Museum of Art.

Lorenzon, G. 1937. *La Basilica dei Santi Felice e Fortunato in Vicenza.* Vicenza, Italy.

Lübke, W. 1878. "Zu den Cosmaten Arbeiten (in Dom zu Civita Castellana)." *Zeitschrift für bildende Kunst* 13: 271–79.

Lucchesi, G. n.d. "Raccolta di varj pavimenti antichi di mosaico che presentamente si vedono in alcune chiese di Roma." Biblioteca Vaticana, Codex Capponi 236.

Lucci, M. L. 1964. "Il porfido nell'antichità." *Archeologia Classica* 16: 226–71.

Luciani, R. 1991. *Sainte-Marie du Transtevere.* Rome: Edit. Fratelli Palombi.

Lugano, P. 1912. *L'Abbazia di Santa Croce di Sassovino.* Rome.

Lydholm, I. 1982. "The Cosmati and the Cathedral at Anagni." In *Analecta Romana Instituti Danici,* vol.10, 7–22. Rome: Odense University Press, Accademia di Danimarca.

Maccarone, M. 1959. "I papi del secolo XII e la vita comune e regolare del clero." *Misc. del Centro di Studio Medioevali III: La vita comune del clero nei s. XI–XII.* Settimana di studio de la Mendola, vol. 1: 361ff.

McClendon, C. 1978. "The Medieval Abbey Church at Farfa." Ph.D. diss., New York University.

McClendon, C. B. 1980. "The Revival of Opus Sectile Pavements in Rome and the Vicinity in the Carolingian Period." *Papers of the British School at Rome* 48: 157–65, plates XXX to XXXIV.

MacDonald, W. L. 1962. *Early Christian and Byzantine Architecture.* New York: George Braziller.

Madoni, E. 1914. *Il pavimento del battisterio fiorentino.* Brescia, Italy.

Mâle, E. 1922. *L'Art religieux du XIIe siècle en France.* Paris.

———. 1923. "Les influences arabes dans l'art roman." *Revue des Deux Mondes* 93: 335.

Malmstrom, R. E. 1975. "The Colonnades of High Medieval Churches at Rome." *Gesta* 14 (2): 37–45.

———. 1981. *Speculations about Cosmati Pavements: A Review of Dorothy F. Glass's "Studies on Cosmatesque Pavements."* Milwaukee, Wisc.

Mandelbrot, B. B. 1983. *The Fractal Geometry of Nature.* W. H. Freeman and Company.

Mango, C. 1959. "The Date of the Narthex Mosaics of the Church of the Dormition at Nicaea." *Dumbarton Oaks Papers* 13: 245–52.

———. 1972. *The Art of the Byzantine Empire 312–1453: Sources and Documents.* Englewood Cliffs, NJ: Prentice-Hall.

Marangoni. 1747. *Storia del Sancta Sanctorum.*

Marçais, G. 1954. *L'architecture musulmane d'Occident.* Paris.

———. 1962. *L'art musulman.* Paris.

Margarucci, B. M. 1985. *Il Titolo di Pammachio: Santi Giovanni e Paolo.* Rome.

Marle, R. van. 1921. *La peinture romaine au moyen-âge, son développment du VI jusqu'à la fin du XIII siècle.* Strasbourg, France.

Marocco, G. 1833–36. *Monumenti dello Stato Pontificio.* Rome.

Martin, C. 1924. *L'art roman en Italie: L'architecture et la décoration.* Paris.

Martínez Montávez, P., and C. Ruíz Bravo-Villasante. 1991. *Europa Islámica: La magia de una civilización milenaria.* Barcelona: Grandes Obras El Sol.

Matas, J., ed. 1994. *Historia Visual del Mundo.* Madrid: El Mundo, Unidad Editorial S.A.

Mathews, T. 1962. "An Early Roman Chancel Arrangement and Its Liturgical Functions." *Rivista di Archeologia Cristiana* 38: 73–95.

———. 1971. *The Early Churches of Constantinople: Architecture and Liturgy.* University Park, Penn.

Matini Morricone, M. L. 1980. *Stuculata pavimenta: Pavimenti con inserti di marmo o di pietra . . . Roma e dintorni . . . sec II a C.* Rome.

Matthew, D. 1989. *Atlas of Medieval Europe.* Oxford.

Matthiae, G. 1942. "Fasi costruttive nella cattedrale di Anagni." *Palladio:* 6 (2): 44–48, Rome, Casa Editrice Carlo Colombo.

———. 1952. "Componenti del gusto decorativo cosmatesco." *Rivista dell'Istituto Nazionale d'Archeologia e Storia dell'Arte,* Nuova Serie 1: 249–81.

———. 1954. "La cultura artistica in Roma del secolo IX." *Rivista dell'Istituto Nazionale d'Archeologia e Storia dell'Arte.* Nuova Serie 3: 257–74.

———. 1959. "Cosmati." *Enciclopedia Universale dell'Arte,* II. Rome, Venice: 737–843.

———. 1962. *Le Chiese di Roma dal IV al X secolo.* Vol. 3 of *Roma Cristiana.* Bologna: Cappelli.

———. 1966a. *Pittura romana del Medioevo.* Rome.

———. 1966b. *San Lorenzo fuori le Mura.* Monograph 89 in the series *Le Chiese di Roma illustrate.* Rome: Casa Ed. Roma.

———. 1967. *Mosaici Medioevali delle Chiese di Roma.* (Testo & tavole) Rome: Istituto Poligrafico dello Stato.

———. n.d. "The Cosmati." In *Encyclopedia of World Art,* vol. 3: 829–35.

Mauceri, E. 1898. "Colonne Tortili." *L'Arte* 377ff.

Mazzanti, F. 1896. "La scultura ornamentale romana dei bassi tempi." *Archivio storico dell'Arte:* 33 ff., 151 ff.

Mazzotti, M. 1954. "La Basilica di Sant'Apollinare in Classe." Studi di Antichità Christiana, 21. Vatican City.

Megaw, A. H. S. 1963. "Notes on the Recent Work of the Byzantine Institute in Istanbul." *Dumbarton Oaks Papers* 17: 333–71.

———. 1976. "Interior Decoration in Early Christian Cyprus." In *XIVᵉ Congrès International d'Etudes Byzantines: Rapports et Co-rapports,* 4–9, plate 5. Athens.

Melani, A. 1894–1904. *Dell' ornamento nell' architettura.* Vols. 1–2 of *L'Architettura nella storia e nella practica., Parte 2.* Milan.

———. 1899. "I cosiddetti Cosmati." *Arte e Storia* (Florence) 18 (4): 26–27.

Melucco Vaccaro, A. 1974. *La II Regione ecclesiastica.* Vol. 3 of *Corpus della Scultura Altomedioevale, 7, La Diocesi di Roma.* Spoleto, Italy.

Mengozzi, G. 1931. *La città italiana nell'Alto Medioevo.* Florence.

Meoli Toulmin, R. 1977. "Pisan Geometric Patterns of the Thirteenth Century and Their Islamic Sources." *Antichità Viva* (Florence: Case Editrice Edam) 16 (1): 3–12.

Merzario, G. 1967. *I maestri comacini* II. Bologna.

Mesnard, M. 1935. "La basilique de Saint Chrysogone à Rome. *Studi di Antichità Cristiana* (Vatican City) 9.

Michelin, 1985. *Tourist Guide, Michelin: Rome.* Middlesex, UK: Michelin Tyre P.L.C.

Michelin, 1987. *Guide Turistica, Michelin: Italia.* Milan: Michelin Italiana S.p.A.

Middleton, R. 1985. "Perfezione e colore: la policromia nell'architettura francese del XVIII e XIX secolo." *Rassegna* (Milan): 7 (23/3, September): 55–67.

Miller, K. 1916. *Itineraria Romana.* Stuttgart.

Millet, G. 1916. *L'ecole grecque dans l'architecture byzantine.* Paris.

Mirabella Roberti, M. 1947–48. "Indagini nel Duomo di Pola." *Rivista di Archeologia Cristiana* 23–24: 209–29.

———. 1963. "La Cattedrale Antica di Milano e il suo battistero." *Arte Lombarda* 8: 77–99.

Monna, D., and P. Pensabene. 1977. *Marmi dell' Asia Minore.* Rome.

Monna, D., P. Pensabene, and J. P. Sodini. 1983. "L'identification des marbres: sa nécessité, ses méthodes, ses limites." *Revue d L'Art* (Paris: Editions du C. N. R. S.) 60: 35–46.

Monneret de Villard, U. 1912. *I monumenti del lago di Como.* Milan.

———. 1914. "L'isola Comacina." *Rivista Archeologica della Provincia e della Antica Diocesi di Como:* 7–243.

———. 1916. "I dati-storici relativi ai musaici pavimentali cristiani di lombardia." *Archivio Storico Lombardo,* ser. 5, 43: 341–92,

Montecassino, A. di. 1935. *Storia de'Normanni di Amato di Montecassino volgarizzata in antico francese.* Edited by V. De Bartolomaeis. Rome: Istituto Storico Italiano per il Medio Evo (Fonti, 76); 3 (52): 175.

Moracchini, G. 1965. "Le pavement en mosaïque de la basilique et du baptistère de Mariana." *Archeologia* 5: 51–59.

Morey, C. R. 1924–25. "The Sources of Medieval Style." *The Art Bulletin* 7: 35–50.

Morghen, R. 1951. *Medioevo cristiano.* Bari, Italy.

Morini, M. 1963. *Atlante di Storia dell'Urbanistica.* Milan.

Morricone Matini, M. L. 1967. *Mosaici Antichi in Italia: Regione Prima. Roma: Reg. X Palatium.* Rome.

Morricone Matini. 1971. "I pavimenti di signino repubblicani di Roma e dintorni." *Mosaici antichi in Italia, Studi monografichi.* Rome.

Mortari, L. 1949. "Nota sui mosaici pavimentali delle chiese Venete tra il IX e il XII secolo." *Bolletino d'Arte*, ser. 4, 34: 261–64.

Mortet, V. 1911. *Recueil de textes relatifs à l'histoire de l'architecture et à la condition des architectes en France, au Moyen Age.* Paris.

Muñoz, A. 1911a. "La decorazione e gli amboni Cosmateschi della basilica di San Pancrazio fuori le mura." *L'Arte* (Rome) 14 (2): 97–106.

———. 1911b. *Le opere dei marmorari romani.* Rome.

———. 1914. *Il restauro della chiesa e del chiostro dei Santi Quattro Coronati.* Rome.

———. 1923. *San Pietro in Vaticano.* Rome.

———. 1944. *La Basilica di San Lorenzo fuori le mura.* Rome: Fratelli Palombi Editori.

———. 1953. "La Basilica di Santa Sabina." *Roma Nobilis* (Rome): 391–95.

———. 1954. "I marmorari romani nei paesi del Lazio." *Rasegna del Lazio* 1 (March–May) (3, 4, 5): 18–20.

Nearls Porter, M. Wi-. 1907. *What Rome Was Built With.* London and Oxford.

Neunheuser, B. 1977. *Storia della liturgia attraverso le epoche culturali.* Rome

Newman, J.-H., R. Oursel, and L. Moulin. 1987. *La civilización de los Monasterios medievales.* Madrid: Edics. Encuentro. Originally published as *L'Europe des monastères* (Milan, 1985).

Nibby, A. 1848–49. *Analisi storico-topografica-antiquaria della carta de' dintori di Roma.* 2d ed. Rome.

Nicolosi, G. 1937, 1939. "La città nel Medioevo." In *Atti del II Convegno Nazionale di Storia dell'Architetture:* 17–36. Assisi 1937, Rome 1939.

Noehles, K. 1961. "Die Fassade von San Pietro in Tuscania: Ein Beitrag zur Frage der Antikenrezeption in 12. und 13. Jahrhundert in Mittelitalien. *Römisches Jahrbuch für Kunstgeschichte* (Vienna and Munich: Verlag Anton Schrooll & Co.) 9–10: 13–72.

———. 1966. "Die Kunst des Cosmaten und die Idee der Renovatio Romae." In *Festschrift Werner Hager*, 17–37. Recklinghausen, Germany.

Nolli, G. B. 1748. "Roma al tempo di Benedetto XIV: La Planta di Roma di Giambattista Nolli dei 1748 riprodotta da una copia Vaticana." In *Le piante maggiori di Roma dei sec. XVI–XVIII.* Vatican City.

Nord-Hagen, P. J. 1962. "The Earliest Decorations in Santa Maria Antiqua and Their Date." In *Acta ad Archeologiam et Artium Historiam Pertinentia,* 53–72, plate III.

Nuti, G. 1964. "Nota sull'esposizione del restauro a Montecasino." In *Marmo* 3, 122–24. Milan and Lucca: Editoriale Metro S.p.A.

Oakeshott, W. 1967. *The Mosaics of Rome.* London.

Orlandos, A. K. 1939. *Archeion ton Byzantinon Mnemeion tes Hellados.* Vol. 5.

———. 1951. *Archeion ton Byzantinon Mnemeion tes Hellados.* Vol. 7.

Orlandos, A. 1951. "Heoen Boiotia mone tou Sagmata." Archeion Ton Byzantinon Mnemeion tes Helledos, 7: 72–110.

Ortolani, S. 1925. *San Giovanni in Laterano.* Monograph in the series *Le Chiese di Roma illustrate.* Rome: Casa Ed. Roma.

———. n.d.(a). *Santa Croce in Gerusalemme.* 3d ed. Monograph 106 in the series *Le Chiese di Roma illustrate.* Rome: Casa Ed. Roma.

——— n.d.(b). *Santi Giovanni e Paolo.* Monograph in the series *Le Chiese di Roma illustrate.* Rome: Casa Ed. Roma.

Oursel, R. 1967. *Living Architecture: Romanesque.* New York: Grosset and Dunlap.

———. 1970. *Invention de l'architecture Romaine.* Saint-Léger.

Ovadiah, A. 1980. *Geometric and Floral Patterns in Ancient Mosaics: A Study of Their Origin in the Mosaics from the Classical Period to the Age of Augustus.* Rome: L'Erma di Bretschneider.

Pajares Ayuela, P. 1993. "Ornamento Arquitectónico: La Ornamentación Geométrica Plana Policroma según los Monumentos de la Ciudad de Roma y del Lazio, Edad Media." In *Accademia Spagnola di Storia, Archeologia e Belle Arti, Roma, 1993,* 87–92. Rome: Dirección General de Relaciones Culturales del Ministerio de Asuntos Exteriores de España.

Panazza, G. 1939. "L'arte medioevale nella città e territorio di Brescia." In *Atti e memorie del terzo congresso storico Lombardo, Cremona 1938,* 5–12. Milan.

Paniagua Soto, J. R. 1993. *Vocabulario básico de arquitectura.* 7th ed. Madrid: Cátedra.

Pani Ermini, L. 1974. *La IV Regione ecclestiaca.* Vol. 1 of *Corpus della Scultura Altomedioevale, 7, La Diocesi di Roma.* Spoleto, Italy.

Pantoni, A. 1973. "Le vicende della Basilica di Montecassino attraverso la documentazione archeologica." *Miscellanea Cassinese* 36, Montecassino.

———. 1980. *Le chiese e gli edifici del monasterio di San Vincenzo al Volturno.* Montecassino.

Panvinio, O. 1570. *Le sette chiese romane.* Rome.

Parlasca, K. 1969. "Mosaici romani e loro colorazione." *Tavolozza* (Basel, Switzerland: Sandoz S. A.) 31: 2–12.

Parlato, E., and S. Romano. 1992. *Roma y el Lacio.* Vol. 18 of *Europa Románica.* Madrid: Edc. Encuentro. Originally published as *Roma e il Lazio* (Saint-Léger Vauban: Zodiaque, and Milan: Editoriale Jaca Book, 1992).

Pastoreau, M. 1985. "Vizi e virtù dei colori nella sesibilità medioevale." *Rassegna* 7 (23/3 September): 5–13. Milan.

Patricolo, A. 1877. "La Chiesa di Santa Maria dell'Ammiraglio." *Archivio Storico Siciliano* 2: 137–71.

———. 1878. "La Chiesa di Santa Maria dell'Ammiraglio." *Archivio Storico Siciliano* 3: 397–406

Paulin, E. 1890. *Thermes de Dioclétien (Restauration des Monuments Antiques par les Architectes pensionnaires de l'Académie de France à Rome).* Paris.

Peitgen, H.-O., H. Jürgens, and D. Saupe. 1989. *Fractals for the Classroom.* Springer-Verlag.

Peitgen, H.-O., and P. Richter. 1986. *The Beauty of Fractals.* Springer-Verlag.

Peitgen, H.-O., and D. Saupe. 1988. *The Science of Fractal Images.* Springer-Verlag.

Pelekanidis, S., and P. Atzaka. 1974. *Corpus Mosaicorum Christianorum Vetustorum Pavimentorum Graecorum.* Vol. 1: *Graecia Insularis.* Tesalonica.

Pensabene, P. 1978. "A Cargo of Marble Shipwrecked at Punta Scifo near Crotone (Italy)." *Nautical Archeology* 7: 105–18, 233.

———. 1983. "Osservazioni sulla diffusione dei marmie e sul loro prezzo nella Roma Imperiale." *Dialoghi di Archeologia* (Rome: Edizioni Quasar), 3d series, 1 (1): 55–63.

Pepe, L. 1898. "La cattedrale di Sessa Aurunca." *Napoli nobilissima* 7: 55–61.

Pera, L. 1938. "La chiesa di San Pietro in Vincoli a Pisa." *I Monumenti Italiani* (Rome) 14.

Pertusi, A. 1975. "Insegne del potere sovrano e delegato a Bisanzio e nei paesi influenza bizantina." *Simboli e simbologia nell'Alto Medioevo,* XXIII: 481–568.

Pertusi, A., C. Heitz, et al. 1975. *Simboli e simbologia nell'Alto Medioevo.* Centro Italiano di Studi sull'Alto Medioevo 23. Vols. 1 and 2. Spoleto, Italy.

Peschlow, U. 1983. "Zum byzantinischen opus sectile-Boden." In *Beiträge zur Altertumskunde Kleinasiens, Festschrift für Kurt Bittel,* 435–47. Mainz.

Phaidon. 1987. *Rome and Latium: A Phaidon Cultural Guide.* Oxford.

Piazzesi, A., V. Mancini, and L. Benevolo, 1954. "Una statistica sul repertorio geometrico dei Cosmati." *Quaderni dell'Istituto di Storia dell'Architettura* (Rome: Facoltà di Architettura Universita di Roma) 5 (July): 11–19.

Piccinato, L, 1941. "Origini dello schema circolare urbano nel medioevo." *Palladio* 5: 120–25.

———. 1943. *Urbanista medievale: Urbanista dall'antichità ad oggi.* Florence.

Pieri, M. 1964. *I marmi d'Italia.* Milan.

———. 1966. *Marmologia: Dizionario di Marmi e Graniti Italiani ed Esteri; Pietre da costruzione ed ornamento naturali e prodotte dall'industria merceologica, mineralogia, geologia dei materiali litoidi e loro cave.* Milan: Ulrico Hoepli.

Pinzi. 1877. *Storia de Viterbo.* Rome.

Pirenne, H. 1963. *Histoire économique et sociale du Moyen Age.* Paris.

Planeta. 1989. *Al-Andalus: musulmanes y cristianos (siglos VIII–XIII).* Vol. 3 of *Historia de España.* Barcelona: Ed. Planeta.

———. 1991. *La Edad del Feudalismo.* Vol. 4 of *Historia Universal Planeta.* Barcelona: Ed. Planeta.

Platón, s. V a de JC. 1956. "Meno." Trans. by W. K. Guthrie in *Protagoras and Meno.* New York: Penguin Classics.

Pliny the Elder. 1946. *Storia delle Arti Antiche.* Translated by S. Ferri. Rome.

———. n.d. *Naturalis Historiae.* Vols. 35 and 36.

Porter, A. K. 1909. *Medieval Architecture.* New York.

———. 1923. *Romanesque Sculpture of the Pilgrimage Roads.* Boston.

Powstenko, O. 1954. "The Cathedral of Saint Sophia in Kiev." *The Annals of the Ukrainian Academy of Arts and Science in the United States,* 3–4.

Prandi, A. 1957. *Santi Giovanni e Paolo.* Monograph 88 in the series *Le Chiese di Roma illustrate.* Rome: Casa Ed. Roma.

———. 1968. *Roma nell'alto Medioevo.* Turin, Italy.

Pressouyre, L. 1966. "Le cosmos platonicien de la cathédrale d'Anagni." *Mélanges d'archéologie et d'histoire publiés par l'Ecole Française de Rome* 78: 551–93.

Priester, A. E. 1990. "The Belltowers of Medieval Rome and the Architecture of Renovatio." Ph.D. diss., Princeton University.

Promis, C. 1836. *Notizie epigrafiche degli artefici marmorari romani dal X al XV secolo.* Turin, Italy.

Prudhomme, R. 1975. "Recherche des Principes de Construction des Mosaïques Géométriques Romaines." In *La Mosaïque Gréco-Romaine 2: IIe Colloque International pour L'Etude de la mosaïque antique, Vienna 1971,* 339–47 and plates CLXI–CLXX. Vienna: A & J Picard with Éditions du CNRS.

Puccinelli, O. 1950. *La basilica di San Frediano in Lucca.* Lucca.

Puig y Cadafalch, J. 1928. *Le premier art roman: L'architecture en Catalogne et dans l'Occident méditerranéen au Xe et XIe siècles.* Paris.

———. 1961. *L'Art wisigothique et ses survivances: Recherches sur les origines et le développment de l'art en France et en Espagne du IVe au XIIe siècle.* Paris.

Pullen, H. W. 1849. *Handbook of Ancient Roman Marbles.* London.

Rash-Fabbri, N. 1971. "Eleventh and Twelfth Century Figurative Mosaic Floors in South Italy." Ph. D. diss., Bryn Mawr College.

Raspi Serra, J. 1972. *La Tuscia Romana: Un territorio come esperienza d'arte: evoluzione urbanistico-architettonica.* Milan: Banco di Santo Spirito, ERI/Edizioni Rai Radiotelevisione Italiana.

———. 1974. *Corpus della scultura altomedievale, 8, Le diocesi dell'Alto Lazio.* Spoleto, Italy: 142–149.

Rathgens, H. 1903. *San Donato zu Murano und ähnliche venezianische Bauten.* Berlin: 75–85.

Ricci, C. 1925. *L'architettura romanica in Italia.* Stuttgart.

Rice Talbot, D. 1954. *Byzantine Art.* London.

Richter, J. P. 1877. "Die Cosmaten Familien." *Zeitschrift für Bildenden Kunst* 12: 337–38.

Robison, D. M. 1946. *Domestic and Public Architecture*. Vol. 12 of *Excavations at Olynthus*. Baltimore.

Robotti, C. 1983a. "La geometria negli impianti musivi: considerazioni su alcuni esempi." *Disegno* 7 (5).

———. 1983b. *Mosaico e Architettura: Disegni, Sinopie, Cartoni*. Naples: Editrice Ferraro.

Rohault de Fleury, C. 1883–89. *La messe: Études archéologiques sur ses monuments*. Paris.

Romanini, A. M., ed. 1991. *Roma nel Duecento*. Turin, Italy: 1–72.

Rossi, P. 1986. *Civita Castellana e le chiese medievali del suo territorio*. Rome: 15–27.

Rushforth, N. 1902. "The Church of Santa Maria Antiqua." *Papers of the British School at Rome* 1: 1–23.

Salazaro, D. 1871–77. *Studi sui monumenti dell'Italia Meridionale dal IV al XIII secolo*. Naples.

———. 1881. "L'arte romano nel medioevo." Appendix to *Monumenti dell'Italia mediovale* 3. Naples.

Salmi, M. 1938, 1948. "Influssi degli edifici antichi di culto sulle chiese dell'alto medioevo in Italia." In *Atti del IV Congresso Internazionale di Archeologia Cristiana*, 231–70. Vatican City, 1938; Rome, 1948.

———. 1954. "L'architettura in Italia durante il periodo carolingio." In *Centro Italiano di Studi sull'Alto Medioevo—Settimane di Studi, 1: I problemi della civilità carolingia*, 227–40. Spoleto, Italy.

———. 1962. "Stucchi e litostrati nell'alto medioevo italiano." In *Atti dell'ottavo congresso sull'Arte dell'alto medioevo*, vol. 1, 21–51. Milan.

———. 1966. *L'abbazia di Pomposa*. 2d ed. Milan.

Salmon., P. 1961. "The Urban and Papal Rites in Seventh- and Eighth-Century Rome." *Sacris Erudiri* 441–87.

———. 1967. "L'office divin au moyen age." *Lex orandi* 43.

Salvadori, R. 1990. *Architects' Guide to Rome*. London: Butterworth Architecture.

Santilli, A. 1925. *La Basilica dei Santi Apostoli*. Monograph in the series *Le Chiese di Roma Illustrate*. Rome: Casa Ed. Roma.

Sapin, C. 1983. "Les marbres sculptés du haut Moyen Age en Bourgogne." In *Artistes, artisans et production artistique au Moyen Age*, vol. 2 (May 1983), 1045–59. Rennes, France.

Sartorio, G.A. 1896. *I marmorari romani nella chiesa di Westminster Abbey*. Rome.

Schaffran, E. 1941. *Die Kunst der Langobarden in Italien*. Jena.

Schlumberger, G. 1896–1905. *L'Epopée Byzantine à la fin du dixième siècle*. Paris.

Schneider, O. 1887. *Ueber den roten Porphyr der Alten*. Dresden: 77ff.

Schultz, H.-W. 1860. *Denkmaler der kunst des Mittel Altersdresden*.

Schultz, R. W., and S. H. Barnsley. 1901. *The Monastery of Saint Luke of Stiris in Phocis*. London.

Serafini, A. 1927. *Torri campanarie di Roma e del Lazio nel Medioevo*. 2 vol. Rome.

Seroux D'Agincourt, G. B. L. G. 1826–29. *Storia dell'Arte dimostrata coi monumenti dalla sua decadenza nel IV secolo fino al suo risorgimento nel XVI*. Prato, Italy.

Serradifalco, D. 1838. *Del duomo di Monreale e di altre chiese siculo normanne*. 2 vol. Palermo.

Settis Frugoni, C. 1968. "Per una lettura del mosaico pavimentale della cattedrale di Otranto." *Bullettino dell'Istituto Storico Italiano per il Medioevo e Archivio Muratoriano* 80: 213–56.

Shelby, L. R. "The Geometric Knowledge of the Medieval Master Masons." *Speculum* 67 (4) Cambridge, Mass.: 295–421.

Sibilia, S. 1914. *La Cattedrale d'Anagni*. Orieto: Tip. Degli Orfanelli.

Slomann, V. 1967. *Bicorporates: Studies in Revivals and Migrations of Arts Motifs*. Copenhagen.

Smith, M. Q. 1965. "Anagni: An Example of Medieval Typological Decoration." *Papers of the British School at Rome,* n.s. 20: 1–47.

Speltz, A. 1915. *L'Ornement Polychrome.* 1, *L'Antiquité.* Leipzig, Germany.

Spesi, P. 1928. *Bibliografia metodico-analitica delle chiese di Roma.*

Spinelli, R. 1925. *Santa Maria sopra Minerva.* Rome.

Spiro, M. 1975. "Critical Corpus of the Mosaic Pavements on the Greek Mainland, Fourth–Sixth Centuries." Ph.D. diss., New York University.

Srbinovski, P. 1983. "Les mosaïques de la Pélagonie: Origines, techniques, datations." In *III Colloquio Internazionale sul Mosaico Antico, Ravenna 1980,* vol. 1, 119–32. Ravenna: Edizioni del Girasole.

Stern, H. 1965. "Ateliers de mosaïstes Rhodaniens d'époque gallo-romaine." In *La mosaïque greco-romaine: Colloques internationaux du centre national de la recherche scientifique, Paris 1963,* 233–41. Paris.

———. 1968. "Le pavement de la basilique de Pomposa (Italie)." *Cahiers Archéologiques* 18: 157–69.

———. 1975. "La funzione del mosaico nella casa antica." *Mosaici in Aquileia e nell'Alto Adriatico* (Udine, Italy): 39–57.

Stevens, R. T. 1988. *Graphic Programming in C.* Redwood City, Calif.: M&T Books.

———. 1989. *Fractal Programming in C.* Redwood City, Calif.: M&T Books.

———. 1990a. *Advanced Fractal Programming in C.* Redwood City, Calif.: M&T Books.

———. 1990b. *Fractal Programming and Ray Tracing with C++.* Redwood City, Calif.: M&T Books.

———. 1990c. *Fractal Programming in Turbo Pascal.* Redwood City, Calif.: M&T Books.

Stevenson, E. H. 1880. "Conferenza della Soc. cultori della cristiana archeologia." *Bulletino d'Archeologia cristiana.* Rome: 59ff.

———. 1884. "Marmorarii Romani." In *Mostra della città di Roma all' Esposizione di Torino nell'anno 1884,* 168–95.

Stewart, C. 1954. *Early Christian, Byzantine, and Romanesque Architecture.* London.

Stikas, E. 1972. "Nouvelles observations sur la date de construction du Catholicon et de l'eglise de la Vierge du Monastère de Saint Luc en Phocide." *Corsi di Cultura sull'Arte Ravvenate e Bizantina* 19: 311–30.

Stroll, M. 1991. *Symbols as Power: The Papacy Following the Investiture Contest.* Leiden, New York, Copenhagen, Cologne.

Studio NE, CE, LU. n.d. *San Giovanni: Basilica Patriarcale, Roma; La Basilique de Saint Jean; La Baslica de San Juan.* Rome.

Swarzenski, G. 1906. "Romanische Plastik und Inkrustationsstil in Florenz." *Repertorium für Kunstwissenschaft* 29: 518–31.

Taracena, B., P. Batlle Huguet, and H. Schlunk. 1947. *Ars Hispaniae: Historia Universal del Arte Hispánico.* Vol 2, *Arte Romano, Arte Paleocristiano, arte Visigodo y Arte Asturiano.* Madrid.

Taurisano, P. I., n.d. *Santa Sabina.* Rome.

Terrasse, H. 1932. *L'Art Hispano-Moresque des origines au XIIIe siècle.* Paris.

Terzi, A. 1915–16. *Venti disegni di decorazioni cosmatesche acquarellati riproducenti chiese Romane e di Palermo.* Rome.

———. 1917. *Disegni di decorazioni cosmateche, n. 38; reproduzioni a colori e oro di musaici ed altro.* Rome.

Texier, C., and R. P. Pullan. 1864. *Byzantine Architecture Illustrated by a Series of the Earliest Edifices in the East.* London.

Thümmler, H. 1938. "Die Kirche San Pietro in Tuscania." *Romisches Jahrbuch für Kunstgeschichte* 2: 265–88.

Thynne, R. 1924. *The Churches of Rome.* London.

Toesca, P. 1927. *Storia dell'Arte italiana dalle origini fino al tredicesimo secolo: Il medioevo* vol. 2. Turin, Italy: 582ff.

———. 1929. "Miniature romane dei secoli XI e XII: Bibbie miniate." *Rivista del R. Istituto di Archeologia e Storia dell'Arte* 1: 69–96.

Tomassetti, G. 1879. "Della campagna romana nel Medio Evo." *Archivio della R. Società Romana di Storia Patria* 2: 1–35, 129–64, 385–408.

———. 1880. "Della campagna romana nel Medio Evo." *Archivio della R. Società Romana di Storia Patria* 3: 135–74, 306–31.

———. 1881. "Della campagna romana nel Medio Evo." *Archivio della R. Società Romana di Storia Patria* 4: 217–49, 358–86.

———. 1882. "Della campagna romana nel Medio Evo." *Archivio della R. Società Romana di Storia Patria* 5: 67–156, 590–653.

———. 1883. "Della campagna romana nel Medio Evo." *Archivio della R. Società Romana di Storia Patria* 6: 173–221.

———. 1884. "Della campagna romana nel Medio Evo." *Archivio della R. Società Romana di Storia Patria* 8: 183–257, 353–462.

———. 1906a. *A. MCMVI quinto centenario dell'Università dei marmorari di Roma.* Rome.

———. 1906b. "Dei sodalizi in genere e dei marmorarii romani." *Bullettino della commissione archeologica comunale di Roma* (Rome) 34: 235–69.

———. 1913. *La campagna romana antica, medioevale e moderna.* Rome. Reissued as vol. 1 of *La Campagna Romana in Genere* 7 vols. Rome: Banco di Roma, 1975.

Toubert, H. 1970. "Le renouveau paléochrétien à Rome au début du XIIe siècle." *Cahiers Archèologiques* 20: 99–154.

Toubert, P. 1974. *Les Structures du Latium médiéval: Le Latium méridional et la Sabine du IXe siècle à la fin du XIIe siècle.* Rome.

Touring Club Italiano. 1977. *Guida d'Italia: Roma e dintorni.* 7th ed. Milan.

———. 1981. *Guida d'Italia: Lazio.* 4th ed. Milan.

———. 1989. *Guida d'Italia: Sicilia.* 6th ed. Milan.

Trinci Cecchelli, M. 1976. *La I Regione ecclesiastica.* Vol. 4 of *Corpus della Scultura Altomedioevale, 7, La Diocesi di Roma.* Spoleto, Italy.

Tronzo, W. 1989. "Apse Decoration, the Liturgy and the Perception of Art in Medieval Rome: Santa Maria in Trastevere and Santa Maria Maggiore." In *Italian Church Decoration of the Middle Ages and Early Renaissance,* edited by W. Tronzo, 167–93. Bologna.

Ullmann, W. 1976. *The Papacy and Political Ideas in the Middle Ages.* London.

Underwood, P. 1955–56. "Notes on the Work of the Byzantine Institute in Istanbul." *Dumbarton Oaks Papers* 9–10: 291–300.

Urbani di Gheltof, G. 1888. "Il pavimento." In *La basilica di San Marco in Venezia,* edited by C. Boito, 227–34. Venice.

Valenti, F. 1932. "L'Arte dell'era normanna." In *Il Regno Niomanno.* Messina, Italy.

van Berchem, M., and E. Cluzot. 1925. *Mosaiques chrétiennes.* Paris.

Van Milligen, A. 1912. *Byzantine Churches in Constantinople.* London.

Varène, P. 1974. "Sur la taille de la pierre antique." Centre de Recherches sur les Techniques gréco-romains, no. 3. Université de Dijon.

Venanzi, C. 1953. *Caratteri costruttivi dei monumenti: Strutture murarie a Roma e nel Lazio.* Rome.

Venditti, A. 1967. *Architettura bizantina nell'Italia meridionale.* Naples.

Venturi, A. 1904. *Storia dell'arte Italiana.* Vol. 3, *L'arte romanica.* Milan: 788f., 884f., 771ff.

Verdier, P. 1940. "La Façade-temple de l'eglise San Pietro in Tuscania." *Mélanges d'Archéologie et d'Histoire* 57: 174–89.

Vergnolle, E. 1980. "Méobecq et Saint-Benoît-sur-Loire: Problèmes de sculture." *Cahiers d'Archéologie et d' Histoire du Berry* 62: 71–83.

Verhoogen, V. 1965. *Apamea in Syrië in de Koninklijke Musea voor Kunst en Geschiedenis,* plate 12. Brussels.

Verzone, P. 1942. *L'architettura religiosa dell'alto medioevo nell'Italia settentrionale.* Turin.

Viollet-le-Duc, E. 1875. *Dictionnaire raisonné de l'architecture française du XIe au XVIe siècle.* Paris.

Vitruvius, M. 1791. *De Architectura.* Translated by W. Newton as "Ten Books of Architecture: The Architecture of M. Vitruvius Pollio." London: 198–9.

———. 1960. *De Architectura.* Vols. 1–7. Rome: S. Ferri.

Vogel, C. 1963–72. *Le Pontifical Romano-germanique du dixieme siècle.* 3 vols. Vatican City.

———. 1975. "Introduction aux sources de l'histoire du culte chrétien au moyen age." Centro Italiano di studi sull alto medioevo, Spoleto, Italy.

Volpe, G. 1961. *Medio Evo Italiano.* Florence.

Voss, I., and P. C. Claussen. 1991–92. "Das Paviment von San Clemente." *Römisches Jahrbuch für Kunstgeschichte* 27/28: 1–22.

Waley, D. 1961. *The Papal State in the Thirteenth Century.* London.

Wander, S. H. 1978. "The Westminster Abbey Sanctuary Pavement." In *Traditio: Studies in Ancient and Medieval History, Thought and Religion,* vol. 35, 137–56. New York: Fordham University Press.

Ward-Perkins, J. B. 1963."Il commercio dei sarcofagi in marmo fra Grecia e Italia Settentrionale." In *Atti del I Congr. Intern. di Archeologia dell'Italia Settentrionale, Turin 1963,* 119–24, and in "Papers of the British School at Rome," 48, 1980, p. 43.

———. 1971. "Quarrying in Antiquity: Technology, Tradition and Social Change." *Proceedings of the British Academy* 52.

Ward-Perkins, J. W. 1980. "The Marble Trade and Its Organization: Evidence from Nicomedia." In *Memoirs of the American Academy in Rome,* vol 36, 325–28. Rome.

Weitzmann, K. 1977. *Late Antique and Early Christian Book Illumination.* London.

White, J. 1966. *Art and Architecture in Italy.* London.

Wulff, O. 1903. "Die Koimesiskirche in Nicäa und ihre Mosaiken." *Zur Kunstgeschichte des Auslandes* (Strassburg) 13: 157–64, plate 6.

Yarza, J. 1980. *Historia del Arte Hispánico II: La Edad Media.* Madrid.

Zahn, W. 1831–33. *Ornamente aller Klassischen Kunstepochen.*

Zambarelli, P. L., n.d. *Santi Bonifacio ed Alessio.* Rome.

Zanetti, V. 1873. *La basilica dei Santi Maria e Donato di Murano.* Venice.

Zocca, M. 1942. "Aspetti dell'Urbanistica Medioevale del Lazio." *Palladio* 6 (1): 1–15. Roma: Casa Editrice Carlo Colombo.

Zoido Zamora, R. n.d. "Análisis y generación de embaldosados." Ph.D. diss., E. T. S. Arquitectura de Madrid.

Zovatto, P. L. 1947–48. "Il battisterio di Grado." *Rivista di Archeologia Cristiana* 23–24: 231–51.

———. 1950. *Antichità cristiane di Verona.* Verona.

———. 1952. "La basilica di Sant'Eufemia di Grado." *Palladio* n.s. 2: 112–25.

———. 1956–1957. "Tappeti musivi del secolo IX a Venezia." In *Atti del XVIII congresso internazionale di storia dell'arte, Venice 1955,* 136–39. Venice, 1956. Also published as "Decorazione musive pavimentali del sec IX in abbazie benedettine del Veneto" in *Settimane di studio del centro italiano di studi sull'alto medioevo,* vol. 4: *Il monachesimo nell'alto medioevo e la formaz . . . ,* 417–22. Spoleto, Italy, 1957.

———. 1962. "I Mosaici altomedioevali di Gazzo Veronese." In *Atti dell'ottavo congresso di studi sull'arte del'alto medioevo, Milan 1959,* vol. 1, 260–72. Milan.

———. 1963. *Mosaici paleocristiani delle Venezie.* Udine, Italy.

CREDITS

Every effort has been made to contact the copyright holders of each of these images. Rights holders of any selection not credited should contact W.W. Norton & Company, Inc., Permissions Department, 500 Fifth Avenue, New York, NY 10010, in order for a correction to be made in the next printing of this book.

All photographs and line drawings not credited below are the property of Paloma Pajares-Ayuela.

Figs. 1-1, 1-3, 1-4, and 1-53: Reproduced by kind permission of Andromeda Oxford Limited, www. andromeda.co.uk.

Fig. 1-2: John McLaughlin.

Fig. 1-5: Departure for the Crusades, for the Battle of Bouquee. Ancienne Chapelle des Templiers, Cressac, France. Giraudon/Art Resource, NY.

Fig. 1-6: © Michelin, Guida Verde Italia—1a edizione (1987)

Figs. 1-7, 1-8, 1-9, 1-10, 1-11, 1-26, 1-29, 1-50, 4-111, and 4-112: From Friedrich Maximilian Hessemer, *Historic Designs and Patterns in Color from Arabic and Italian Sources*. Mineola, NY: Dover, 1990. Reprinted with permission of the publisher.

Fig. 1-12: From Pedro Martínez Montávez and Carmen Ruíz Bravo-Villasante, *Europa Islámica*. Barcelona: El Sol, 1991.

Figs. 1-14 and 1-15: Giotto di Bondone (1266–1336). Homage of a Simple Man; St. Francis giving his Mantle to a Poor Knight; Dream of the Palace. Three frescoes. S. Francesco, Assisi, Italy. Scala/Art Resource, NY.

Figs. 1-16 and 1-17: © National Gallery, London.

Figs. 1-18, 1-19, 1-20, 5-42, and 5-43: From Michèle Blanchard-Lemée, *Recueil Géneral des Mosaïques de la Gaulle*. Paris: Editions du Centre National de la Recherche Scientifique, 1991.

Figs. 1-24 and 1-25: From Pierre Gascar, *Saint-Marc*. Zurich: Delpire Editeur, 1964.

Figs. 1-27 and 1-28: From Pedro Martínez Montávez and Carmen Ruíz Bravo-Villasante, *Europa Islámica*. Barcelona: El Sol, 1991.

Figs. 1-34, 1-35, 3-4, 4-26, 4-100, 4-101, 5-54, 5-55, 5-56, and 5-57: Courtesy Richard Foster. From *Patterns of Thought: The Hidden Meaning of the Great Pavement of Westminster Abbey* by Richard Foster.

Fig. 1-51: Robert Harding Picture Library.

Fig. 1-52: © Kümmerly + Frey AG, CH-3052 Zollikofen-Bern

Fig. 1-54: Map is *Mapa de Italia* published 1990 by Touring Club Italiano, Milan. Modified to show sites of Cosmatesque ornamentation by the author.

Fig. 2-1: Map is *Plano de Roma* published 1992 by Ufficio Speciale per gli Interventi sul Centro Storico, Rome. Modified to show sites of Cosmatesque ornamentation by the author.

Fig. 2-3: Cover from brochure entitled *La Basilica e L'area Archeologica di S. Clemente in Roma*. Published in Rome, 1990.

Fig. 2-4, 2-6, 2-7, 2-10, 2-47, 2-188, and 2-197: Krautheimer, Richard; *Profile of a City, 312–1308*. Copyright ©1980 by Richard Krautheimer. Reprinted by permission of Princeton University Press.

Fig. 2-5: From Gabriella Delfini Filippi, *Guide del Vaticano 2: San Pietro*. Rome: Fratelli Palombi Editori, 1991.

Figs. 2-8, 2-40, 2-100, 2-102, 2-114, 2-115, 2-116, 2-119, 4-53, and 6-2: Reprinted from *Les Edifices de Rome Moderne*, Princeton Architectural Press.

Figs. 2-11 and 2-12: From José Ramón Paniagua, *Vocabulario básico de arquitectura*, 8th ed., Madrid, Ed. Cátedra, 1998, plates IX y IX bis.

Figs. 2-19, 2-169, 2-170, 4-11, 4-52, and 5-36: From Giovanni Battista de Rossi, *Musaici cristiani e saggi dei pavimenti delle Chiese di Roma anteriori al secolo XV*. Rome: Libreria Spithöver di Guglielmo Haass, 1873–99.

Figs. 2-27 and 2-111: From Guglielmo Matthiae, *La Chiese di Roma dal IV al X secolo*. Bologna: Cappelli, 1962.

Figs. 2-43, 5-18, 5-19, 5-20, 5-22, 5-23, 5-24, 5-25, 5-27, 5-29, 5-30, and 5-31: From Richard Krautheimer, *Early Christian and Byzantine Architecture*. Penguin Books, 1965.

Figs. 2-64, 2-163, 4-60, and 4-96: Alinari/Art Resource, NY.

Figs. 2-72, 3-15d, 3-16e, 3-17d, 3-19a through 3-19h, 3-21a through 3-21h, 4-12, 4-15, 4-16, 4-17, 4-18, 4-24, 4-25, 4-32, 4-36, 4-37, 4-48, 4-49, 4-65, 5-3, 5-32, 5-33, 5-34, 5-35, and 5-36: From Dorothy F. Glass, *Studies on Cosmatesque Pavements*. Oxford, England: BAR, 1980. Reprinted by permission of BAR.

Fig. 2-129: Paschal candelabrum. Alinari/Art Resource, NY.

Figs. 2-135 and 6-3: From Leonard Boyle, *Pequeña Guía de San Clemente*. Published in Rome, 1991.

Fig. 2-157: From Studio NE, CE, LU, *San Giovanni. Basilica Patriarcale. Roma. La Basilique de Saint Jean. La Basílica de S. Juan*.

Figs. 2-189 and 4-51: From Carla Faldi Guglielmi, *Roma, Basilica di S. Lorenzo al Verano (fuori le mura)*. Bologna: publisher unknown, n.d.

Fig. 2-200: From Maria Giulia Barberini, *I Santi Quattro Coronati a Roma*. Courtesy Fratelli Palombi Editori.

Figs. 3-1 and 3-2: From Owen Jones, *The Grammar of Ornament*.

Fig. 3-3: Chromolithograph by Heinrich Dolmetsch. From *Der Ornamentenschatz*, 1883.

Figs. 3-5a through 3-5e; 3-15a through 3-15c; 3-16a through 3-16d; 3-17a through 3-17c; 3-18a through 3-18h; 3-20a through 3-20h; 3-22a, 3-22b; 3-24a through 3-24d; 3-26a, 3-26b; 3-28a through 3-28d; 3-30a through 3-30d; and 3-32a through 3-32d: From Balmelle, Blanchard-Lemée, Christophe, et al., *Le décor géométrique de la mosaïque romaine*. © *Le décor géométrique de la mosaïque romaine*. Picard 1985.

Figs. 3-6, 5-26, 5-38, 5-41, 5-45, 5-50, 5-66, 5-68a, 5-68b, 5-69: From *Historia Universal Planeta, Vol. IV: La Edad del Feudalismo*. Published in Barcelona, 1991.

Figs. 3-7, 3-9, 3-10, 3-12, and 3-13: From Guiglia Guidobaldi, *Tradizione locale e influenze Bizantine nei pavimenti Cosmateschi*. Rome: Ministeri per i Beni Culturali e Ambientali, 1984.

Figs. 3-8 and 5-28: From *Intorno all'origine e per una nuova denominazione dei mosaici "cosmateschi"* by Goffredo Bendinelli.

Fig. 3-11: Small basilica, 5th century, Heraclea Lynkestis, Yugoslavia. Vanni/Art Resource, NY.

Fig. 3-14: Imrahor Camii (St. John of Stoudios), pavement. Vanni/Art Resource, NY.

Figs. 3-23a, 3-23b, 3-25a through 3-25d, 3-27a, 3-27b, 3-29a through 3-29d, 3-31a through 3-31d; 3-33a through 3-33d; 4-66a through 4-66h; 4-68; and 4-110: From Piazzesi, Mancini, and Benevolo, *Una statistica sul repertorio geometrico dei Cosmati*. Published by Università de Roma, 1954.

Figs. 3-34 and 4-109: From G. Becatti, *Edificio con opus sectile fuori Porta Marina, Scavi di Ostia* Vol. VI, and *Mosaici e pavimenti marmorei* Vol. IV. Reprinted with the permission of Istituto Poligrafico e Zecca dello Stato, Rome.

Figs. 4-33, 4-106, 4-107, and 5-10 through 5-14: From Asher Ovadiah, *Geometric and Floral Patterns in Ancient Mosaics*. Rome: L'Erma di Bretschneider, 1980. Reprinted by permission of the publisher.

Figs. 4-38, 4-39, 4-58, 4-59, 4-63, 4-64, 4-72, 4-73, 4-74, 4-75, 4-77, 4-91, 4-92, 4-93, 4-94, 4-95, 4-102, 4-103, 4-104, and 4-105: From Andrea Terzi, *Venti disegni di decorazioni cosmatesche acquarellati riproducenti chiese Romane e di Palermo*. Rome, 1915–16.

Figs. 4-42 and 5-1: From Ib Lydholm, *The Cosmati and the Cathedral at Anagni*. Rome: Odense University Press, 1982.

Fig. 4-46: From P. Elia Jarawan, *S. Maria in Cosmedin*. Published in Rome, 1987.

Figs. 4-55 and 4-56: From Antonio Muñoz, *La basilica di S. Lorenzo fuori le mura*. Rome: Fratelli Palombi Editori, 1944. Reprinted by permission of the publisher.

Fig. 4-69: From Edward Hutton, *The Cosmati: The Roman Marble Workers of the XII and XIII Centuries*. Published in London, 1950.

Figs. 4-97, 4-98, and 4-108: From Raniero Gnoli, *Marmora Romana*. Rome: Edizioni dell'Elefante, 1971.

Fig. 4-113: From *Notices of the AMS*, 46, No. 10, 1999. Courtesy of the American Mathematical Society.

Fig. 4-117: From "Mathematical Recreations" by A. K. Dewdney. Copyright © 1990 by Scientific American, Inc. All rights reserved.

Fig. 4-119: Bottom two triangles from "The Language of Fractals" by Harmut Jürgens, Heinz-Otto Peitgen, and Dietmar Saupe. Copyright © 1990 by Scientific American, Inc. All rights reserved.

Fig. 5-2: From Richard Prudhomme, *La Mosaïque Gréco-Romaine II; IIe Colloque International pour l'etude de la mosaïque antique*. Published in Vienna, 1975.

Figs. 5-15a through 5-15d: From Dimas Fernández Galiano, *Influencias orientales en la musiva hispánica*. Colloquio Internazionale sul Mosaico Antico, Ravenna, Italy: Edizioni del Girasole srl, 1983. Reprinted by permission of the publisher.

Fig. 5-16: From Guglielmo Matthiae, *Rivista dell'Istituto Nazionale d'Archeologia e Storia dell'Arte*, 1952.

Fig. 5-17: From Raffaella Olivieri Farioli, *I mosaici pavimentali della chiesa di S. Giovanni Evangelista in Ravenna*. Published in Ravenna, 1970.

Fig. 5-21: Courtesy of the British School at Rome. Illustration from page 107 of M. H. Ballance, "Cumanin Cami'i at Antalya: a Byzantine Church," *Papers of the British School at Rome* 23, 1955.

Figs. 5-39a and 5-39b: From postcards of S. Marco. Fig. 6-6: From postcard of S. Clemente. Author's collection.

Fig. 5-40: © Michelin, Guida Verde Italia—1a edizione (1987).

Figs. 5-44a and 5-44b: From G. Galassi, *Roma o Bisanzio*. Published in Rome, 1930. Reprinted with the permission of Istituto Poligrafico e Zecca dello Stato, Rome.

Figs. 5-46 and 5-47: cliché Bibliothèque nationale de France Paris.

Fig. 5-48: Illustration from manuscript—Gonville & Caius MS 428/458, f.23v. By permission of the Master and Fellows of Gonville & Caius College, Cambridge.

Fig. 5-49: By permission of the Fellows and Scholars of St. John's College, Oxford.

Figs. 5-51, 5-58, 5-59, 5-60, and 5-81: From Marie-Thérèse D'Alverny, *L'homme comme symbole. Le microcosme* in *Simboli e simbologia nell'Alto Medioevo*. Spoleto, Italy: Centro Italiano Studi sull'Alto Medioevo, 1975.

Fig. 5-52: From *Rome and Latium: A Phaidon Cultural Guide*. Published in Oxford, England, 1987.

Fig. 5-53: Bayerische Staatsbibliothek, Munich.

Figs. 5-61, 5-67, and 5-88: From Jaume Matas and Luis Sylvestre, *Historia Visual del Mundo*. Madrid: El Mundo, 1994.

Figs. 5-62 and 5-63: From Richard Krautheimer, *Tre Capitali Cristiane. Topografia e politica*. Torino, Italy: G. Einaudi Editore, 1983.

Fig. 5-64. SEF/Art Resource, NY.

Figs. 5-68c through 5-68f, 5-86, and 5-89: From *Historia de España, Vol. 3: Al-Andalus, musulmanes y cristianos (siglos VIII–XIII)*. Barcelona: Editorial Planeta, 1989.

Figs. 5-70, 5-72, 5-85, 5-90, and 5-91: From Blas Taracena, Pedro Batlle Huguet, and Helmut Schlunk, *Ars Hispaniae, Historia Universal del Arte Hispánico, Vol. II: Arte Romano, Arte Paleocristiano, Arte Visigodo y Arte Asturiano*. Madrid: publisher unknown, 1947.

Figs. 5-71 and 5-73: From José Gudiol Ricart and Juan Antonio Gaya Nuño, *Ars Hispaniae, Historia Universal del Arte Hispanico, Vol. V: Arquitectura y Escultura Románicas*. Madrid: publisher unknown, 1948.

Figs. 5-74, 5-75, and 5-84: From Joaquin Yarza, *Historia del Arte Hispanico II: La Edad Media*. Madrid: publisher unknown, 1980.

Figs. 5-76, 5-77, and 6-1: From Enrico Parlato and Serena Romano, *Roma y el Lacio*. Madrid: Ediciones Encuentro, n.d. Reprinted by permission of Zodiaque.

Fig. 5-78: From Bianca Maria Margarucci Italiani, *Il Titolo di Pammachio, Santi Giovanni e Paolo*. Rome: publisher unknown, 1985.

Figs. 5-79 and 5-80: Scala/Art Resource, NY.

Fig. 5-82: Erich Lessing/Art Resource, NY.

Fig. 5-83: The Metropolitan Museum of Art, The Cloisters Collection, 1947. (47.101.32) Photograph © 1985 The Metropolitan Museum of Art.

Fig. 5-87: The Pierpont Morgan Library, New York. Ms M. 1.

Figs. 5-95, 5-96, 5-99, 5-100, 5-101, 5-103, 5-105, and 5-106: From Gérad de Champeux and Dom Sébastien Sterckx, *Introducción a los símbolos*. Madrid: Ediciones Encuentro, 1984. Reprinted by permission of Zodiaque.

Fig. 5-97: The Pierpont Morgan Library, New York. M. 644, f. 222v.

Fig. 5-98: The Pierpont Morgan Library, New York. M. 644, f. 87.

Fig. 5-104: Photo Dieuzaide-Zodiaque.

Fig. 6-37: From Federico Guidobaldi, in *Marmi Antichi*, edited by P. Pensabene. Rome, 1985.

INDEX